Ichigo Takano presents

Dreamin'
Sun

2

volume
two

Dreamin'
Sun

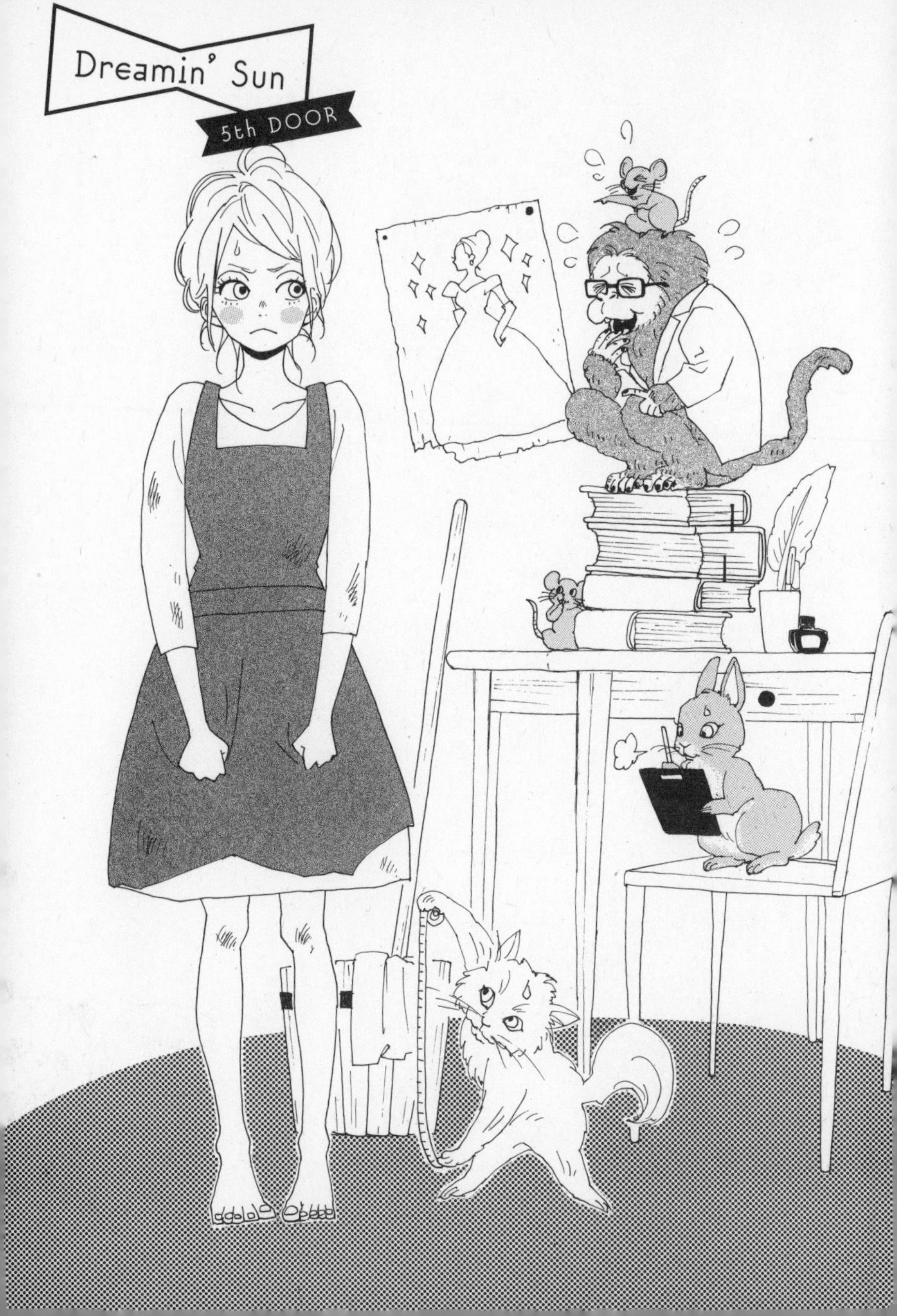
Dreamin' Sun
5th DOOR

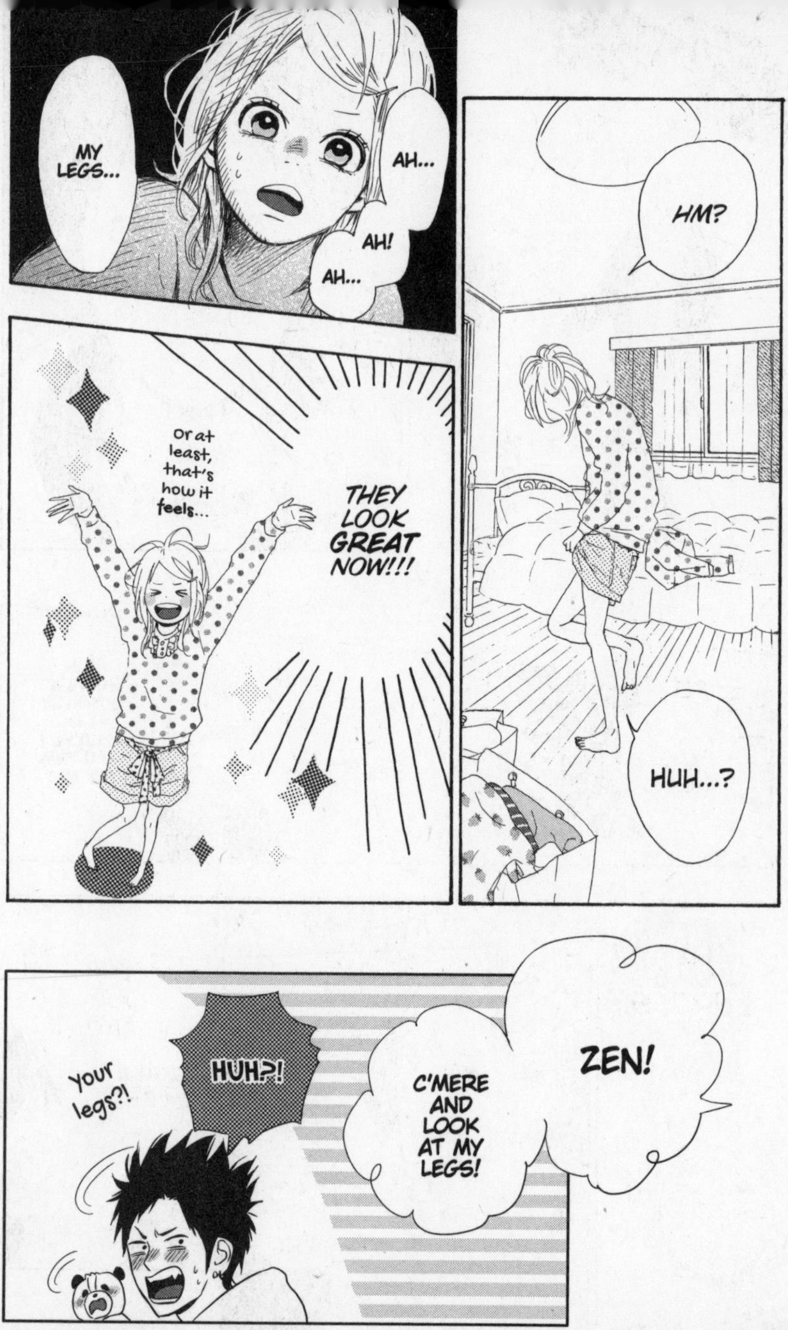
HM?
HUH...?
AH...
AH!
AH...
MY LEGS...
THEY LOOK GREAT NOW!!!
Or at least, that's how it feels...
ZEN!
C'MERE AND LOOK AT MY LEGS!
HUH?!
your legs?!

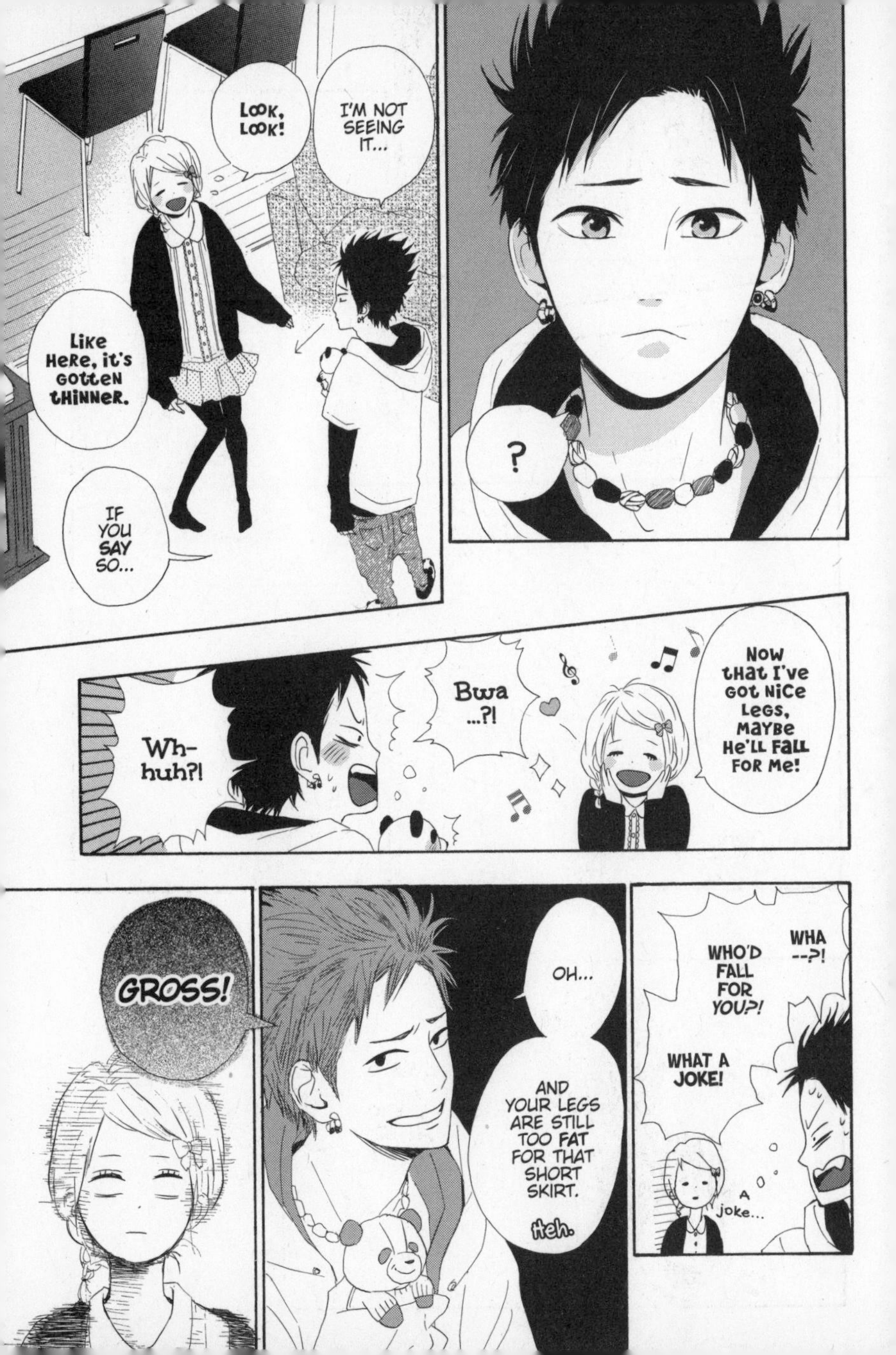
?
LOOK, LOOK!
I'M NOT SEEING IT...
Like Here, it's gotten thinner.
IF YOU SAY SO...
Now that I've got nice legs, maybe he'll fall for me!
Bwa ...?!
Wh-huh?!
WHA --?!
WHO'D FALL FOR YOU?!
WHAT A JOKE!
A joke...
OH...
AND YOUR LEGS ARE STILL TOO FAT FOR THAT SHORT SKIRT.
Heh.
GROSS!

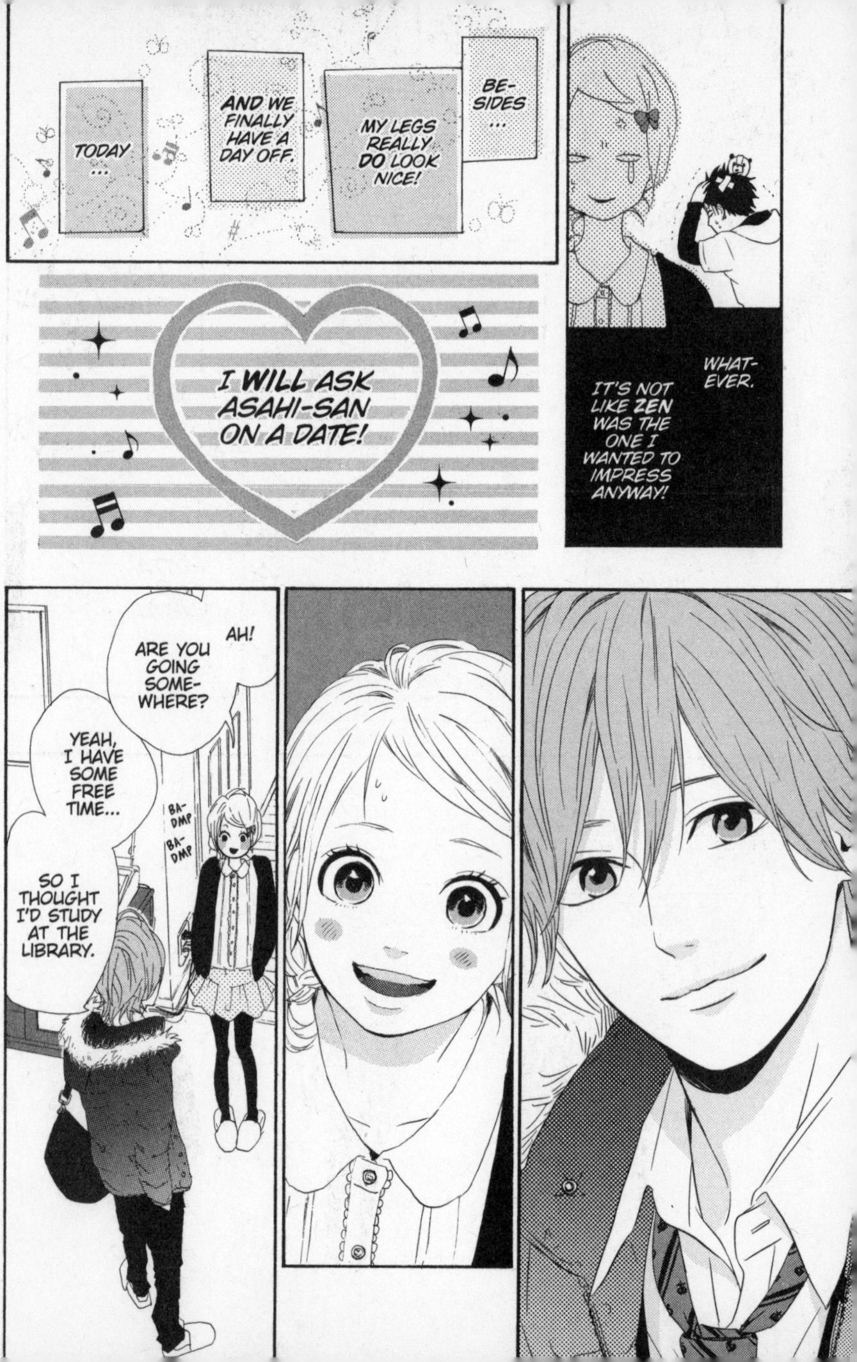
WHAT-EVER.
IT'S NOT LIKE ZEN WAS THE ONE I WANTED TO IMPRESS ANYWAY!
BE-SIDES ...
MY LEGS REALLY DO LOOK NICE!
AND WE FINALLY HAVE A DAY OFF.
TODAY ...
I WILL ASK ASAHI-SAN ON A DATE!
AH!
ARE YOU GOING SOME-WHERE?
YEAH, I HAVE SOME FREE TIME...
BA-DMP
BA-DMP
SO I THOUGHT I'D STUDY AT THE LIBRARY.

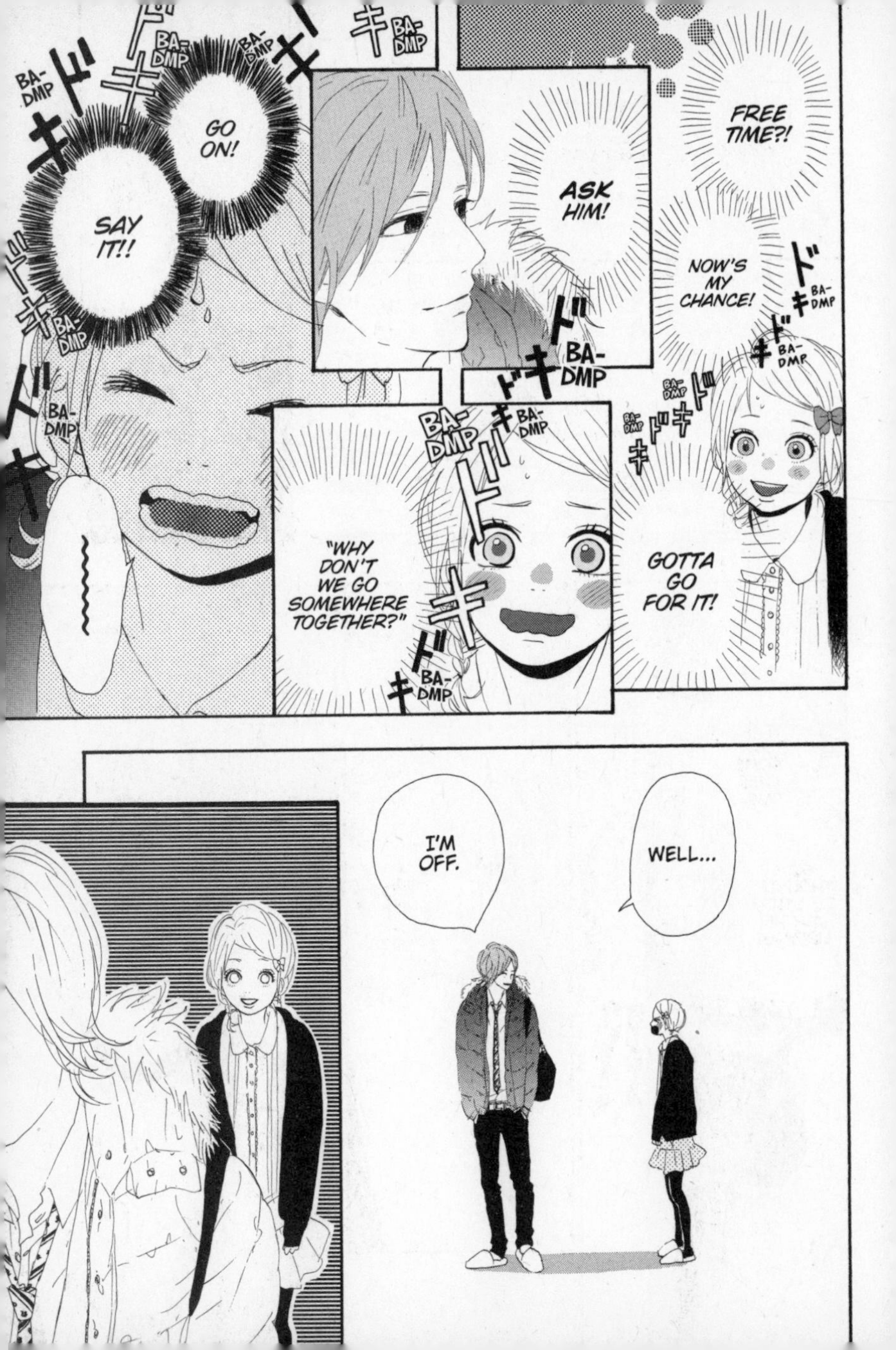
BA-DMP
FREE TIME?!
NOW'S MY CHANCE!
BA-DMP
BA-DMP
ASK HIM!
BA-DMP
BA-DMP
BA-DMP
GO ON!
BA-DMP
SAY IT!!
BA-DMP
BA-DMP
GOTTA GO FOR IT!
BA-DMP
BA-DMP
"WHY DON'T WE GO SOMEWHERE TOGETHER?"
BA-DMP
BA-DMP
WELL...
I'M OFF.

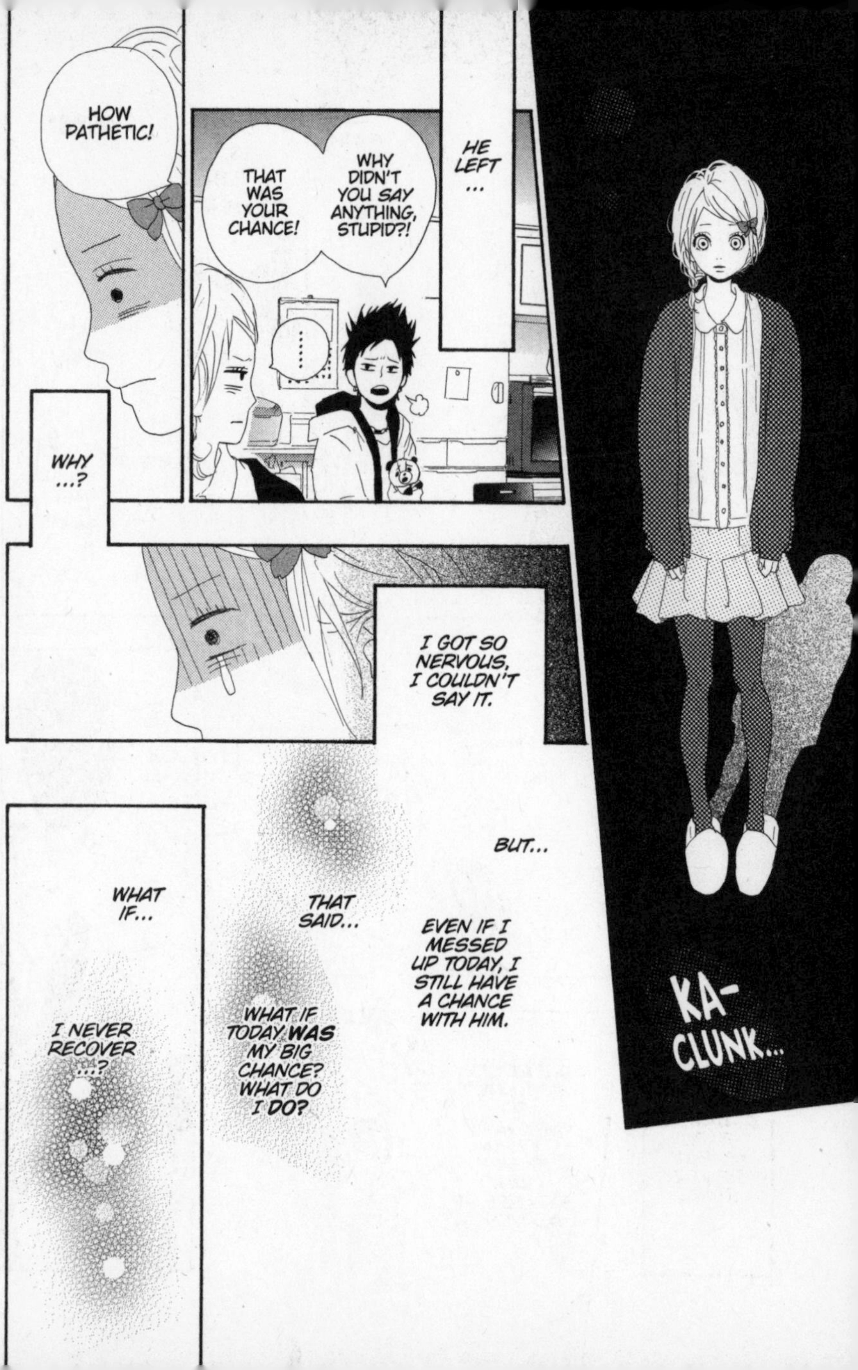
KA-CLUNK...
HE LEFT...
WHY DIDN'T YOU SAY ANYTHING, STUPID?!
THAT WAS YOUR CHANCE!
......
HOW PATHETIC!
WHY...?
I GOT SO NERVOUS, I COULDN'T SAY IT.
BUT...
EVEN IF I MESSED UP TODAY, I STILL HAVE A CHANCE WITH HIM.
THAT SAID...
WHAT IF TODAY WAS MY BIG CHANCE? WHAT DO I DO?
WHAT IF...
I NEVER RECOVER...?

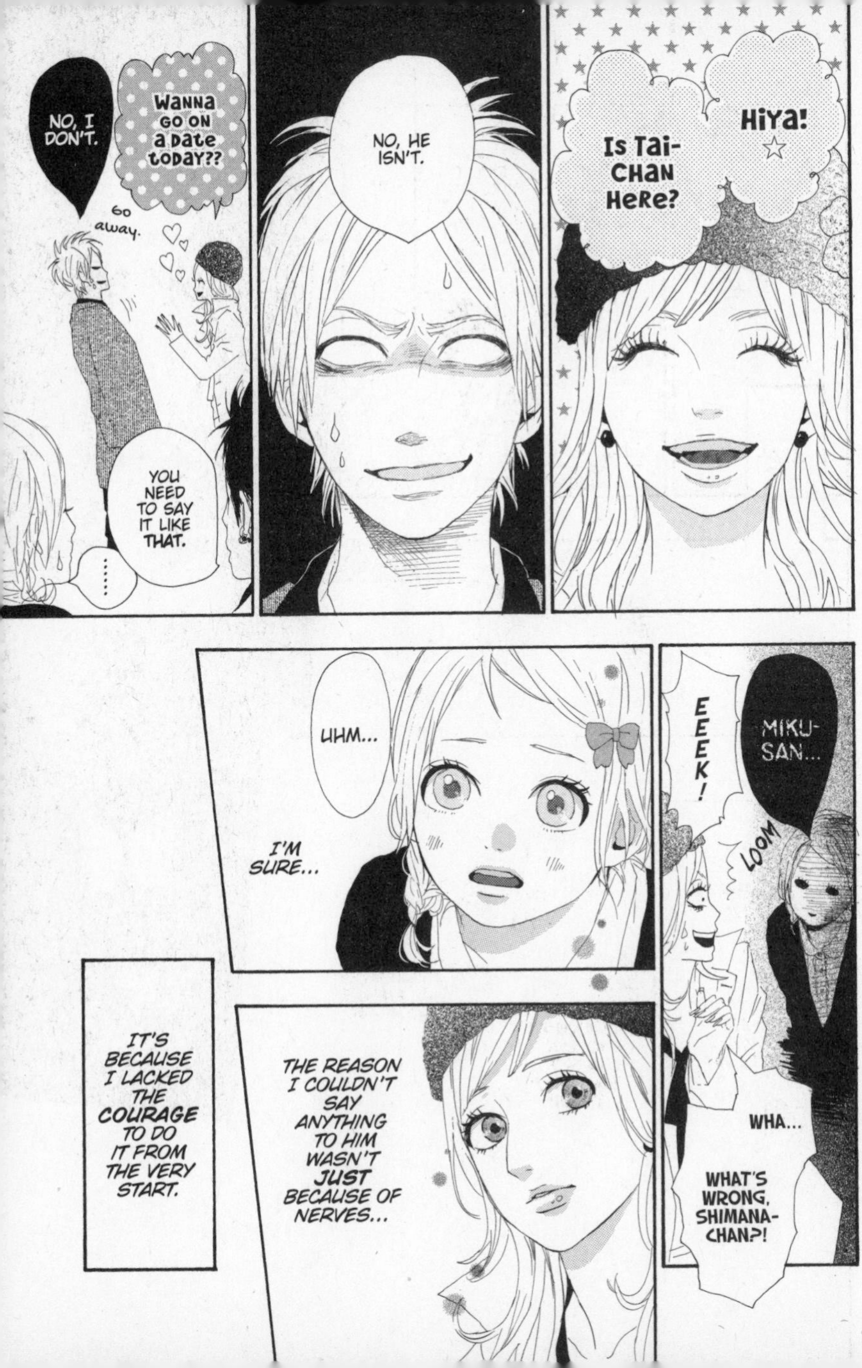

HiYA! ☆
Is Tai-CHAN HeRe?
NO, HE ISN'T.
WANNA GO ON A DATE TODAY??
NO, I DON'T.
Go away.
YOU NEED TO SAY IT LIKE THAT.
......
MIKU-SAN...
EEEK!
LOOM
WHA...
WHAT'S WRONG, SHIMANA-CHAN?!
UHM...
I'M SURE...
THE REASON I COULDN'T SAY ANYTHING TO HIM WASN'T JUST BECAUSE OF NERVES...
IT'S BECAUSE I LACKED THE COURAGE TO DO IT FROM THE VERY START.

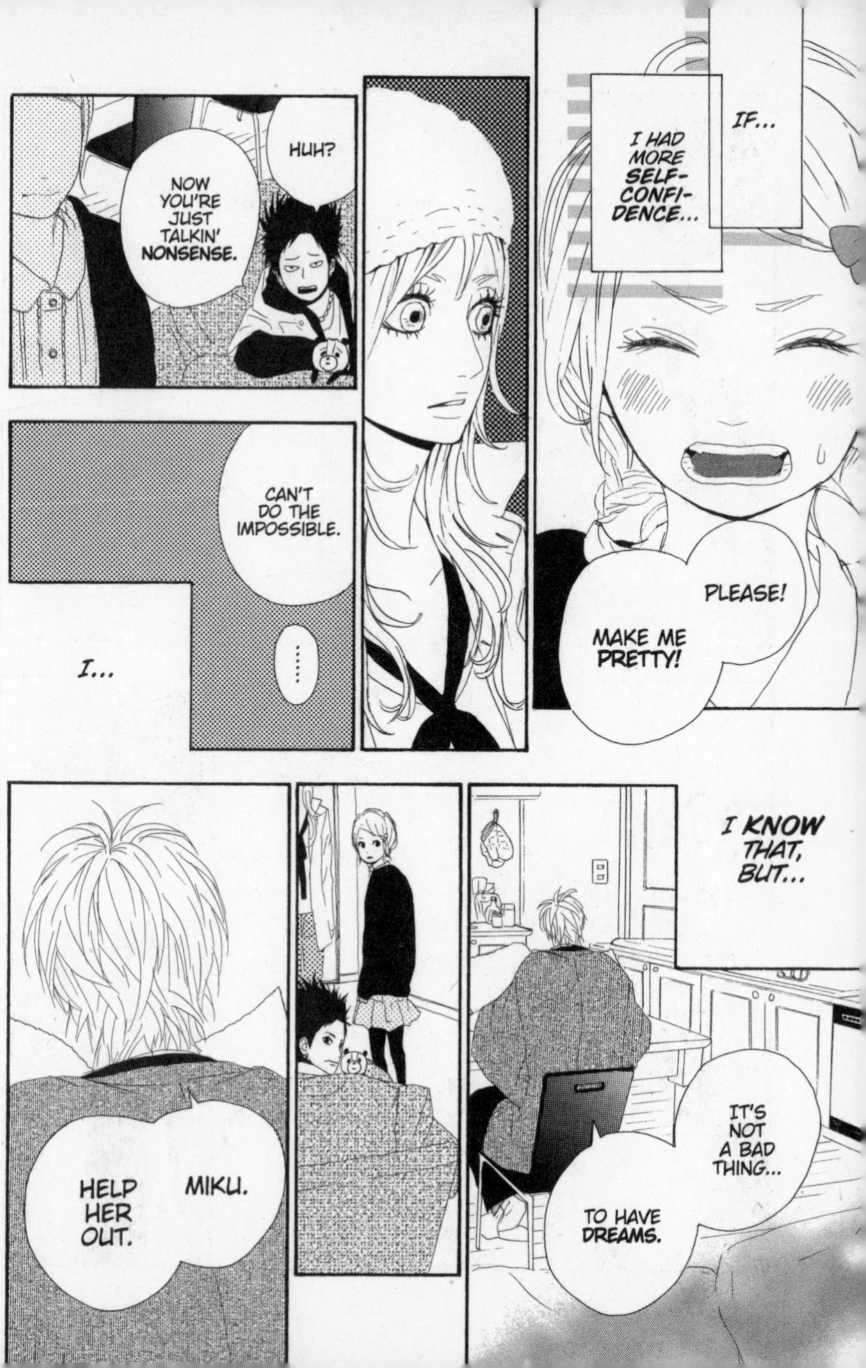
IF...
I HAD MORE SELF-CONFIDENCE...
PLEASE!
MAKE ME PRETTY!
HUH?
NOW YOU'RE JUST TALKIN' NONSENSE.
CAN'T DO THE IMPOSSIBLE.
......
I...
I KNOW THAT, BUT...
IT'S NOT A BAD THING...
TO HAVE DREAMS.
MIKU.
HELP HER OUT.

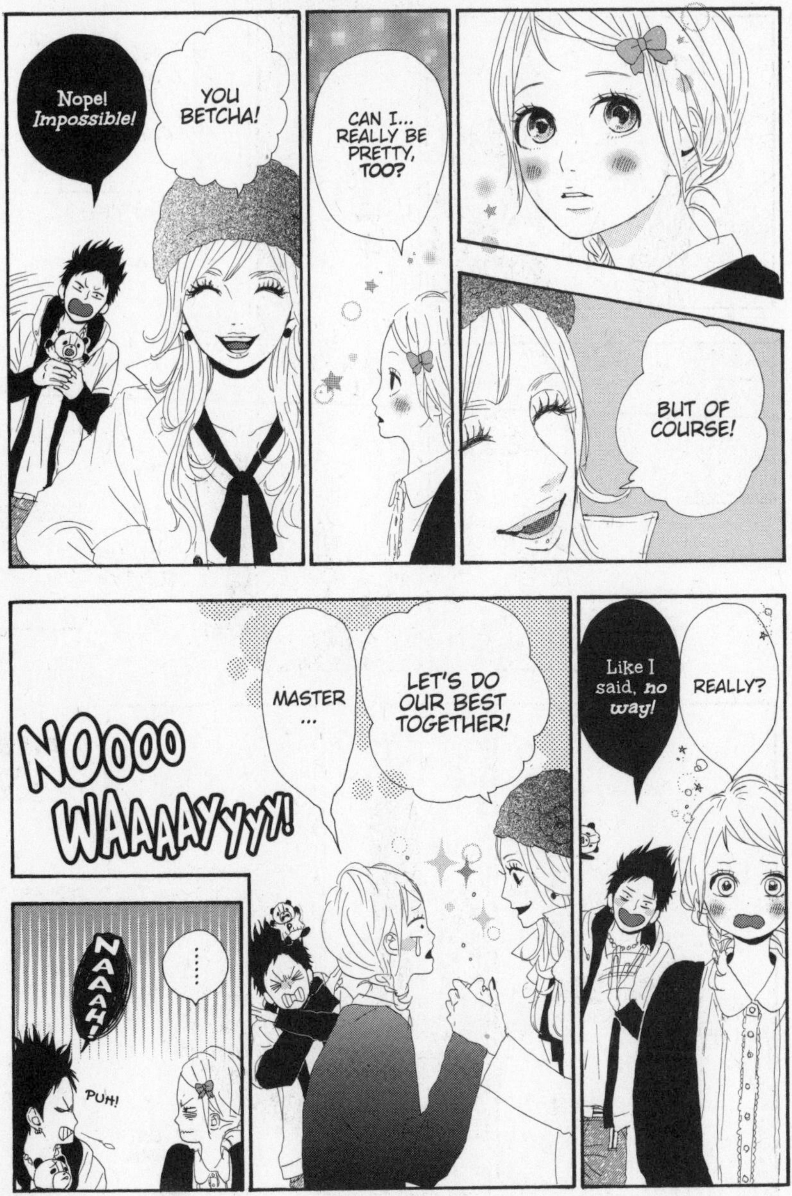
CAN I... REALLY BE PRETTY, TOO?
BUT OF COURSE!
YOU BETCHA!
Nope! *Impossible!*
REALLY?
Like I said, *no way!*
LET'S DO OUR BEST TOGETHER!
MASTER...
NOOOO WAAAAYyyY!
......
NAAAH!
PUH!

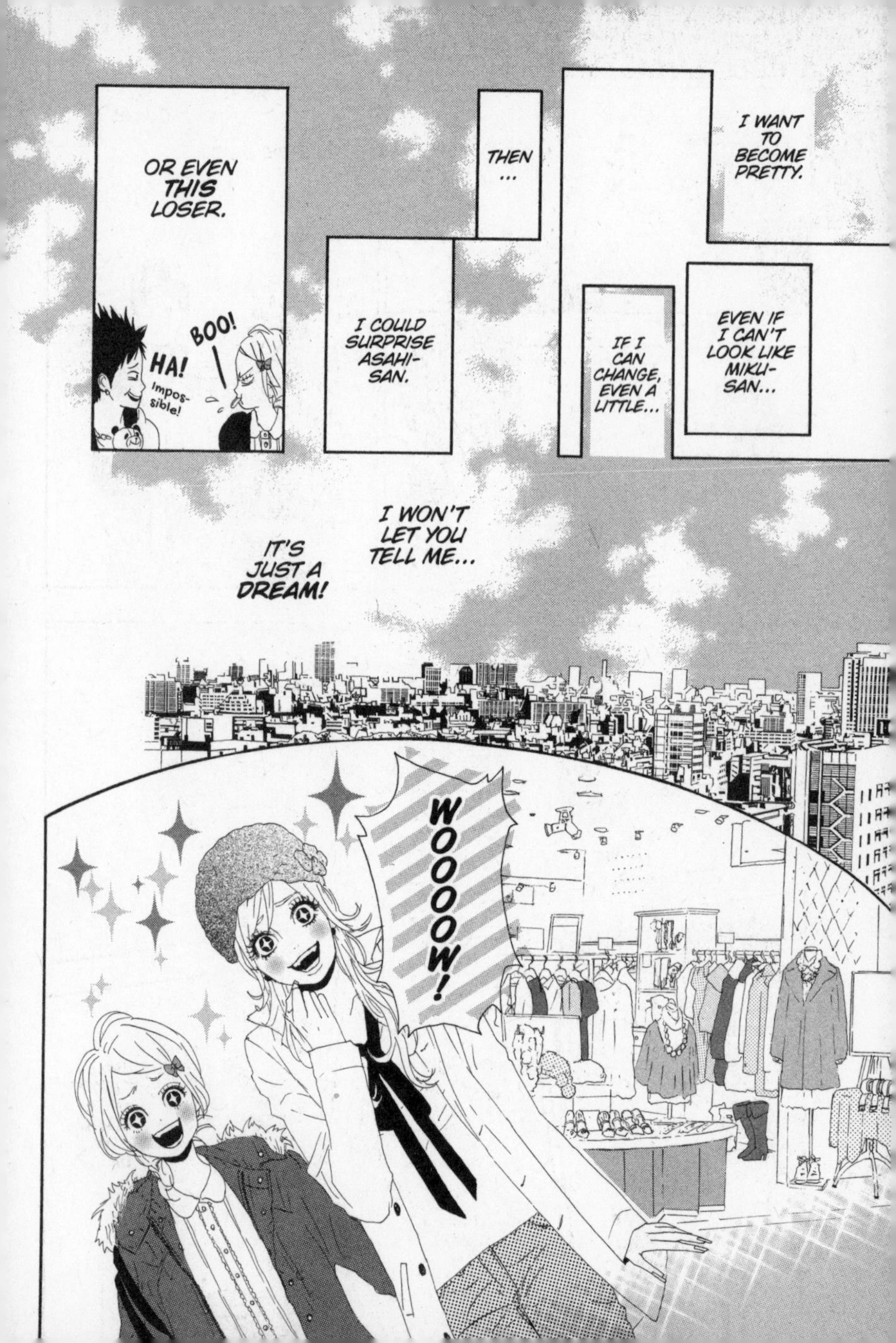
I WANT TO BECOME PRETTY.
EVEN IF I CAN'T LOOK LIKE MIKU-SAN...
IF I CAN CHANGE, EVEN A LITTLE...
THEN...
I COULD SURPRISE ASAHI-SAN.
OR EVEN THIS LOSER.
HA! Impossible!
BOO!
I WON'T LET YOU TELL ME...
IT'S JUST A DREAM!
WOOOOOW!

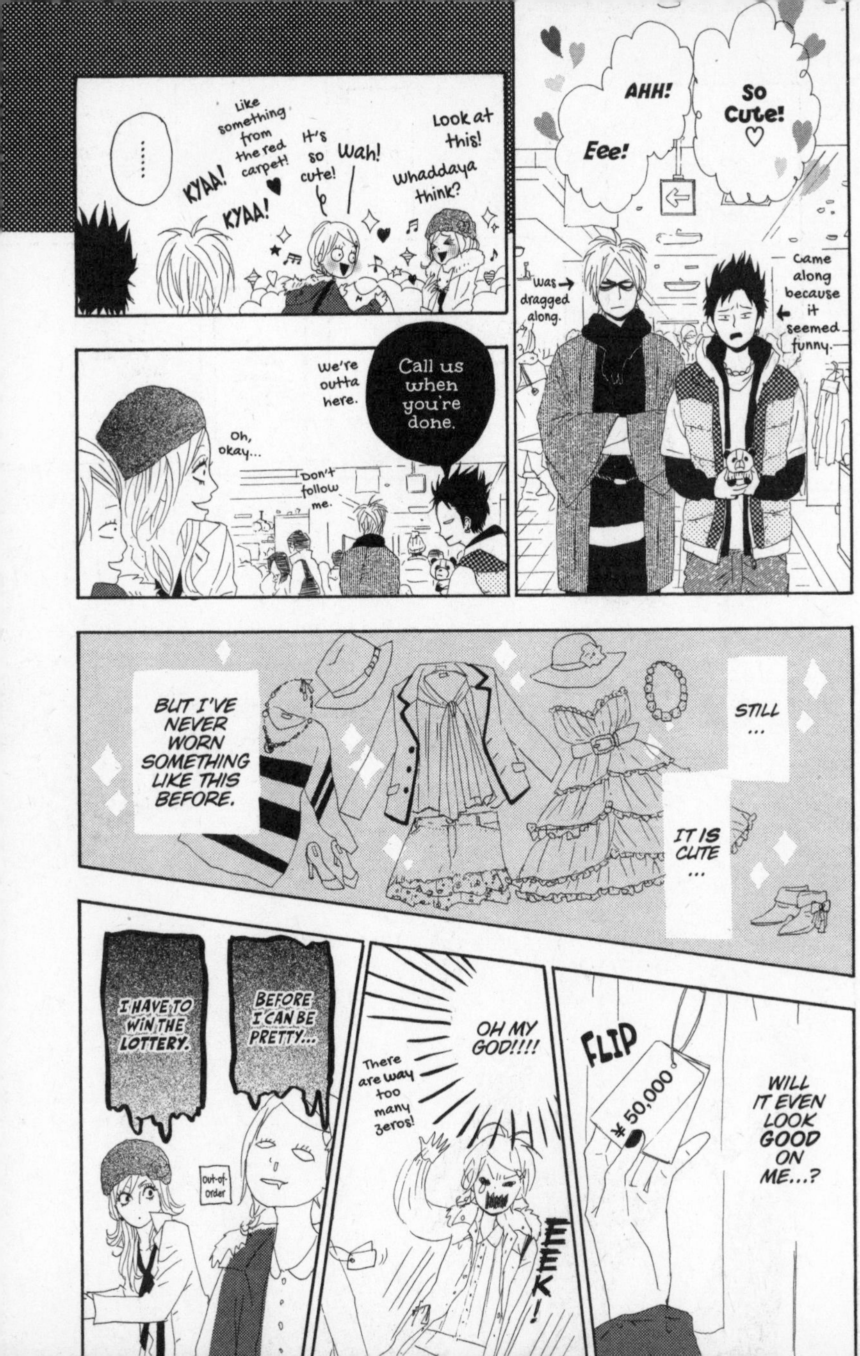

So Cute! ♥
AHH!
Eee!
Came along because it seemed funny.
Was dragged along.
Look at this!
Whaddaya think?
Wah!
It's so cute!
Like something from the red carpet!
KYAA!
KYAA!
......
Call us when you're done.
We're outta here.
Don't follow me.
Oh, okay...
STILL...
IT IS CUTE...
BUT I'VE NEVER WORN SOMETHING LIKE THIS BEFORE.
FLIP
¥50,000
WILL IT EVEN LOOK GOOD ON ME...?
OH MY GOD!!!!
There are way too many zeros!
EEEK!
BEFORE I CAN BE PRETTY...
I HAVE TO WIN THE LOTTERY.
Out-of-Order

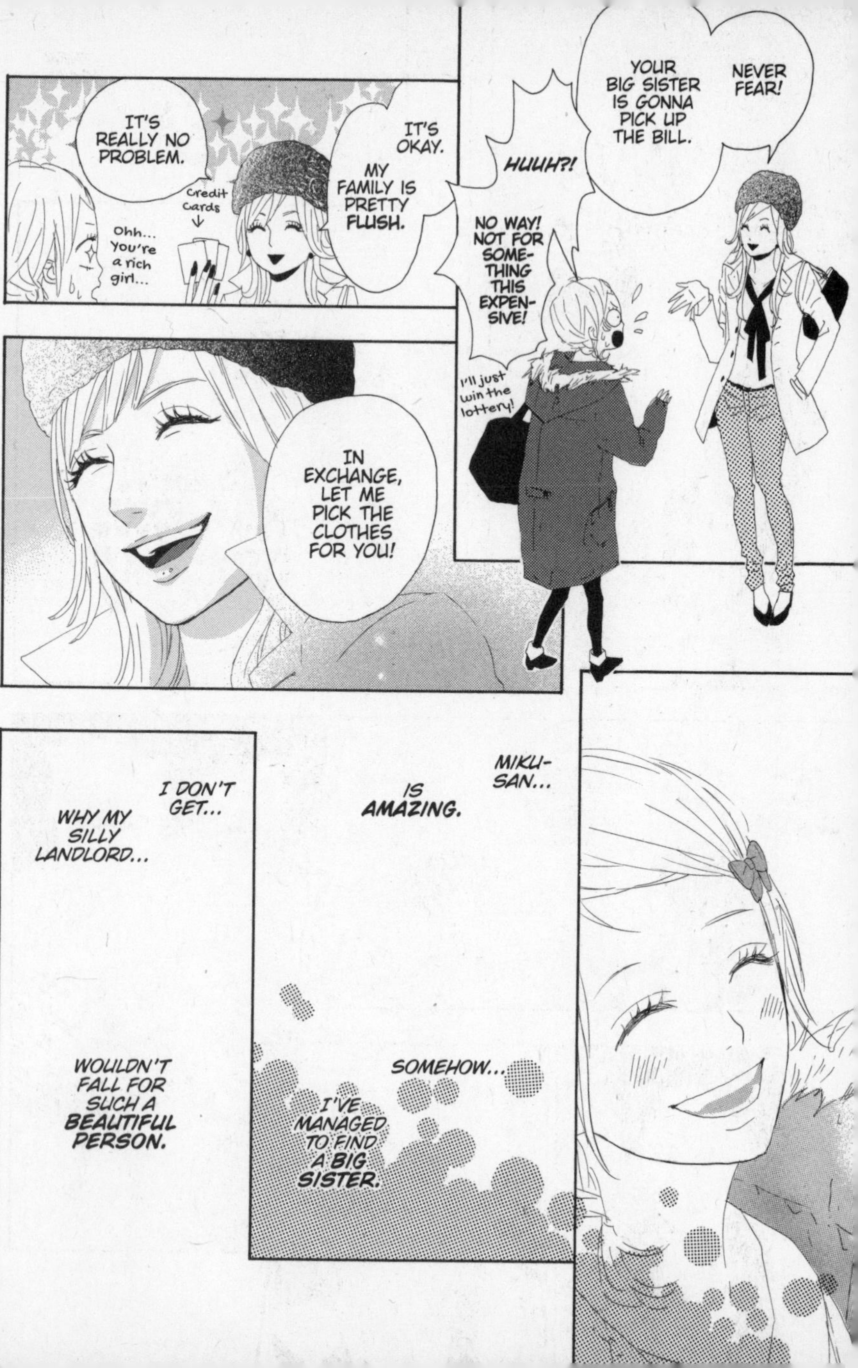
NEVER FEAR!
YOUR BIG SISTER IS GONNA PICK UP THE BILL.
HUUH?!
NO WAY! NOT FOR SOMETHING THIS EXPENSIVE!
I'll just win the lottery!
IT'S OKAY.
MY FAMILY IS PRETTY FLUSH.
IT'S REALLY NO PROBLEM.
Credit Cards
Ohh... You're a rich girl...
IN EXCHANGE, LET ME PICK THE CLOTHES FOR YOU!
MIKU-SAN...
IS AMAZING.
SOMEHOW...
I'VE MANAGED TO FIND A BIG SISTER.
I DON'T GET...
WHY MY SILLY LANDLORD...
WOULDN'T FALL FOR SUCH A BEAUTIFUL PERSON.

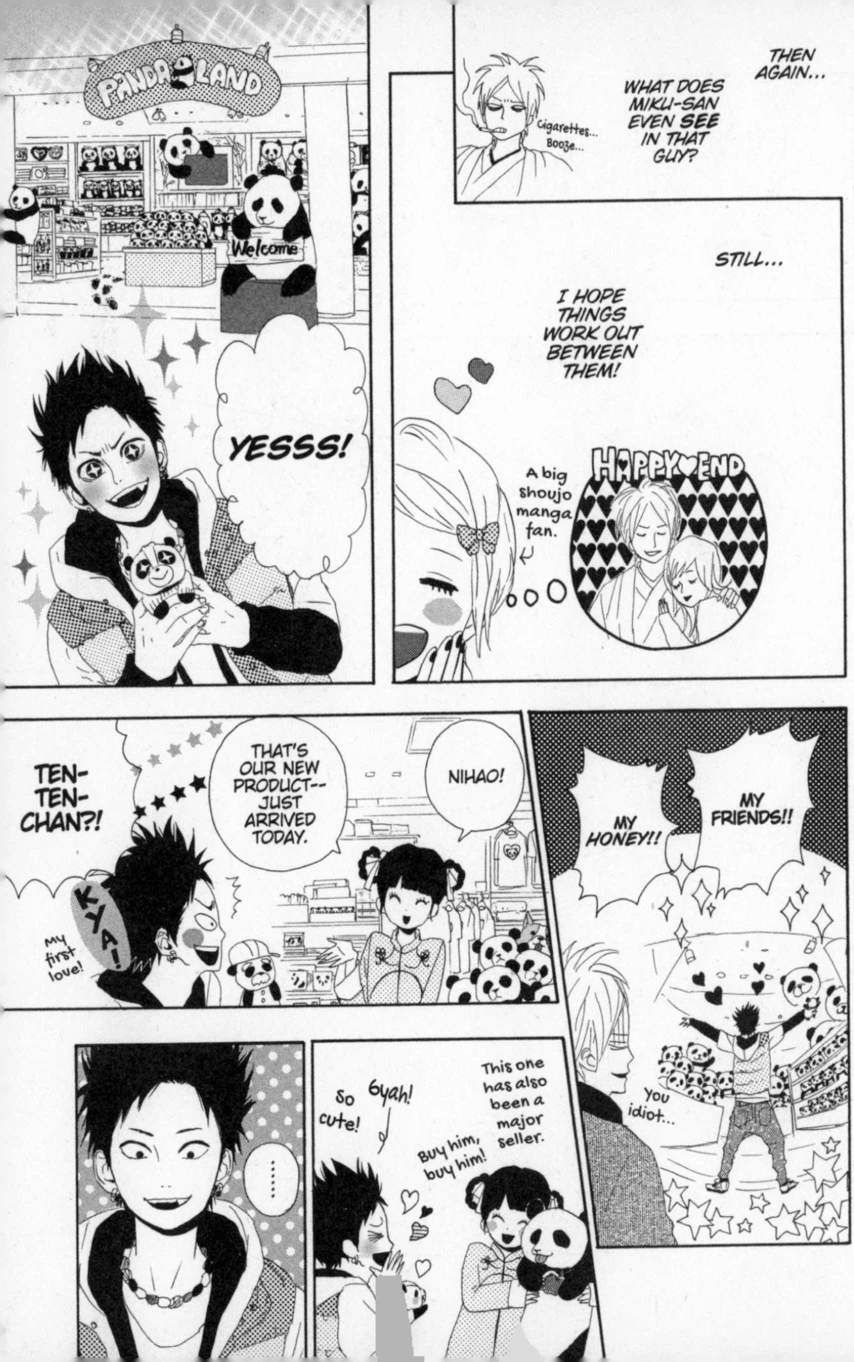
THEN AGAIN...
WHAT DOES MIKU-SAN EVEN SEE IN THAT GUY?
Cigarettes... Booze...
STILL...
I HOPE THINGS WORK OUT BETWEEN THEM!
HAPPY♥END
A big shoujo manga fan.
PANDA LAND
Welcome
YESSS!
MY FRIENDS!!
MY HONEY!!
You idiot...
NIHAO!
THAT'S OUR NEW PRODUCT--JUST ARRIVED TODAY.
TEN-TEN-CHAN?!
KYA!
My first love!
This one has also been a major seller.
Buy him, buy him!
Gyah!
So cute!
......

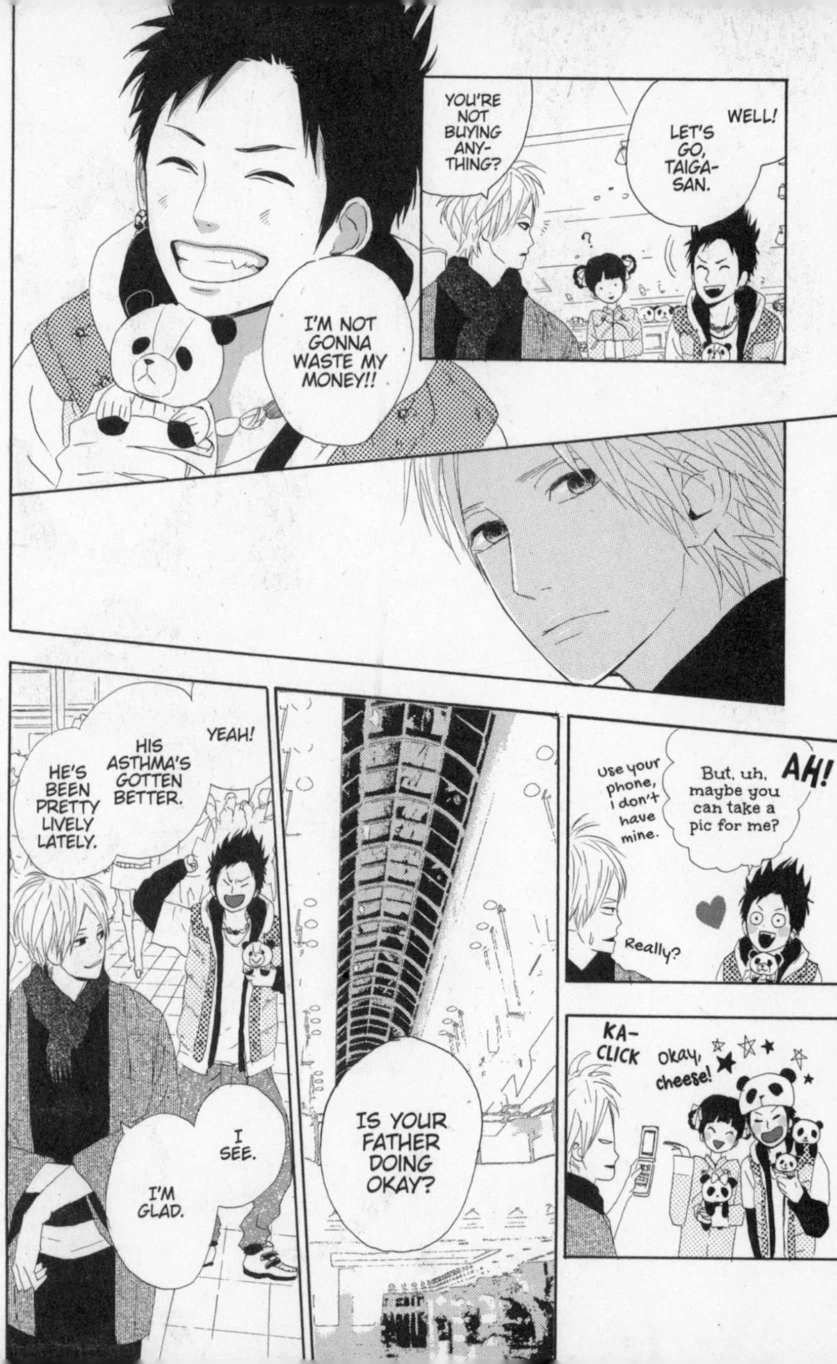
WELL! LET'S GO, TAIGA-SAN.
YOU'RE NOT BUYING ANY-THING?
I'M NOT GONNA WASTE MY MONEY!!
AH!
But, uh, maybe you can take a pic for me?
Use your phone, I don't have mine.
Really?
KA-CLICK
Okay, cheese!
IS YOUR FATHER DOING OKAY?
YEAH!
HIS ASTHMA'S GOTTEN BETTER.
HE'S BEEN PRETTY LIVELY LATELY.
I SEE.
I'M GLAD.

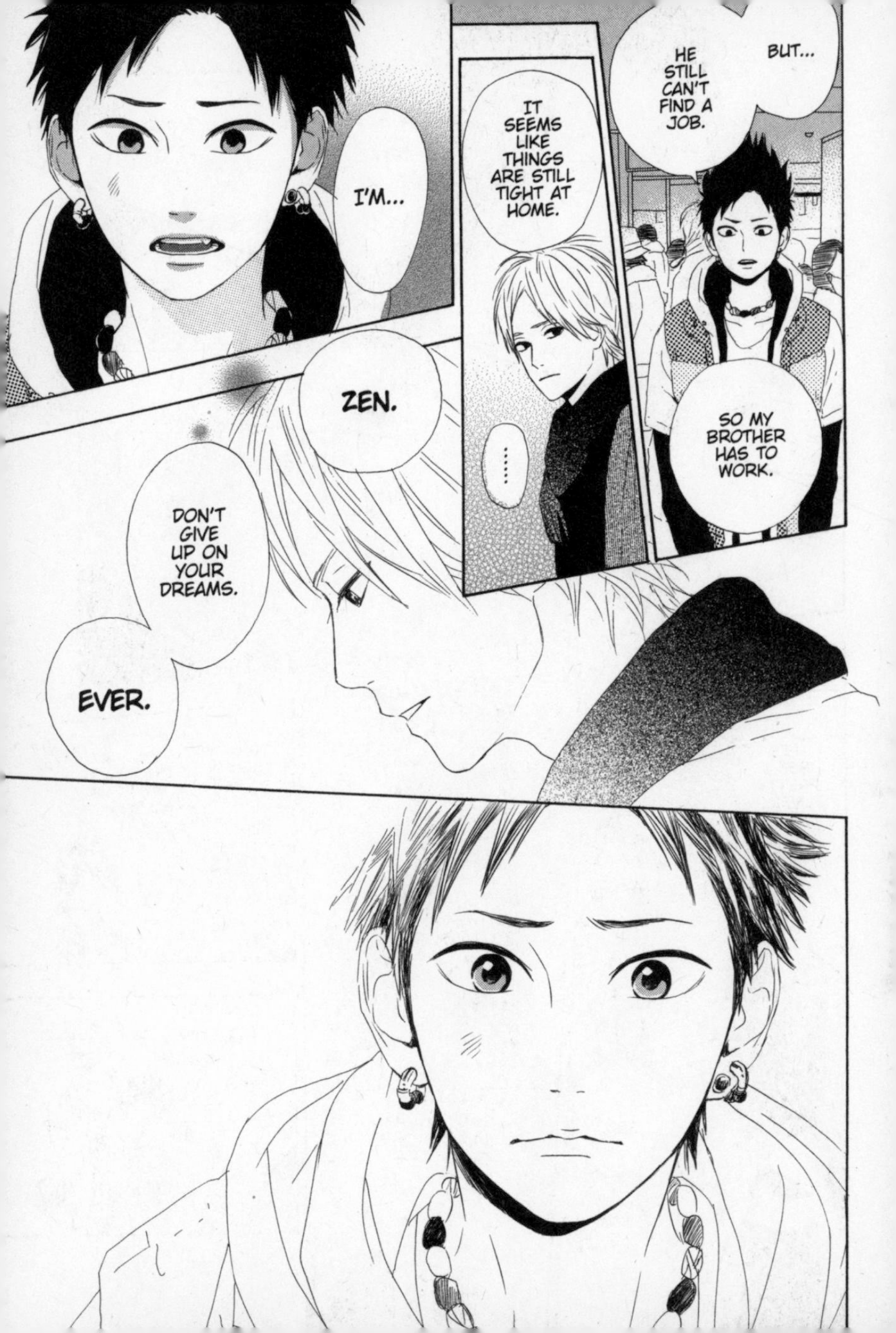
BUT...
HE STILL CAN'T FIND A JOB.
SO MY BROTHER HAS TO WORK.
IT SEEMS LIKE THINGS ARE STILL TIGHT AT HOME.
......
I'M...
ZEN.
DON'T GIVE UP ON YOUR DREAMS.
EVER.

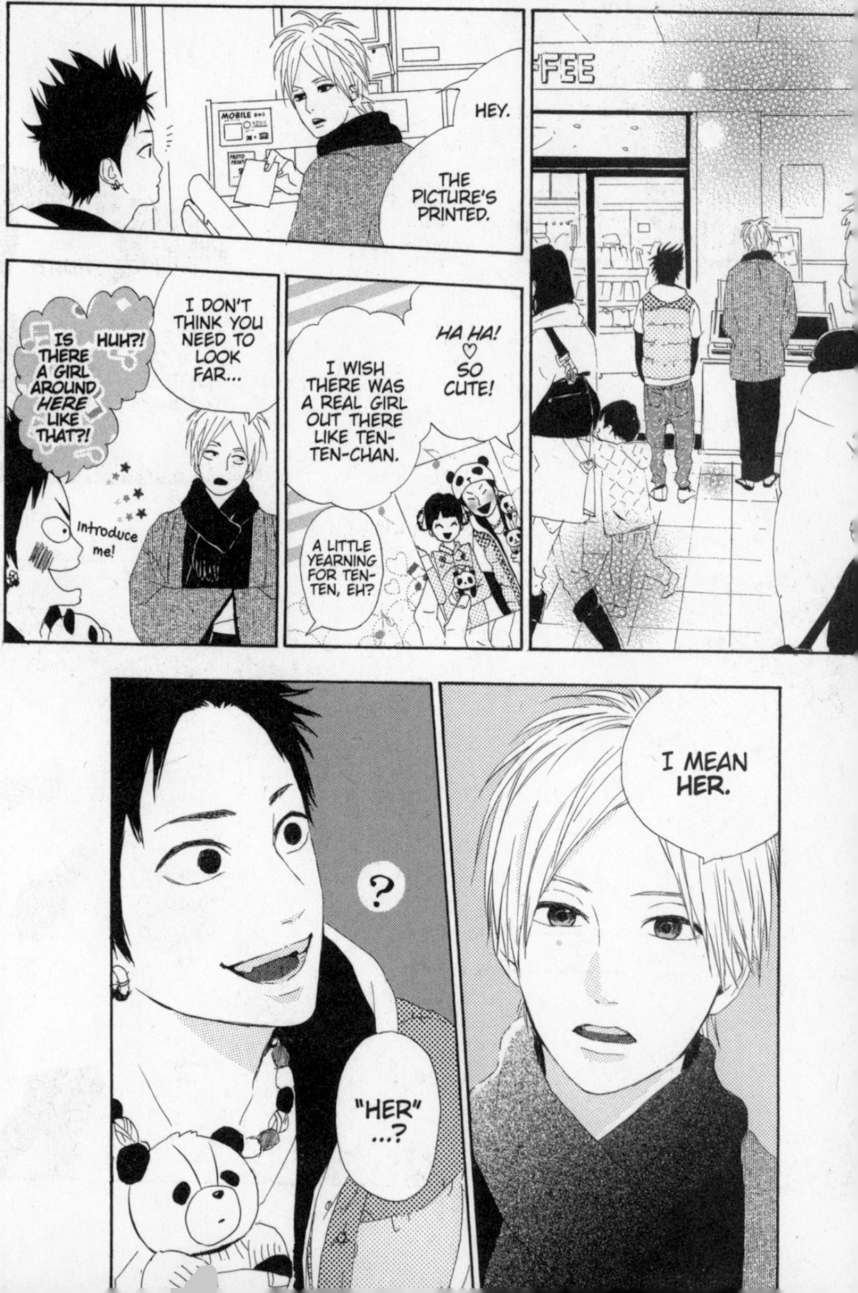
FEE
HEY.
THE PICTURE'S PRINTED.
MOBILE
HA HA! ♡ SO CUTE!
I WISH THERE WAS A REAL GIRL OUT THERE LIKE TEN-TEN-CHAN.
A LITTLE YEARNING FOR TEN-TEN, EH?
I DON'T THINK YOU NEED TO LOOK FAR...
HUH?!
IS THERE A GIRL AROUND HERE LIKE THAT?!
Introduce me!
I MEAN HER.
?
"HER" ...?

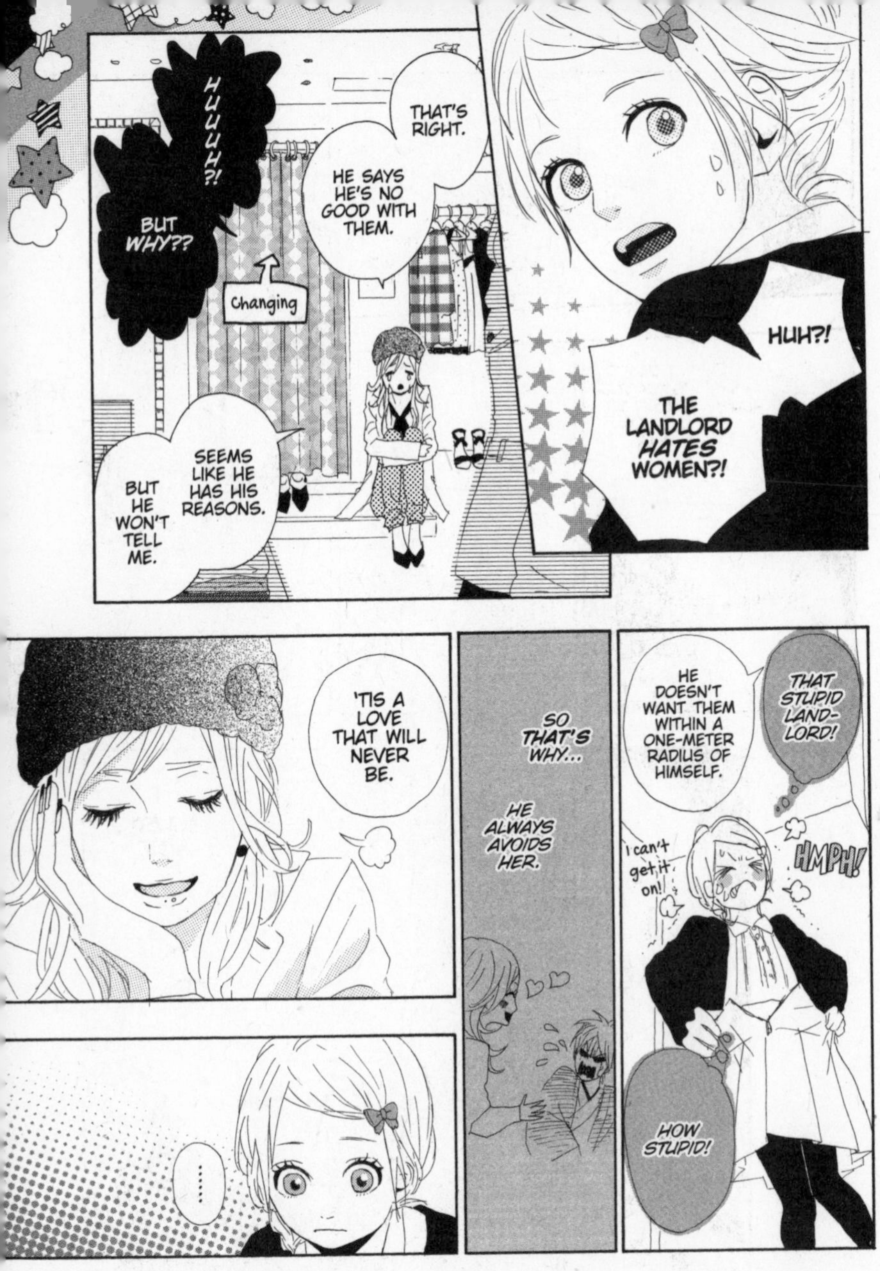
HUH?!
THE LANDLORD HATES WOMEN?!
THAT'S RIGHT.
HE SAYS HE'S NO GOOD WITH THEM.
HUUUH?!
BUT WHY??
Changing
SEEMS LIKE HE HAS HIS REASONS.
BUT HE WON'T TELL ME.
HE DOESN'T WANT THEM WITHIN A ONE-METER RADIUS OF HIMSELF.
THAT STUPID LAND-LORD!
I can't get it on!
HMPH!
HOW STUPID!
SO THAT'S WHY...
HE ALWAYS AVOIDS HER.
'TIS A LOVE THAT WILL NEVER BE.
......

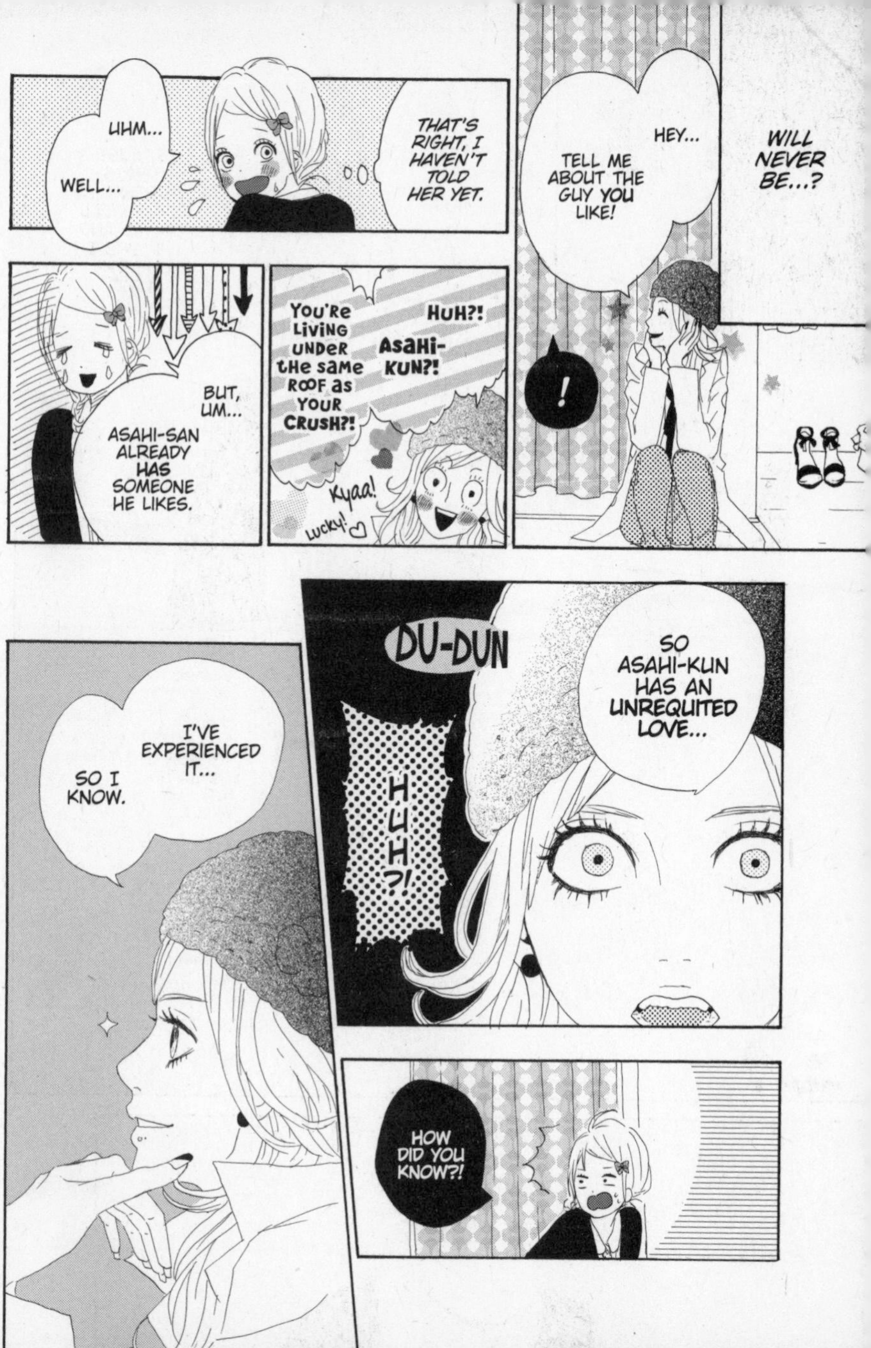

WILL NEVER BE...?
HEY... TELL ME ABOUT THE GUY YOU LIKE!
!
THAT'S RIGHT, I HAVEN'T TOLD HER YET.
UHM... WELL...
HUH?! ASAHI-KUN?!
You're living under the same roof as your crush?!
Kyaa! Lucky!♡
BUT, UM... ASAHI-SAN ALREADY HAS SOMEONE HE LIKES.
DU-DUN
SO ASAHI-KUN HAS AN UNREQUITED LOVE...
HUH?!
HOW DID YOU KNOW?!
I'VE EXPERIENCED IT... SO I KNOW.

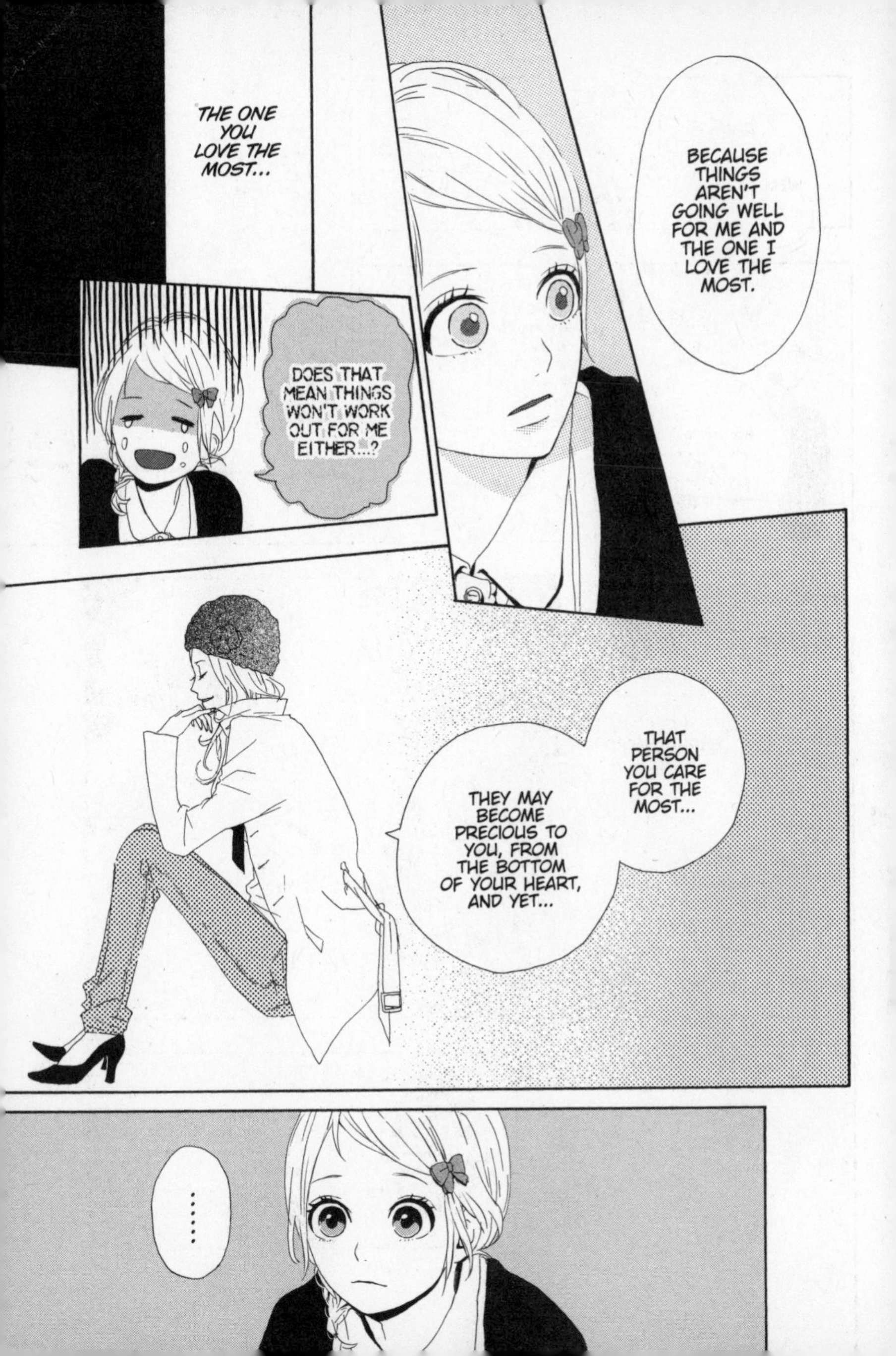
BECAUSE THINGS AREN'T GOING WELL FOR ME AND THE ONE I LOVE THE MOST.
THE ONE YOU LOVE THE MOST...
DOES THAT MEAN THINGS WON'T WORK OUT FOR ME EITHER...?
THAT PERSON YOU CARE FOR THE MOST...
THEY MAY BECOME PRECIOUS TO YOU, FROM THE BOTTOM OF YOUR HEART, AND YET...
......

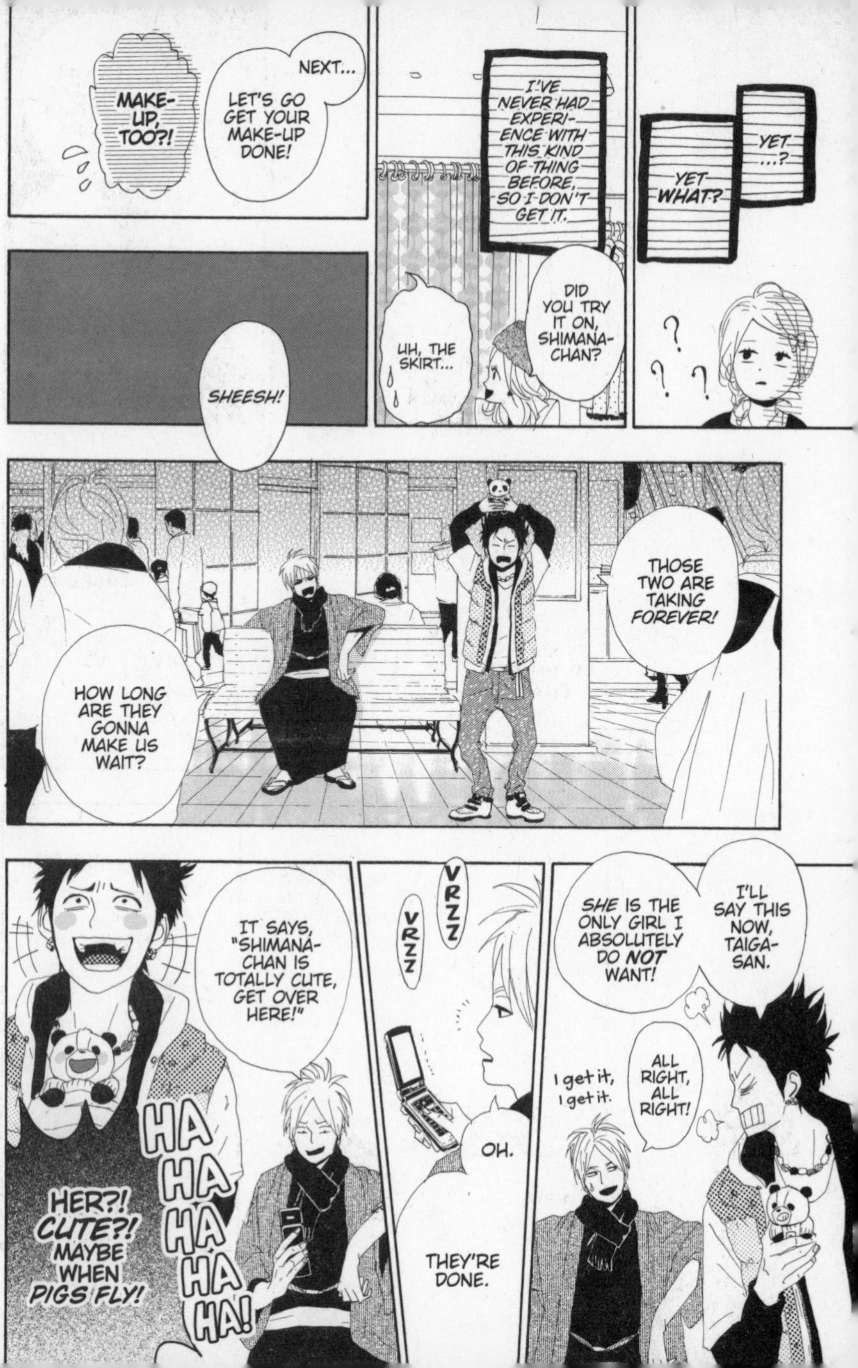
YET ...?
YET WHAT?
I'VE NEVER HAD EXPERIENCE WITH THIS KIND OF THING BEFORE, SO I DON'T GET IT.
DID YOU TRY IT ON, SHIMANA-CHAN?
UH, THE SKIRT...
NEXT...
LET'S GO GET YOUR MAKE-UP DONE!
MAKE-UP, TOO?!
SHEESH!
THOSE TWO ARE TAKING FOREVER!
HOW LONG ARE THEY GONNA MAKE US WAIT?
I'LL SAY THIS NOW, TAIGA-SAN.
SHE IS THE ONLY GIRL I ABSOLUTELY DO NOT WANT!
ALL RIGHT, ALL RIGHT!
I get it, I get it.
VRZZ
VRZZ
OH.
THEY'RE DONE.
IT SAYS, "SHIMANA-CHAN IS TOTALLY CUTE, GET OVER HERE!"
HA HA HA HA HA HA!
HER?! CUTE?! MAYBE WHEN PIGS FLY!

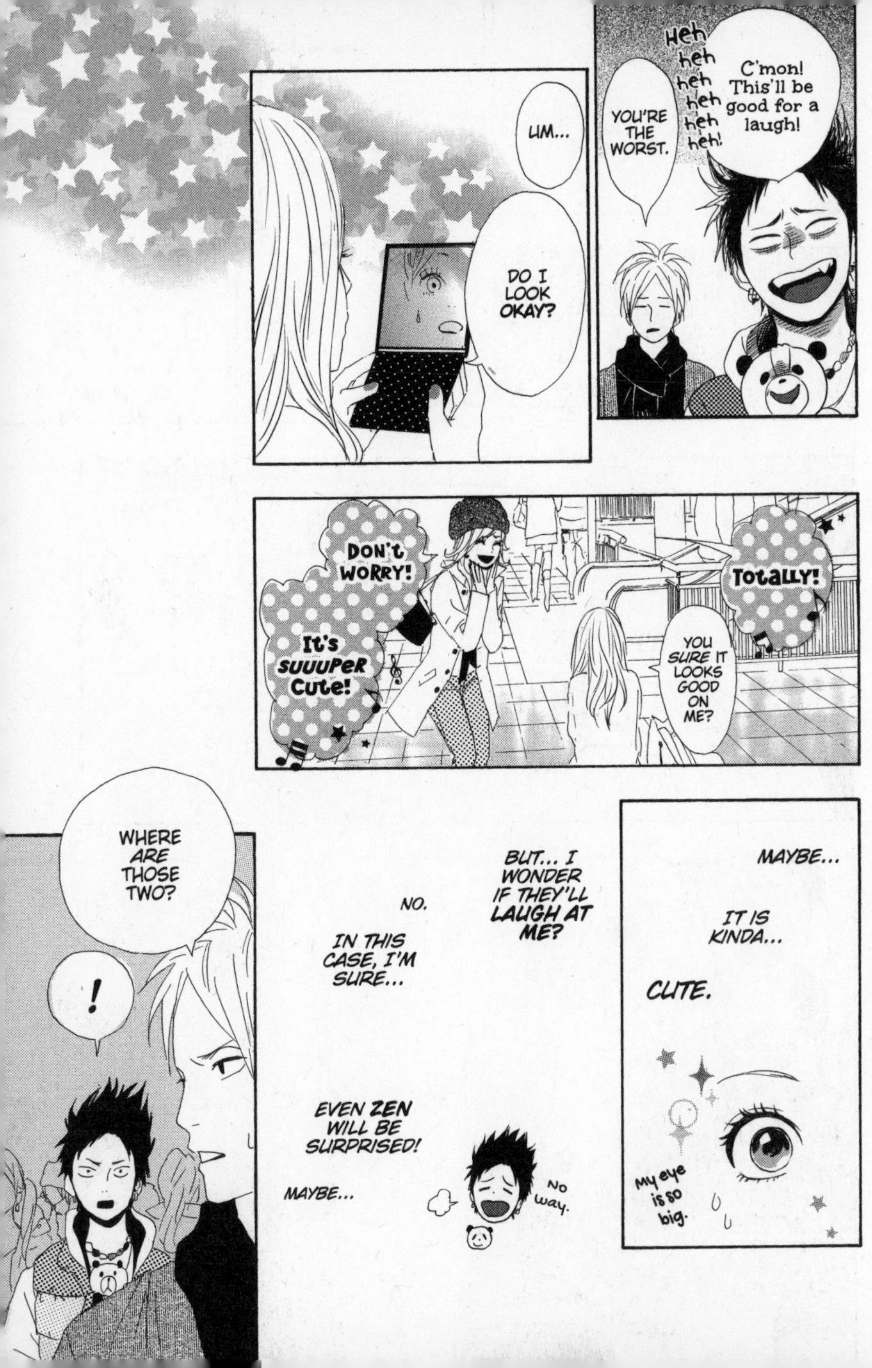
C'mon! This'll be good for a laugh!
Heh heh heh heh heh heh!
YOU'RE THE WORST.
UM...
DO I LOOK OKAY?
YOU SURE IT LOOKS GOOD ON ME?
Totally!
Don't worry!
It's suuuper Cute!
MAYBE...
IT IS KINDA...
CUTE.
My eye is so big.
BUT... I WONDER IF THEY'LL LAUGH AT ME?
NO.
IN THIS CASE, I'M SURE...
EVEN ZEN WILL BE SURPRISED!
MAYBE...
No way.
WHERE ARE THOSE TWO?
!

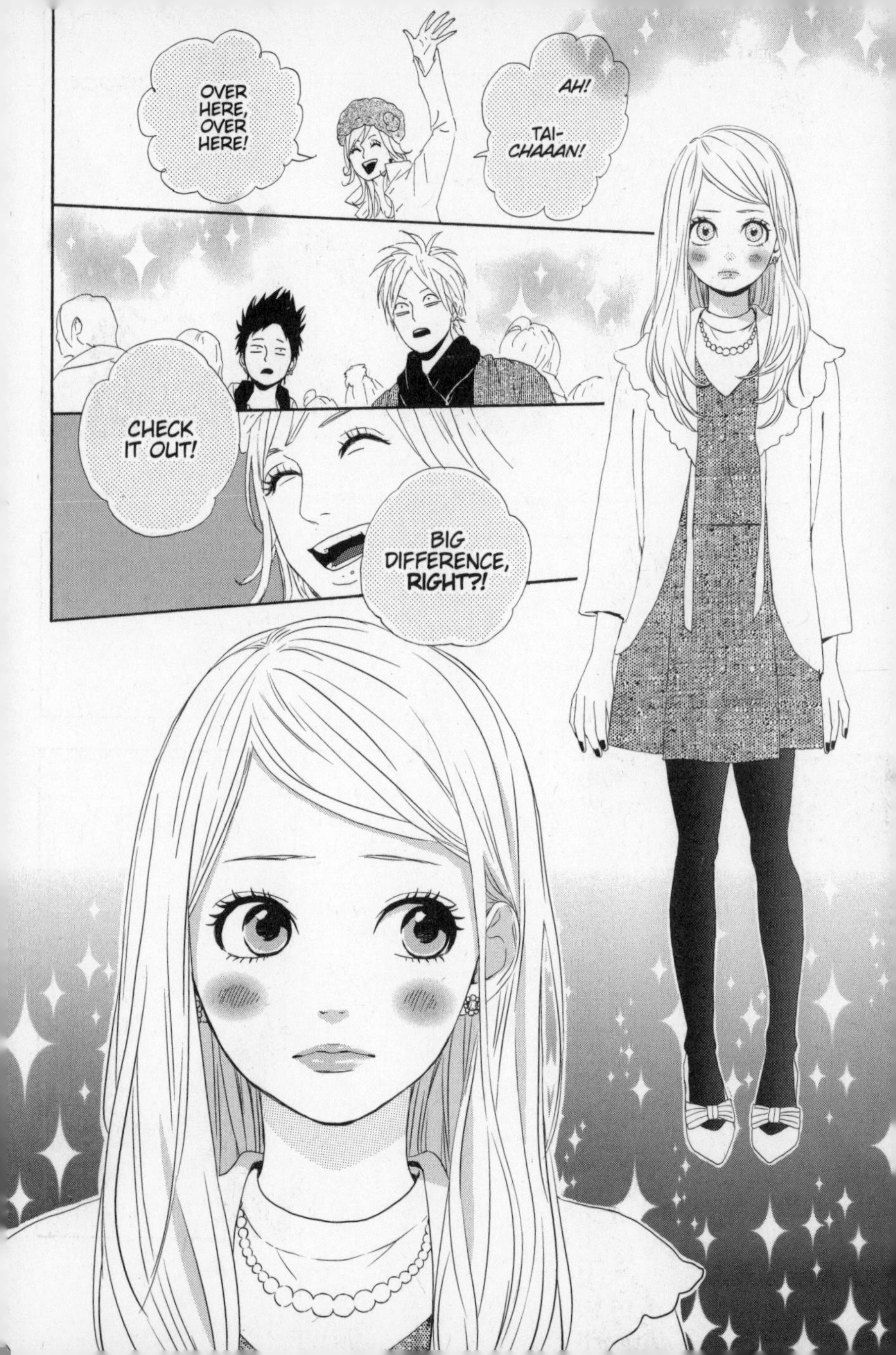
AH!
TAI-CHAAAN!
OVER HERE, OVER HERE!
CHECK IT OUT!
BIG DIFFERENCE, RIGHT?!

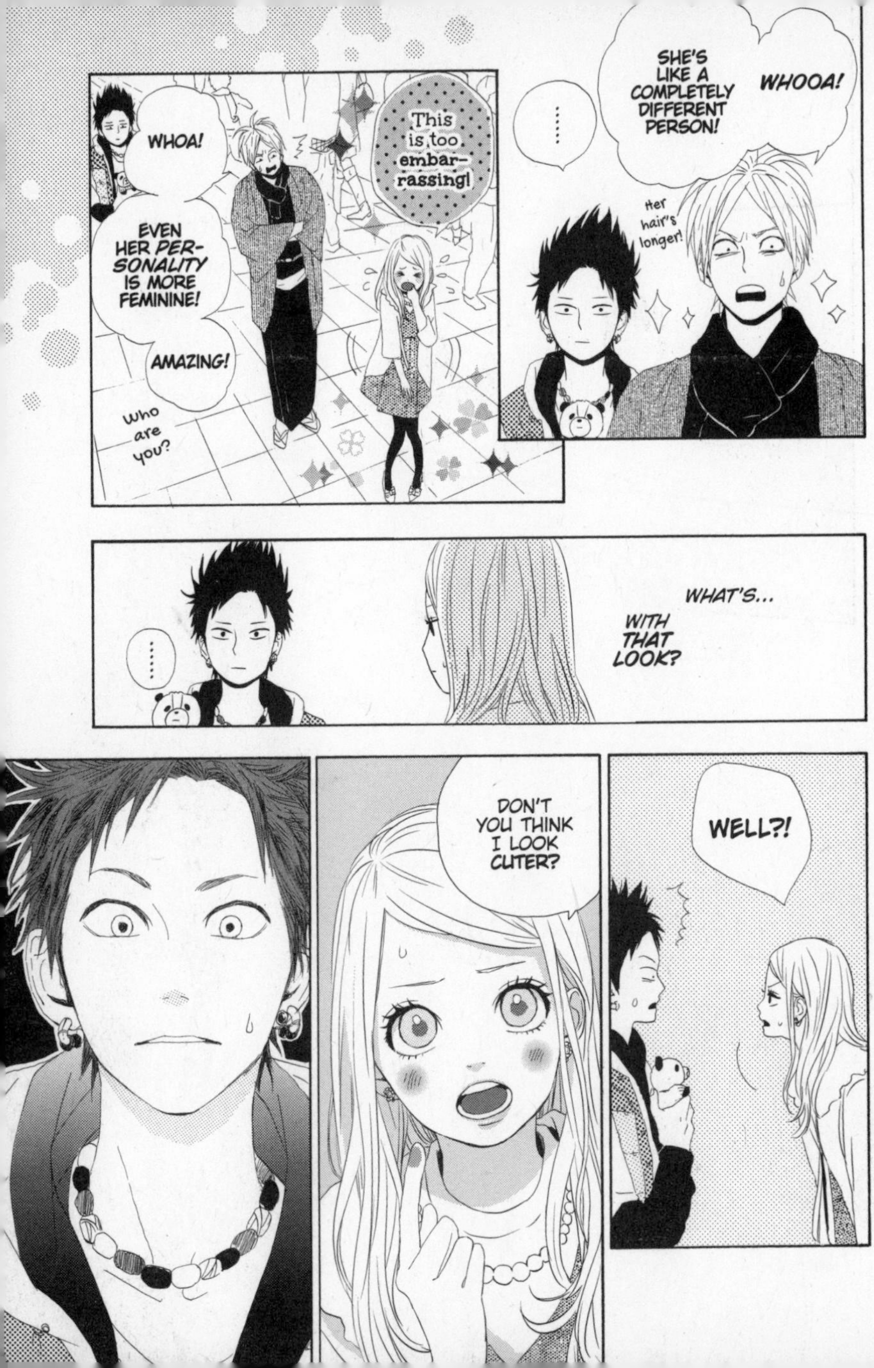
WHOOA!
SHE'S LIKE A COMPLETELY DIFFERENT PERSON!
......
Her hair's longer!
This is too embarrassing!
WHOA!
EVEN HER PERSONALITY IS MORE FEMININE!
AMAZING!
Who are you?
WHAT'S... WITH THAT LOOK?
......
WELL?!
DON'T YOU THINK I LOOK CUTER?

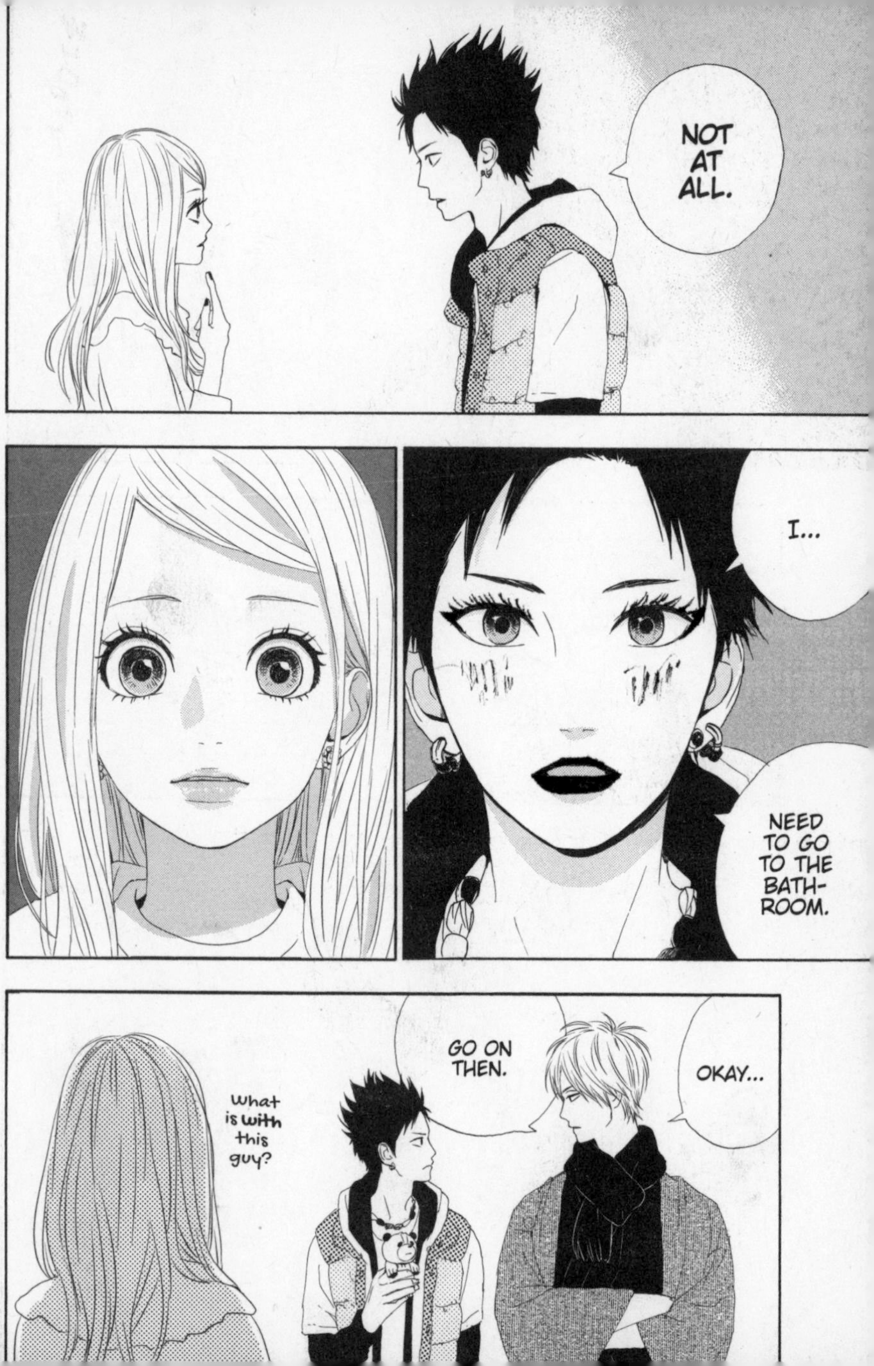
NOT AT ALL.
I...
NEED TO GO TO THE BATH-ROOM.
OKAY...
GO ON THEN.
What is with this guy?

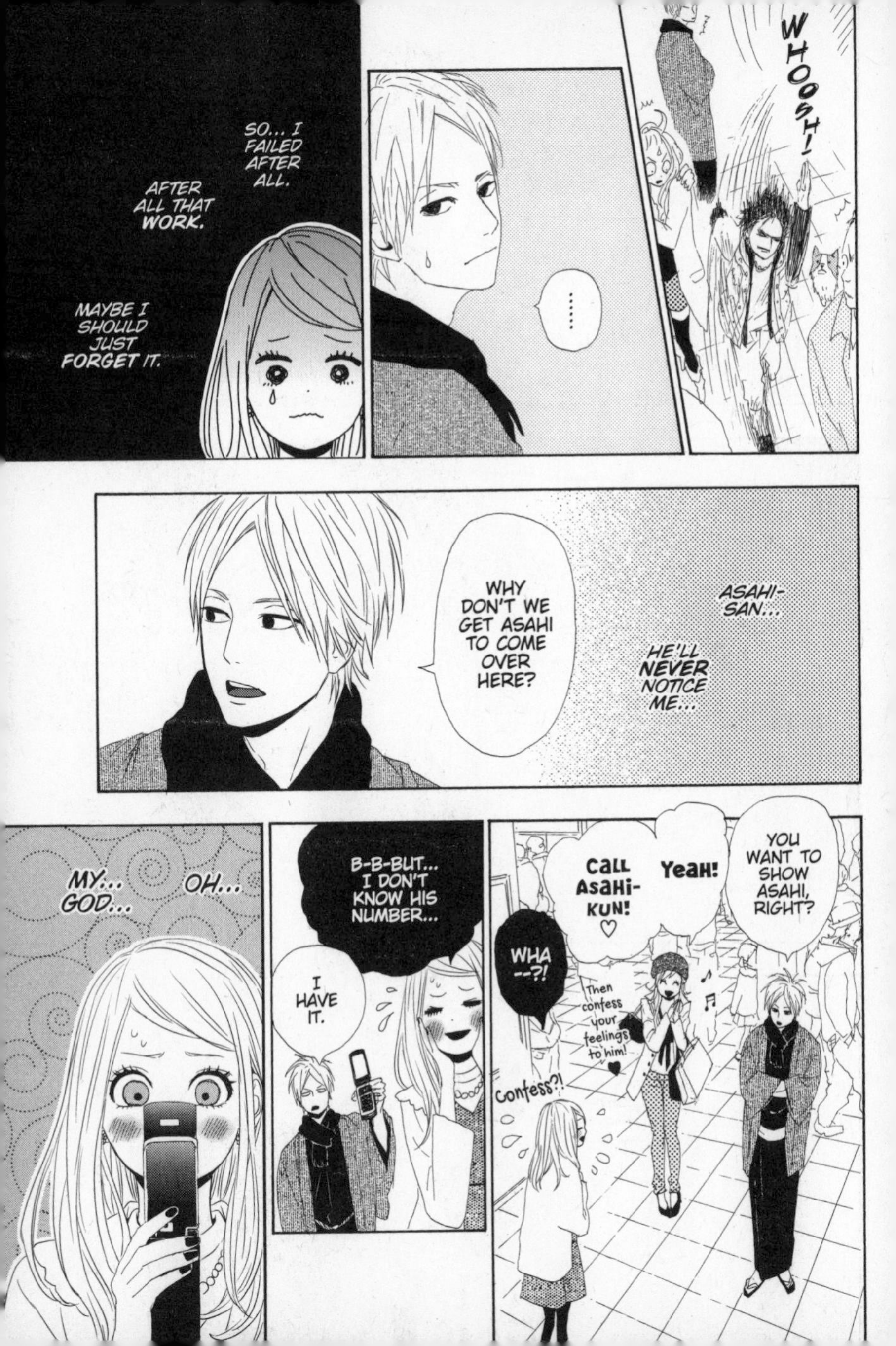
WHOOSH!
......
SO... I FAILED AFTER ALL.
AFTER ALL THAT WORK.
MAYBE I SHOULD JUST FORGET IT.
ASAHI-SAN...
HE'LL NEVER NOTICE ME...
WHY DON'T WE GET ASAHI TO COME OVER HERE?
YOU WANT TO SHOW ASAHI, RIGHT?
Yeah!
Call Asahi-kun! ♡
WHA--?!
Then confess your feelings to him! ♥
Confess?!
B-B-BUT... I DON'T KNOW HIS NUMBER...
I HAVE IT.
OH...
MY... GOD...

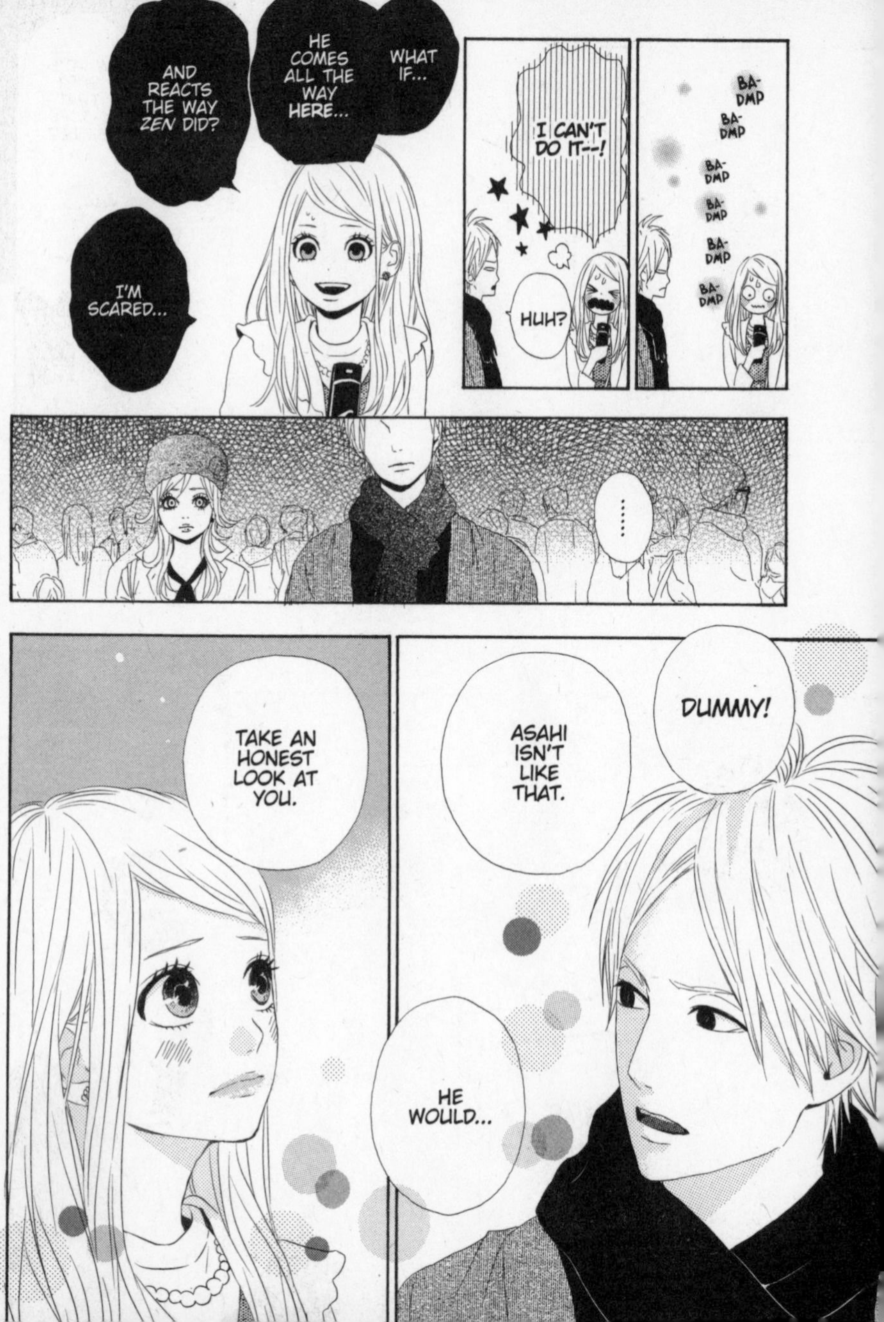
BA-DMP
BA-DMP
BA-DMP
BA-DMP
BA-DMP
BA-DMP
I CAN'T DO IT--!
HUH?
WHAT IF...
HE COMES ALL THE WAY HERE...
AND REACTS THE WAY ZEN DID?
I'M SCARED...
......
DUMMY!
ASAHI ISN'T LIKE THAT.
HE WOULD...
TAKE AN HONEST LOOK AT YOU.

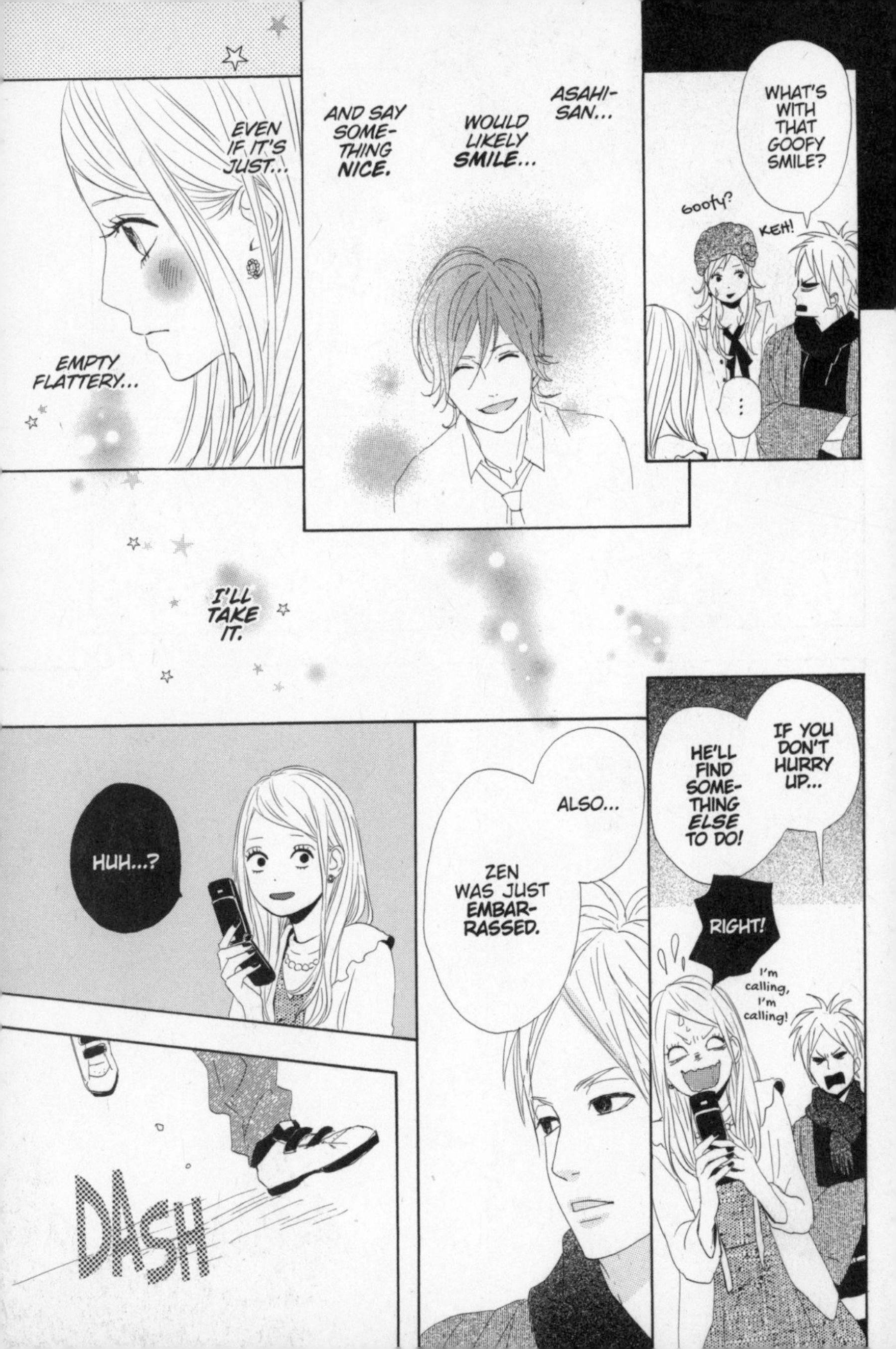
WHAT'S WITH THAT GOOFY SMILE?
Goofy?
KEH!
...
ASAHI-SAN...
WOULD LIKELY SMILE...
AND SAY SOME-THING NICE.
EVEN IF IT'S JUST...
EMPTY FLATTERY...
I'LL TAKE IT.
IF YOU DON'T HURRY UP...
HE'LL FIND SOME-THING ELSE TO DO!
RIGHT!
I'm calling, I'm calling!
ALSO...
ZEN WAS JUST EMBAR-RASSED.
HUH...?
DASH

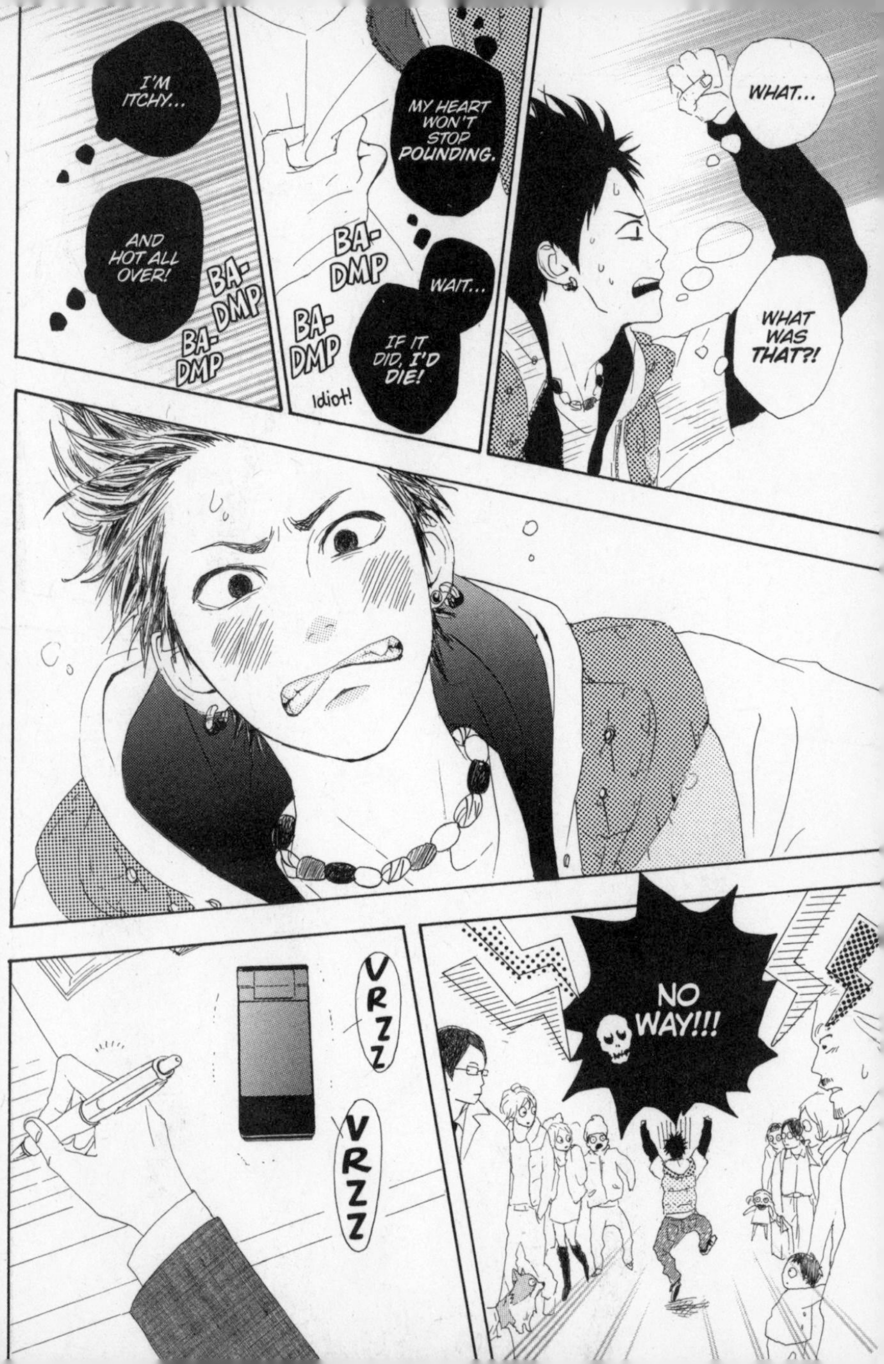
WHAT...
WHAT WAS THAT?!
MY HEART WON'T STOP POUNDING.
BA-DMP
WAIT...
IF IT DID, I'D DIE!
BA-DMP
Idiot!
I'M ITCHY...
AND HOT ALL OVER!
BA-DMP
BA-DMP
NO WAY!!!
VRZZ
VRZZ

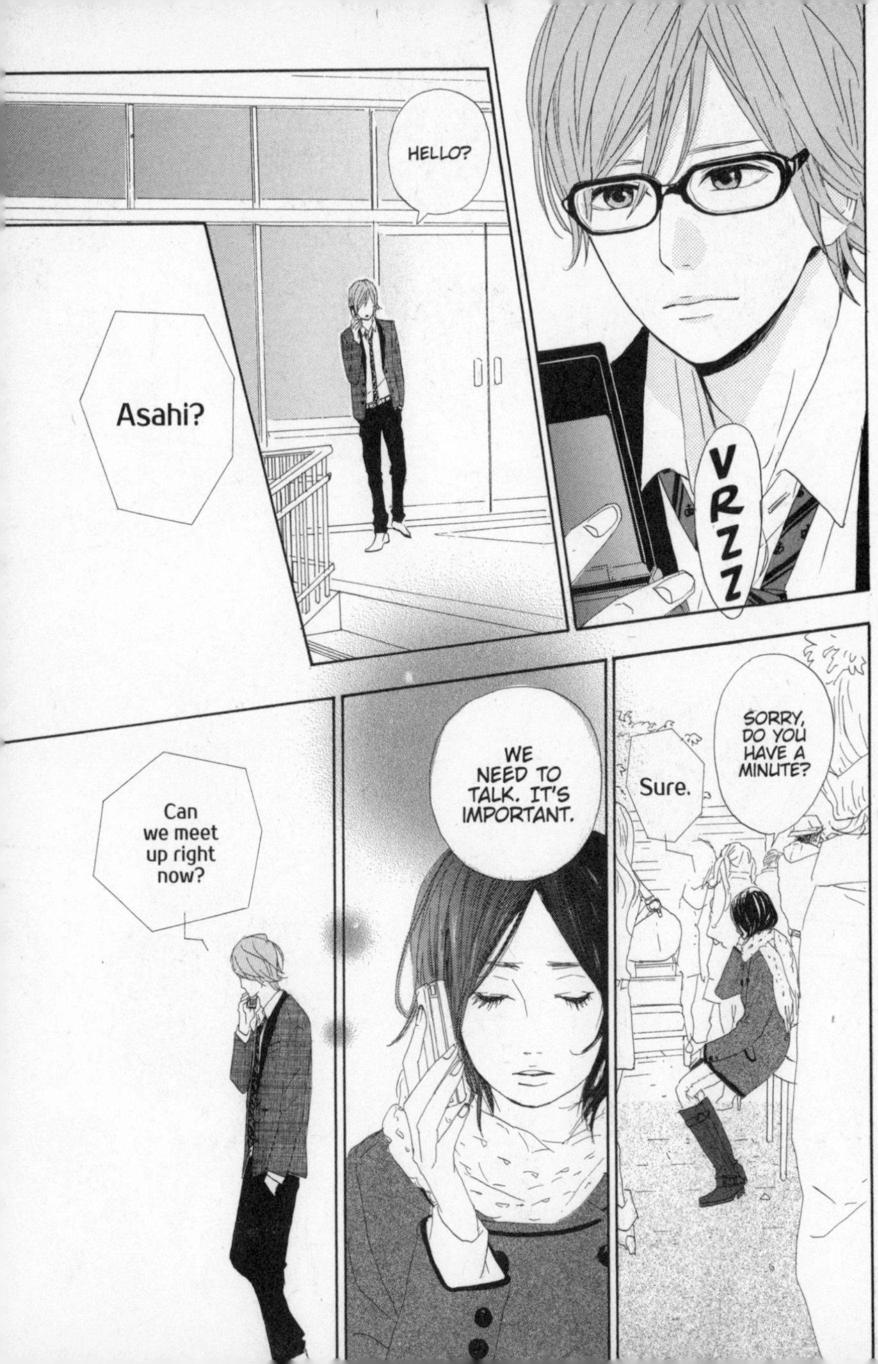
VRZZ
HELLO?
Asahi?
SORRY, DO YOU HAVE A MINUTE?
Sure.
WE NEED TO TALK. IT'S IMPORTANT.
Can we meet up right now?

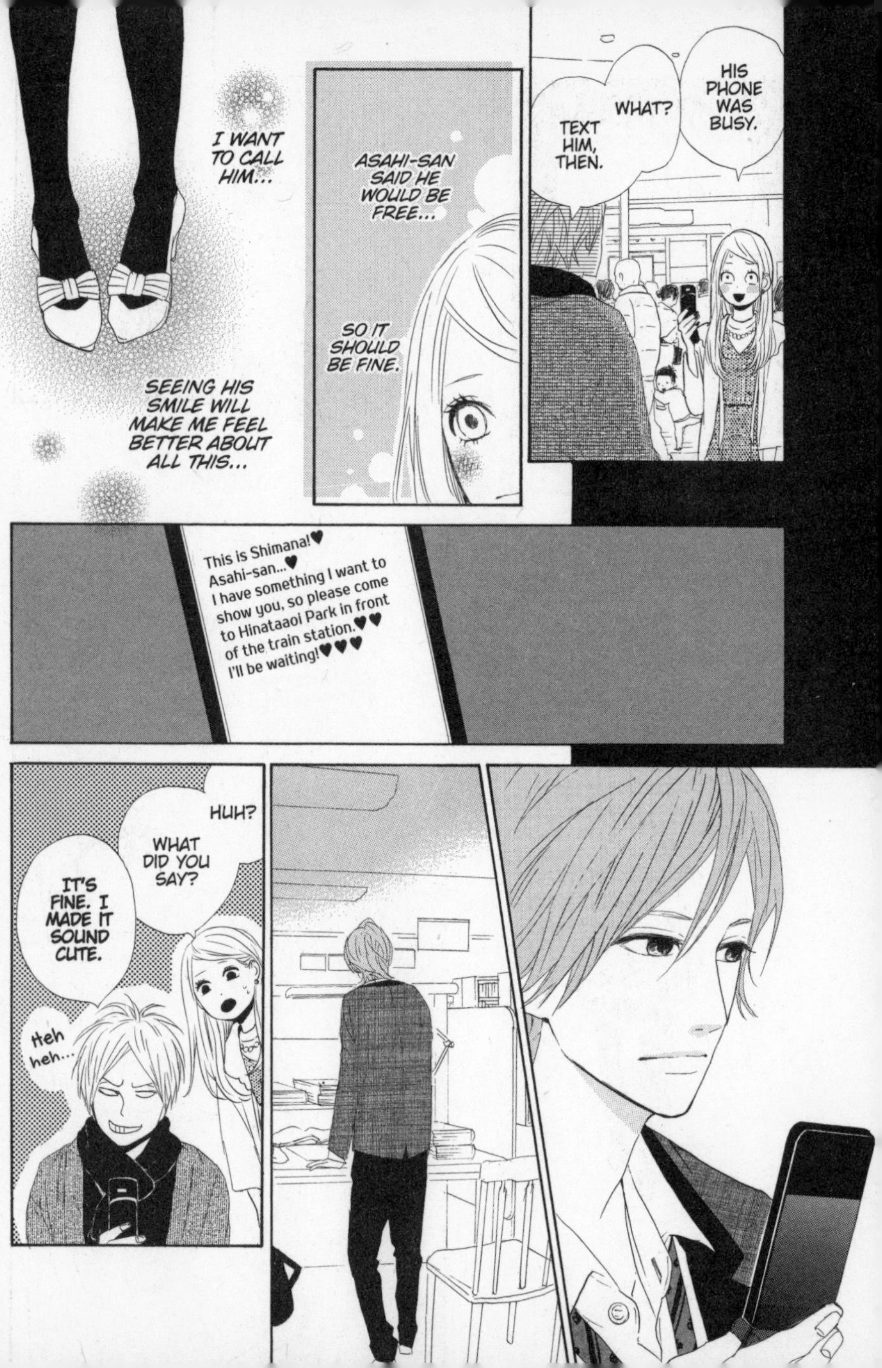
HIS PHONE WAS BUSY.
WHAT?
TEXT HIM, THEN.
ASAHI-SAN SAID HE WOULD BE FREE...
SO IT SHOULD BE FINE.
I WANT TO CALL HIM...
SEEING HIS SMILE WILL MAKE ME FEEL BETTER ABOUT ALL THIS...
This is Shimana!♥ Asahi-san...♥ I have something I want to show you, so please come to Hinataaoi Park in front of the train station.♥♥ I'll be waiting!♥♥♥
HUH? WHAT DID YOU SAY?
IT'S FINE. I MADE IT SOUND CUTE.
Heh heh...

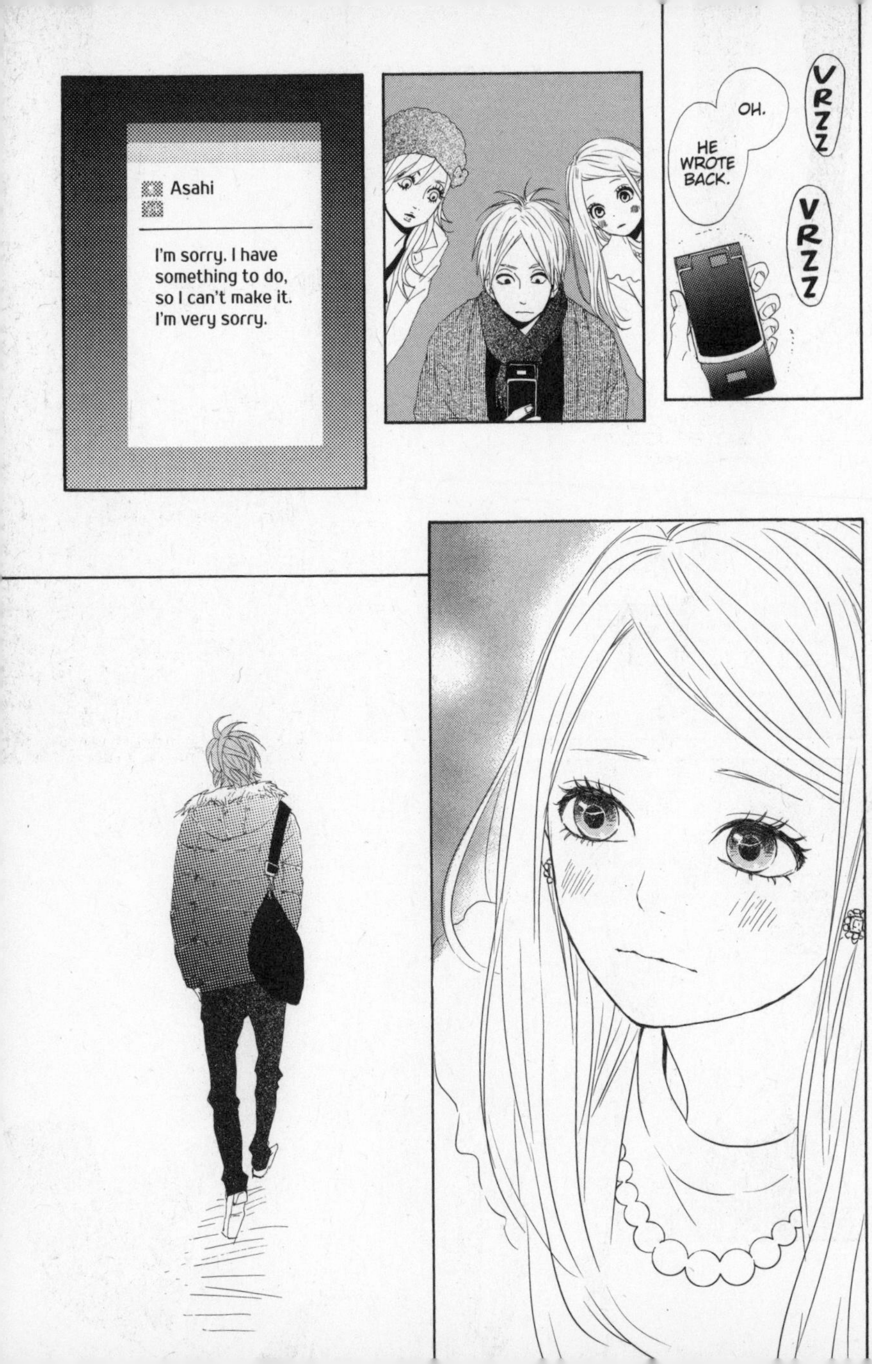
OH.
HE WROTE BACK.
VRZZ
VRZZ
Asahi
I'm sorry. I have something to do, so I can't make it. I'm very sorry.

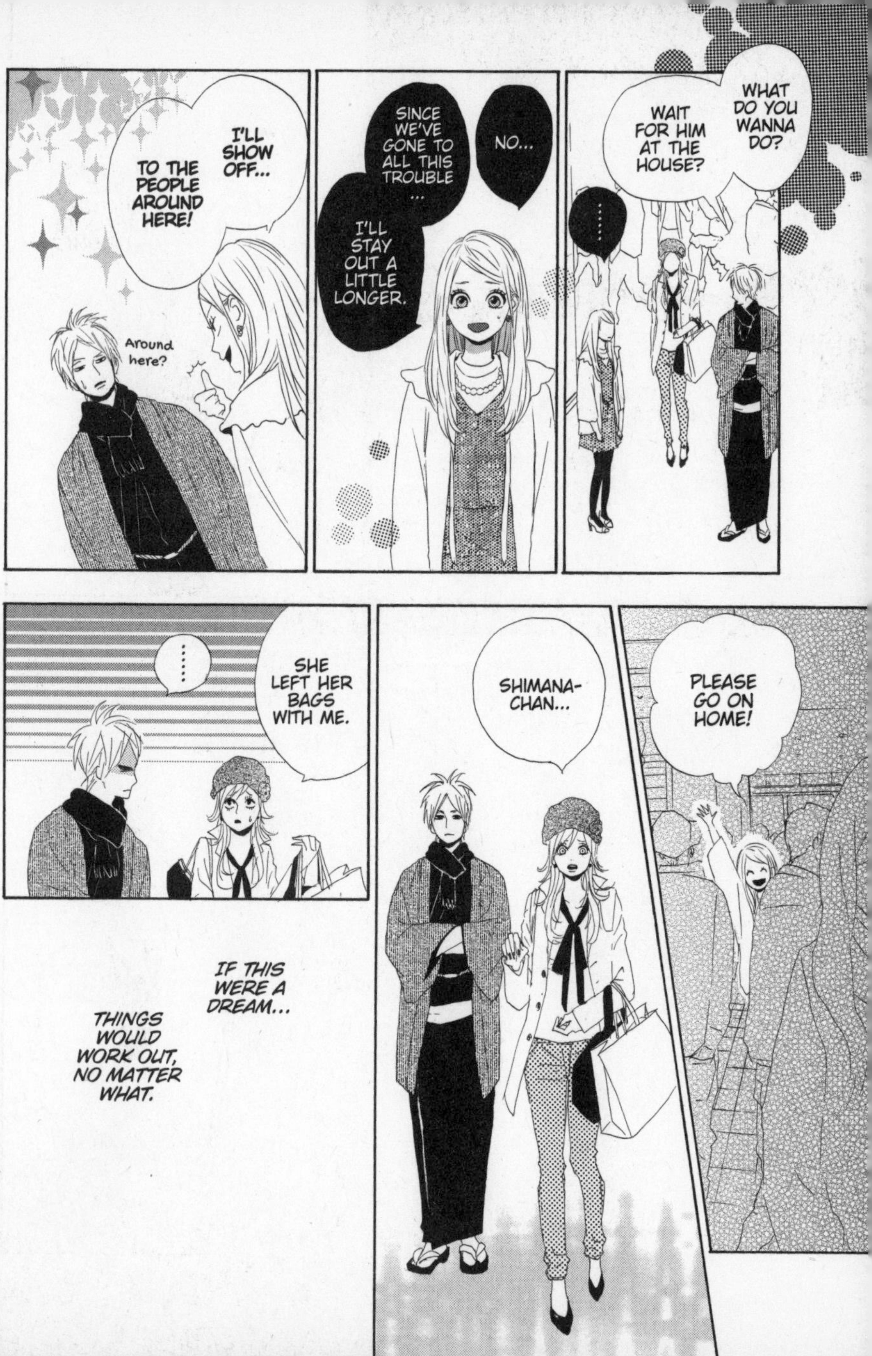
WHAT DO YOU WANNA DO?
WAIT FOR HIM AT THE HOUSE?
......
NO...
SINCE WE'VE GONE TO ALL THIS TROUBLE...
I'LL STAY OUT A LITTLE LONGER.
I'LL SHOW OFF...
TO THE PEOPLE AROUND HERE!
Around here?
PLEASE GO ON HOME!
SHIMANA-CHAN...
SHE LEFT HER BAGS WITH ME.
......
IF THIS WERE A DREAM...
THINGS WOULD WORK OUT, NO MATTER WHAT.

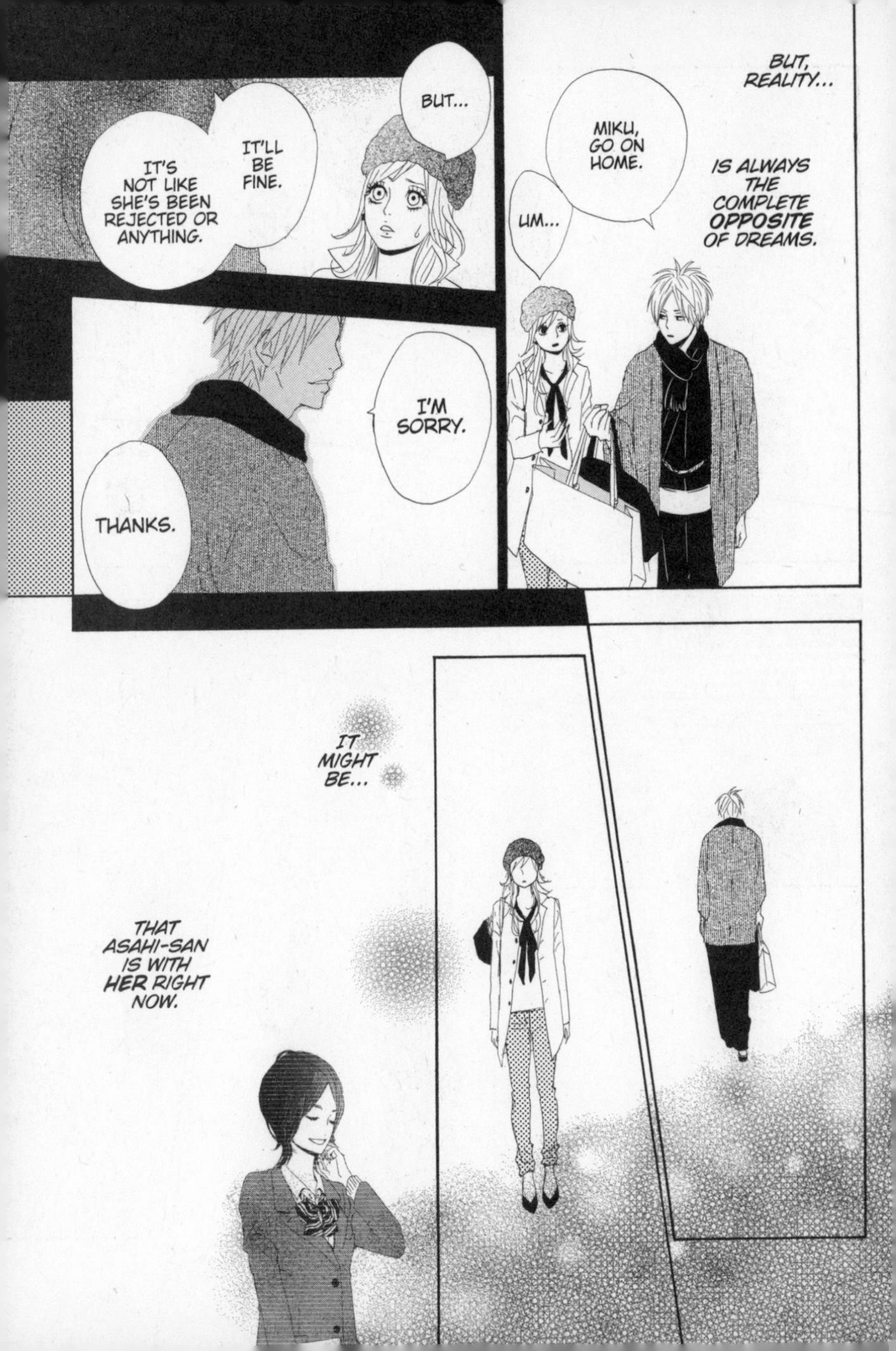
BUT, REALITY...
MIKU, GO ON HOME.
UM...
IS ALWAYS THE COMPLETE OPPOSITE OF DREAMS.
BUT...
IT'LL BE FINE.
IT'S NOT LIKE SHE'S BEEN REJECTED OR ANYTHING.
I'M SORRY.
THANKS.
IT MIGHT BE...
THAT ASAHI-SAN IS WITH HER RIGHT NOW.

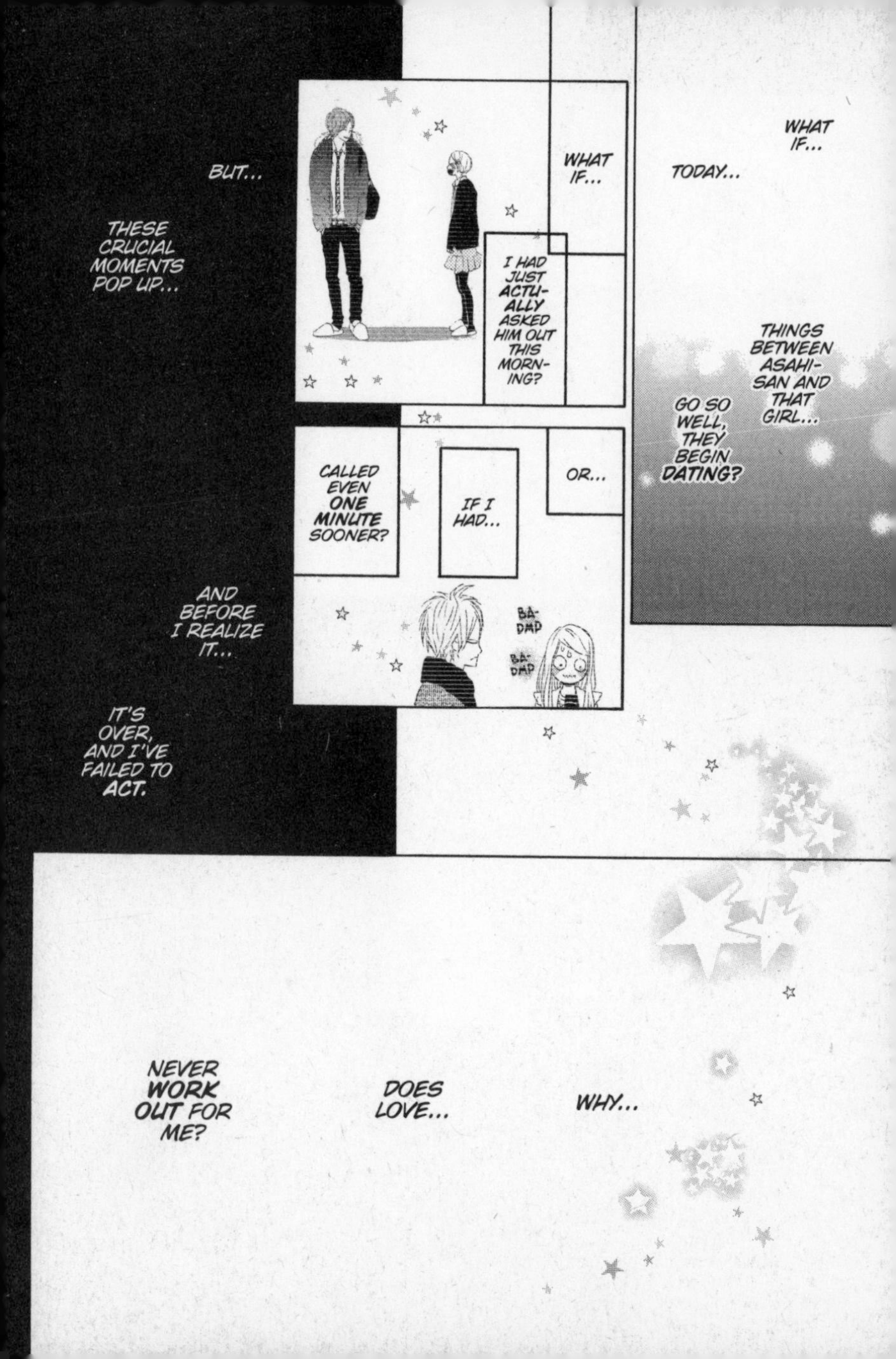
WHAT IF...
TODAY...
THINGS BETWEEN ASAHI-SAN AND THAT GIRL...
GO SO WELL, THEY BEGIN DATING?
WHAT IF...
I HAD JUST ACTUALLY ASKED HIM OUT THIS MORNING?
OR...
IF I HAD...
CALLED EVEN ONE MINUTE SOONER?
BA-DMP
BA-DMP
BUT...
THESE CRUCIAL MOMENTS POP UP...
AND BEFORE I REALIZE IT...
IT'S OVER, AND I'VE FAILED TO ACT.
WHY...
DOES LOVE...
NEVER WORK OUT FOR ME?

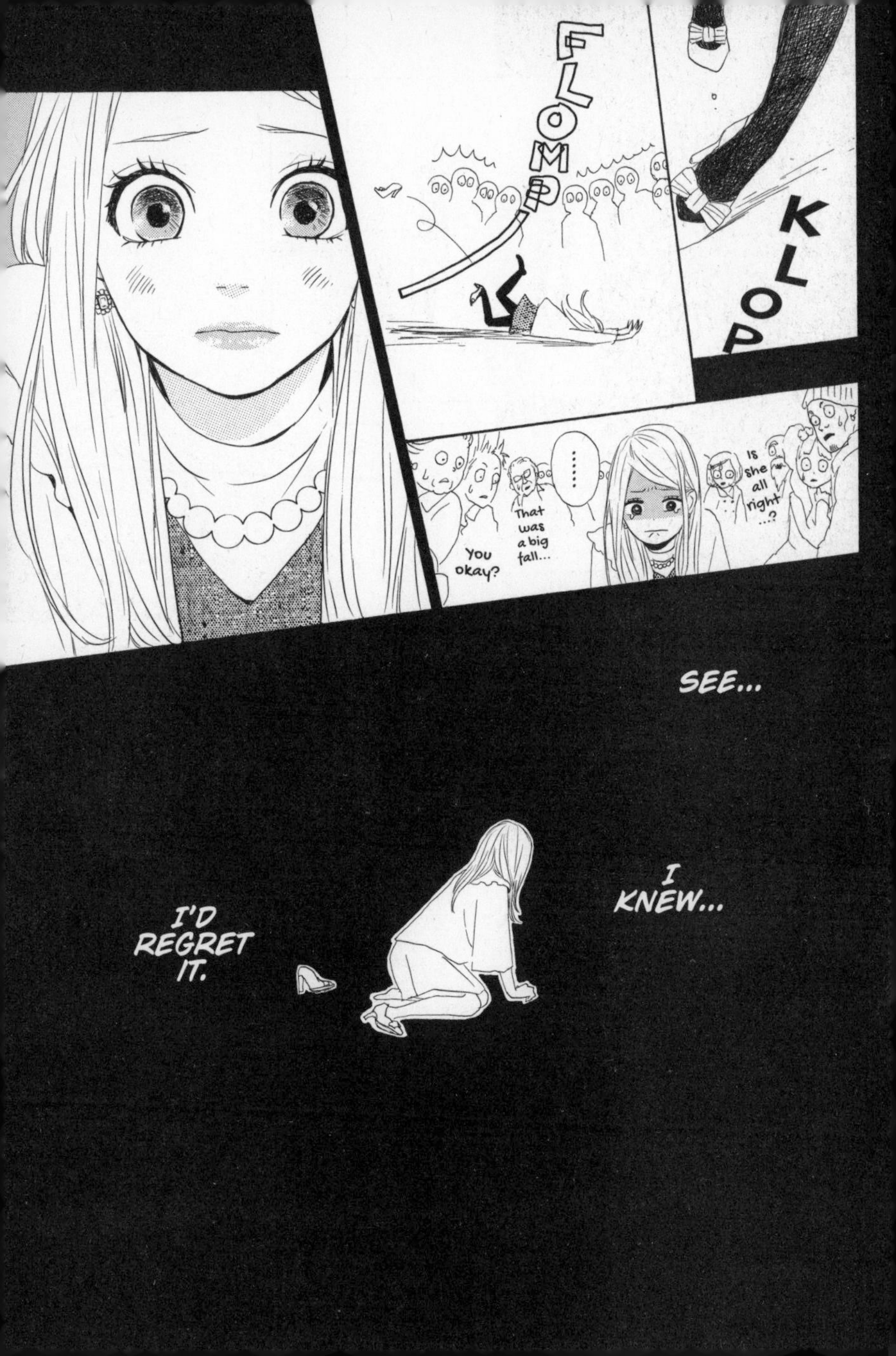
KLOP
FLOMP
Is she all right ...?
......
That was a big fall...
You okay?
SEE...
I KNEW...
I'D REGRET IT.

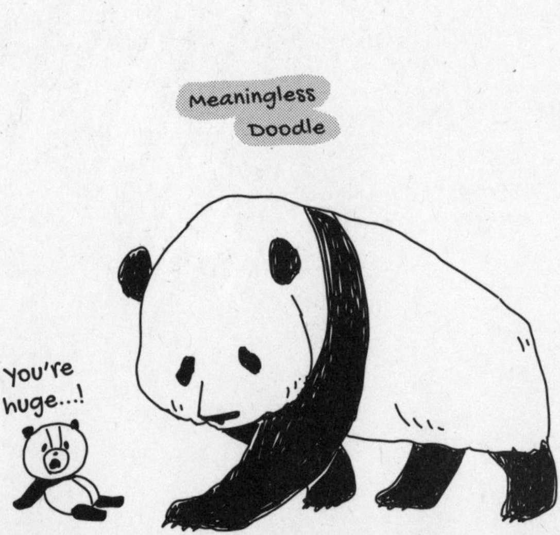
Meaningless Doodle
You're huge...!

Dreamin' Sun

6th DOOR

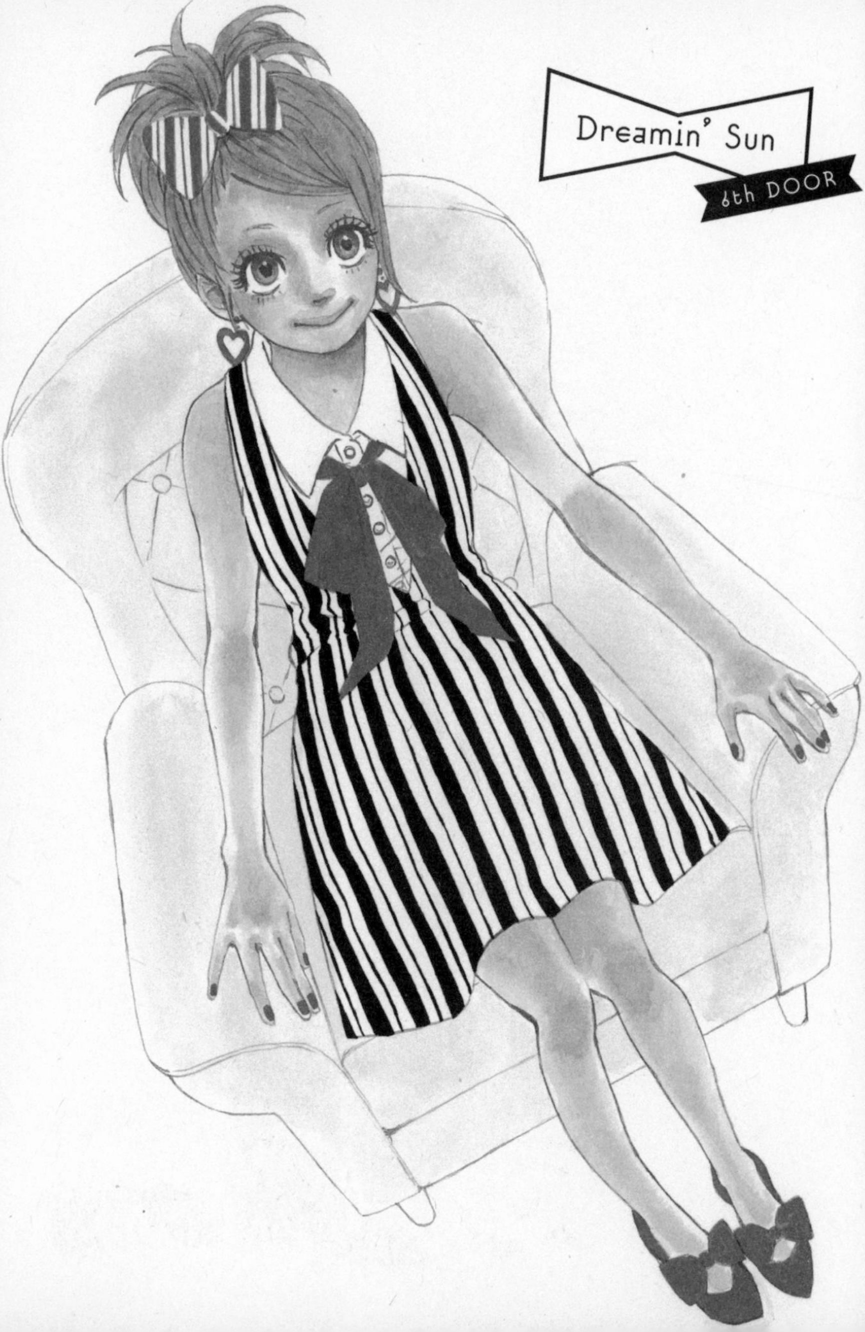

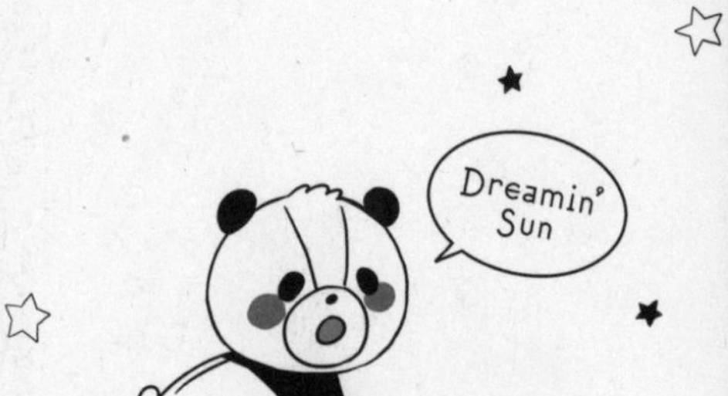
Dreamin' Sun

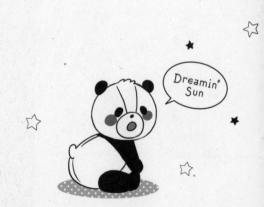

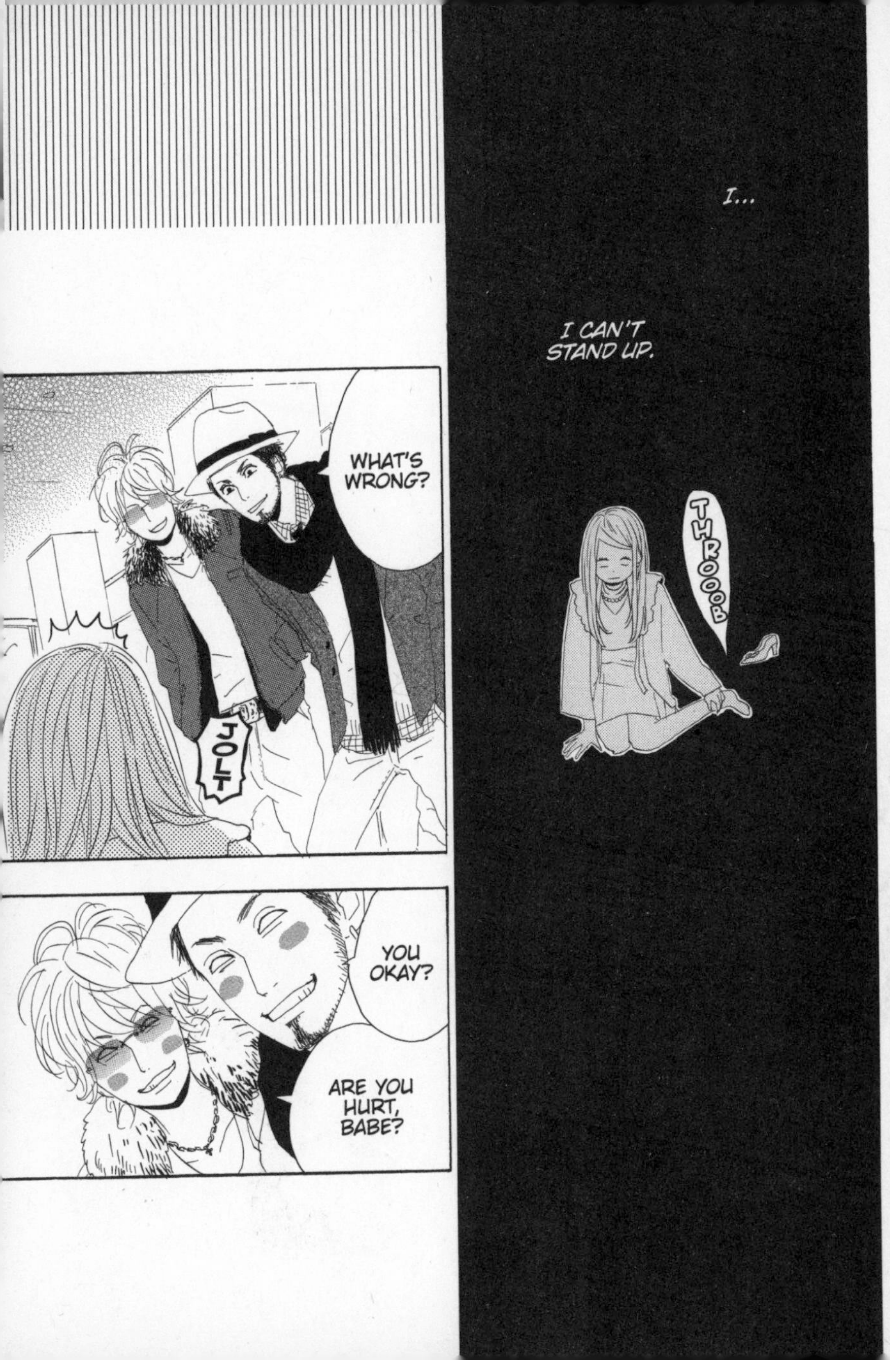
I...
I CAN'T STAND UP.
THROOOB
WHAT'S WRONG?
JOLT
YOU OKAY?
ARE YOU HURT, BABE?

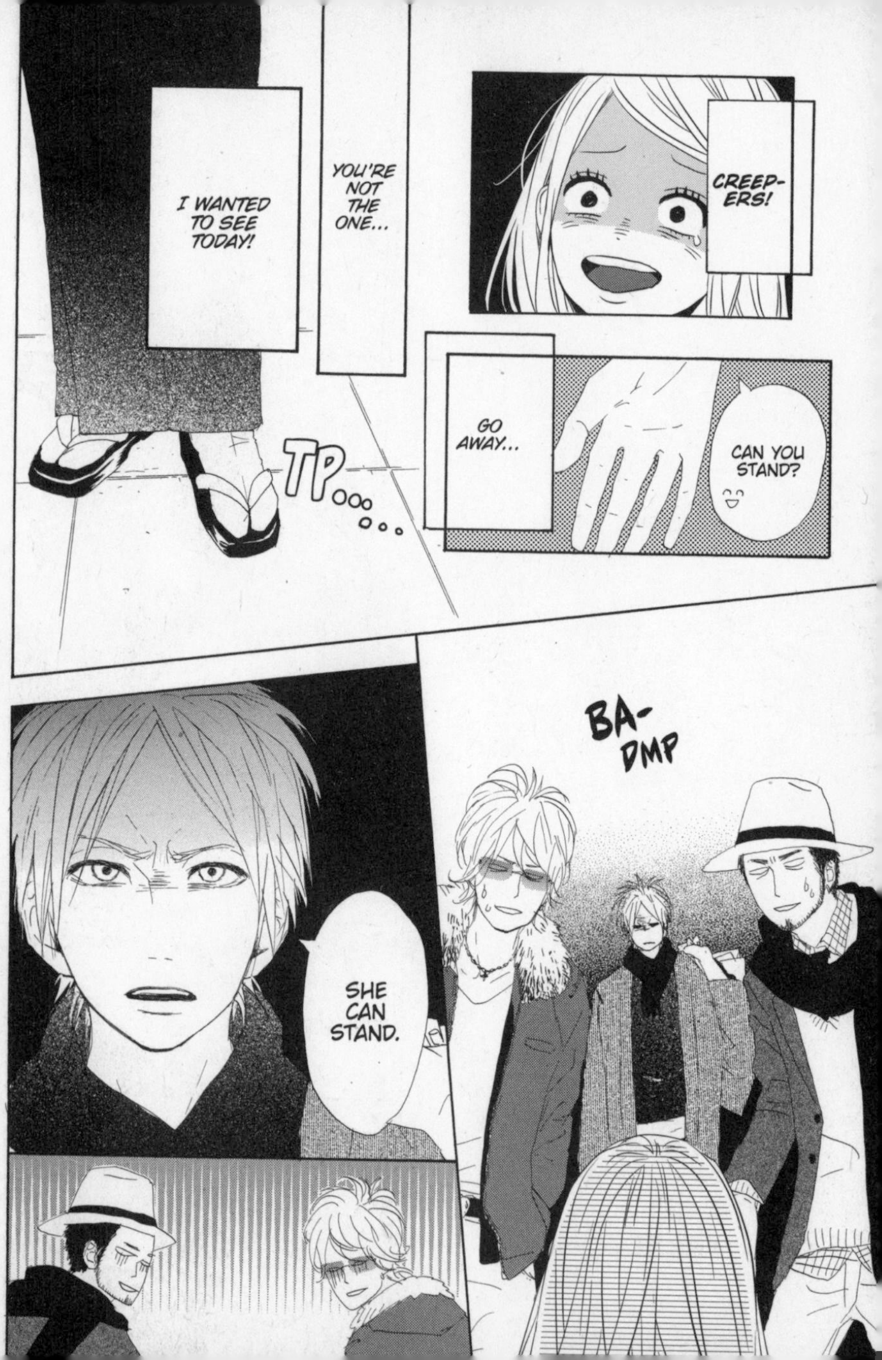
CREEP-ERS!
CAN YOU STAND?
GO AWAY...
YOU'RE NOT THE ONE...
I WANTED TO SEE TODAY!
TP...
BA-DMP
SHE CAN STAND.

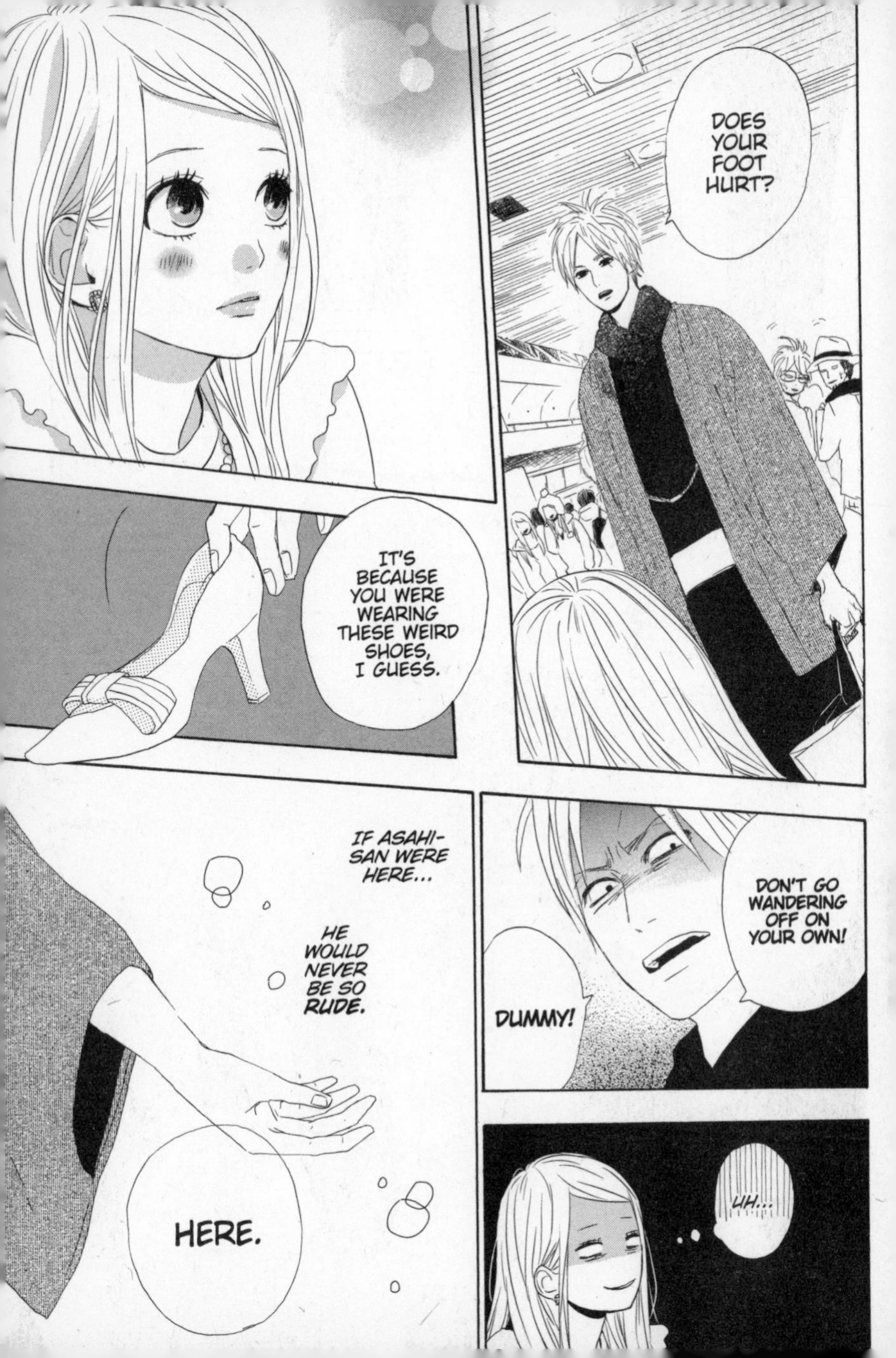
DOES YOUR FOOT HURT?
IT'S BECAUSE YOU WERE WEARING THESE WEIRD SHOES, I GUESS.
DON'T GO WANDERING OFF ON YOUR OWN!
DUMMY!
UH...
IF ASAHI-SAN WERE HERE...
HE WOULD NEVER BE SO RUDE.
HERE.

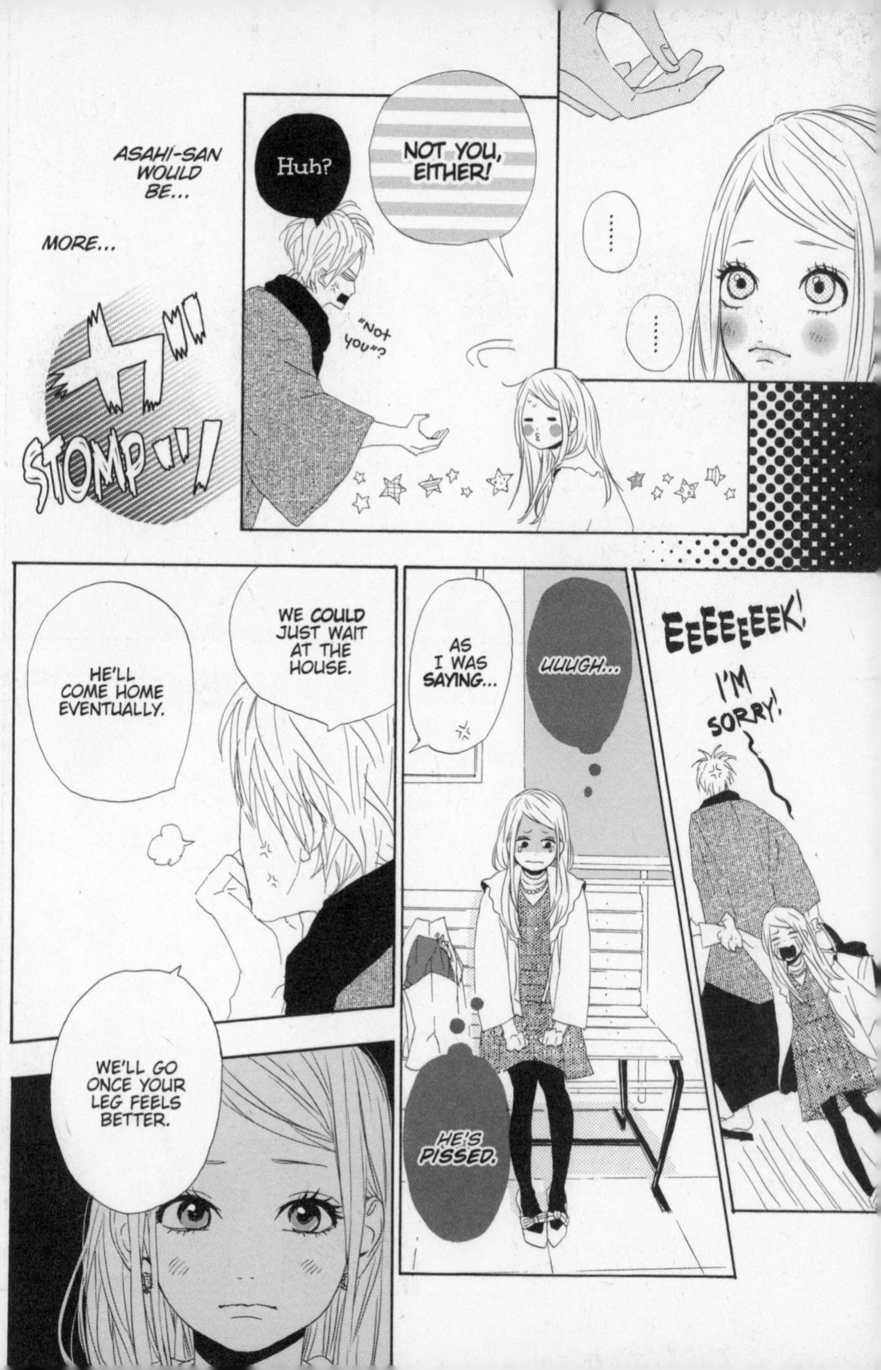
......
......
NOT YOU, EITHER!
Huh?
"Not you"?
ASAHI-SAN WOULD BE...
MORE...
STOMP!!
EEEEEEEK!
I'M SORRY!
UUUGH...
AS I WAS SAYING...
HE'S PISSED.
WE COULD JUST WAIT AT THE HOUSE.
HE'LL COME HOME EVENTUALLY.
WE'LL GO ONCE YOUR LEG FEELS BETTER.

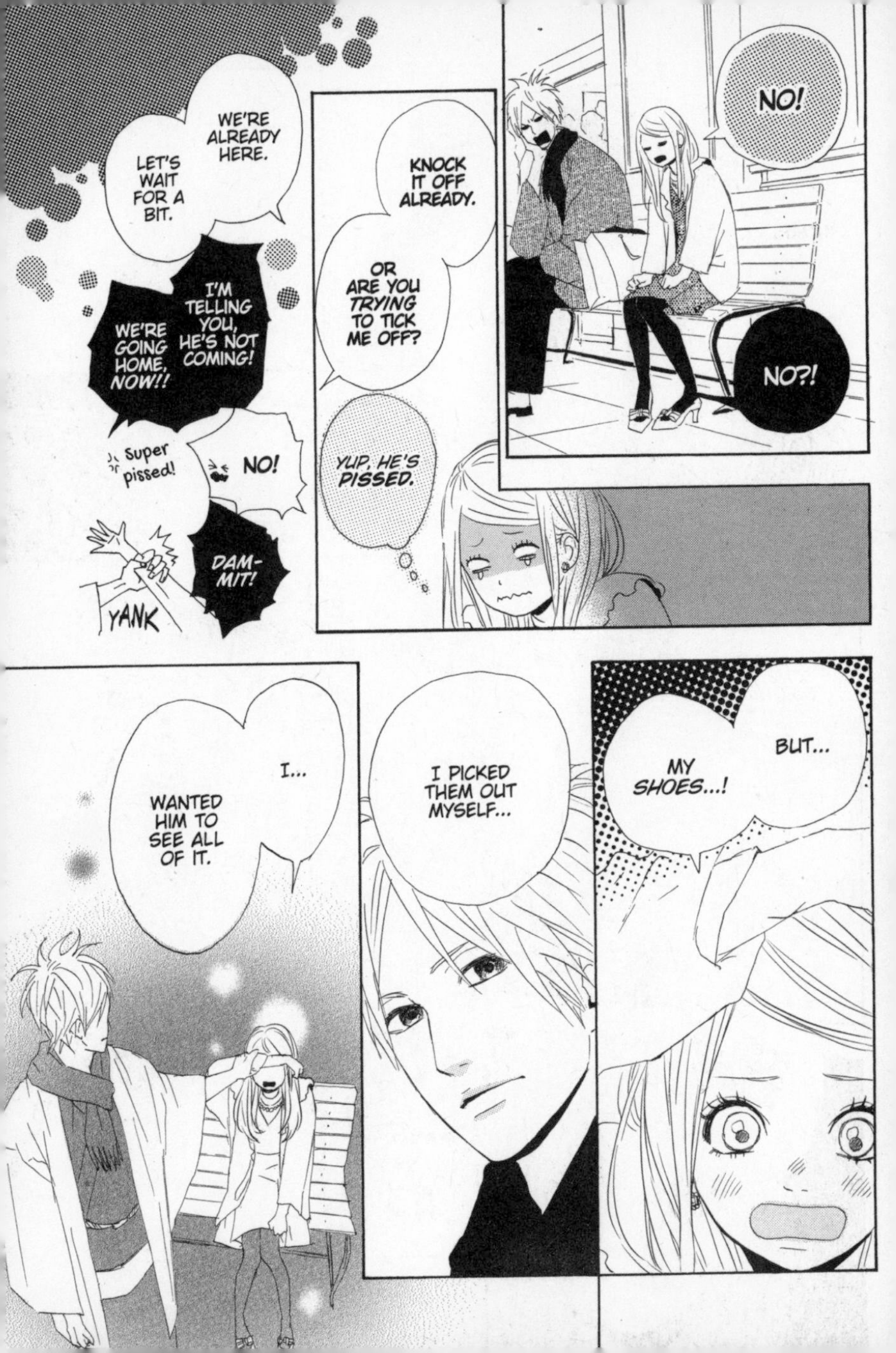
NO!
NO?!
KNOCK IT OFF ALREADY.
OR ARE YOU TRYING TO TICK ME OFF?
YUP, HE'S PISSED.
WE'RE ALREADY HERE.
LET'S WAIT FOR A BIT.
I'M TELLING YOU, HE'S NOT COMING!
WE'RE GOING HOME, NOW!!
NO!
Super pissed!
DAM-MIT!
YANK
BUT...
MY SHOES...!
I PICKED THEM OUT MYSELF...
I...
WANTED HIM TO SEE ALL OF IT.

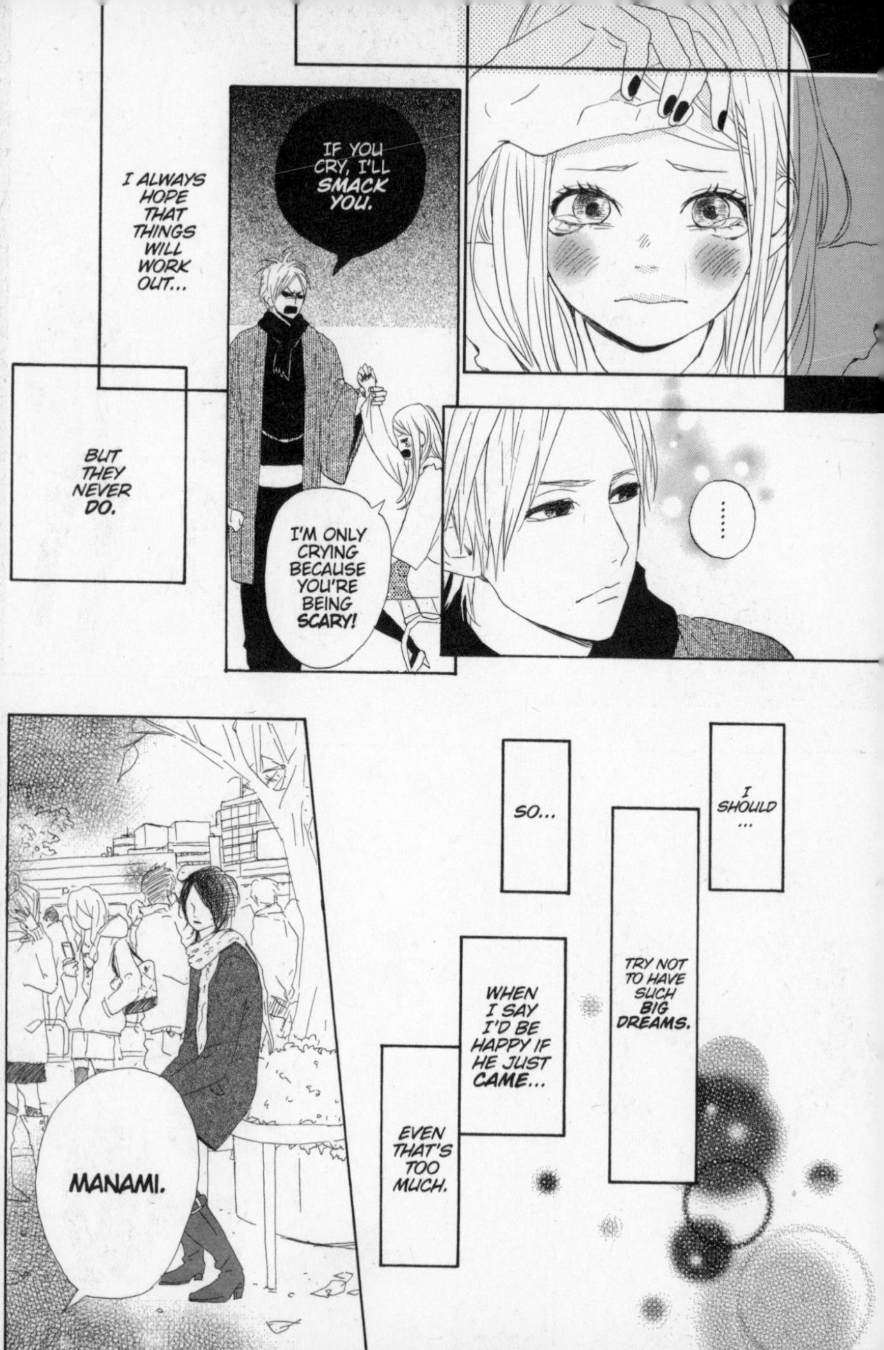
IF YOU CRY, I'LL SMACK YOU.
I'M ONLY CRYING BECAUSE YOU'RE BEING SCARY!
......
I ALWAYS HOPE THAT THINGS WILL WORK OUT...
BUT THEY NEVER DO.
I SHOULD ...
SO...
TRY NOT TO HAVE SUCH BIG DREAMS.
WHEN I SAY I'D BE HAPPY IF HE JUST CAME...
EVEN THAT'S TOO MUCH.
MANAMI.

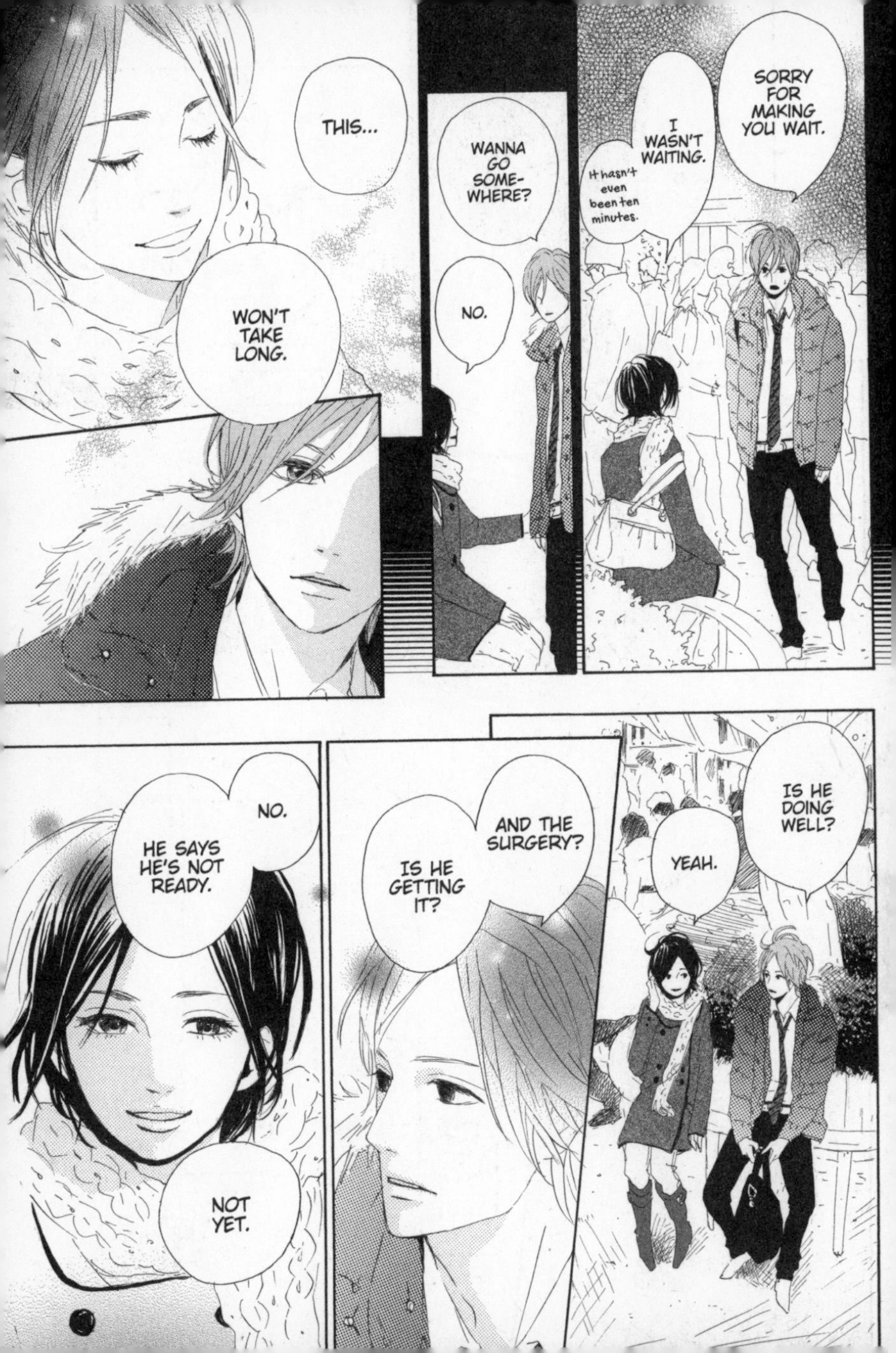
SORRY FOR MAKING YOU WAIT.
I WASN'T WAITING.
It hasn't even been ten minutes.
WANNA GO SOME-WHERE?
NO.
THIS...
WON'T TAKE LONG.
IS HE DOING WELL?
YEAH.
AND THE SURGERY?
IS HE GETTING IT?
NO.
HE SAYS HE'S NOT READY.
NOT YET.

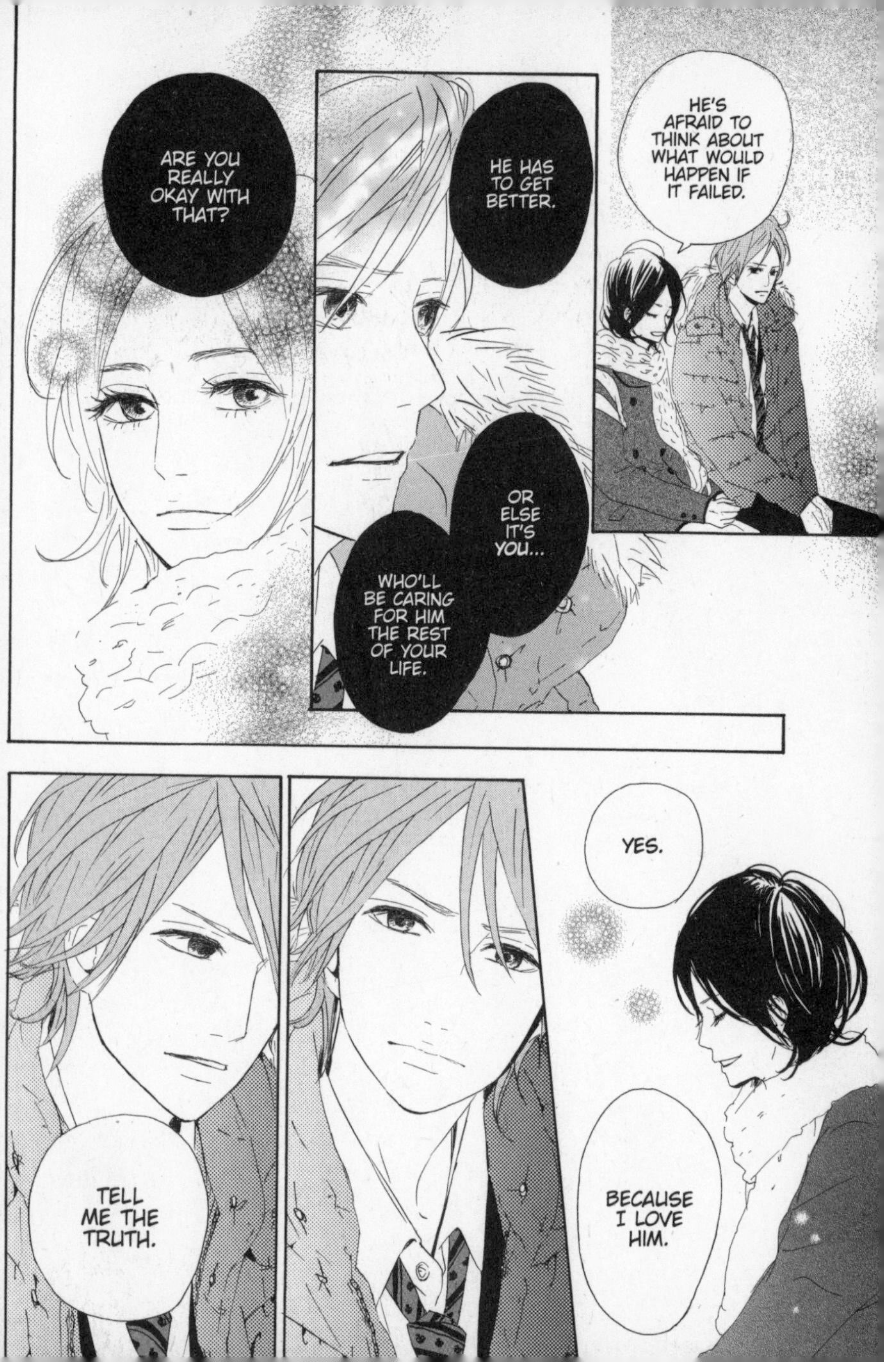
HE'S AFRAID TO THINK ABOUT WHAT WOULD HAPPEN IF IT FAILED.
HE HAS TO GET BETTER.
OR ELSE IT'S YOU...
WHO'LL BE CARING FOR HIM THE REST OF YOUR LIFE.
ARE YOU REALLY OKAY WITH THAT?
YES.
BECAUSE I LOVE HIM.
TELL ME THE TRUTH.

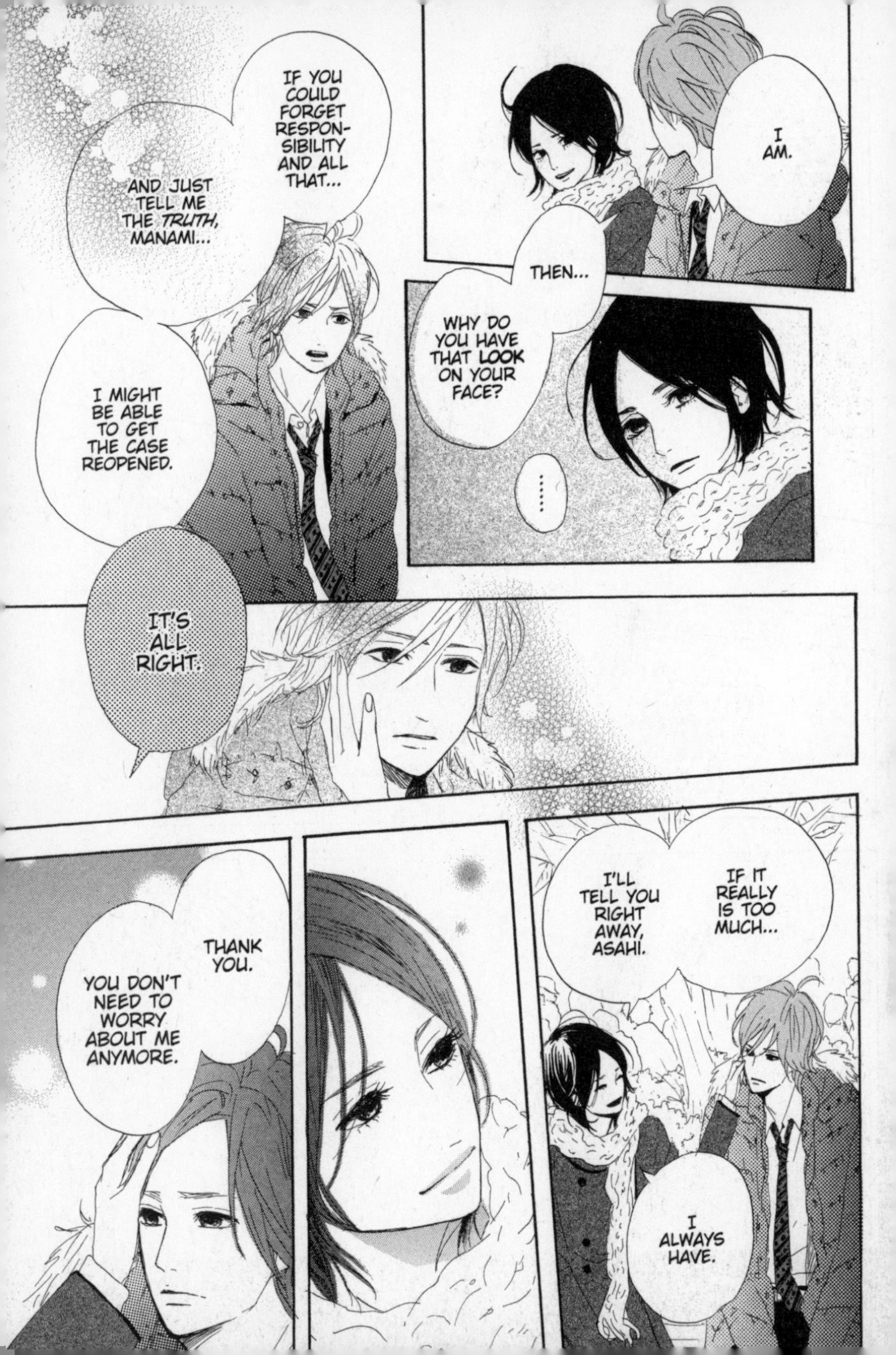

I AM.
THEN...
WHY DO YOU HAVE THAT LOOK ON YOUR FACE?
......
IF YOU COULD FORGET RESPONSIBILITY AND ALL THAT...
AND JUST TELL ME THE *TRUTH*, MANAMI...
I MIGHT BE ABLE TO GET THE CASE REOPENED.
IT'S ALL RIGHT.
IF IT REALLY IS TOO MUCH...
I'LL TELL YOU RIGHT AWAY, ASAHI.
I ALWAYS HAVE.
THANK YOU.
YOU DON'T NEED TO WORRY ABOUT ME ANYMORE.

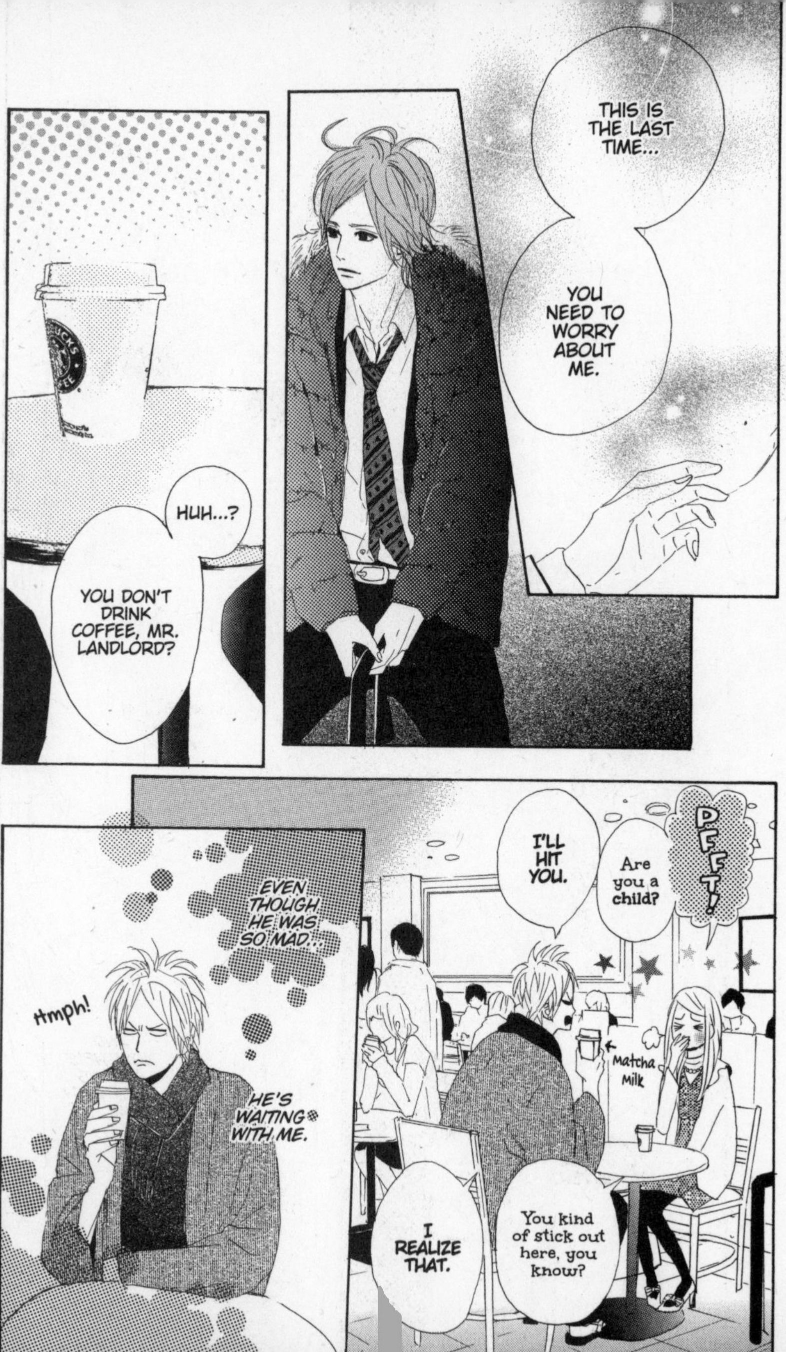
THIS IS THE LAST TIME...
YOU NEED TO WORRY ABOUT ME.
HUH...?
YOU DON'T DRINK COFFEE, MR. LANDLORD?
PFFT!
Are you a child?
I'LL HIT YOU.
Matcha Milk
You kind of stick out here, you know?
I REALIZE THAT.
EVEN THOUGH HE WAS SO MAD...
Hmph!
HE'S WAITING WITH ME.

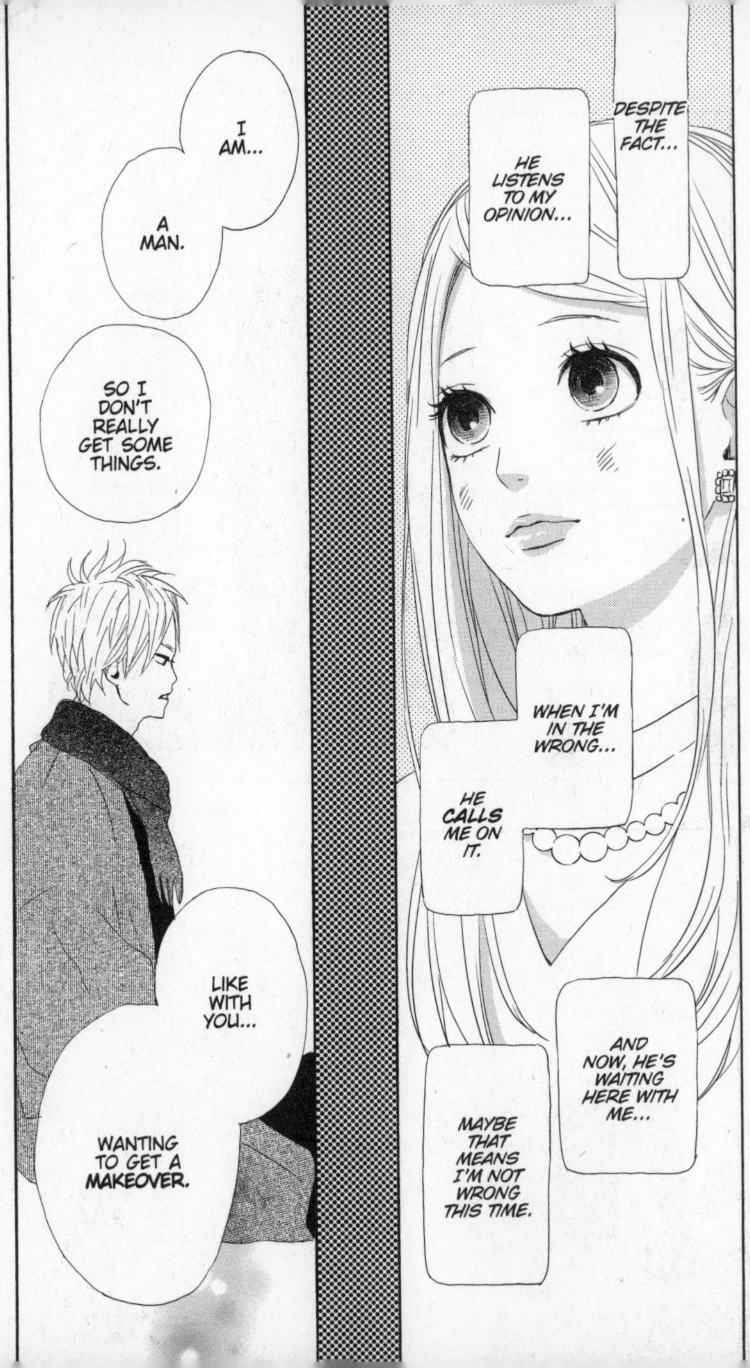
DESPITE THE FACT...
HE LISTENS TO MY OPINION...
WHEN I'M IN THE WRONG...
HE CALLS ME ON IT.
AND NOW, HE'S WAITING HERE WITH ME...
MAYBE THAT MEANS I'M NOT WRONG THIS TIME.
I AM...
A MAN.
SO I DON'T REALLY GET SOME THINGS.
LIKE WITH YOU...
WANTING TO GET A MAKEOVER.

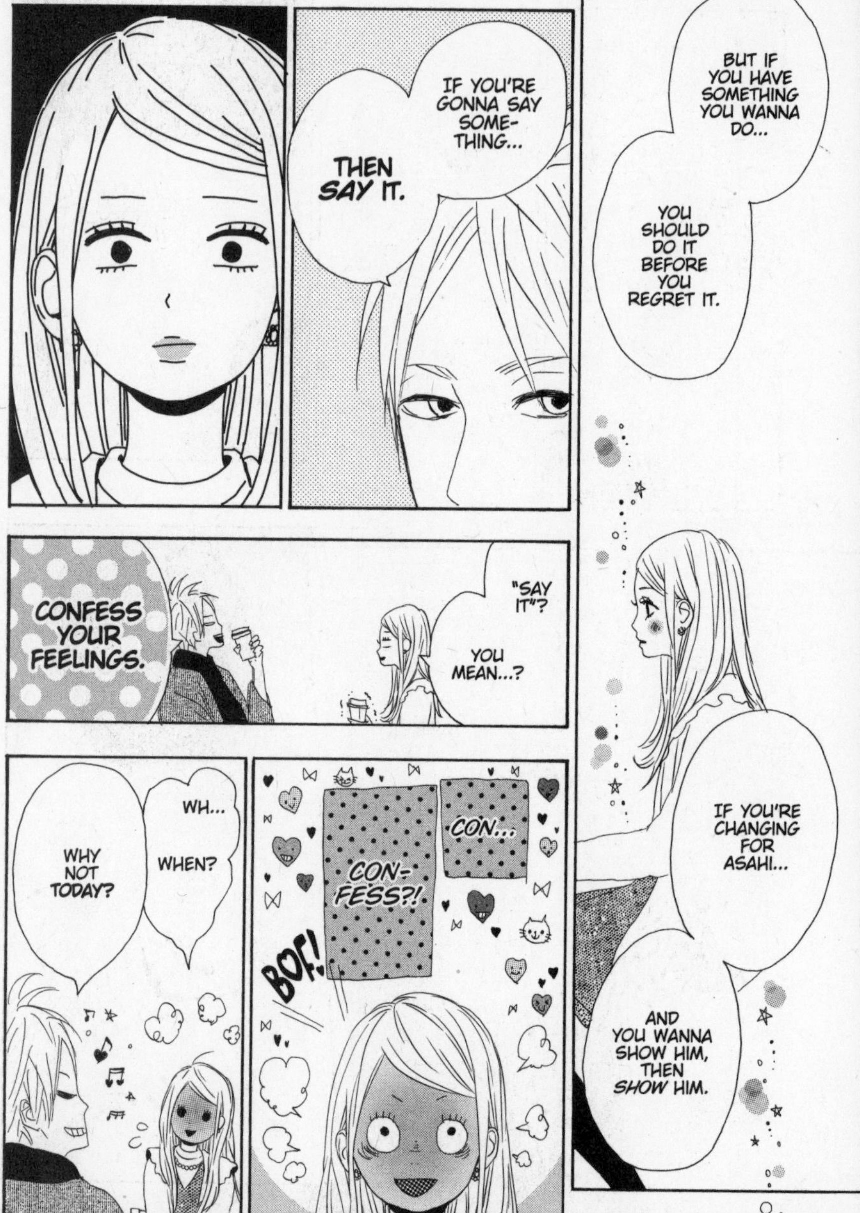
BUT IF YOU HAVE SOMETHING YOU WANNA DO...
YOU SHOULD DO IT BEFORE YOU REGRET IT.
IF YOU'RE CHANGING FOR ASAHI...
AND YOU WANNA SHOW HIM, THEN SHOW HIM.
IF YOU'RE GONNA SAY SOME-THING...
THEN SAY IT.
"SAY IT"?
YOU MEAN...?
CONFESS YOUR FEELINGS.
CON...
CON-FESS?!
BOF!
WH...
WHEN?
WHY NOT TODAY?

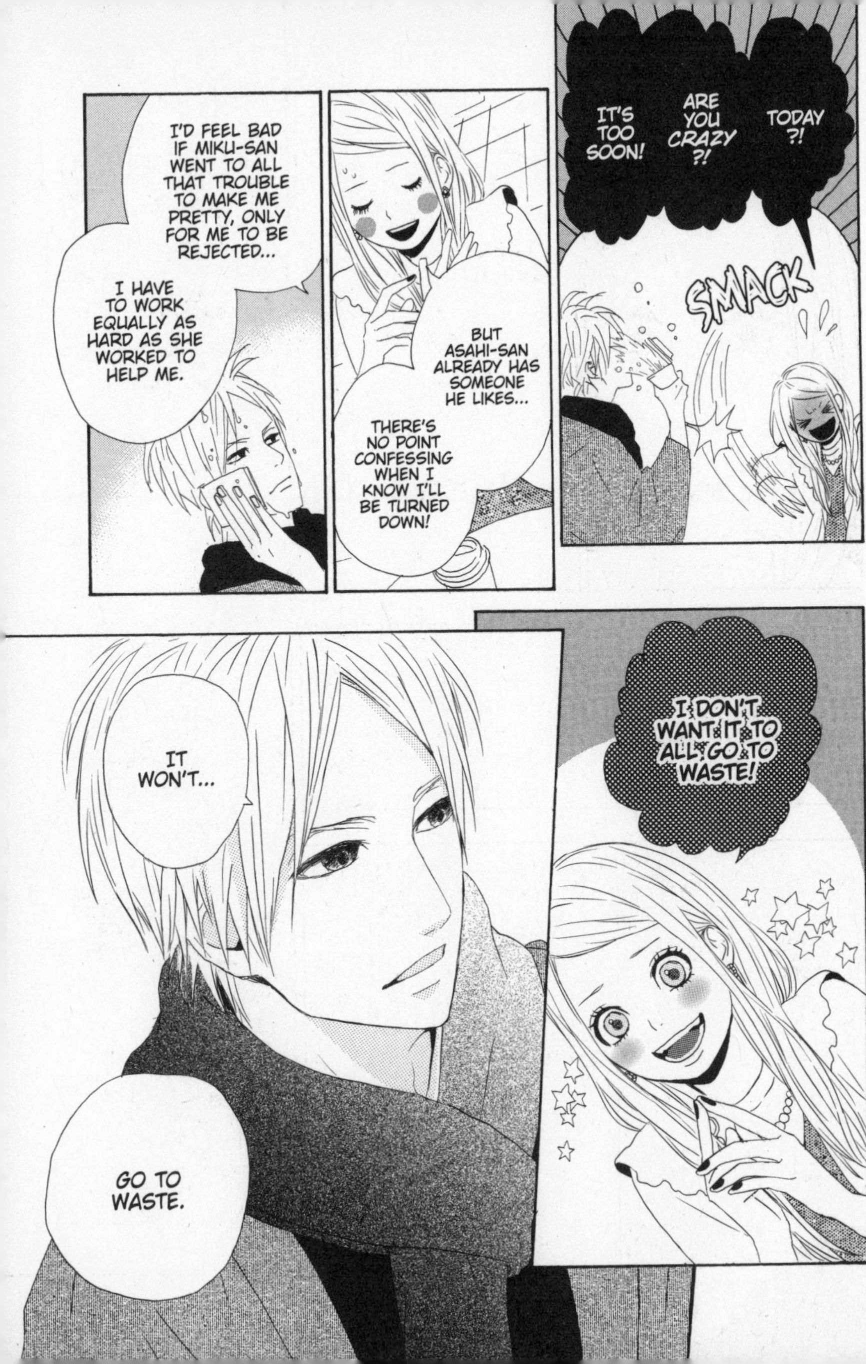
TODAY ?!
ARE YOU CRAZY ?!
IT'S TOO SOON!
SMACK
BUT ASAHI-SAN ALREADY HAS SOMEONE HE LIKES...
THERE'S NO POINT CONFESSING WHEN I KNOW I'LL BE TURNED DOWN!
I'D FEEL BAD IF MIKU-SAN WENT TO ALL THAT TROUBLE TO MAKE ME PRETTY, ONLY FOR ME TO BE REJECTED...
I HAVE TO WORK EQUALLY AS HARD AS SHE WORKED TO HELP ME.
I DON'T WANT IT TO ALL GO TO WASTE!
IT WON'T...
GO TO WASTE.

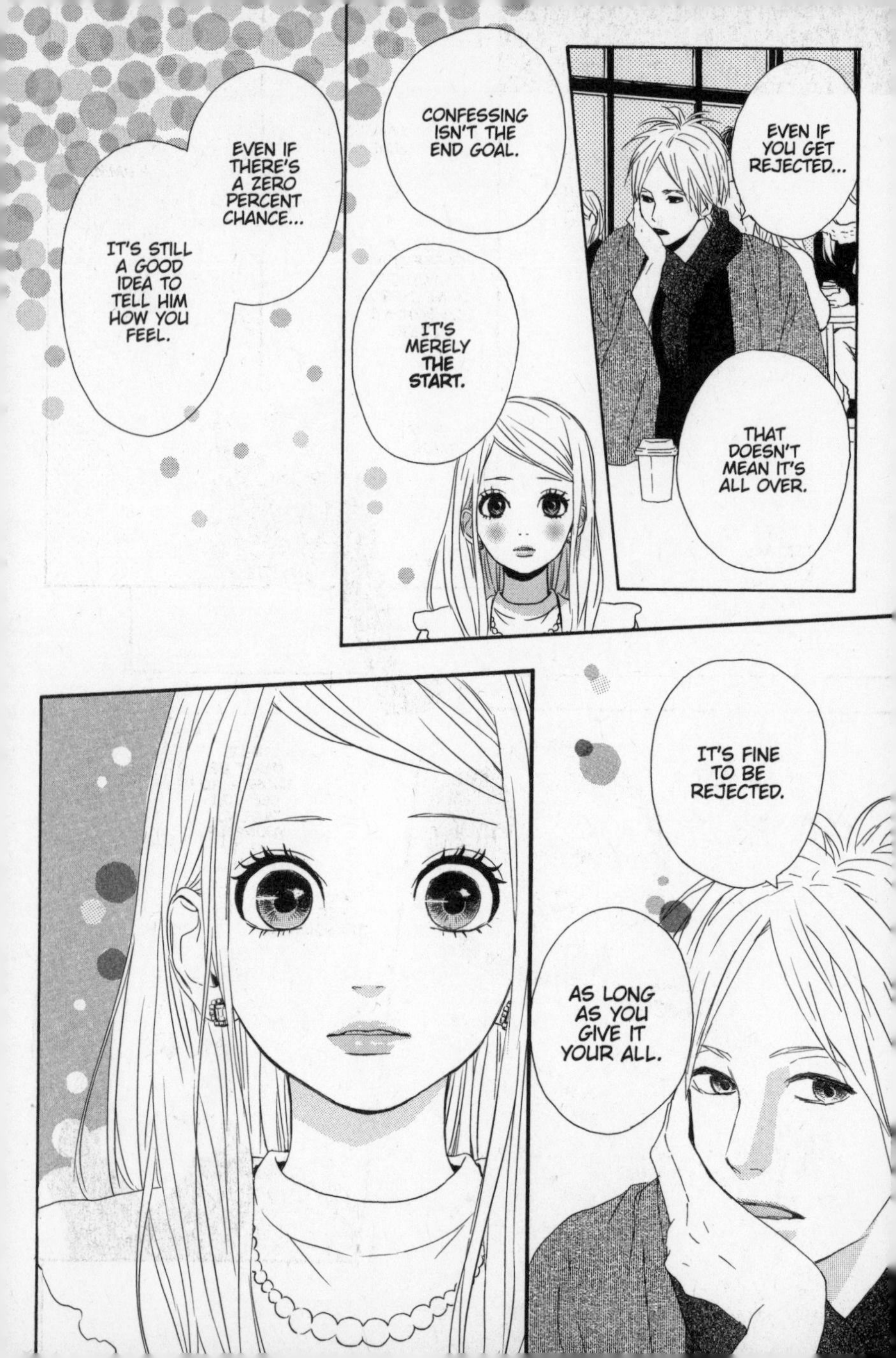
EVEN IF YOU GET REJECTED...
THAT DOESN'T MEAN IT'S ALL OVER.
CONFESSING ISN'T THE END GOAL.
IT'S MERELY THE START.
EVEN IF THERE'S A ZERO PERCENT CHANCE...
IT'S STILL A GOOD IDEA TO TELL HIM HOW YOU FEEL.
IT'S FINE TO BE REJECTED.
AS LONG AS YOU GIVE IT YOUR ALL.

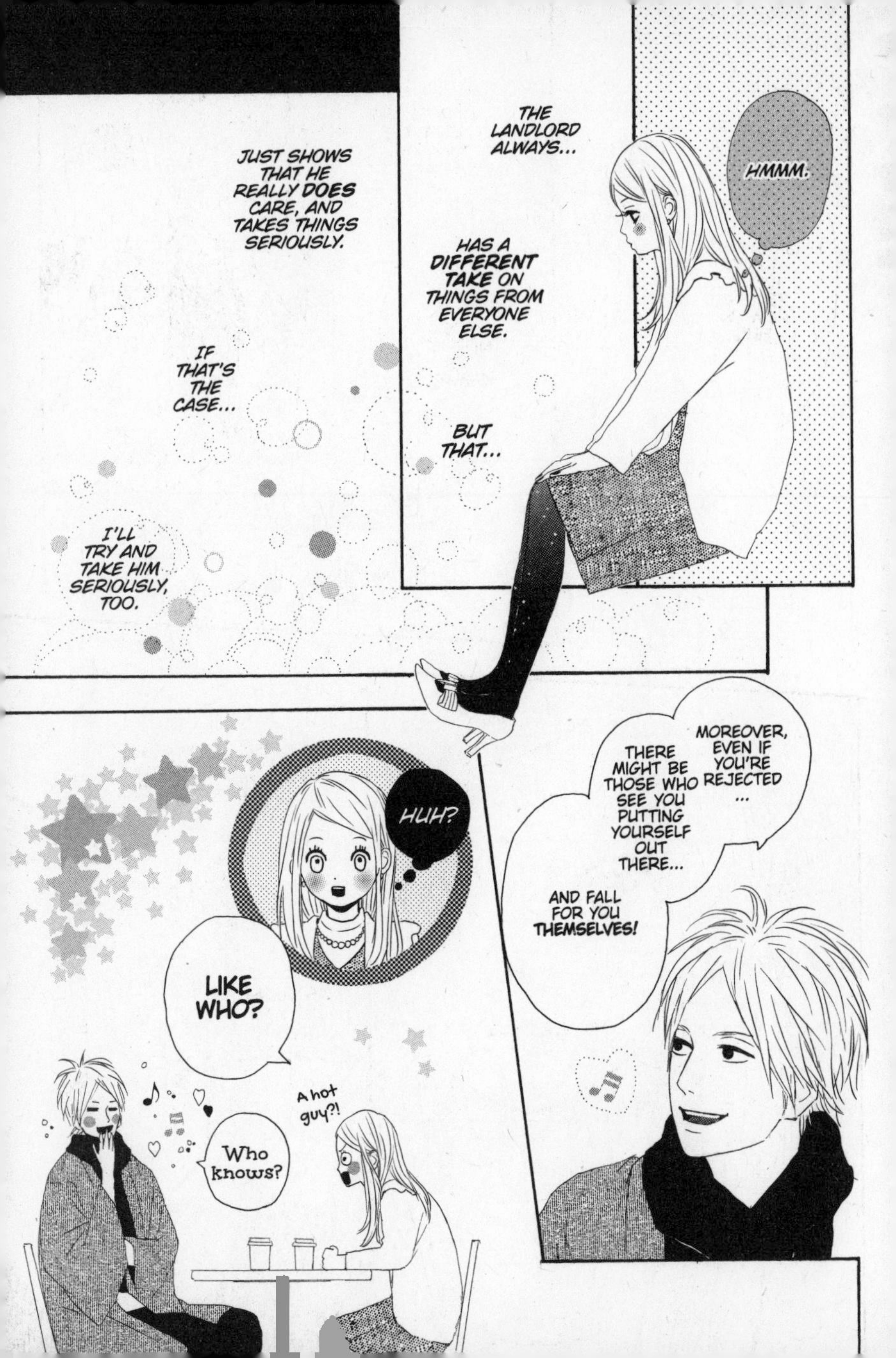
HMMM.
THE LANDLORD ALWAYS...
HAS A DIFFERENT TAKE ON THINGS FROM EVERYONE ELSE.
BUT THAT...
JUST SHOWS THAT HE REALLY DOES CARE, AND TAKES THINGS SERIOUSLY.
IF THAT'S THE CASE...
I'LL TRY AND TAKE HIM SERIOUSLY, TOO.
MOREOVER, EVEN IF YOU'RE REJECTED ...
THERE MIGHT BE THOSE WHO SEE YOU PUTTING YOURSELF OUT THERE...
AND FALL FOR YOU THEMSELVES!
HUH?
LIKE WHO?
A hot guy?!
Who knows?

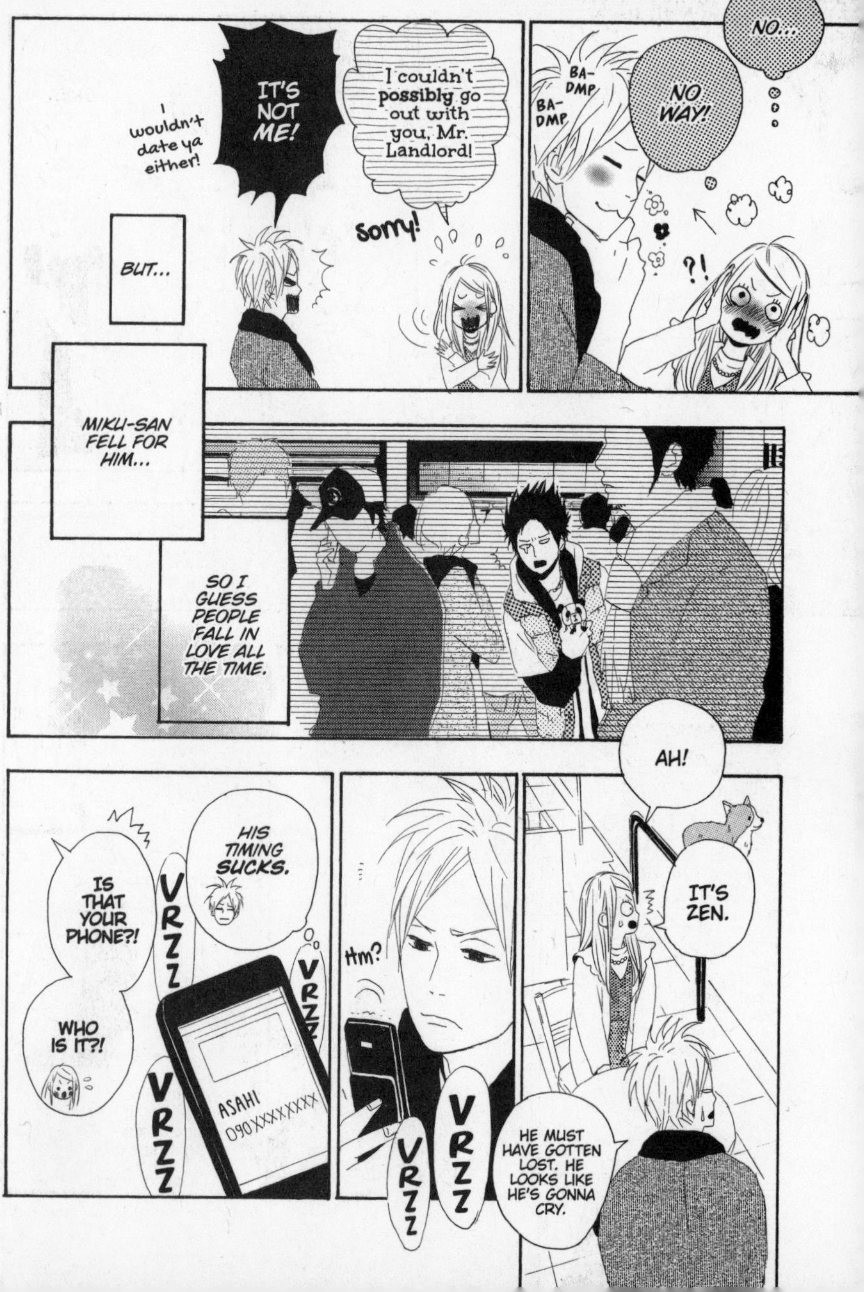
NO...
NO WAY!
BA-DMP
BA-DMP
?!
I couldn't possibly go out with you, Mr. Landlord!
Sorry!
IT'S NOT ME!
I wouldn't date ya either!
BUT...
MIKU-SAN FELL FOR HIM...
SO I GUESS PEOPLE FALL IN LOVE ALL THE TIME.
AH!
IT'S ZEN.
HE MUST HAVE GOTTEN LOST. HE LOOKS LIKE HE'S GONNA CRY.
Hm?
VRZZ
VRZZ
HIS TIMING SUCKS.
IS THAT YOUR PHONE?!
WHO IS IT?!
VRZZ
VRZZ
VRZZ
ASAHI
090XXXXXXXX

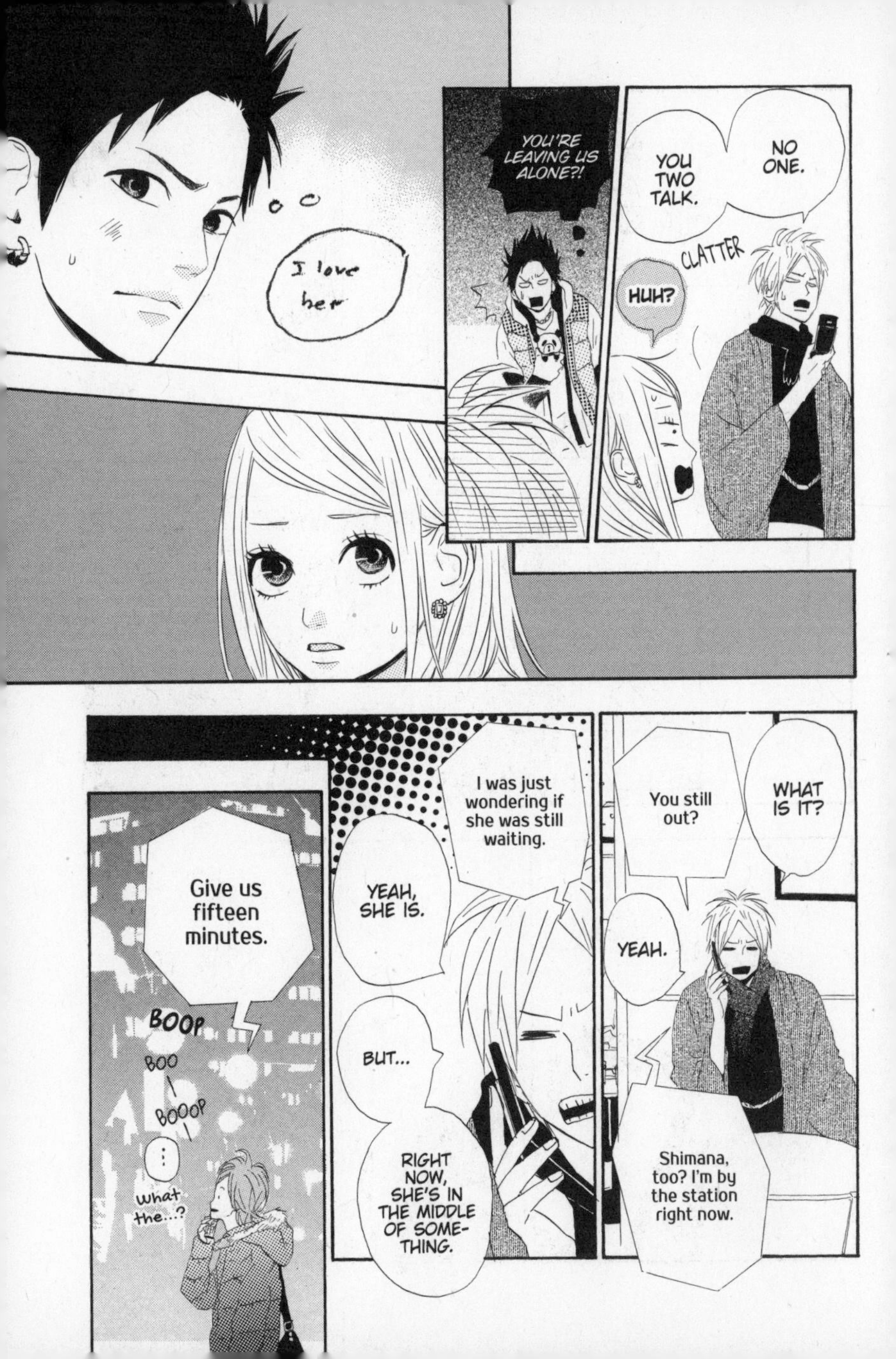
NO ONE.
YOU TWO TALK.
CLATTER
HUH?
YOU'RE LEAVING US ALONE?!
I love her
WHAT IS IT?
You still out?
YEAH.
Shimana, too? I'm by the station right now.
I was just wondering if she was still waiting.
YEAH, SHE IS.
BUT...
RIGHT NOW, SHE'S IN THE MIDDLE OF SOME-THING.
Give us fifteen minutes.
BOOP
BOO
BOOOP
...
what the...?

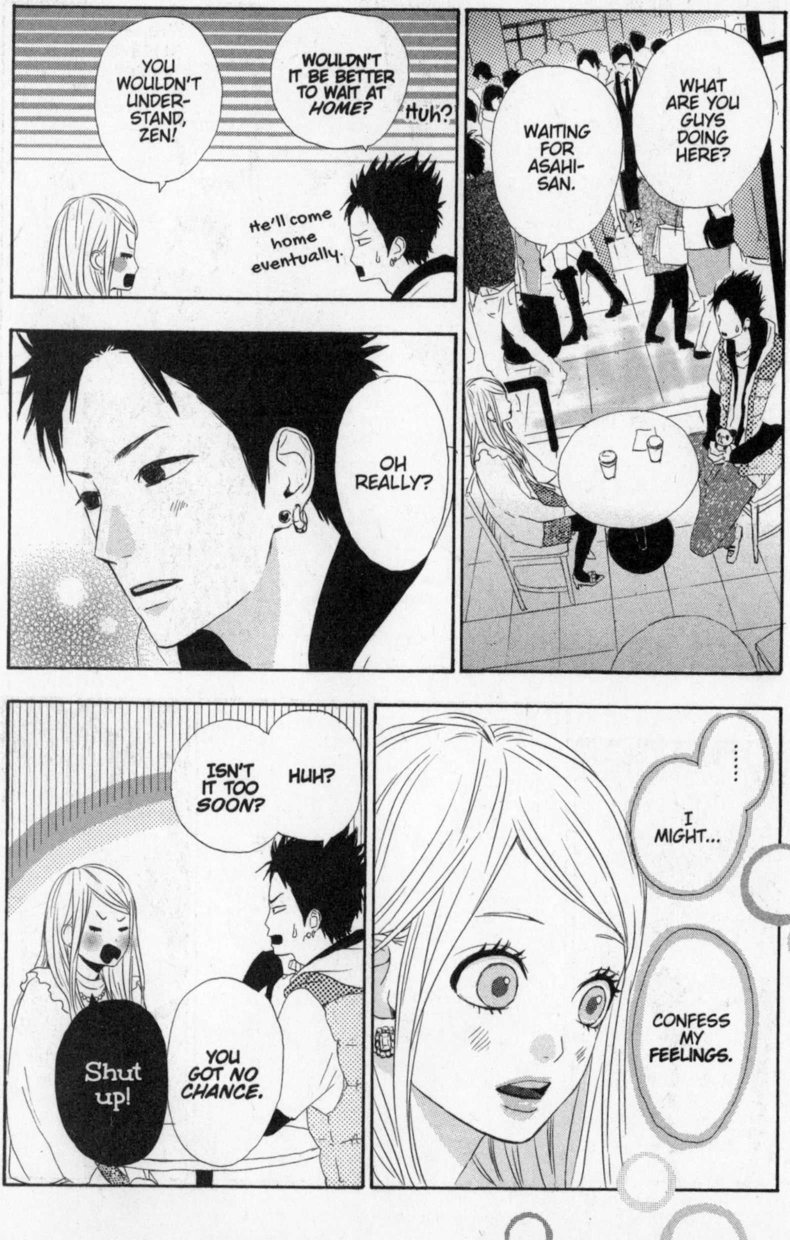
WHAT ARE YOU GUYS DOING HERE?
WAITING FOR ASAHI-SAN.
WOULDN'T IT BE BETTER TO WAIT AT HOME?
Huh?
YOU WOULDN'T UNDER-STAND, ZEN!
He'll come home eventually.
OH REALLY?
......
I MIGHT...
CONFESS MY FEELINGS.
HUH?
ISN'T IT TOO SOON?
YOU GOT NO CHANCE.
Shut up!

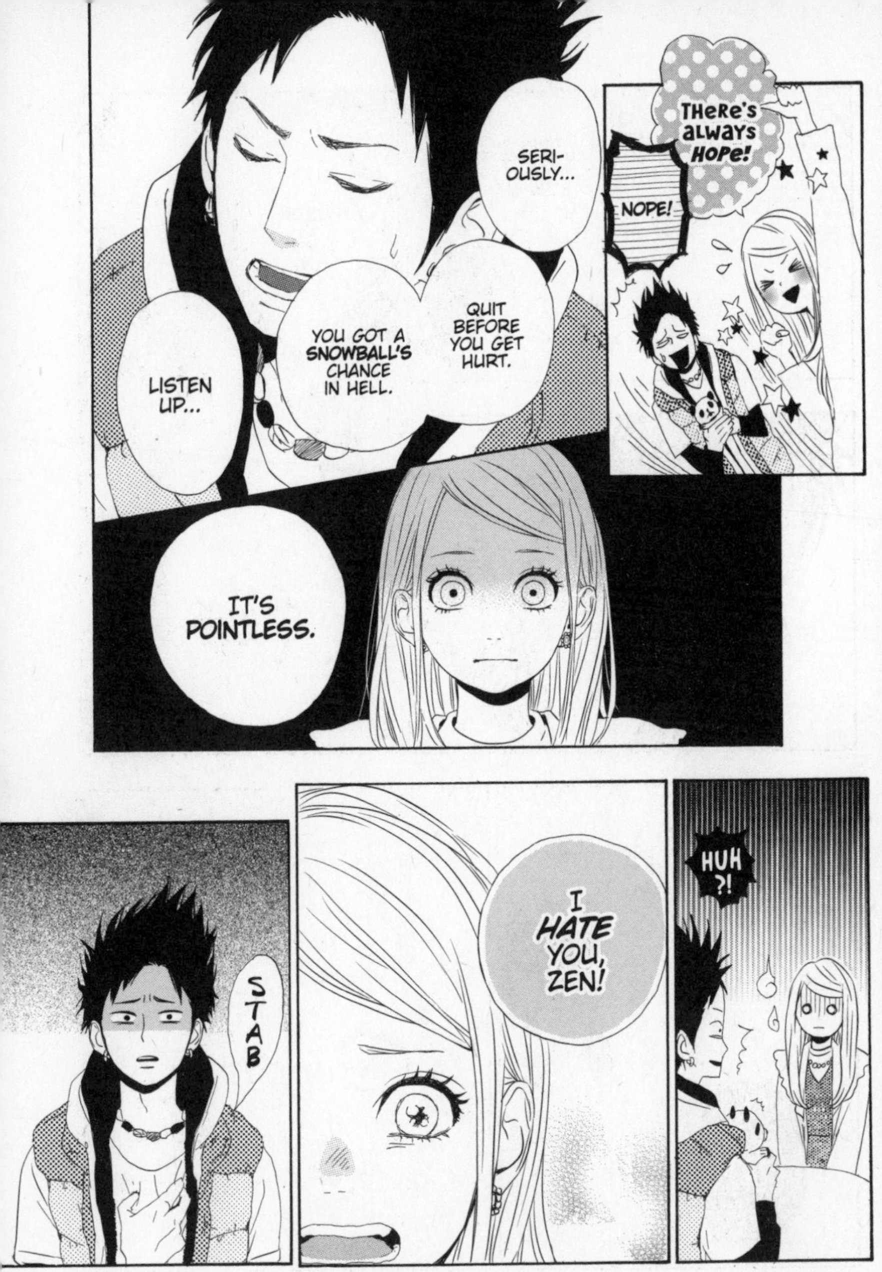
There's always HOPE!
NOPE!
SERI-OUSLY...
QUIT BEFORE YOU GET HURT.
YOU GOT A SNOWBALL'S CHANCE IN HELL.
LISTEN UP...
IT'S POINTLESS.
HUH?!
I HATE YOU, ZEN!
STAB

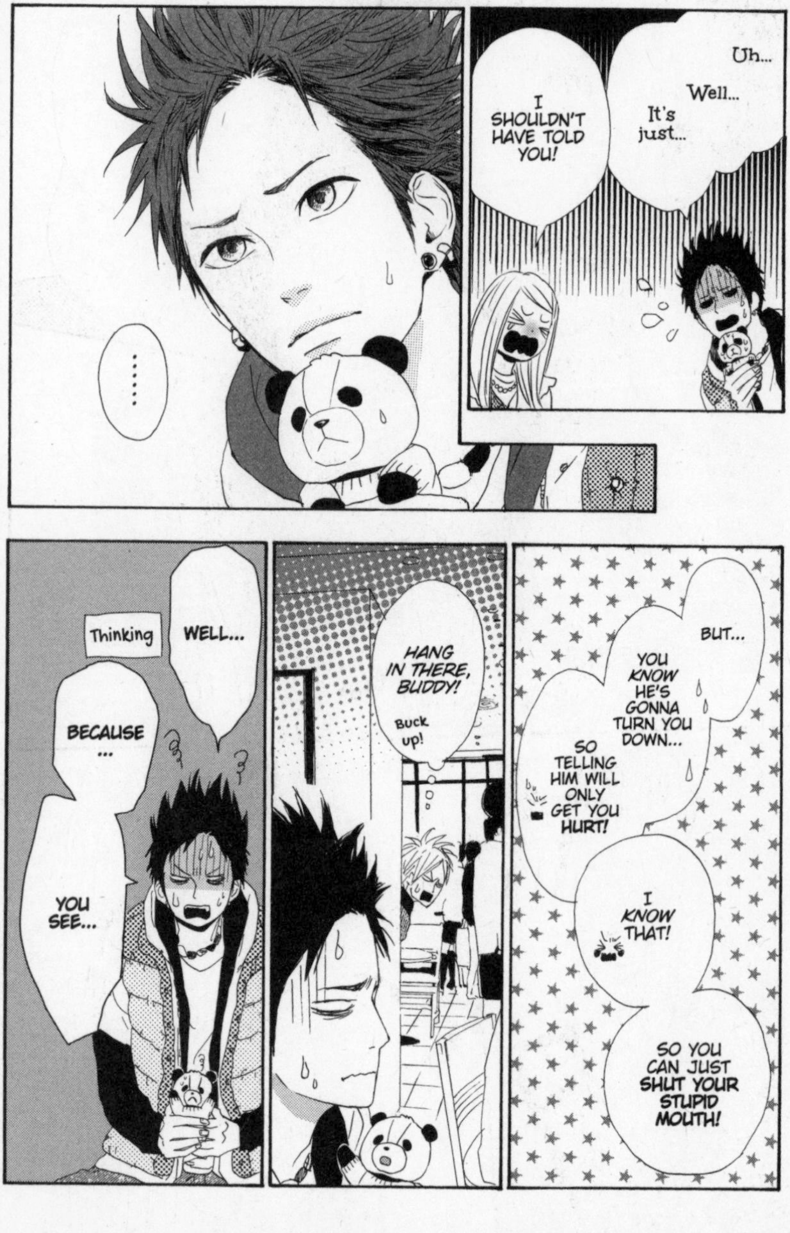
Uh... Well... It's just...
I SHOULDN'T HAVE TOLD YOU!
......
BUT... YOU KNOW HE'S GONNA TURN YOU DOWN...
SO TELLING HIM WILL ONLY GET YOU HURT!
I KNOW THAT!
SO YOU CAN JUST SHUT YOUR STUPID MOUTH!
HANG IN THERE, BUDDY!
Buck up!
WELL...
Thinking
BECAUSE...
YOU SEE...

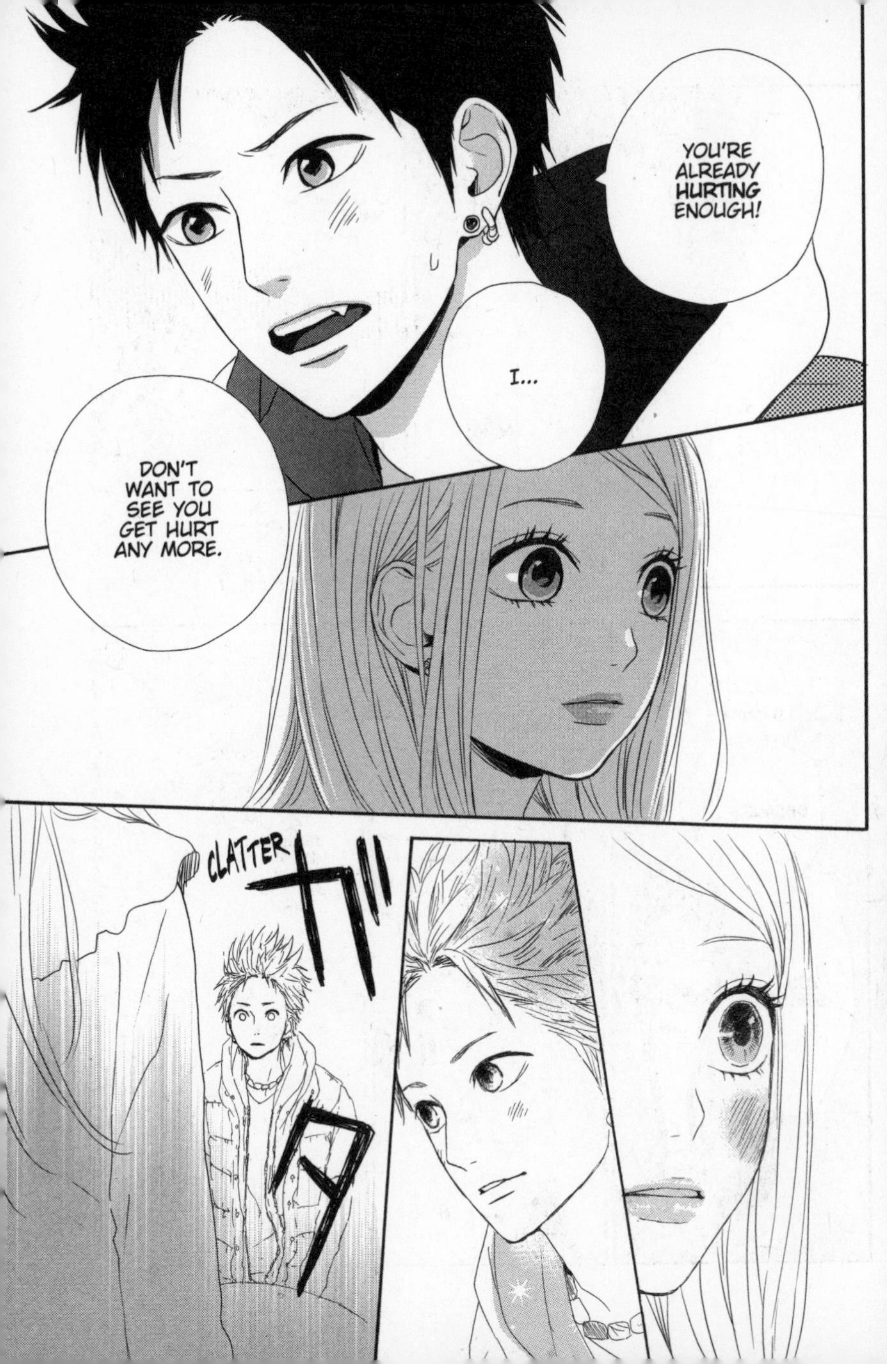
YOU'RE ALREADY HURTING ENOUGH!
I...
DON'T WANT TO SEE YOU GET HURT ANY MORE.
CLATTER

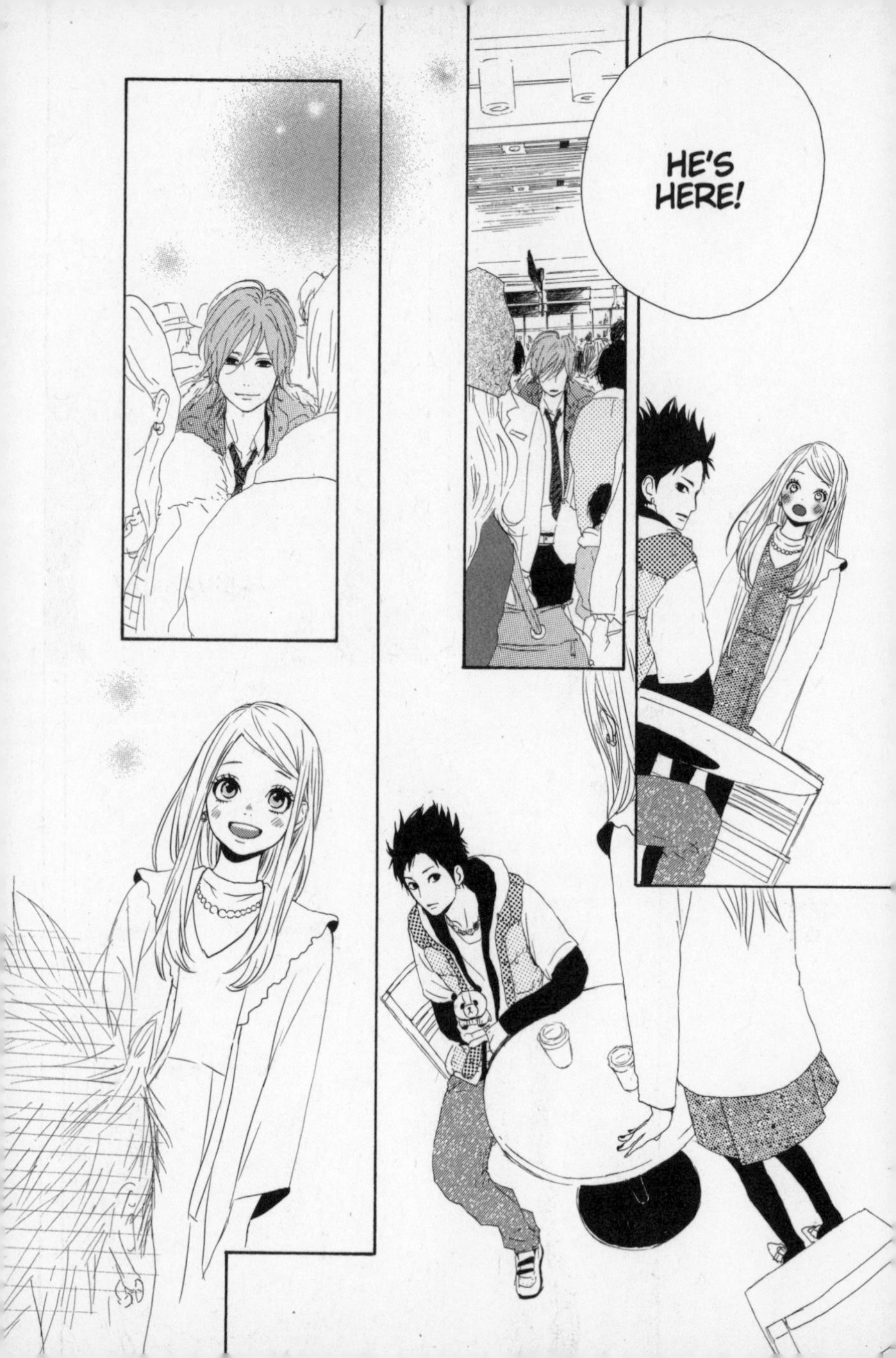
HE'S HERE!

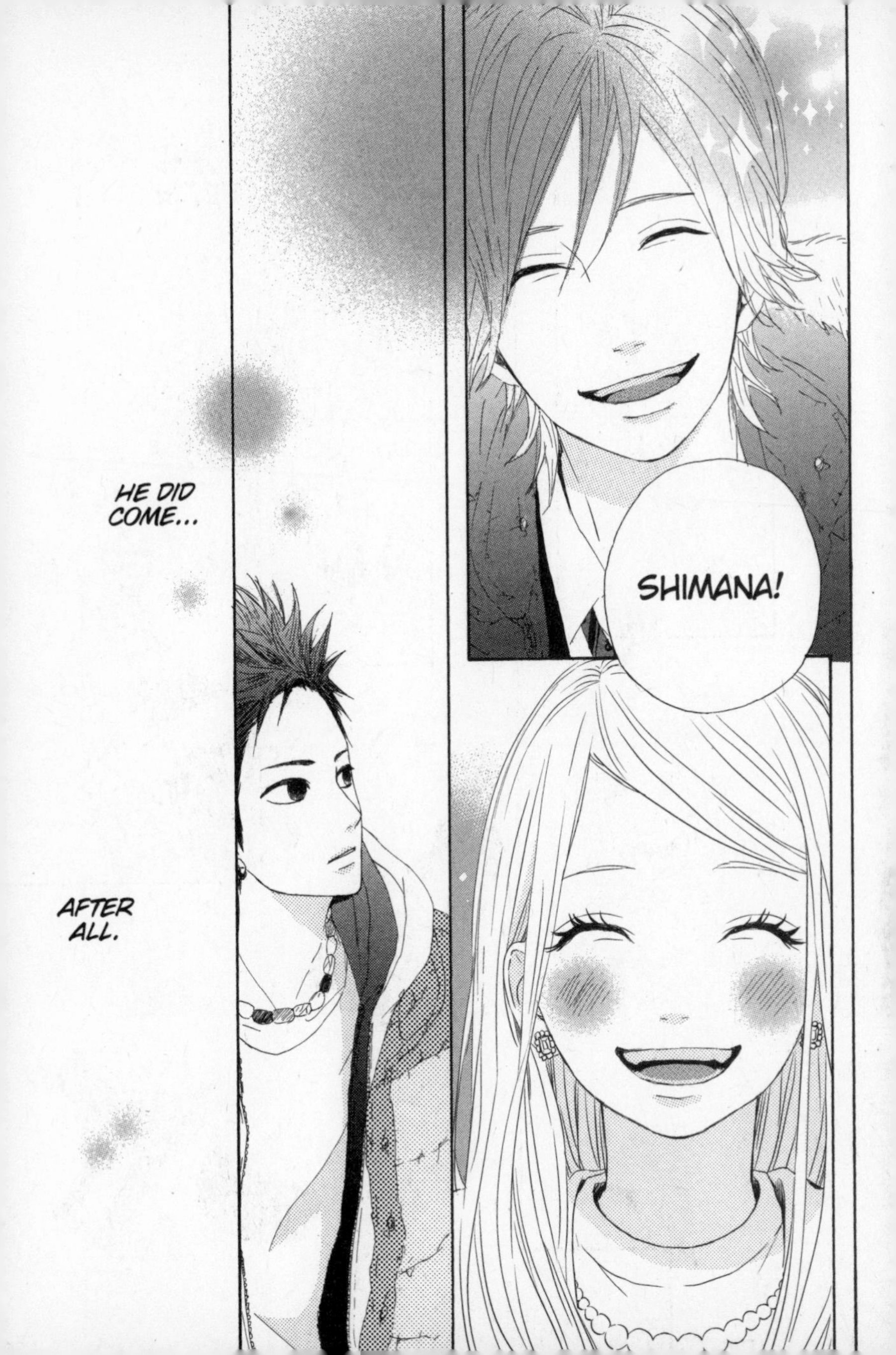
SHIMANA!
HE DID COME...
AFTER ALL.

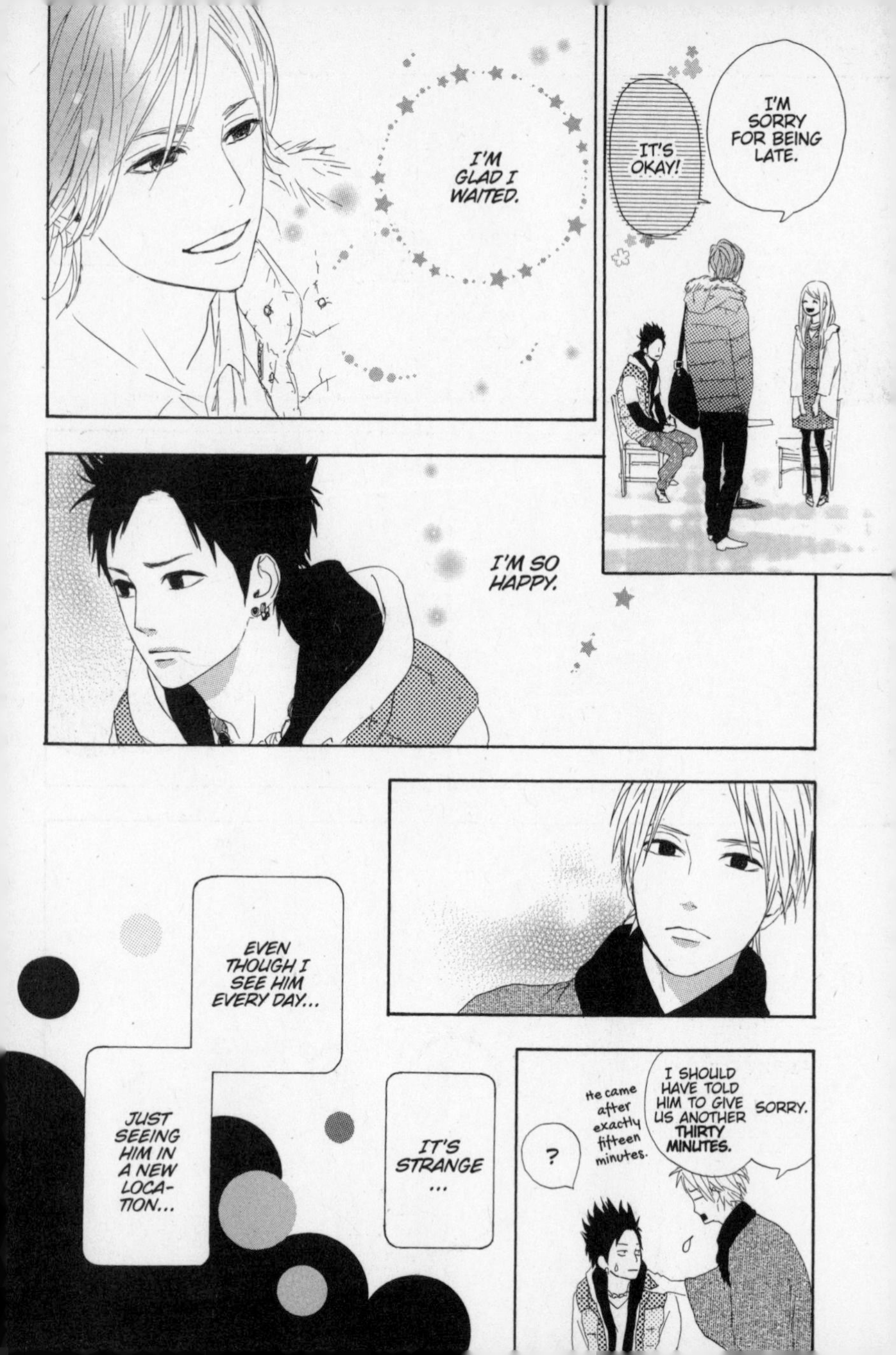
I'M SORRY FOR BEING LATE.
IT'S OKAY!
I'M GLAD I WAITED.
I'M SO HAPPY.
EVEN THOUGH I SEE HIM EVERY DAY...
SORRY.
I SHOULD HAVE TOLD HIM TO GIVE US ANOTHER THIRTY MINUTES.
He came after exactly fifteen minutes.
?
JUST SEEING HIM IN A NEW LOCATION...
IT'S STRANGE...

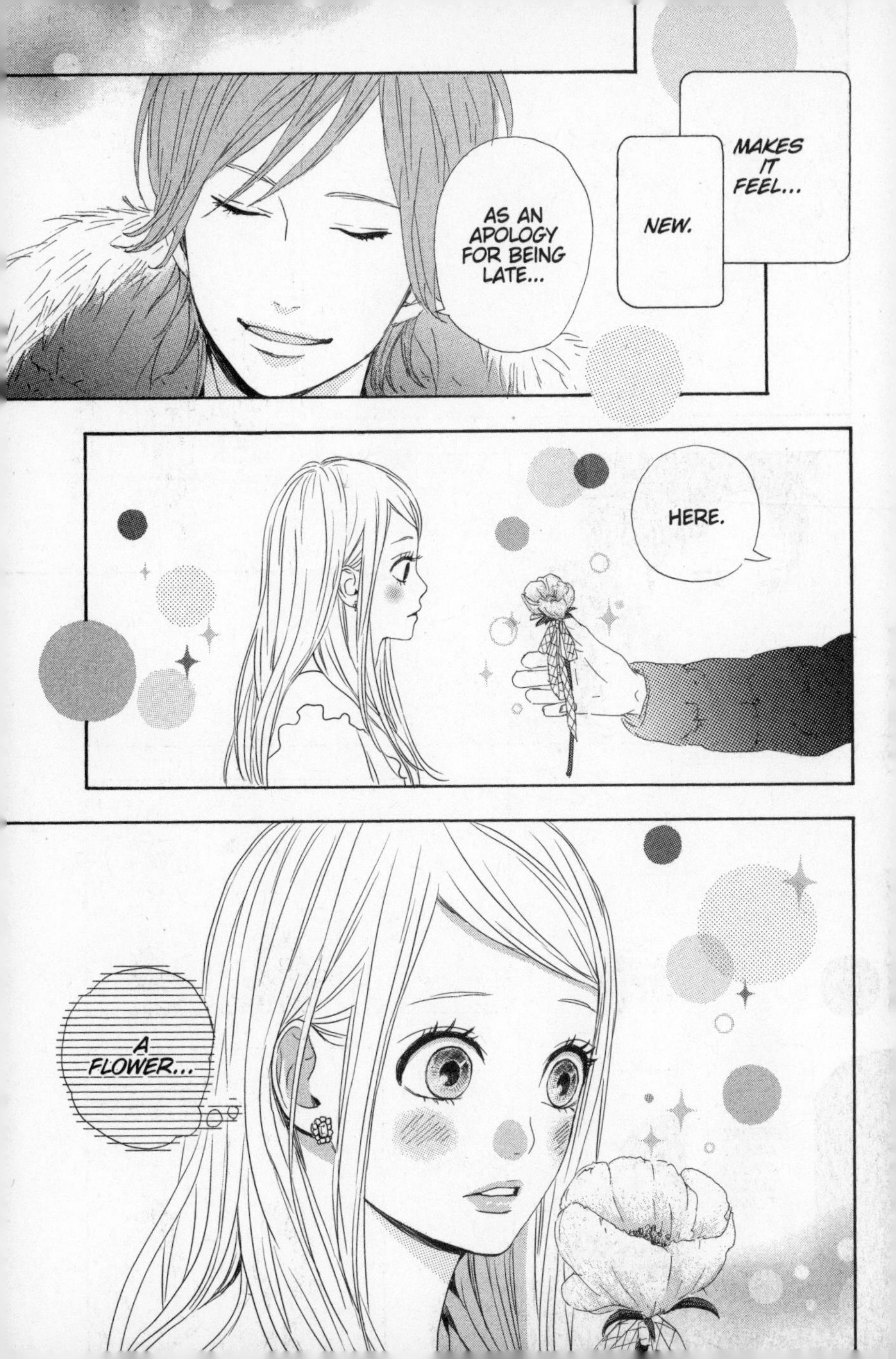
MAKES IT FEEL...
NEW.
AS AN APOLOGY FOR BEING LATE...
HERE.
A FLOWER...

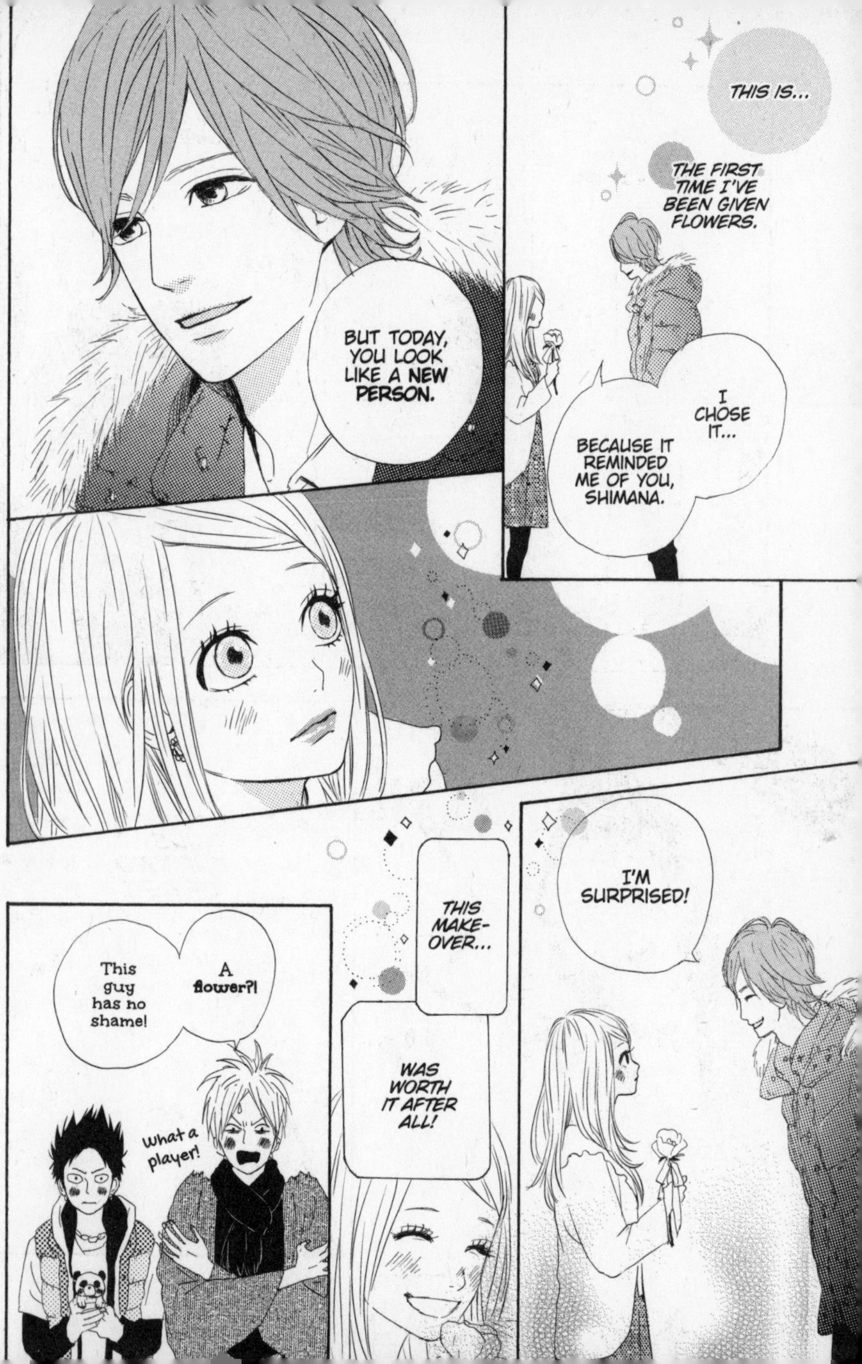
THIS IS...
THE FIRST TIME I'VE BEEN GIVEN FLOWERS.
I CHOSE IT...
BECAUSE IT REMINDED ME OF YOU, SHIMANA.
BUT TODAY, YOU LOOK LIKE A NEW PERSON.
I'M SURPRISED!
THIS MAKEOVER...
WAS WORTH IT AFTER ALL!
A flower?!
This guy has no shame!
What a player!

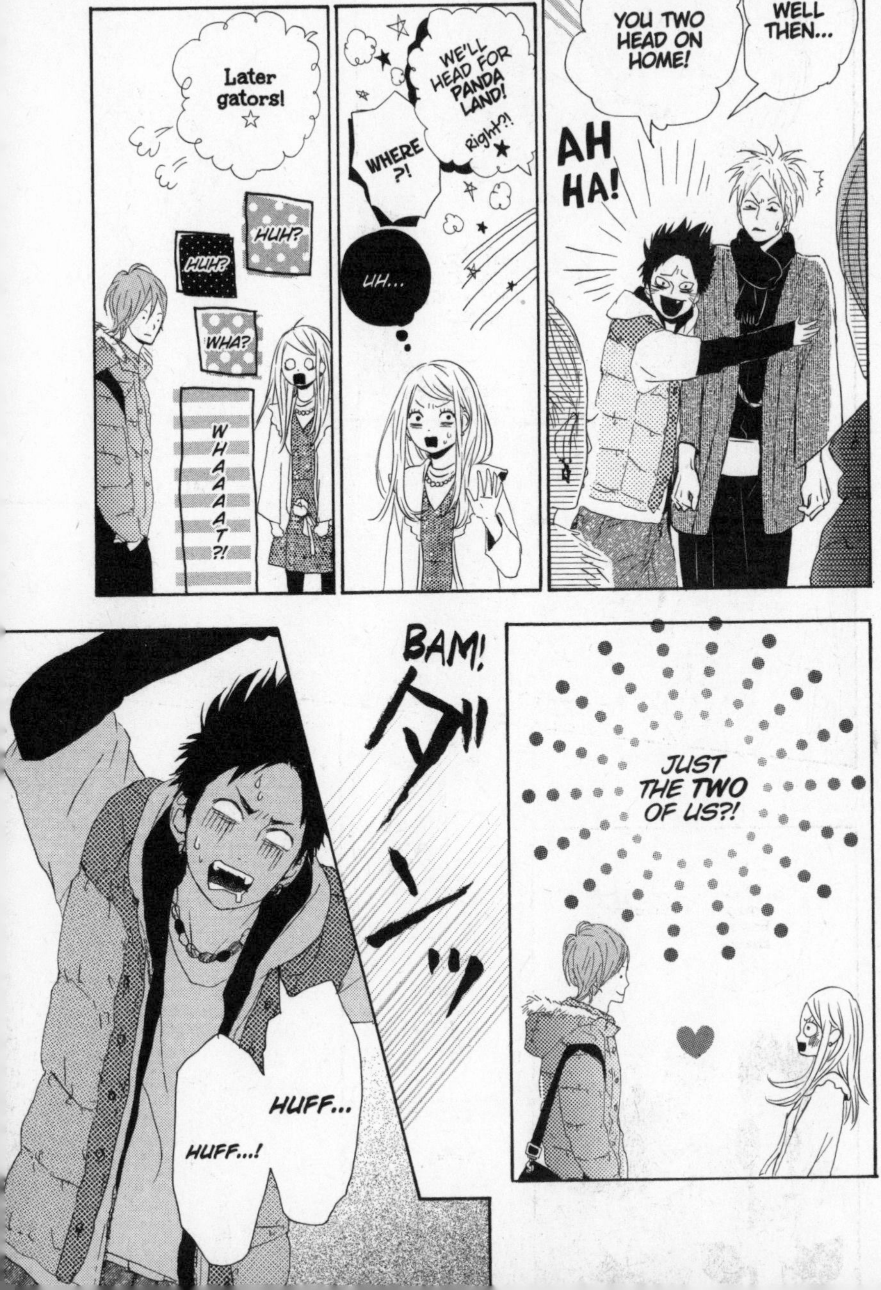
WELL THEN...
YOU TWO HEAD ON HOME!
AH HA!
WE'LL HEAD FOR PANDA LAND!
Right?! ★
WHERE ?!
UH...
Later gators! ☆
HUH?
HUH?
WHA?
WHAAAAAT?!
JUST THE TWO OF US?!
BAM!
HUFF...
HUFF...!

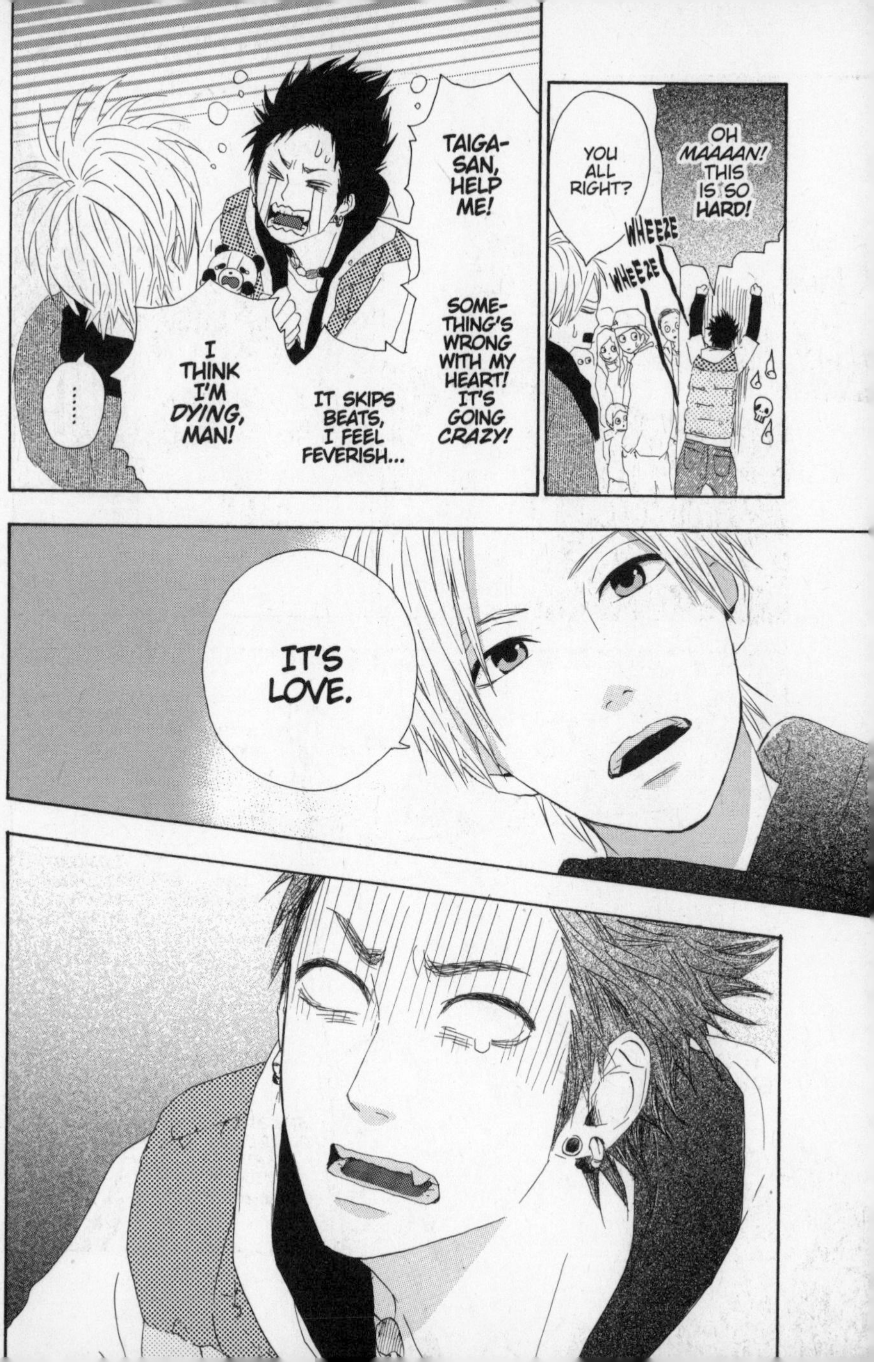
OH MAAAAN! THIS IS SO HARD!
YOU ALL RIGHT?
WHEEZE
WHEEZE
TAIGA-SAN, HELP ME!
SOMETHING'S WRONG WITH MY HEART! IT'S GOING CRAZY!
IT SKIPS BEATS, I FEEL FEVERISH...
I THINK I'M DYING, MAN!
......
IT'S LOVE.

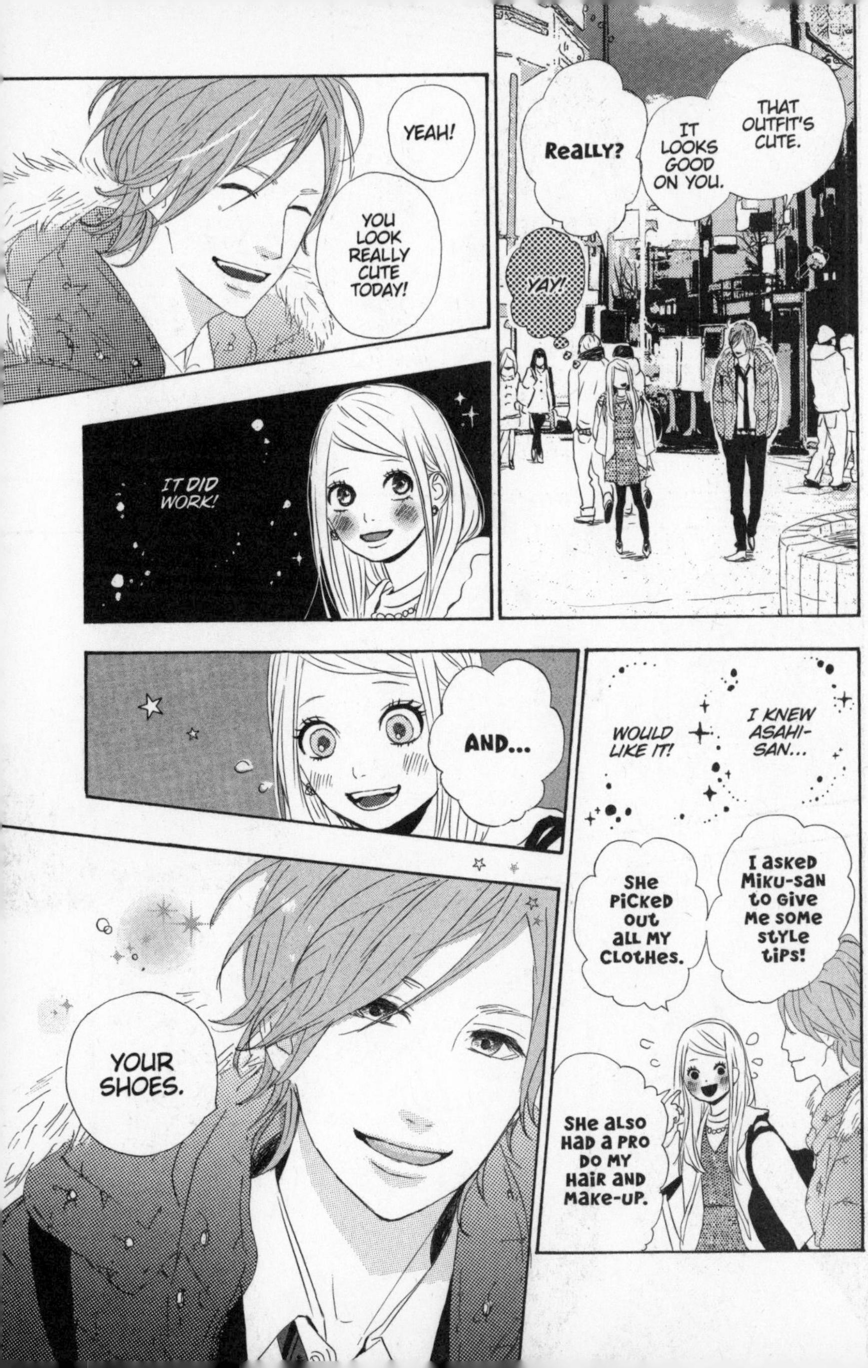
THAT OUTFIT'S CUTE.
IT LOOKS GOOD ON YOU.
Really?
YAY!
YEAH!
YOU LOOK REALLY CUTE TODAY!
IT DID WORK!
I KNEW ASAHI-SAN...
WOULD LIKE IT!
I asked Miku-san to give me some style tips!
She picked out all my clothes.
She also had a pro do my hair and make-up.
AND...
YOUR SHOES.

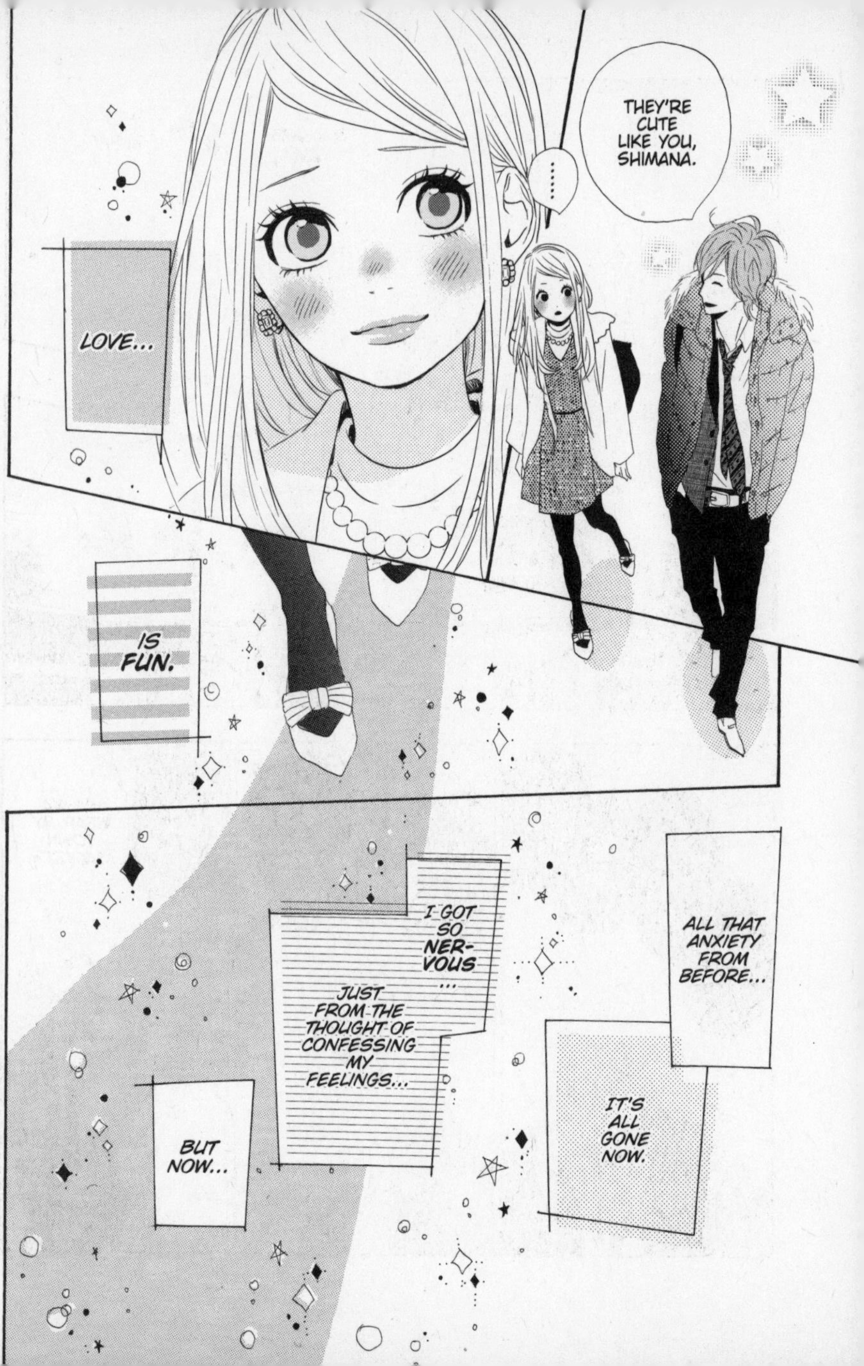
THEY'RE CUTE LIKE YOU, SHIMANA.
......
LOVE...
IS FUN.
ALL THAT ANXIETY FROM BEFORE...
IT'S ALL GONE NOW.
I GOT SO NER-VOUS...
JUST FROM THE THOUGHT OF CONFESSING MY FEELINGS...
BUT NOW...

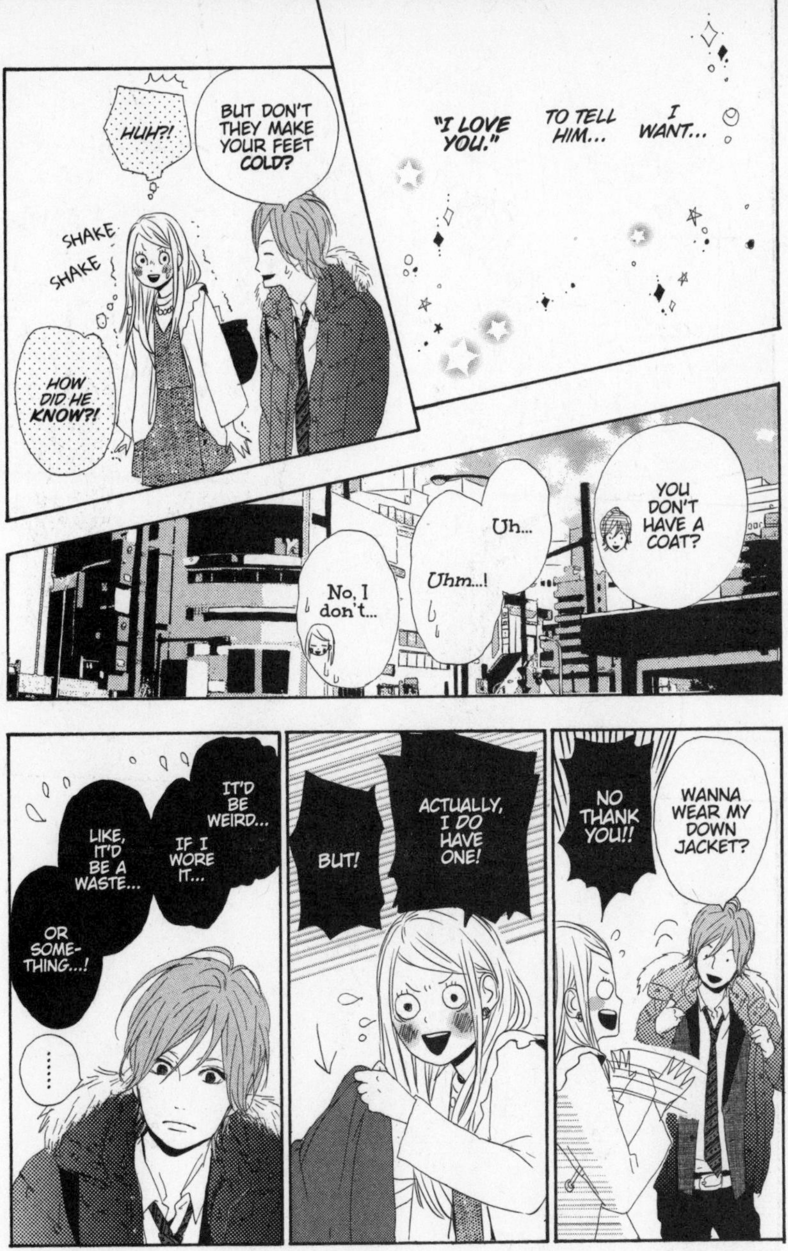
I WANT...
TO TELL HIM...
"I LOVE YOU."
BUT DON'T THEY MAKE YOUR FEET COLD?
HUH?!
SHAKE
SHAKE
HOW DID HE KNOW?!
YOU DON'T HAVE A COAT?
Uh...
Uhm...!
No, I don't...
WANNA WEAR MY DOWN JACKET?
NO THANK YOU!!
ACTUALLY, I DO HAVE ONE!
BUT!
IT'D BE WEIRD...
IF I WORE IT...
LIKE, IT'D BE A WASTE...
OR SOME-THING...!
......

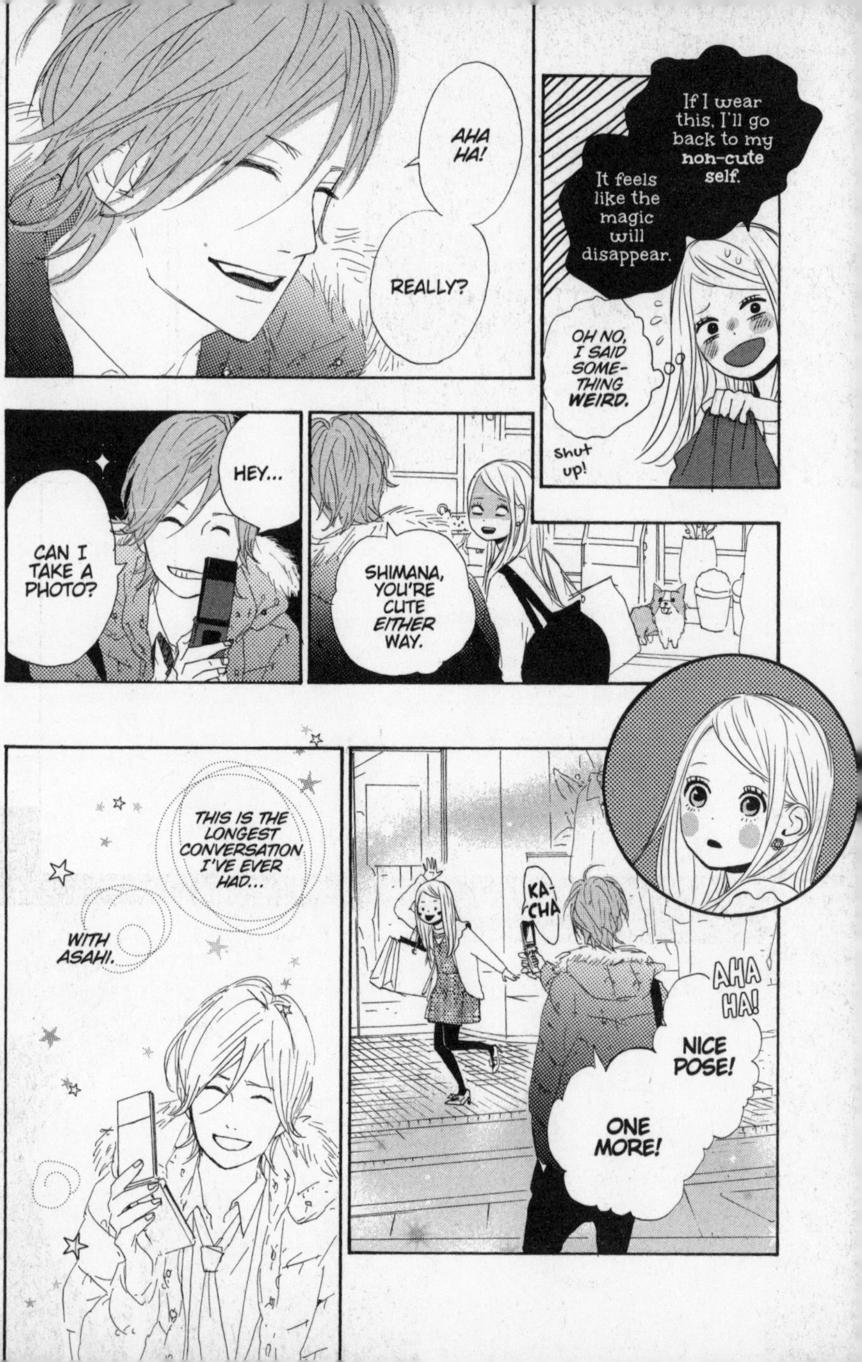
If I wear this, I'll go back to my non-cute self.
It feels like the magic will disappear.
OH NO, I SAID SOME-THING WEIRD.
Shut up!
AHA HA!
REALLY?
SHIMANA, YOU'RE CUTE EITHER WAY.
HEY...
CAN I TAKE A PHOTO?
AHA HA!
NICE POSE!
ONE MORE!
KA-CHA
THIS IS THE LONGEST CONVERSATION I'VE EVER HAD...
WITH ASAHI.

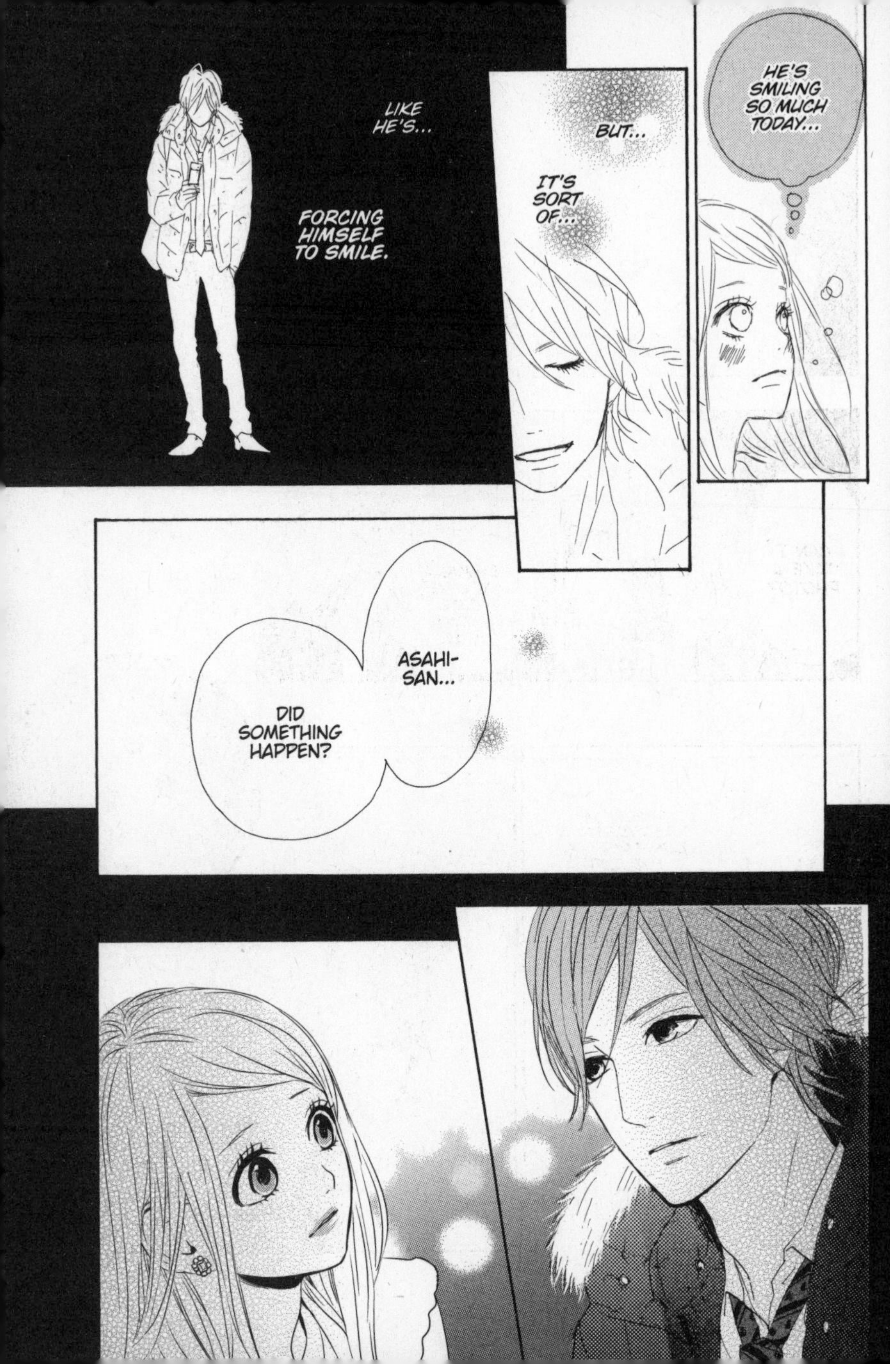
HE'S SMILING SO MUCH TODAY...
BUT...
IT'S SORT OF...
LIKE HE'S...
FORCING HIMSELF TO SMILE.
ASAHI-SAN...
DID SOMETHING HAPPEN?

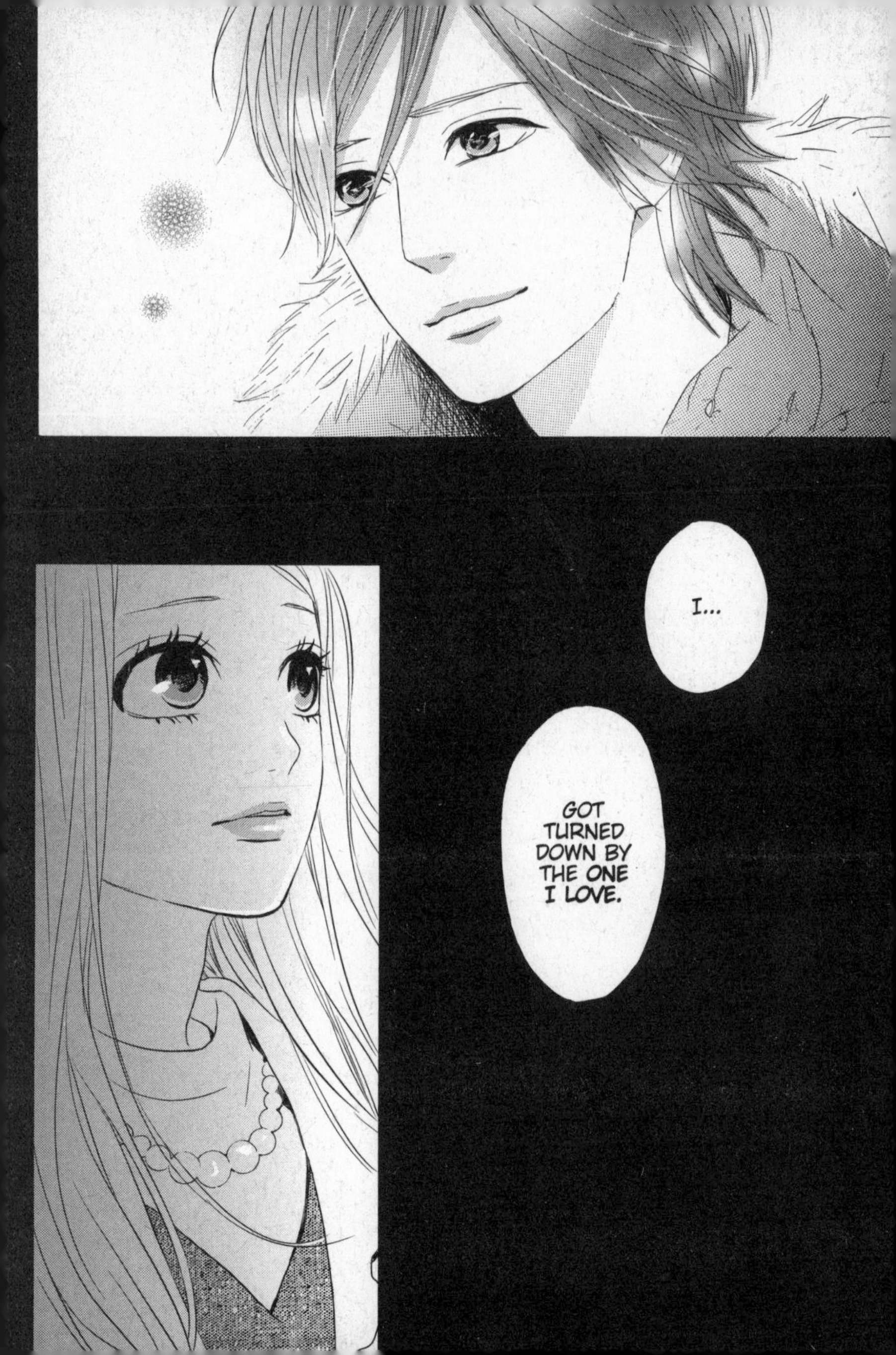
I...
GOT TURNED DOWN BY THE ONE I LOVE.

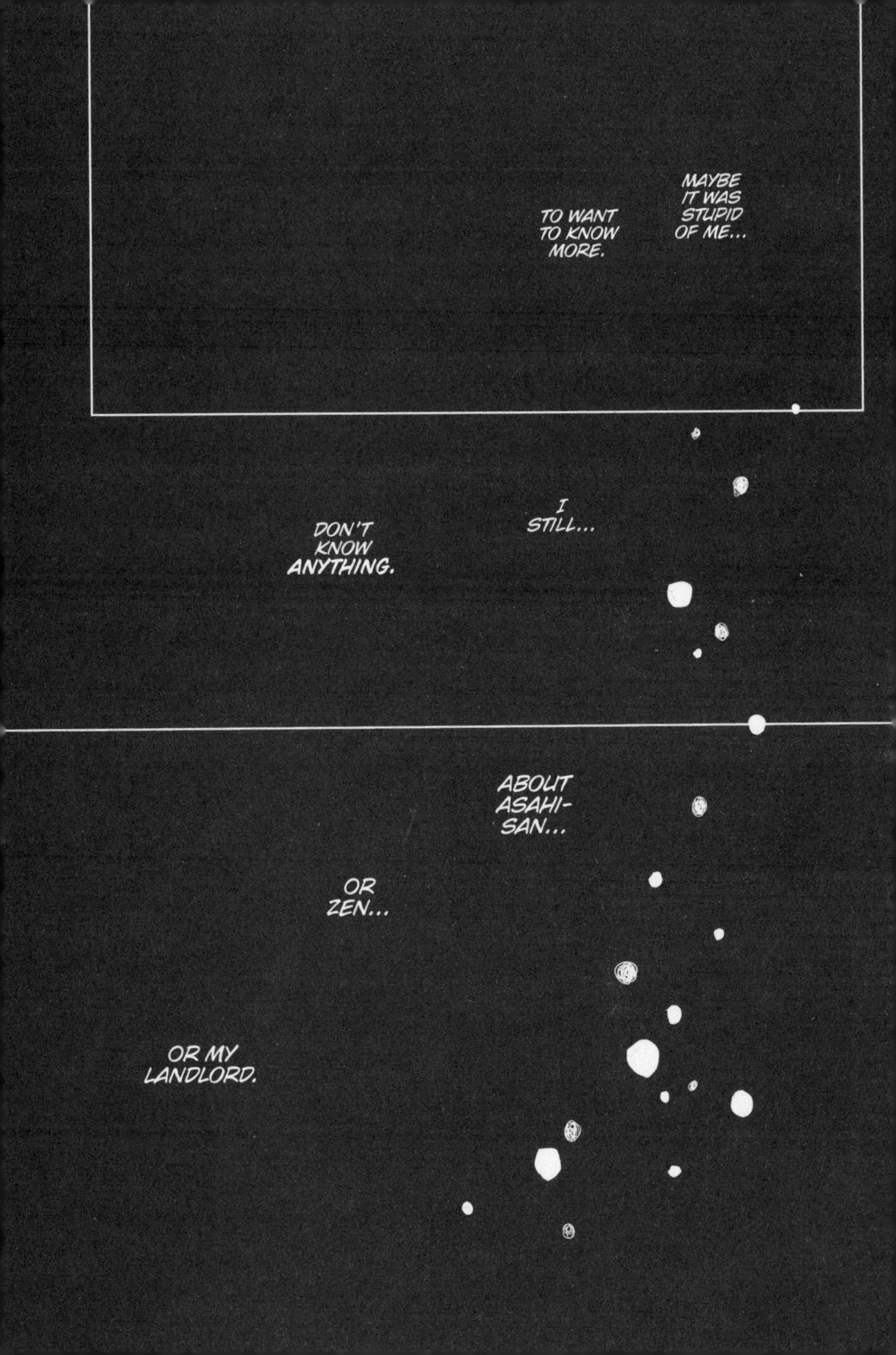
MAYBE IT WAS STUPID OF ME...
TO WANT TO KNOW MORE.
I STILL...
DON'T KNOW ANYTHING.
ABOUT ASAHI-SAN...
OR ZEN...
OR MY LANDLORD.

Meaningless Doodle

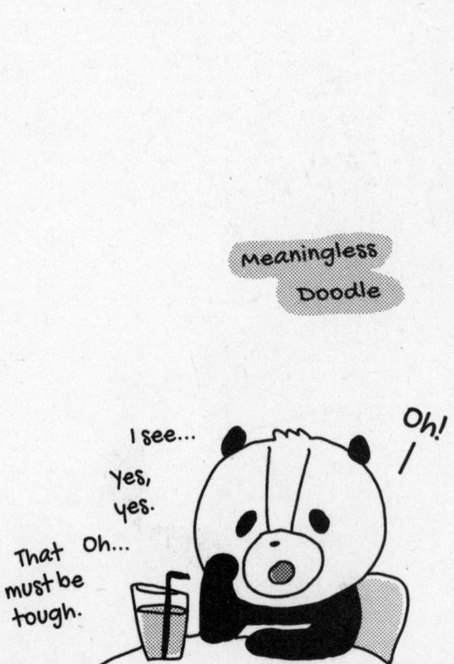
Oh!
I see...
Yes, yes.
Oh...
That must be tough.

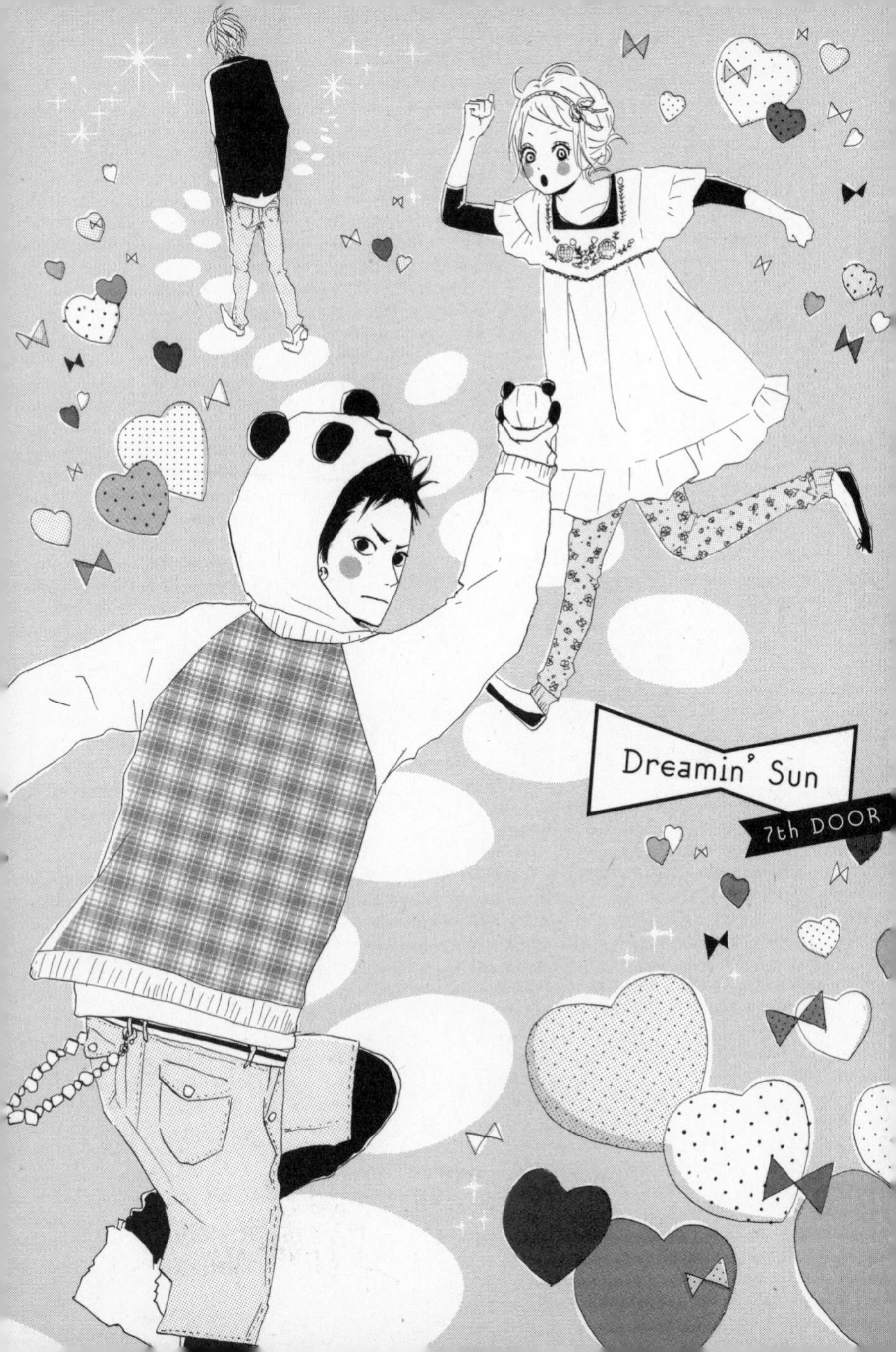
Dreamin' Sun
7th DOOR

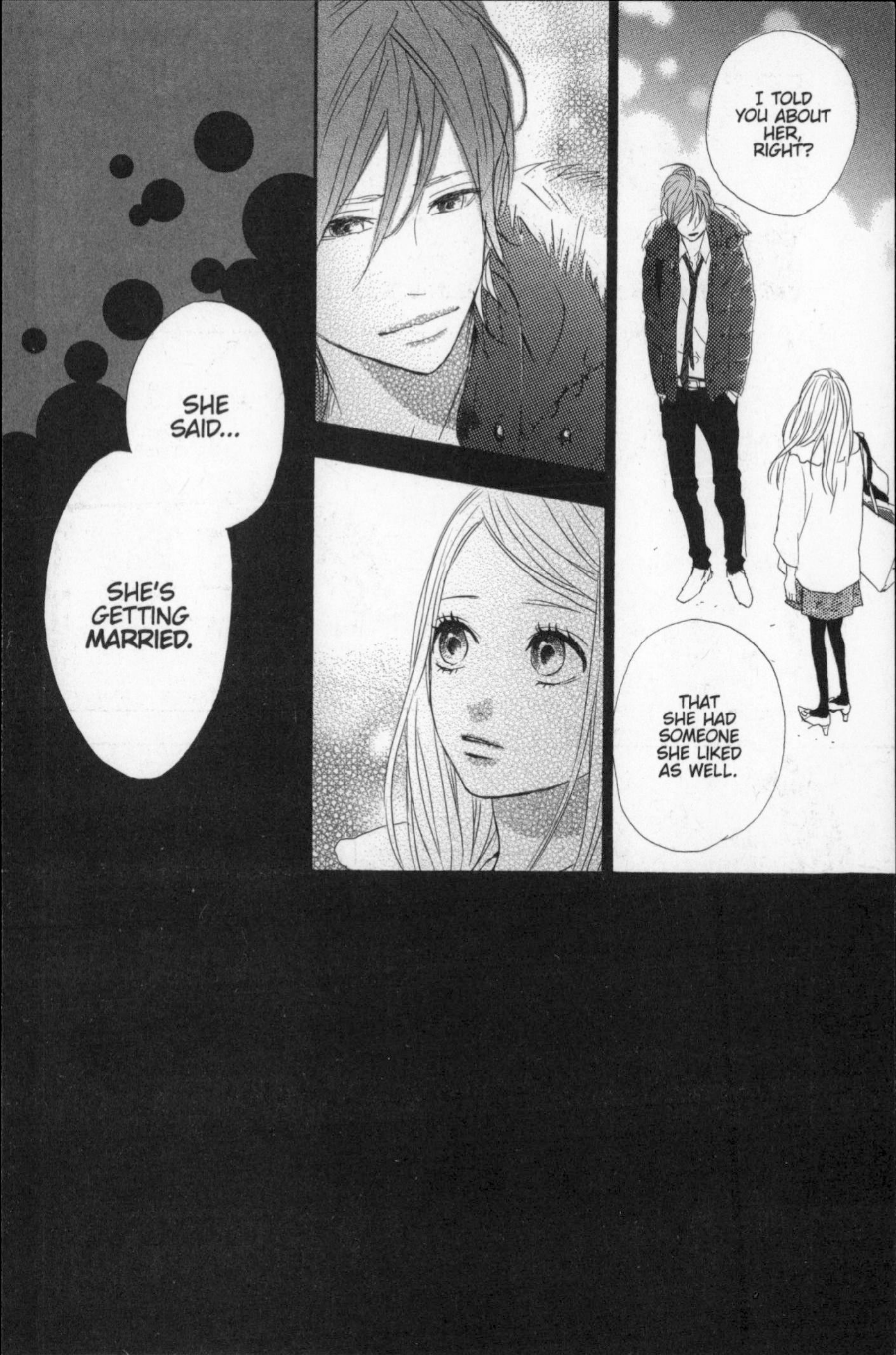
I TOLD YOU ABOUT HER, RIGHT?
THAT SHE HAD SOMEONE SHE LIKED AS WELL.
SHE SAID...
SHE'S GETTING MARRIED.

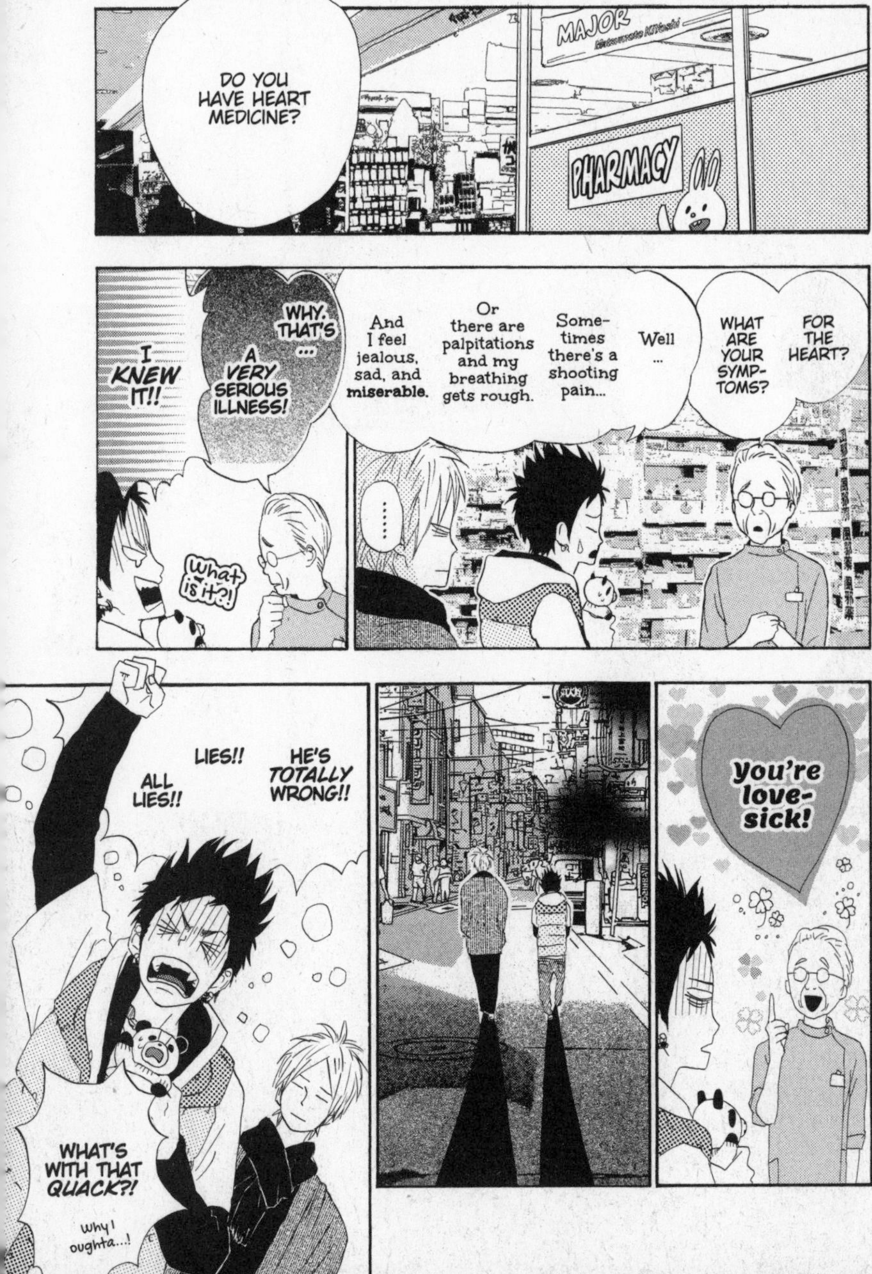
MAJOR
PHARMACY
DO YOU HAVE HEART MEDICINE?
FOR THE HEART?
WHAT ARE YOUR SYMPTOMS?
Well ...
Sometimes there's a shooting pain...
Or there are palpitations and my breathing gets rough.
And I feel jealous, sad, and **miserable**.
......
WHY. THAT'S ...
A *VERY* SERIOUS ILLNESS!
I *KNEW* IT!!
what is it?!
you're love-sick!
LIES!!
ALL LIES!!
HE'S *TOTALLY* WRONG!!
WHAT'S WITH THAT *QUACK*?!
Why I oughta...!

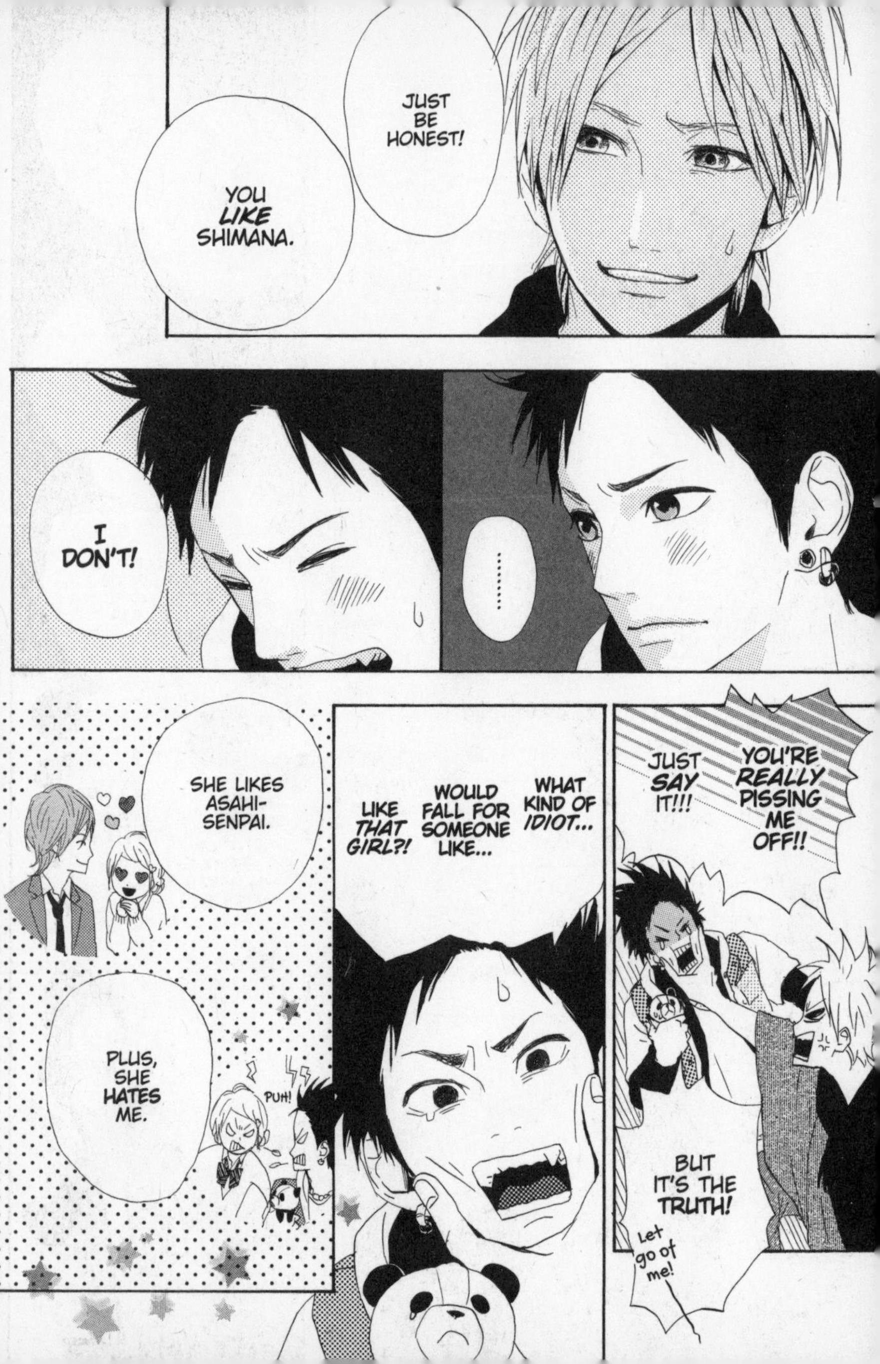
JUST BE HONEST!
YOU LIKE SHIMANA.
......
I DON'T!
YOU'RE REALLY PISSING ME OFF!!
JUST SAY IT!!!
BUT IT'S THE TRUTH!
Let go of me!
WHAT KIND OF IDIOT...
WOULD FALL FOR SOMEONE LIKE...
LIKE THAT GIRL?!
SHE LIKES ASAHI-SENPAI.
PLUS, SHE HATES ME.
PUH!

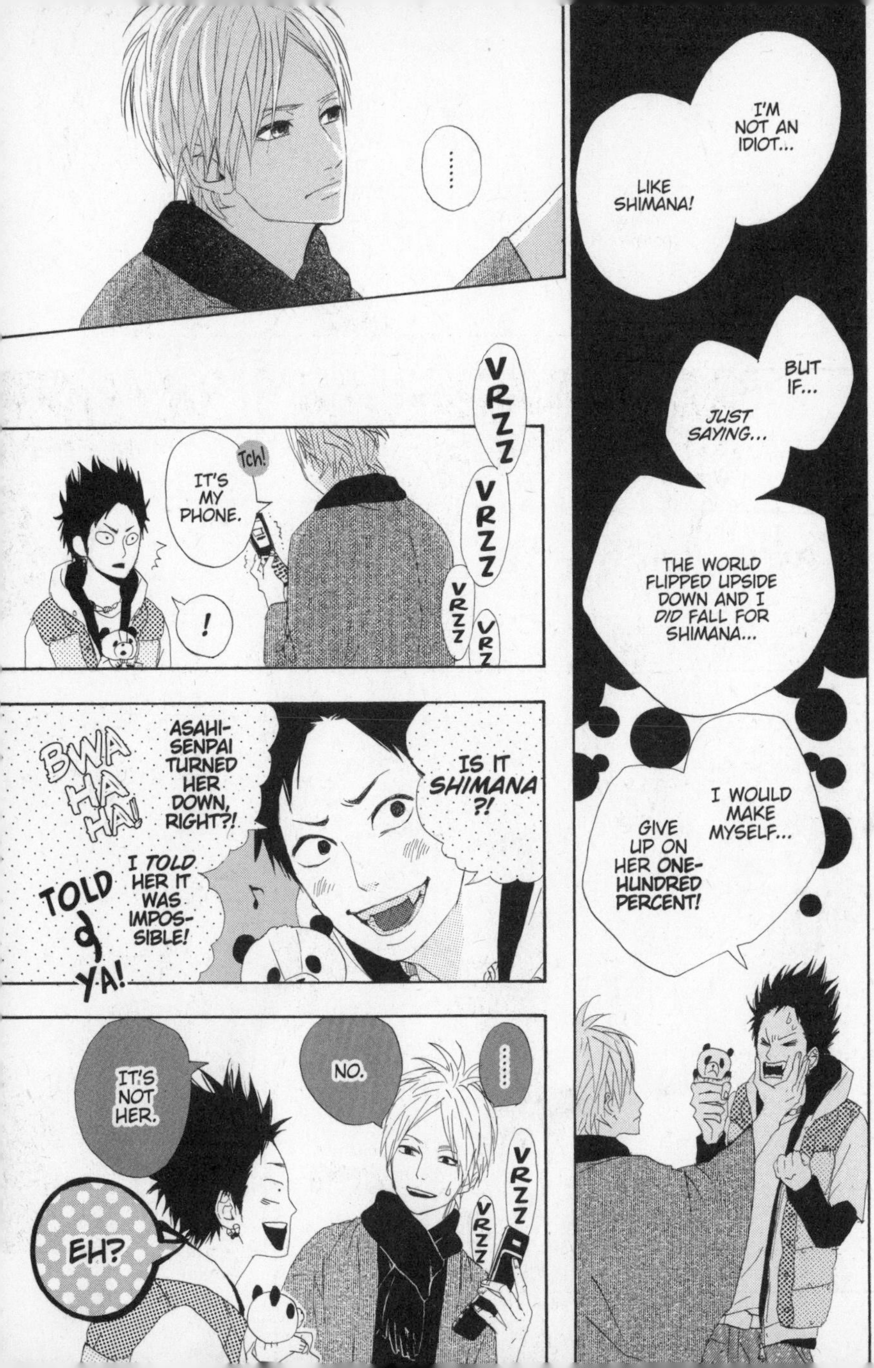
I'M NOT AN IDIOT... LIKE SHIMANA!
BUT IF... JUST SAYING...
THE WORLD FLIPPED UPSIDE DOWN AND I *DID* FALL FOR SHIMANA...
I WOULD MAKE MYSELF... GIVE UP ON HER ONE-HUNDRED PERCENT!
......
VRZZ VRZZ VRZZ VRZZ VRZ
Tch!
IT'S MY PHONE.
!
IS IT *SHIMANA*?!
ASAHI-SENPAI TURNED HER DOWN, RIGHT?!
BWA HA HA!
I *TOLD* HER IT WAS IMPOSSIBLE!
TOLD 'YA!
......
NO.
IT'S NOT HER.
VRZZ VRZZ
EH?

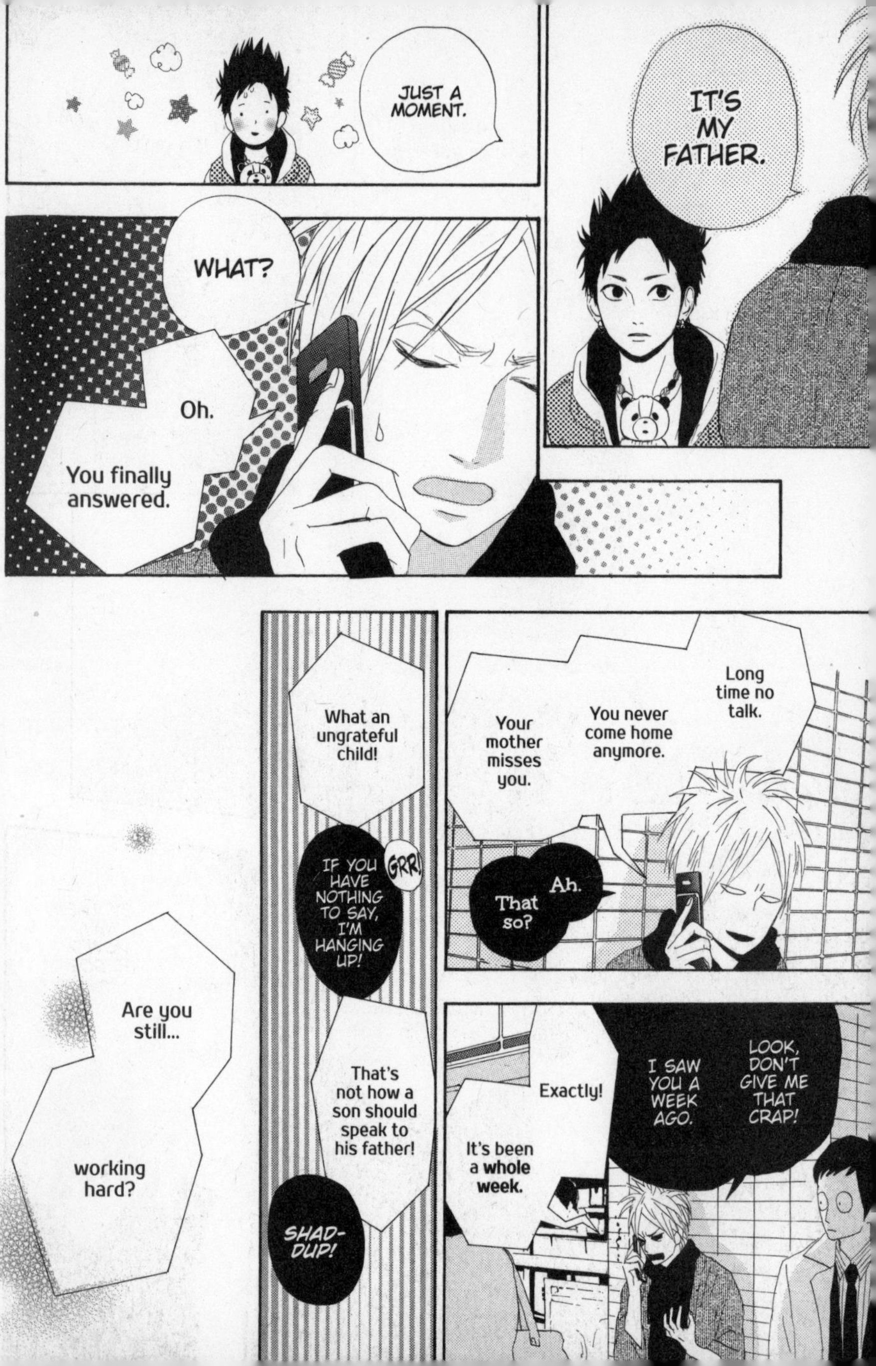
IT'S MY FATHER.
JUST A MOMENT.
WHAT?
Oh.
You finally answered.
Long time no talk.
You never come home anymore.
Your mother misses you.
Ah.
That so?
LOOK, DON'T GIVE ME THAT CRAP!
I SAW YOU A WEEK AGO.
Exactly!
It's been a whole week.
What an ungrateful child!
GRR!
IF YOU HAVE NOTHING TO SAY, I'M HANGING UP!
That's not how a son should speak to his father!
SHAD-DUP!
Are you still...
working hard?

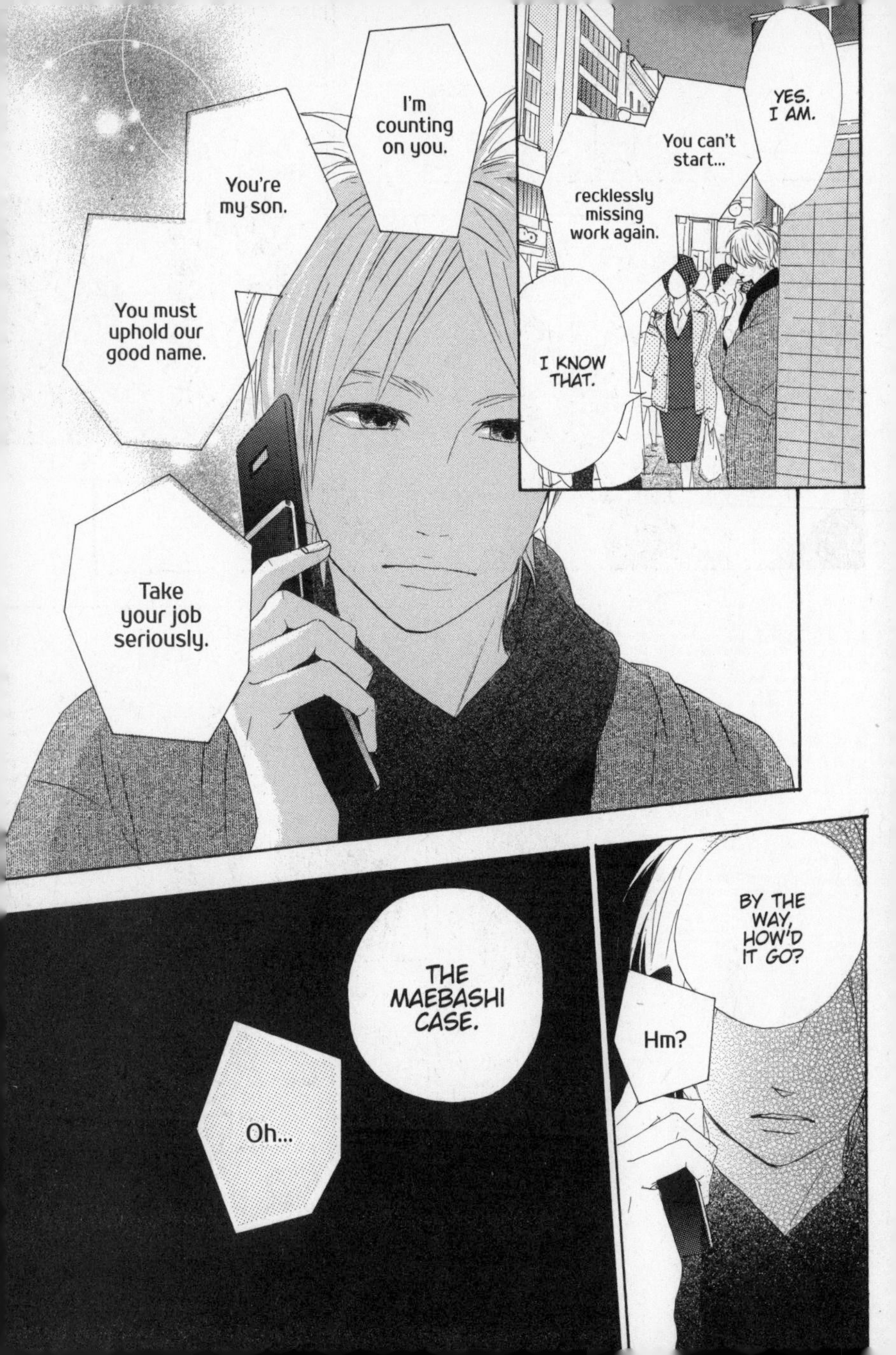
YES. I AM.
You can't start...
recklessly missing work again.
I KNOW THAT.
I'm counting on you.
You're my son.
You must uphold our good name.
Take your job seriously.
BY THE WAY, HOW'D IT GO?
Hm?
THE MAEBASHI CASE.
Oh...

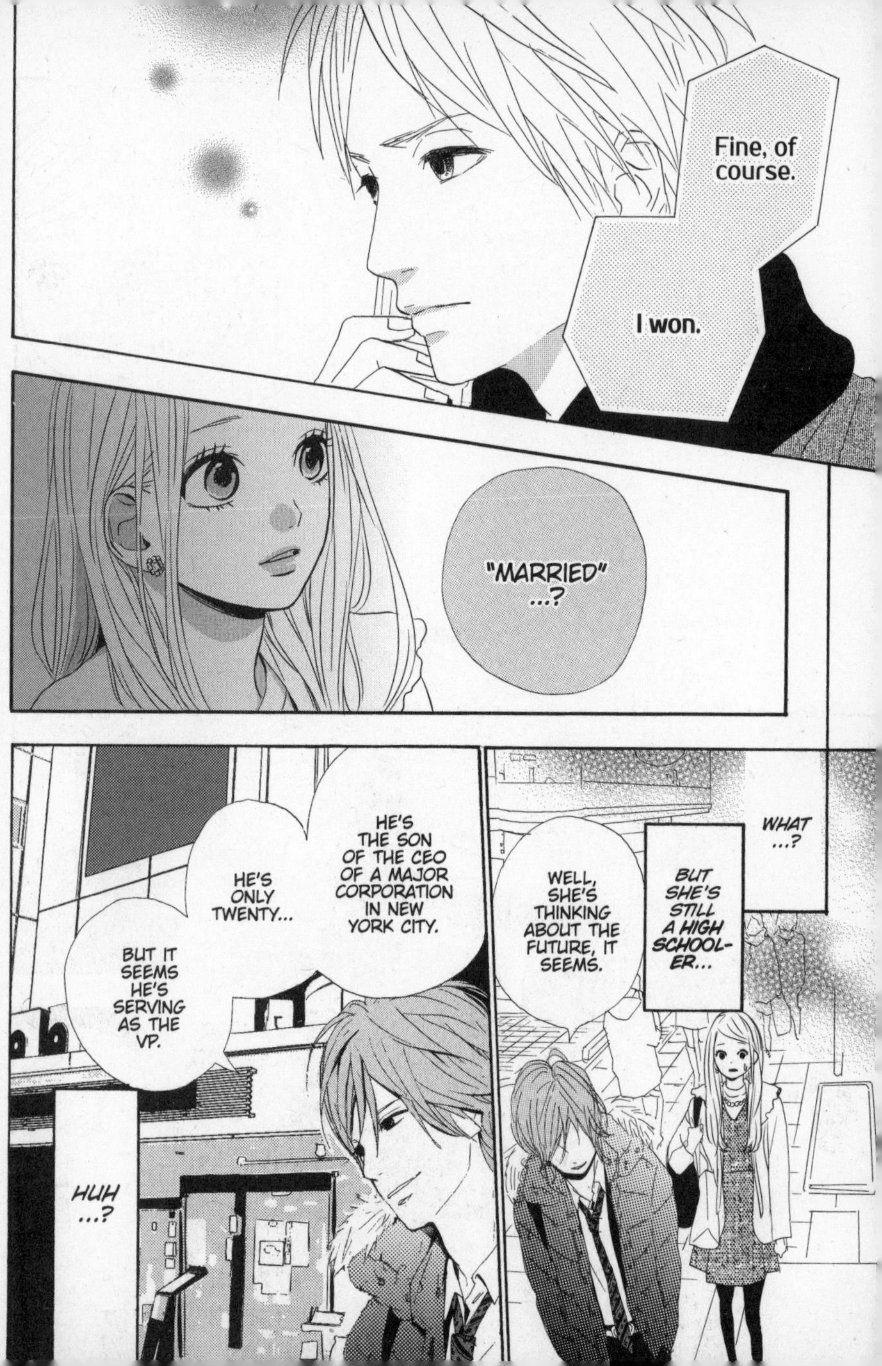
Fine, of course.
I won.
"MARRIED" ...?
WHAT ...?
BUT SHE'S STILL A HIGH SCHOOLER...
WELL, SHE'S THINKING ABOUT THE FUTURE, IT SEEMS.
HE'S THE SON OF THE CEO OF A MAJOR CORPORATION IN NEW YORK CITY.
HE'S ONLY TWENTY...
BUT IT SEEMS HE'S SERVING AS THE VP.
HUH ...?

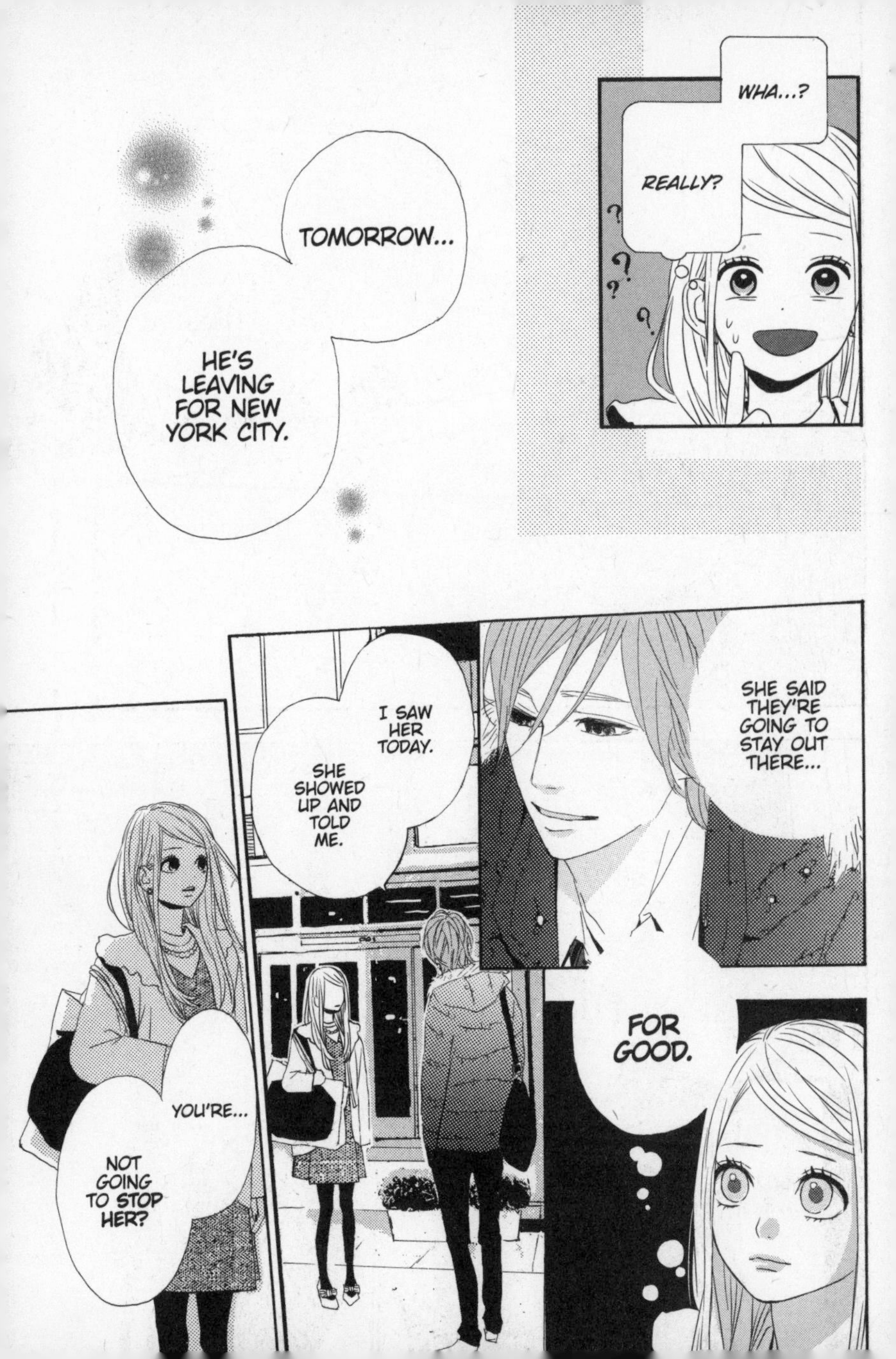
WHA...?
REALLY?
TOMORROW...
HE'S LEAVING FOR NEW YORK CITY.
I SAW HER TODAY.
SHE SHOWED UP AND TOLD ME.
SHE SAID THEY'RE GOING TO STAY OUT THERE...
FOR GOOD.
YOU'RE...
NOT GOING TO STOP HER?

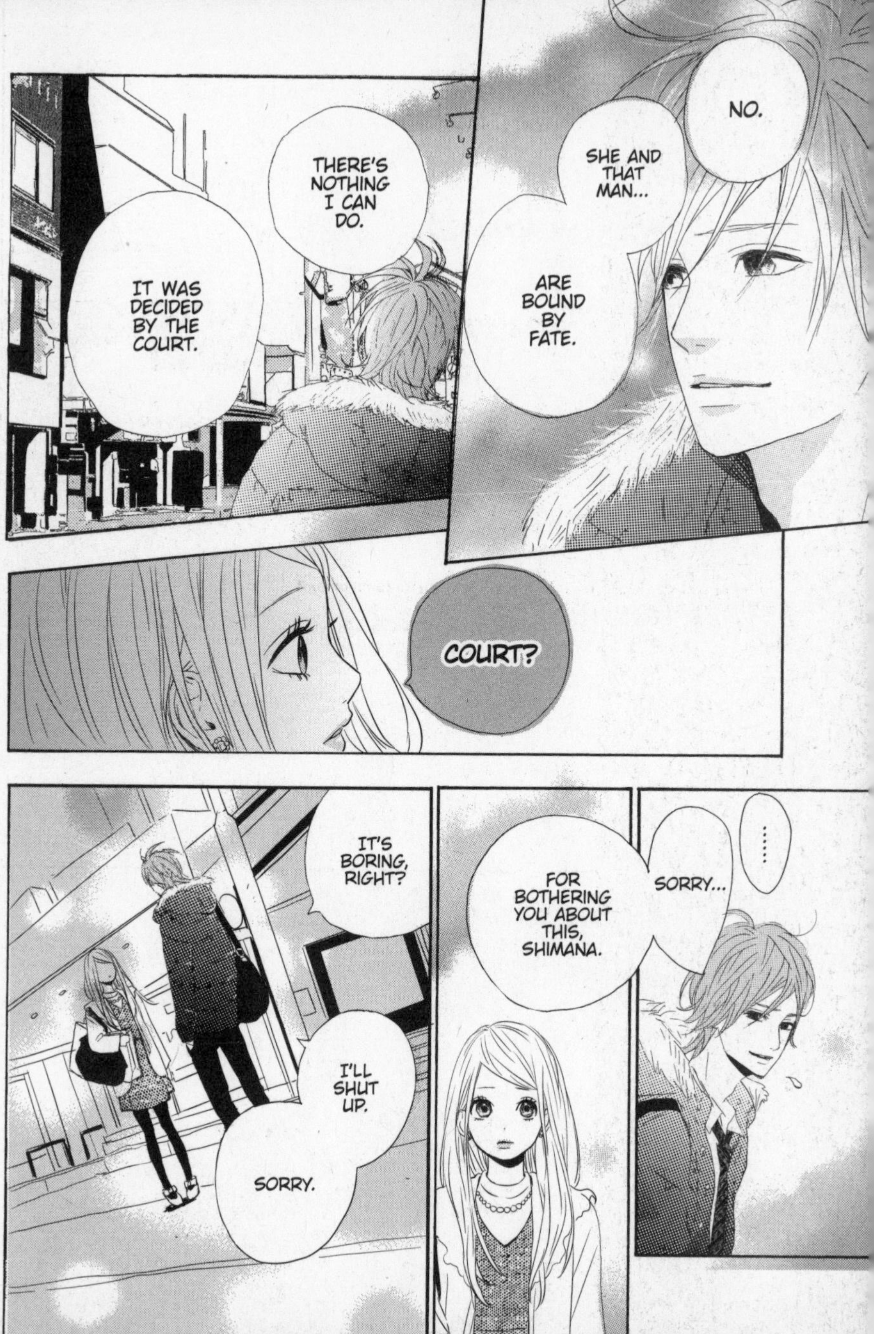
NO.
SHE AND THAT MAN...
ARE BOUND BY FATE.
THERE'S NOTHING I CAN DO.
IT WAS DECIDED BY THE COURT.
COURT?
......
SORRY...
FOR BOTHERING YOU ABOUT THIS, SHIMANA.
IT'S BORING, RIGHT?
I'LL SHUT UP.
SORRY.

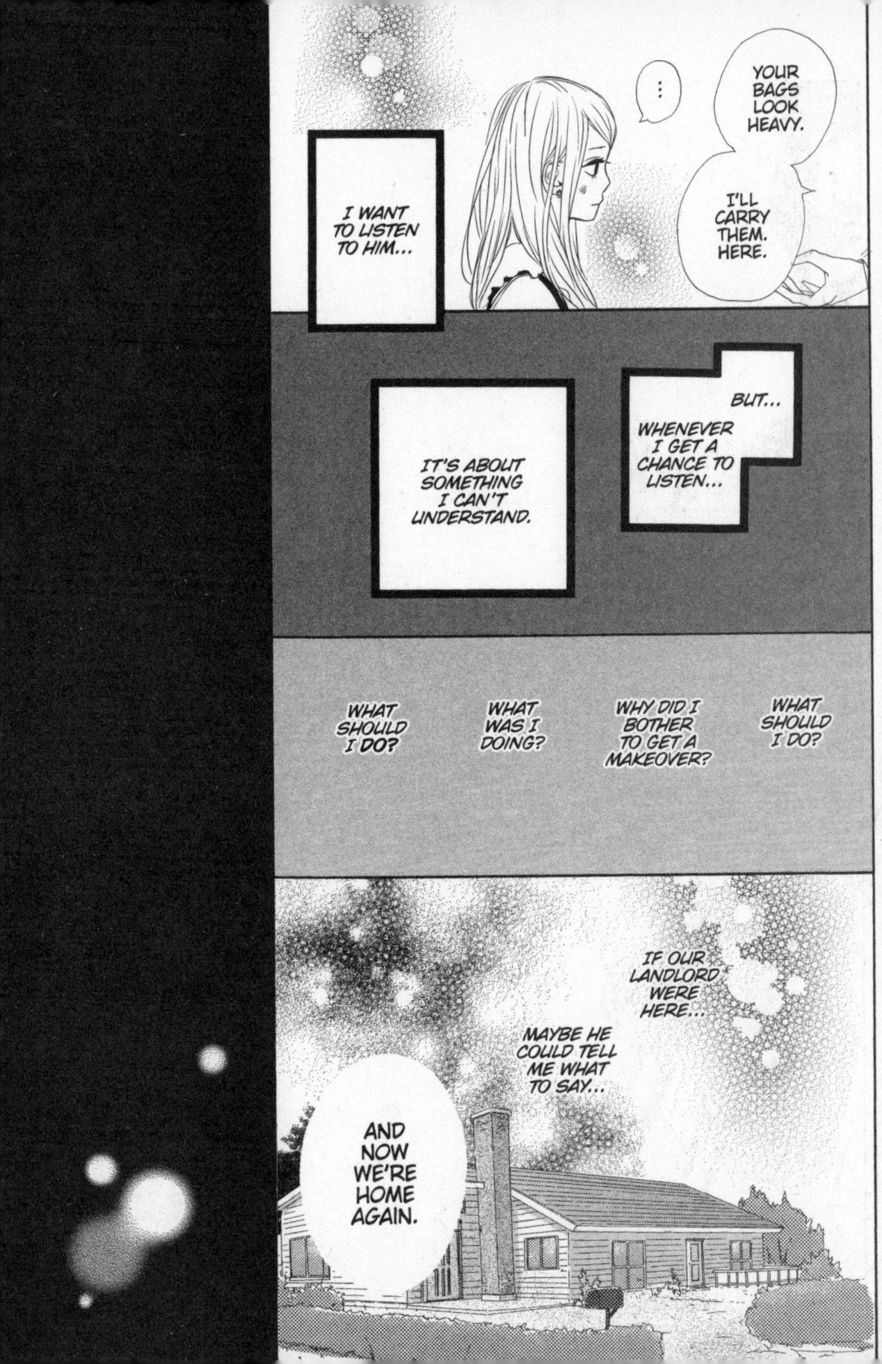
YOUR BAGS LOOK HEAVY.
I'LL CARRY THEM. HERE.
...
I WANT TO LISTEN TO HIM...
BUT...
WHENEVER I GET A CHANCE TO LISTEN...
IT'S ABOUT SOMETHING I CAN'T UNDERSTAND.
WHAT SHOULD I DO?
WHY DID I BOTHER TO GET A MAKEOVER?
WHAT WAS I DOING?
WHAT SHOULD I DO?
IF OUR LANDLORD* WERE HERE...
MAYBE HE COULD TELL ME WHAT TO SAY...
AND NOW WE'RE HOME AGAIN.

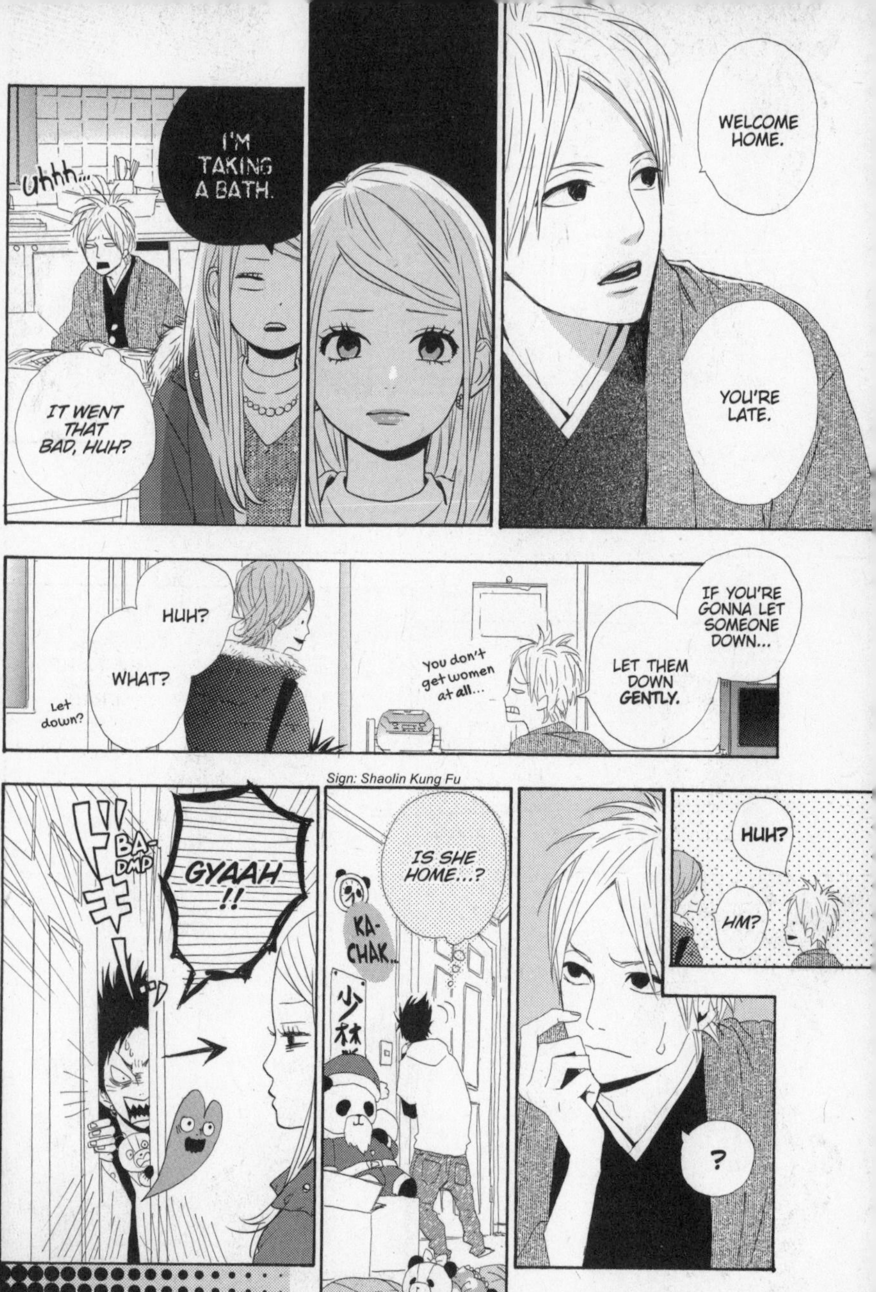
WELCOME HOME.
YOU'RE LATE.
I'M TAKING A BATH.
Uhhh...
IT WENT THAT BAD, HUH?
IF YOU'RE GONNA LET SOMEONE DOWN...
LET THEM DOWN GENTLY.
You don't get women at all...
HUH?
WHAT?
Let down?
Sign: Shaolin Kung Fu
HUH?
HM?
?
IS SHE HOME...?
KA-CHAK...
GYAAH!!
BA-DMP

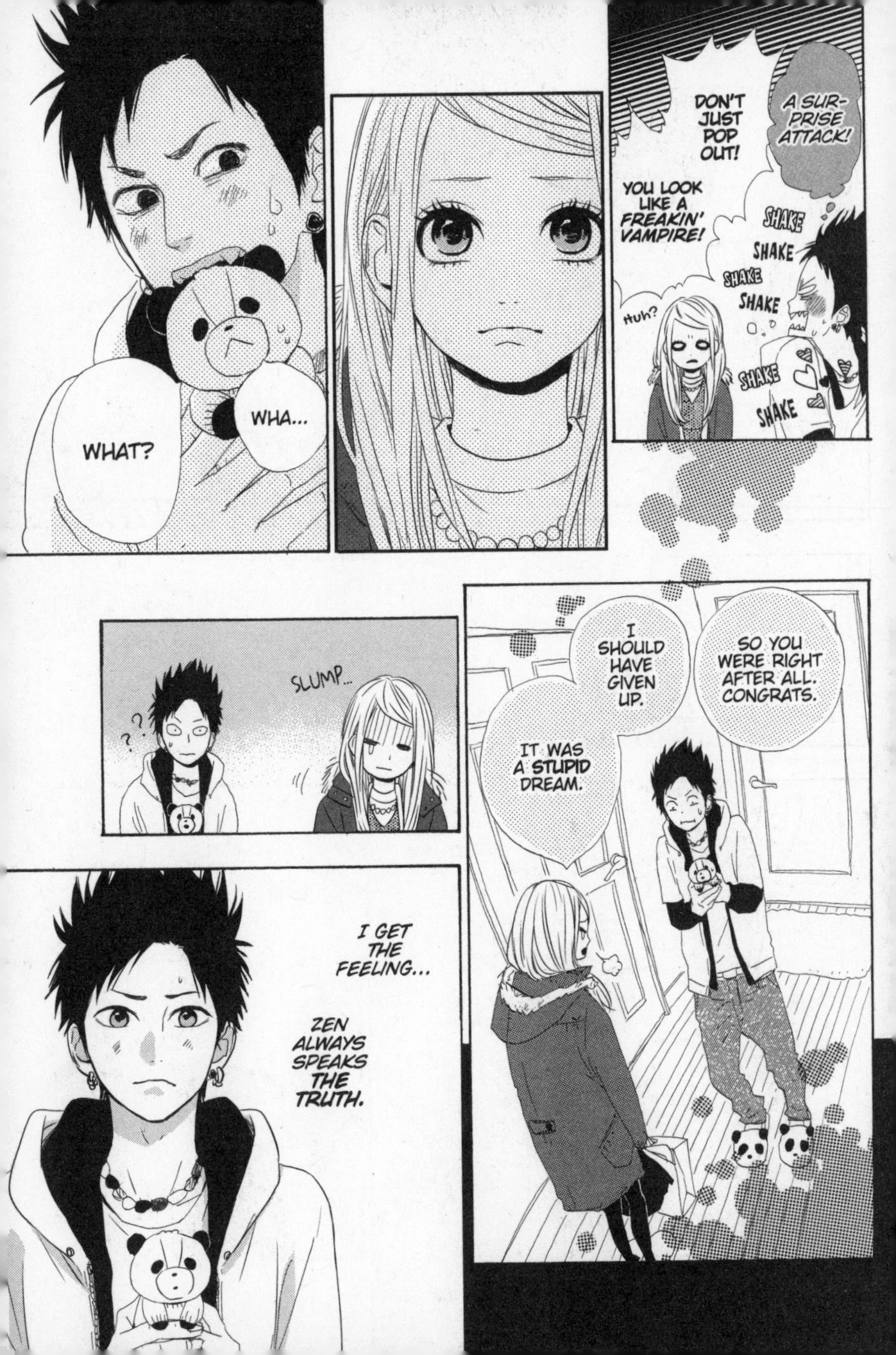
A SUR-PRISE ATTACK!
DON'T JUST POP OUT!
YOU LOOK LIKE A FREAKIN' VAMPIRE!
SHAKE
SHAKE
SHAKE
SHAKE
SHAKE
SHAKE
Huh?
WHA...
WHAT?
SO YOU WERE RIGHT AFTER ALL. CONGRATS.
I SHOULD HAVE GIVEN UP.
IT WAS A STUPID DREAM.
SLUMP...
I GET THE FEELING...
ZEN ALWAYS SPEAKS THE TRUTH.

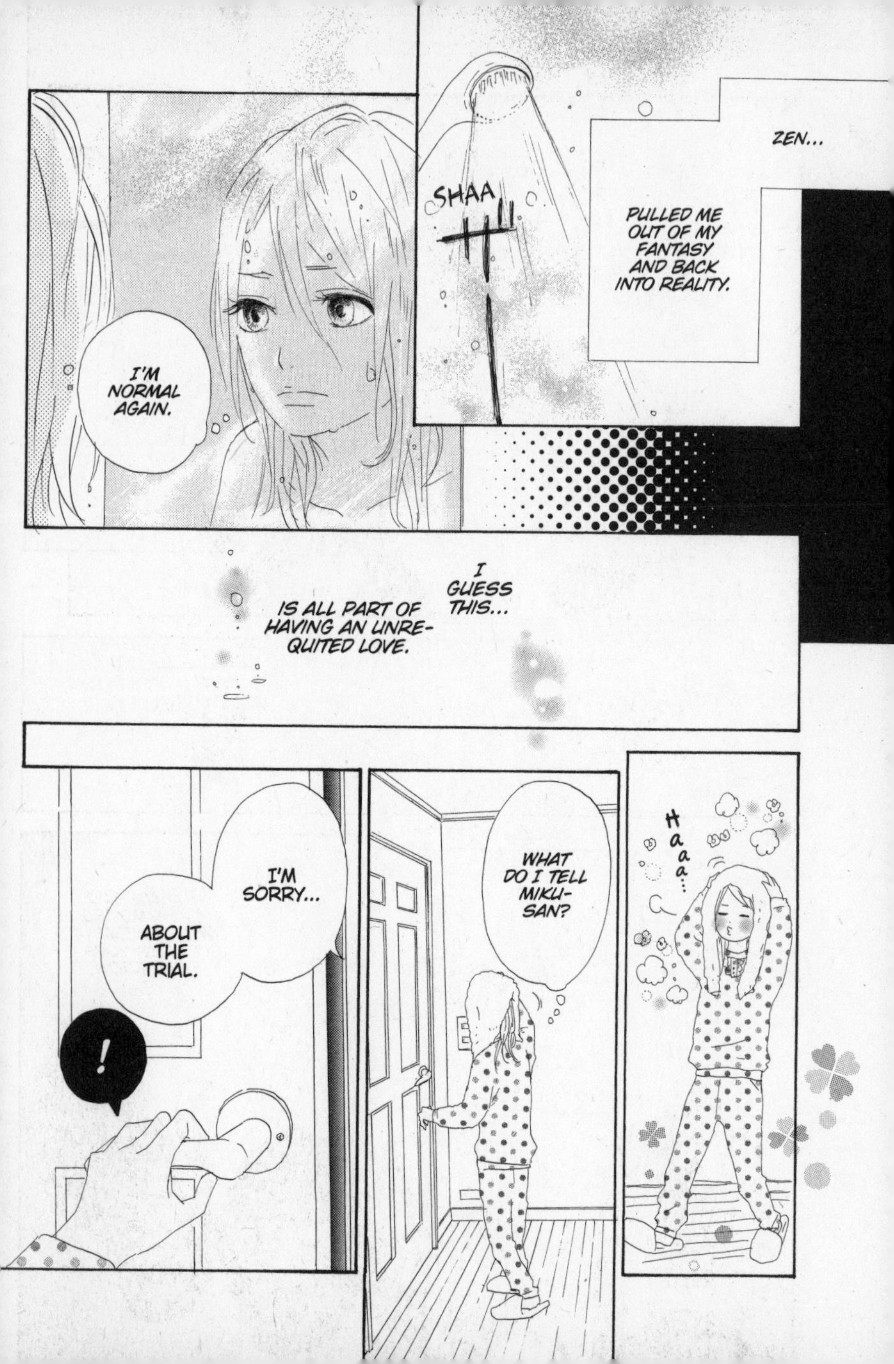
SHAA
ZEN...
PULLED ME OUT OF MY FANTASY AND BACK INTO REALITY.
I'M NORMAL AGAIN.
I GUESS THIS...
IS ALL PART OF HAVING AN UNRE-QUITED LOVE.
Haaa...
WHAT DO I TELL MIKU-SAN?
I'M SORRY...
ABOUT THE TRIAL.
!

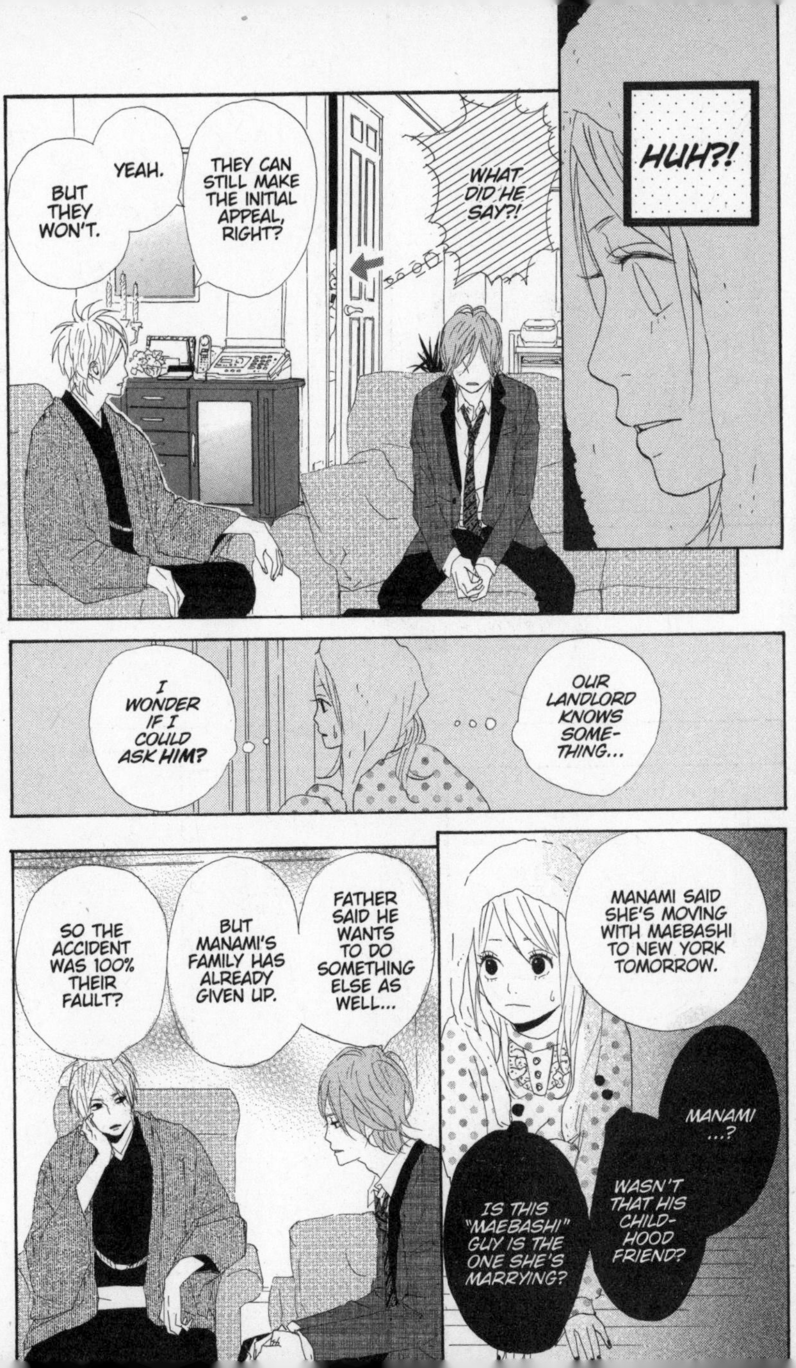
HUH?!
WHAT DID HE SAY?!
THEY CAN STILL MAKE THE INITIAL APPEAL, RIGHT?
YEAH.
BUT THEY WON'T.
OUR LANDLORD KNOWS SOME-THING...
I WONDER IF I COULD ASK HIM?
MANAMI SAID SHE'S MOVING WITH MAEBASHI TO NEW YORK TOMORROW.
MANAMI ...?
WASN'T THAT HIS CHILD-HOOD FRIEND?
IS THIS "MAEBASHI" GUY IS THE ONE SHE'S MARRYING?
FATHER SAID HE WANTS TO DO SOMETHING ELSE AS WELL...
BUT MANAMI'S FAMILY HAS ALREADY GIVEN UP.
SO THE ACCIDENT WAS 100% THEIR FAULT?

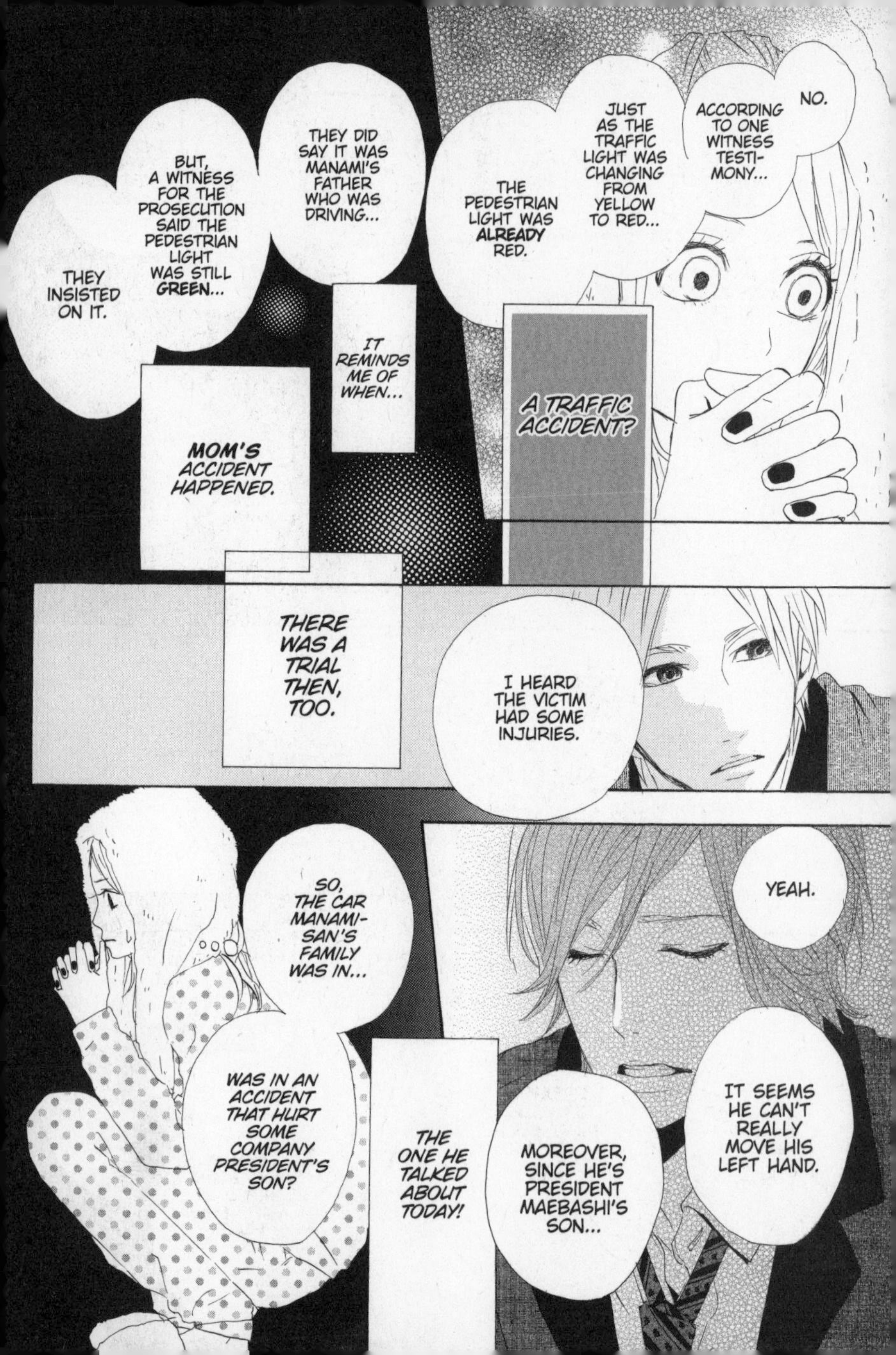
NO.
ACCORDING TO ONE WITNESS TESTIMONY...
JUST AS THE TRAFFIC LIGHT WAS CHANGING FROM YELLOW TO RED...
THE PEDESTRIAN LIGHT WAS ALREADY RED.
A TRAFFIC ACCIDENT?
THEY DID SAY IT WAS MANAMI'S FATHER WHO WAS DRIVING...
BUT, A WITNESS FOR THE PROSECUTION SAID THE PEDESTRIAN LIGHT WAS STILL GREEN...
THEY INSISTED ON IT.
IT REMINDS ME OF WHEN...
MOM'S ACCIDENT HAPPENED.
I HEARD THE VICTIM HAD SOME INJURIES.
THERE WAS A TRIAL THEN, TOO.
YEAH.
IT SEEMS HE CAN'T REALLY MOVE HIS LEFT HAND.
MOREOVER, SINCE HE'S PRESIDENT MAEBASHI'S SON...
THE ONE HE TALKED ABOUT TODAY!
SO, THE CAR MANAMI-SAN'S FAMILY WAS IN...
WAS IN AN ACCIDENT THAT HURT SOME COMPANY PRESIDENT'S SON?

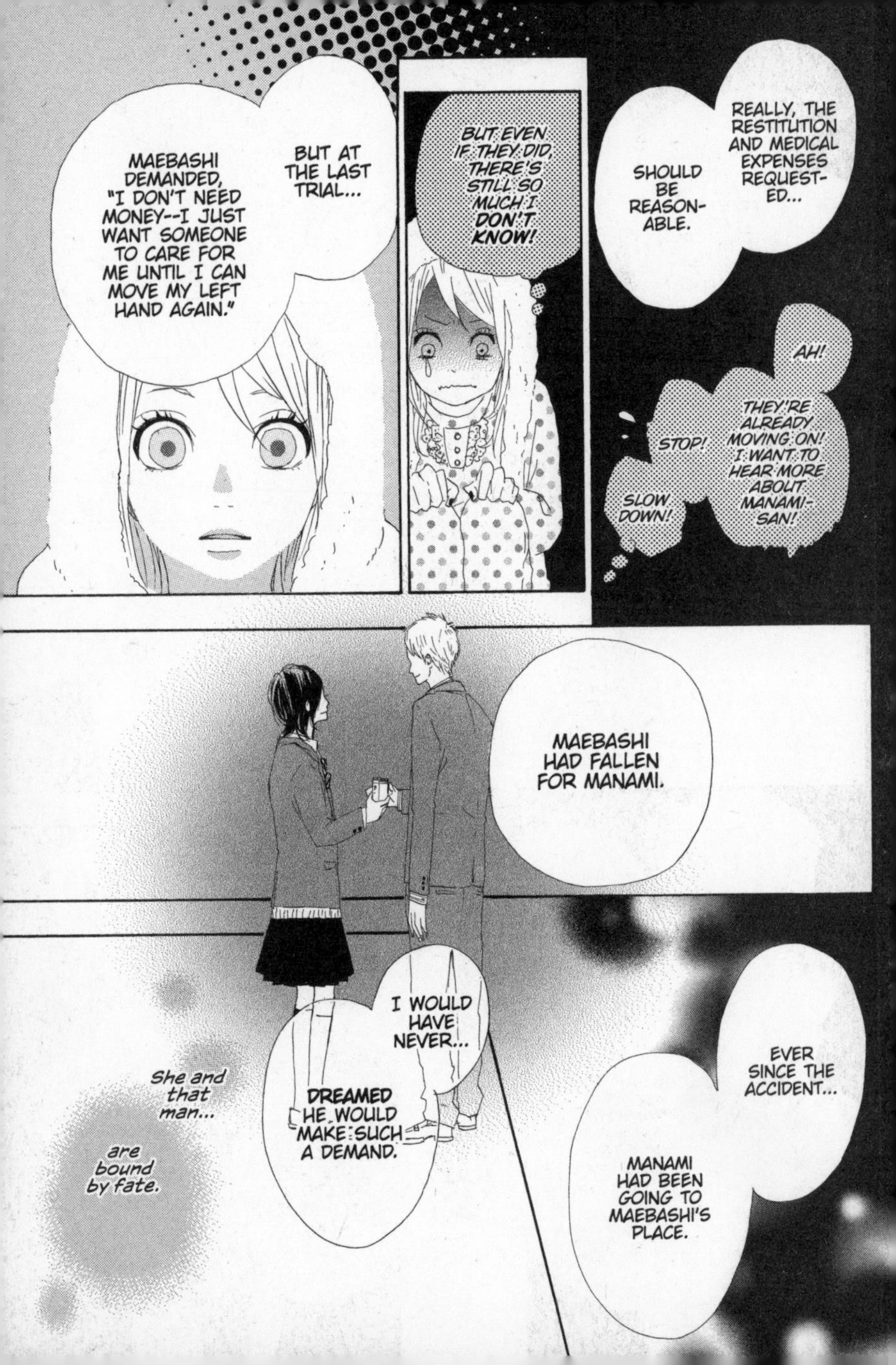
REALLY, THE RESTITUTION AND MEDICAL EXPENSES REQUESTED...
SHOULD BE REASONABLE.
AH!
THEY'RE ALREADY MOVING ON! I WANT TO HEAR MORE ABOUT MANAMI-SAN!
STOP!
SLOW DOWN!
BUT EVEN IF THEY DID, THERE'S STILL SO MUCH I DON'T KNOW!
BUT AT THE LAST TRIAL...
MAEBASHI DEMANDED, "I DON'T NEED MONEY--I JUST WANT SOMEONE TO CARE FOR ME UNTIL I CAN MOVE MY LEFT HAND AGAIN."
I WOULD HAVE NEVER...
DREAMED HE WOULD MAKE SUCH A DEMAND.
EVER SINCE THE ACCIDENT...
MANAMI HAD BEEN GOING TO MAEBASHI'S PLACE.
MAEBASHI HAD FALLEN FOR MANAMI.
She and that man...
are bound by fate.

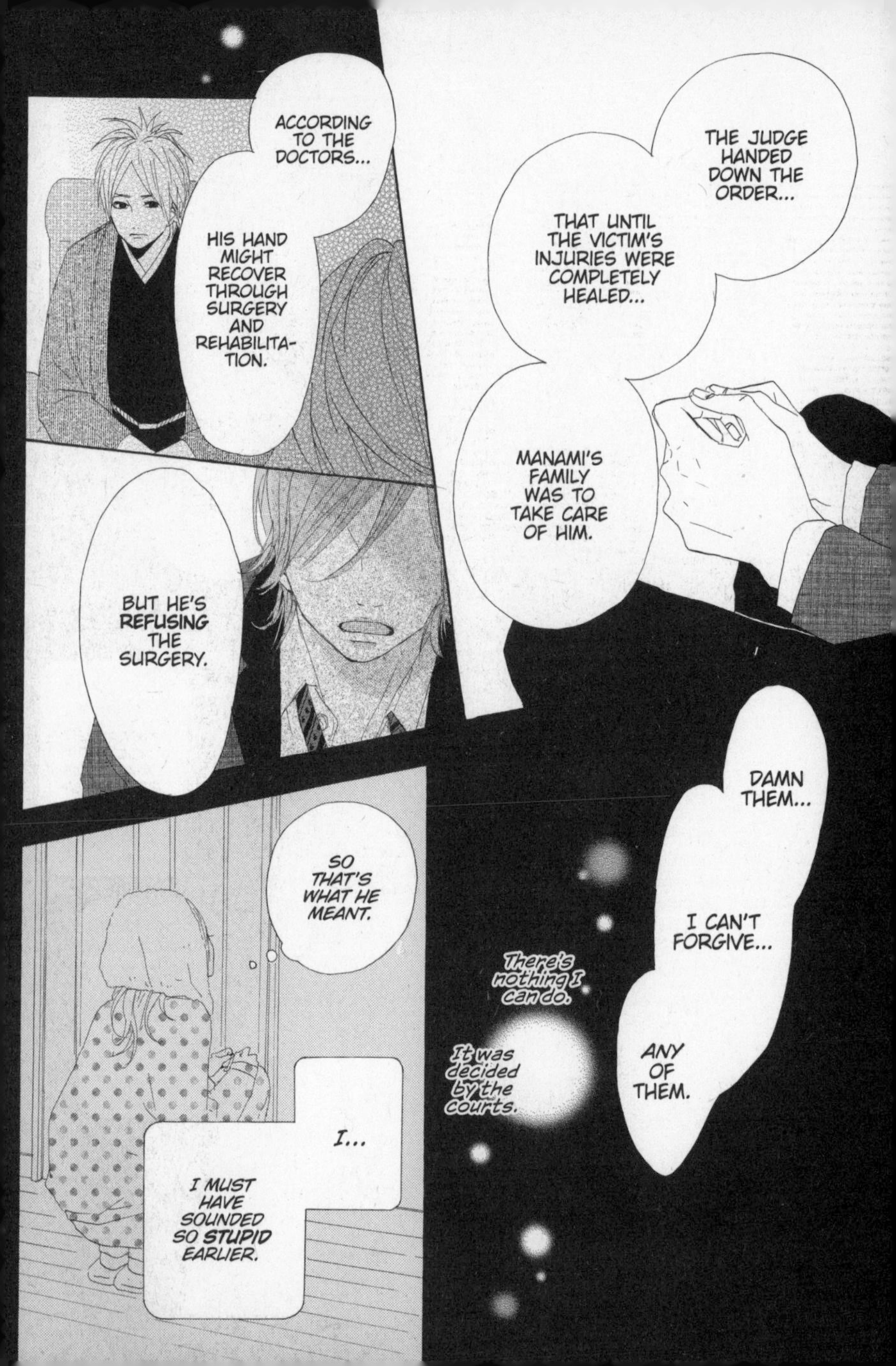
THE JUDGE HANDED DOWN THE ORDER...
THAT UNTIL THE VICTIM'S INJURIES WERE COMPLETELY HEALED...
MANAMI'S FAMILY WAS TO TAKE CARE OF HIM.
ACCORDING TO THE DOCTORS...
HIS HAND MIGHT RECOVER THROUGH SURGERY AND REHABILITATION.
BUT HE'S REFUSING THE SURGERY.
DAMN THEM...
I CAN'T FORGIVE...
ANY OF THEM.
There's nothing I can do.
It was decided by the courts.
SO THAT'S WHAT HE MEANT.
I...
I MUST HAVE SOUNDED SO STUPID EARLIER.

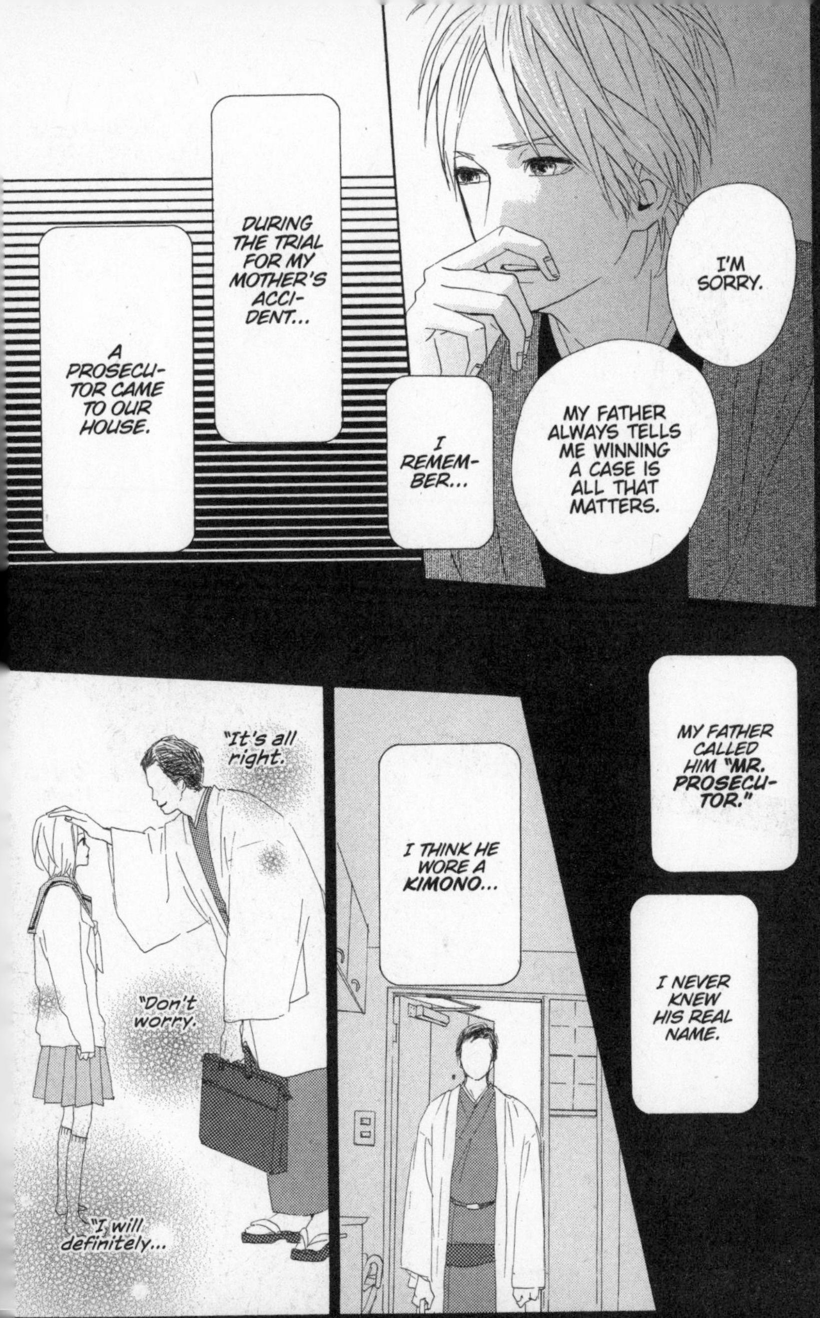
I'M SORRY.
MY FATHER ALWAYS TELLS ME WINNING A CASE IS ALL THAT MATTERS.
I REMEMBER...
DURING THE TRIAL FOR MY MOTHER'S ACCIDENT...
A PROSECUTOR CAME TO OUR HOUSE.
MY FATHER CALLED HIM "MR. PROSECUTOR."
I NEVER KNEW HIS REAL NAME.
I THINK HE WORE A KIMONO...
"It's all right.
"Don't worry.
"I will definitely...

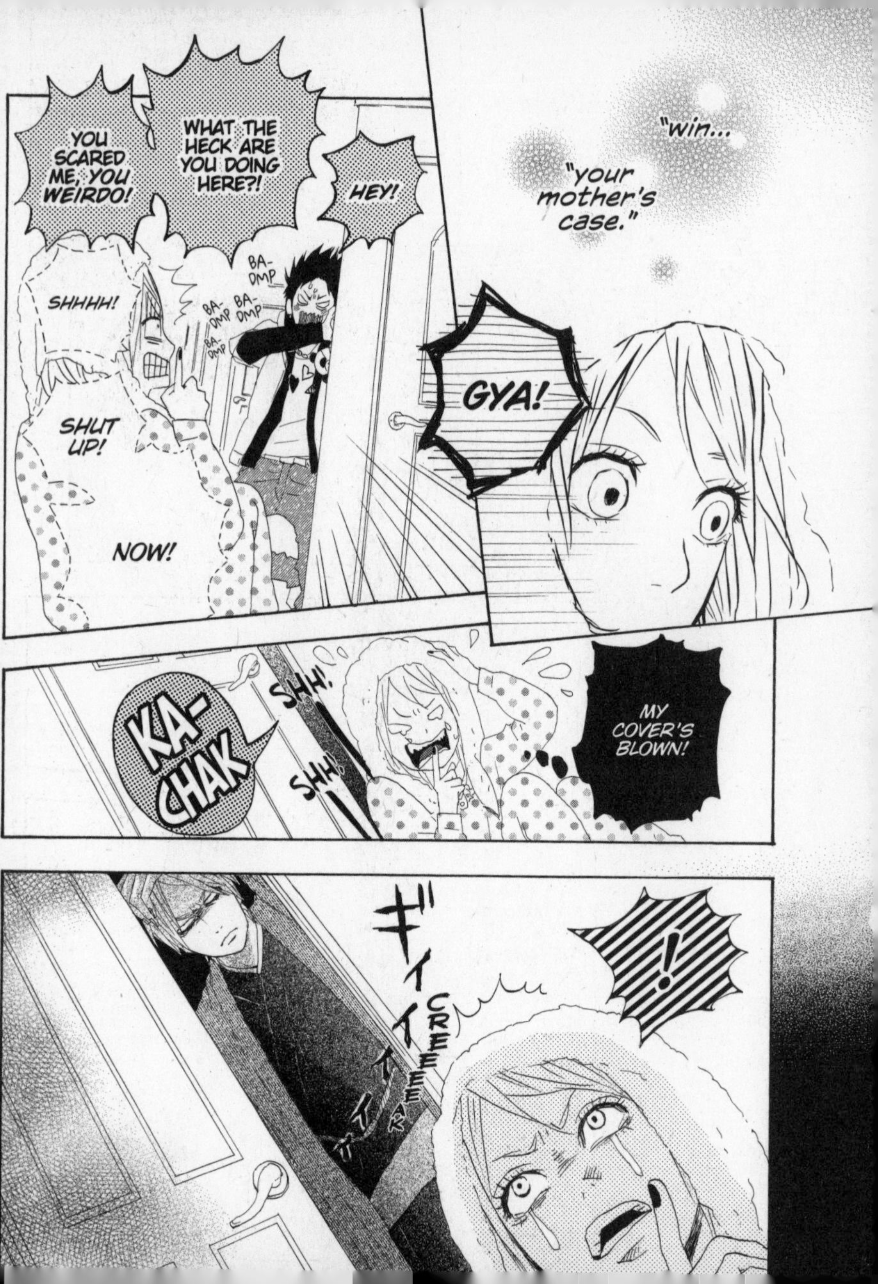
"win...
"your mother's case."
GYA!
HEY!
WHAT THE HECK ARE YOU DOING HERE?!
YOU SCARED ME, YOU WEIRDO!
BA-DMP
BA-DMP BA-DMP
BA-DMP
SHHHH!
SHUT UP!
NOW!
MY COVER'S BLOWN!
SHH!
SHH!
KA-CHAK
!
ギイイイイ
CREEEE

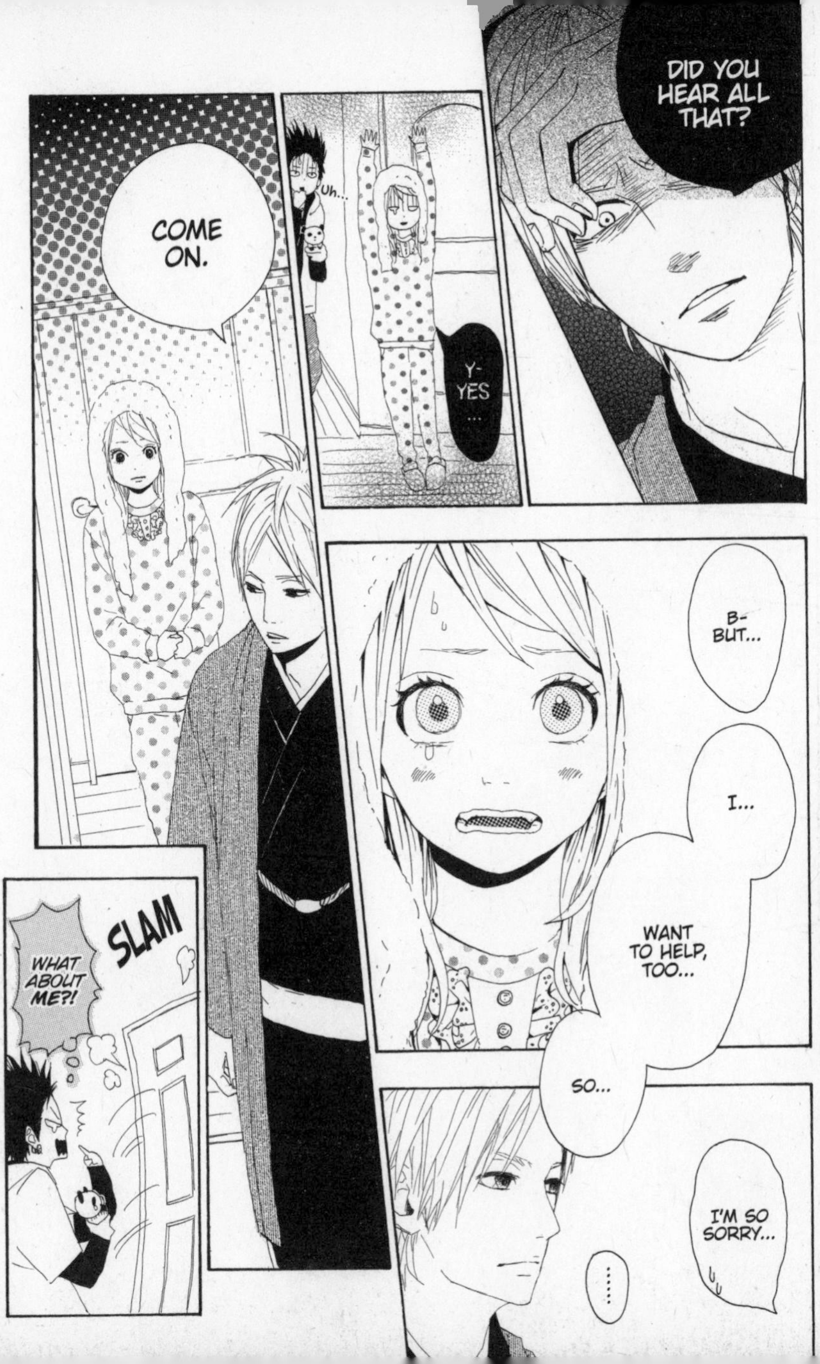
DID YOU HEAR ALL THAT?
Uh...
Y-YES...
COME ON.
SLAM
WHAT ABOUT ME?!
B-BUT...
I...
WANT TO HELP, TOO...
SO...
I'M SO SORRY...
......

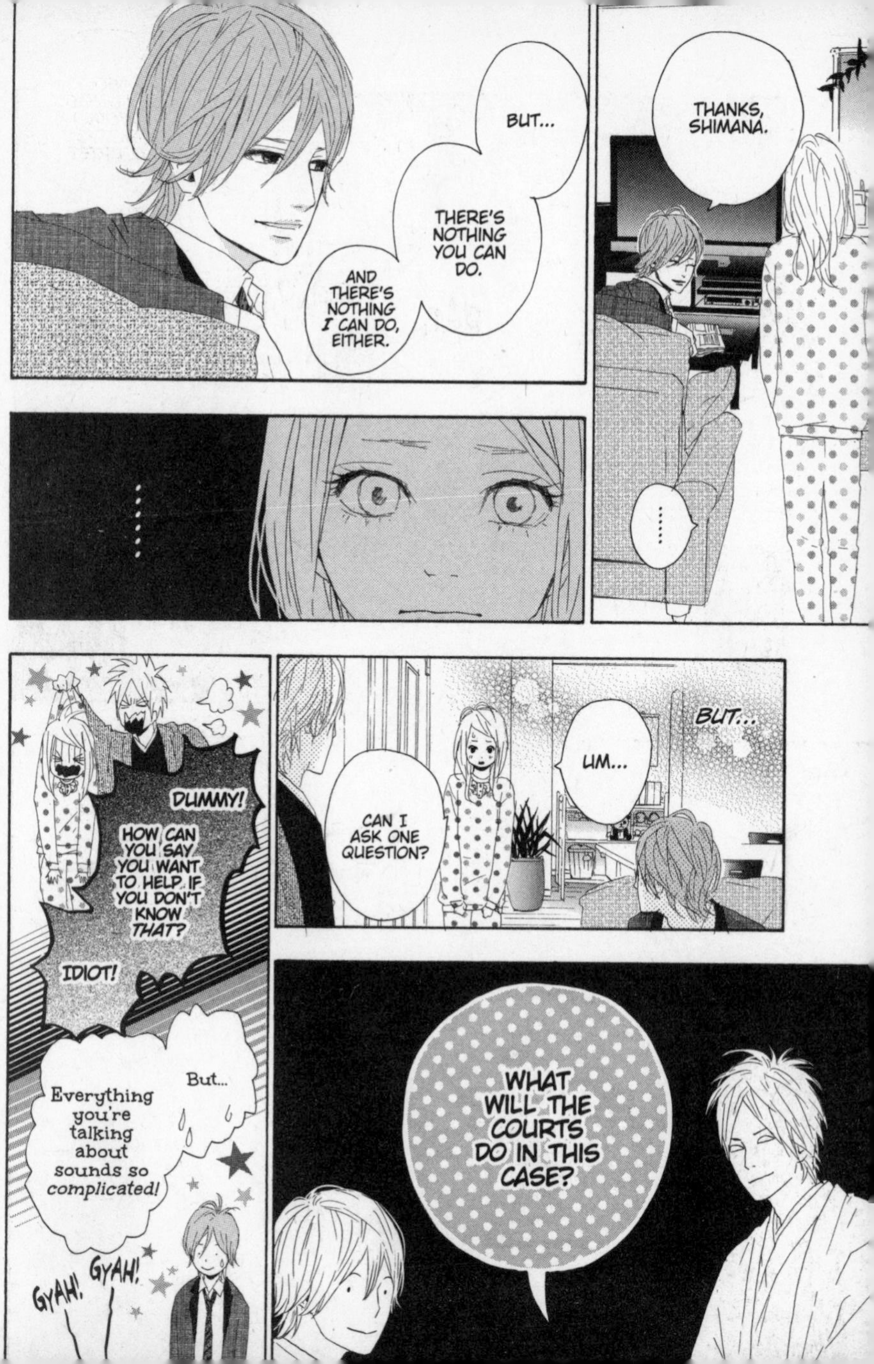
THANKS, SHIMANA.
......
BUT...
THERE'S NOTHING YOU CAN DO.
AND THERE'S NOTHING I CAN DO, EITHER.
......
BUT...
UM...
CAN I ASK ONE QUESTION?
WHAT WILL THE COURTS DO IN THIS CASE?
DUMMY!
HOW CAN YOU SAY YOU WANT TO HELP IF YOU DON'T KNOW THAT?
IDIOT!
But...
Everything you're talking about sounds so complicated!
GYAH! GYAH!

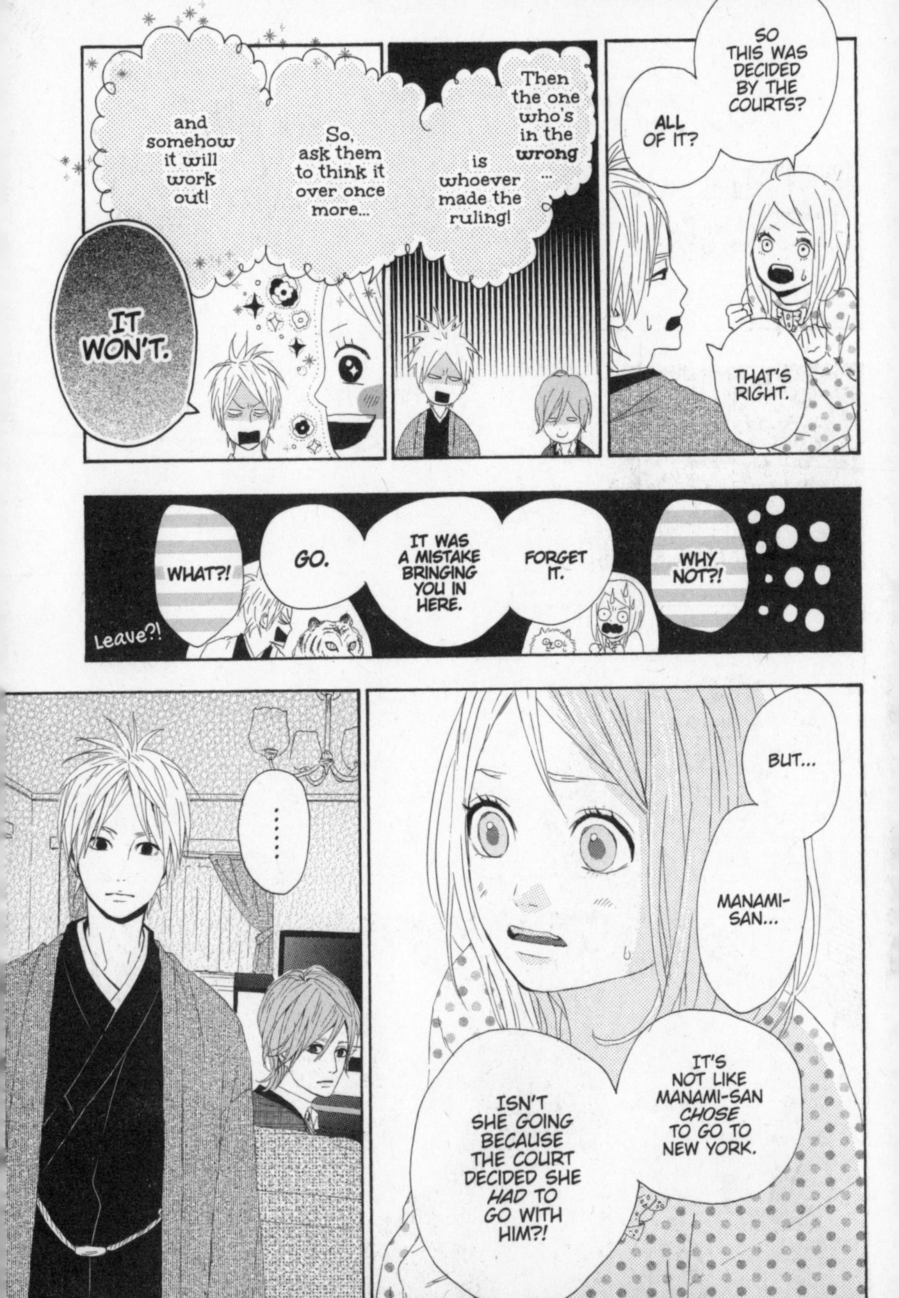
SO THIS WAS DECIDED BY THE COURTS?
ALL OF IT?
THAT'S RIGHT.
Then the one who's in the **wrong**...
is whoever made the ruling!
So, ask them to think it over once more...
and somehow it will work out!
IT WON'T.
WHY NOT?!
FORGET IT.
IT WAS A MISTAKE BRINGING YOU IN HERE.
GO.
WHAT?!
Leave?!
BUT...
MANAMI-SAN...
IT'S NOT LIKE MANAMI-SAN *CHOSE* TO GO TO NEW YORK.
ISN'T SHE GOING BECAUSE THE COURT DECIDED SHE *HAD* TO GO WITH HIM?!
......

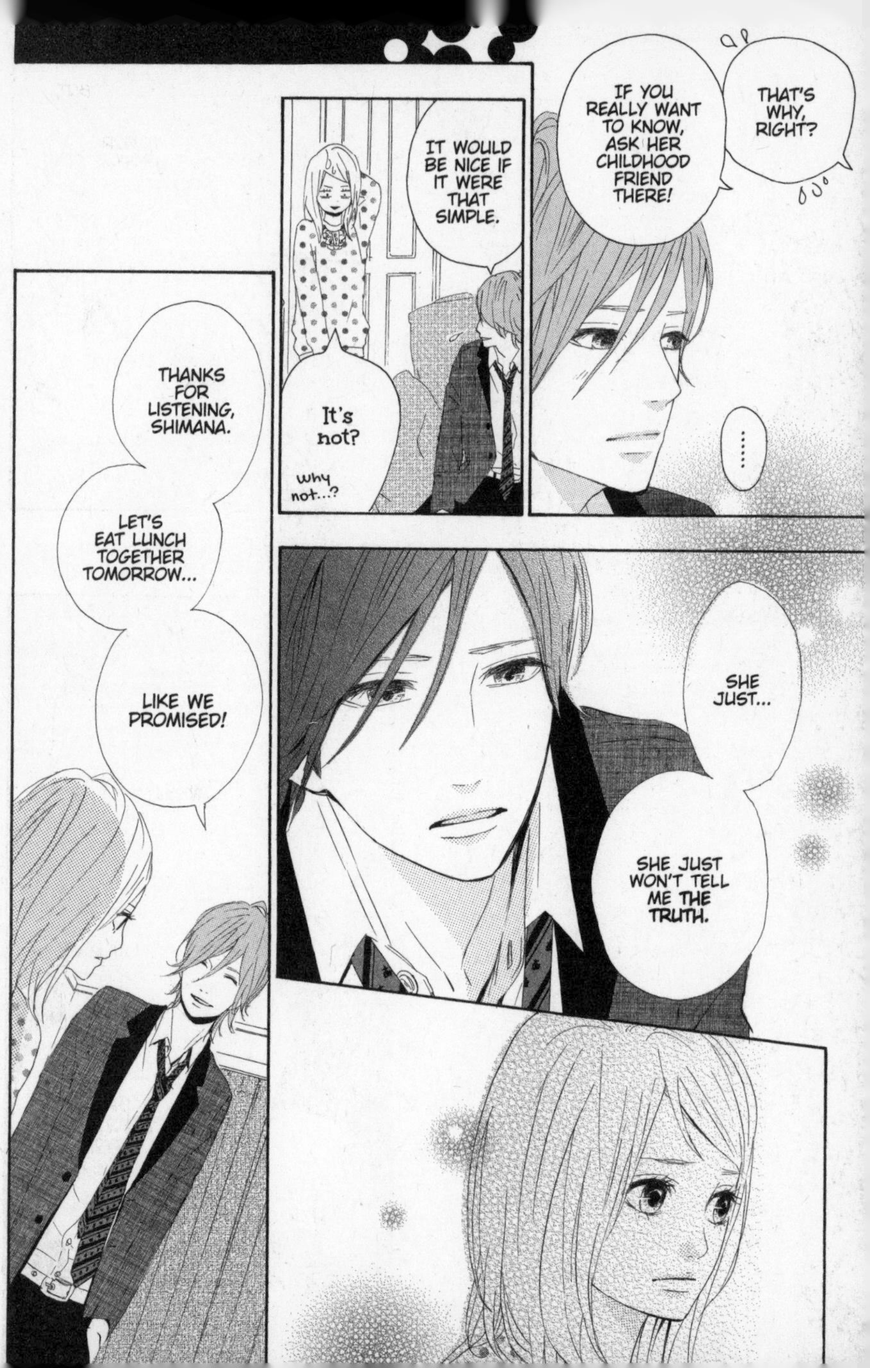
THAT'S WHY, RIGHT?
IF YOU REALLY WANT TO KNOW, ASK HER CHILDHOOD FRIEND THERE!
......
IT WOULD BE NICE IF IT WERE THAT SIMPLE.
It's not?
why not...?
SHE JUST...
SHE JUST WON'T TELL ME THE TRUTH.
THANKS FOR LISTENING, SHIMANA.
LET'S EAT LUNCH TOGETHER TOMORROW...
LIKE WE PROMISED!

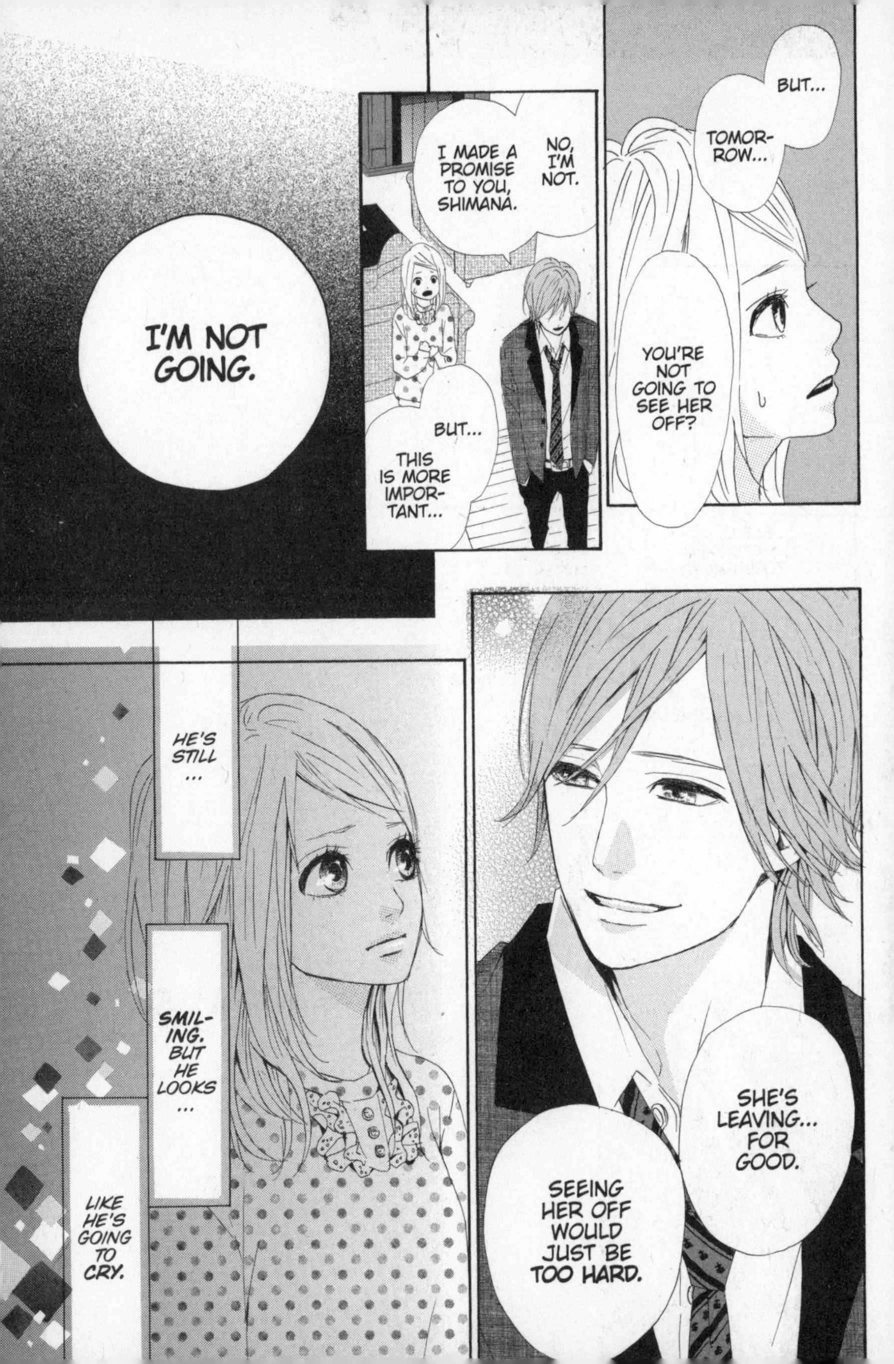
BUT... TOMORROW...
YOU'RE NOT GOING TO SEE HER OFF?
NO, I'M NOT.
I MADE A PROMISE TO YOU, SHIMANA.
BUT... THIS IS MORE IMPORTANT...
I'M NOT GOING.
SHE'S LEAVING... FOR GOOD.
SEEING HER OFF WOULD JUST BE TOO HARD.
HE'S STILL ...
SMILING. BUT HE LOOKS ...
LIKE HE'S GOING TO CRY.

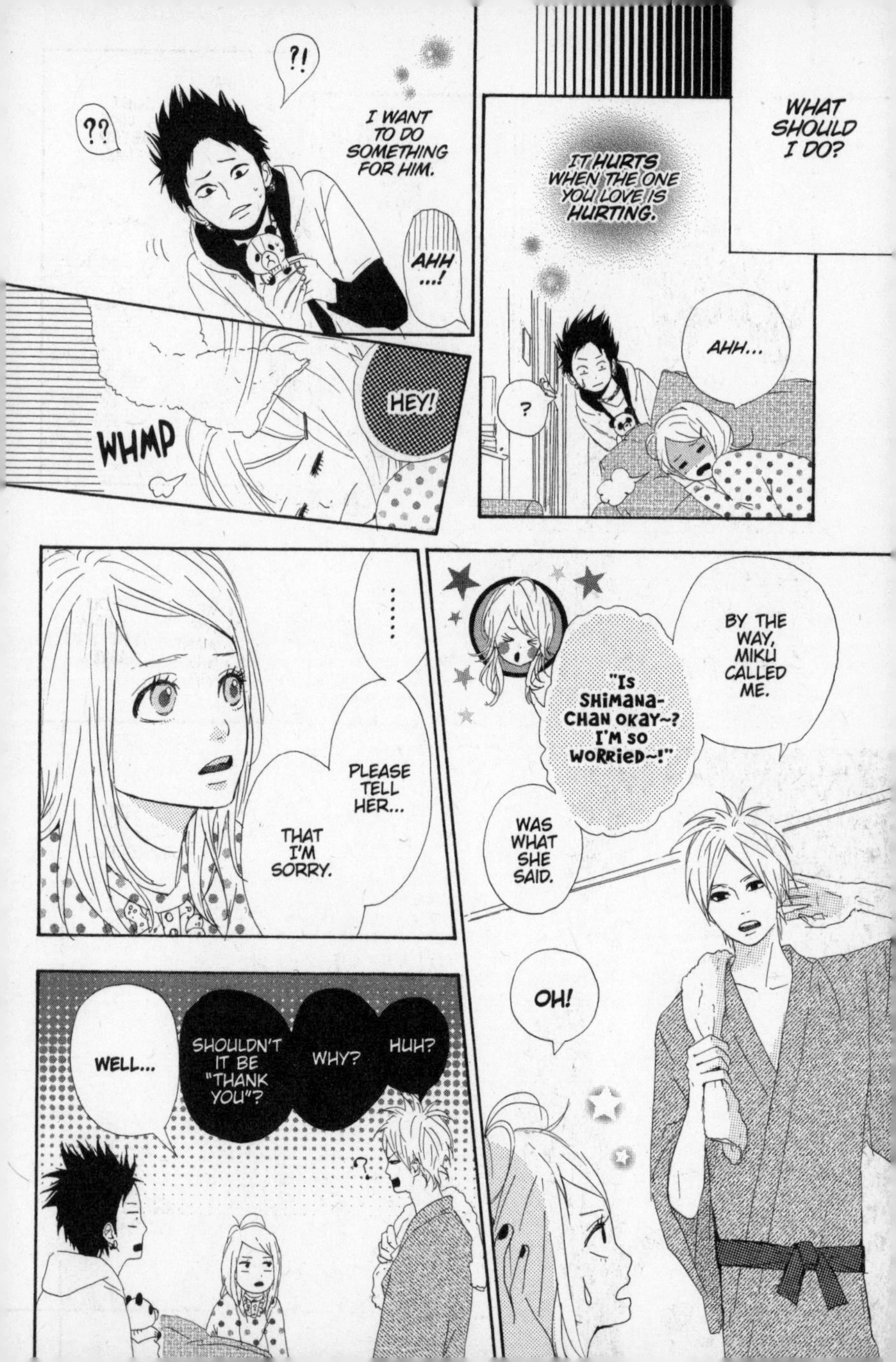
WHAT SHOULD I DO?
IT HURTS WHEN THE ONE YOU LOVE IS HURTING.
AHH...
?
I WANT TO DO SOMETHING FOR HIM.
?!
??
AHH ...!
HEY!
WHMP
BY THE WAY, MIKU CALLED ME.
"IS SHIMANA-CHAN OKAY~? I'M SO WORRIED~!"
WAS WHAT SHE SAID.
OH!
......
PLEASE TELL HER...
THAT I'M SORRY.
HUH?
WHY?
SHOULDN'T IT BE "THANK YOU"?
WELL...

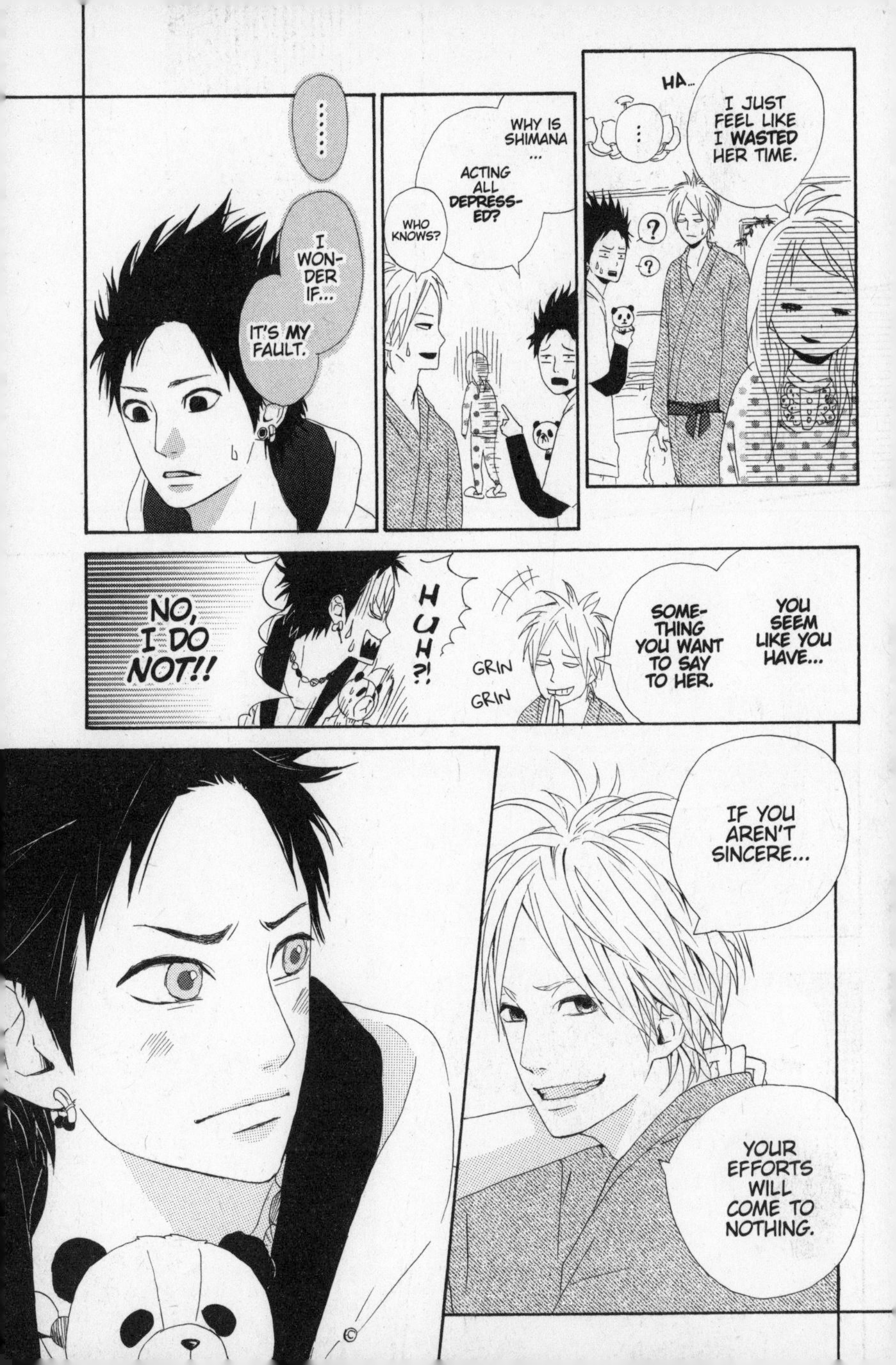
HA...
I JUST FEEL LIKE I WASTED HER TIME.
...
?
?
WHY IS SHIMANA ... ACTING ALL DEPRESSED?
WHO KNOWS?
......
I WONDER IF...
IT'S MY FAULT.
YOU SEEM LIKE YOU HAVE...
SOMETHING YOU WANT TO SAY TO HER.
GRIN GRIN
HUH?!
NO, I DO NOT!!
IF YOU AREN'T SINCERE...
YOUR EFFORTS WILL COME TO NOTHING.

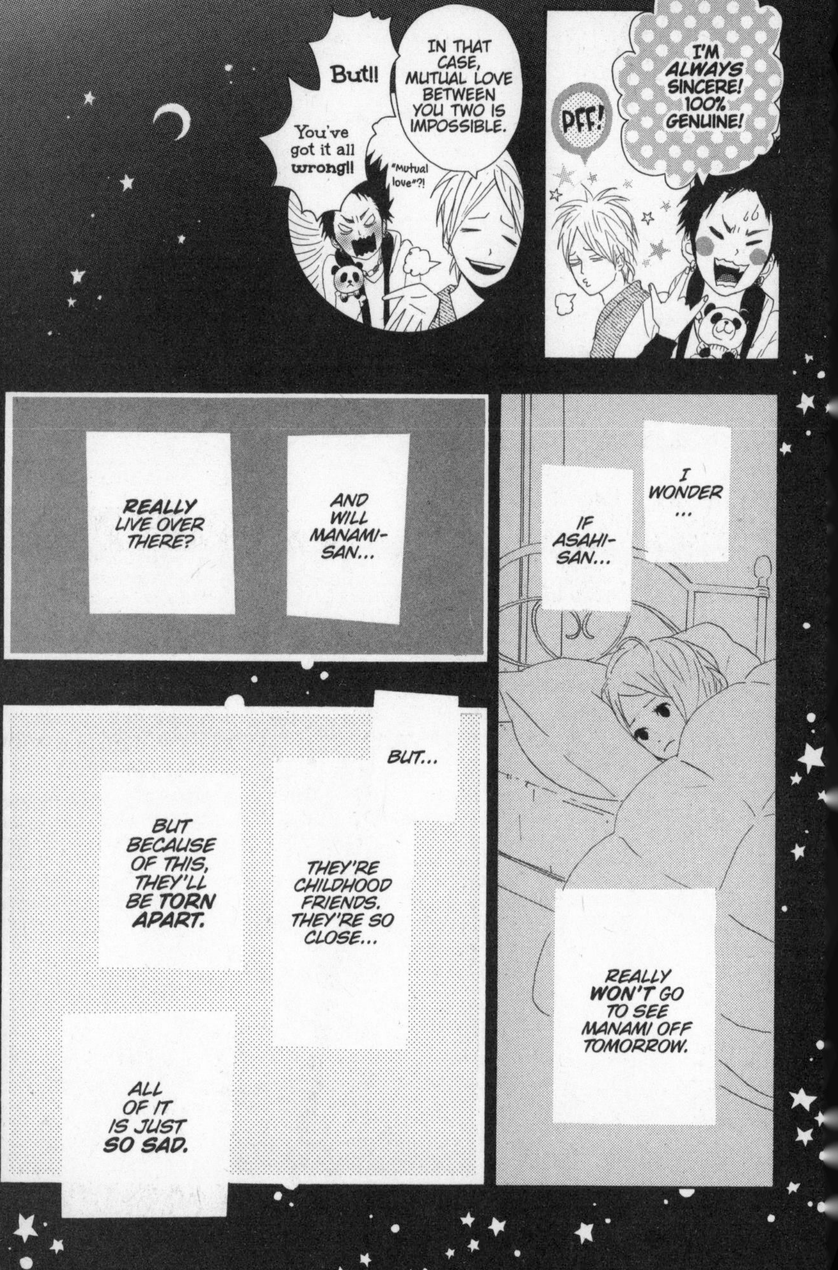
I'M ALWAYS SINCERE! 100% GENUINE!
PFF!
IN THAT CASE, MUTUAL LOVE BETWEEN YOU TWO IS IMPOSSIBLE.
But!!
You've got it all wrong!!
"Mutual love"?!
I WONDER...
IF ASAHI-SAN...
REALLY WON'T GO TO SEE MANAMI OFF TOMORROW.
AND WILL MANAMI-SAN...
REALLY LIVE OVER THERE?
BUT...
THEY'RE CHILDHOOD FRIENDS. THEY'RE SO CLOSE...
BUT BECAUSE OF THIS, THEY'LL BE TORN APART.
ALL OF IT IS JUST SO SAD.

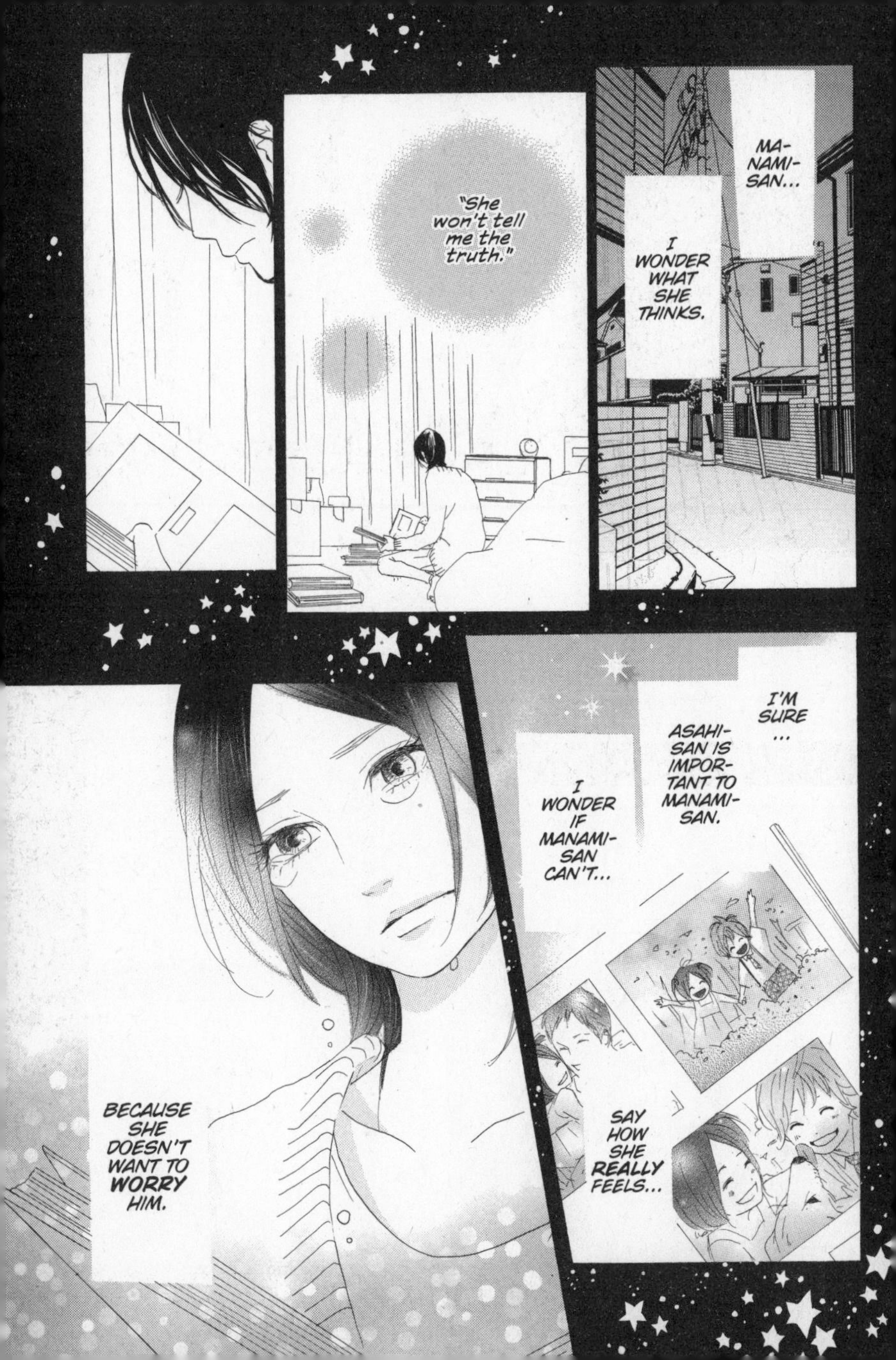
MA-NAMI-SAN...
I WONDER WHAT SHE THINKS.
"She won't tell me the truth."
I'M SURE ...
ASAHI-SAN IS IMPORTANT TO MANAMI-SAN.
I WONDER IF MANAMI-SAN CAN'T...
SAY HOW SHE REALLY FEELS...
BECAUSE SHE DOESN'T WANT TO WORRY HIM.

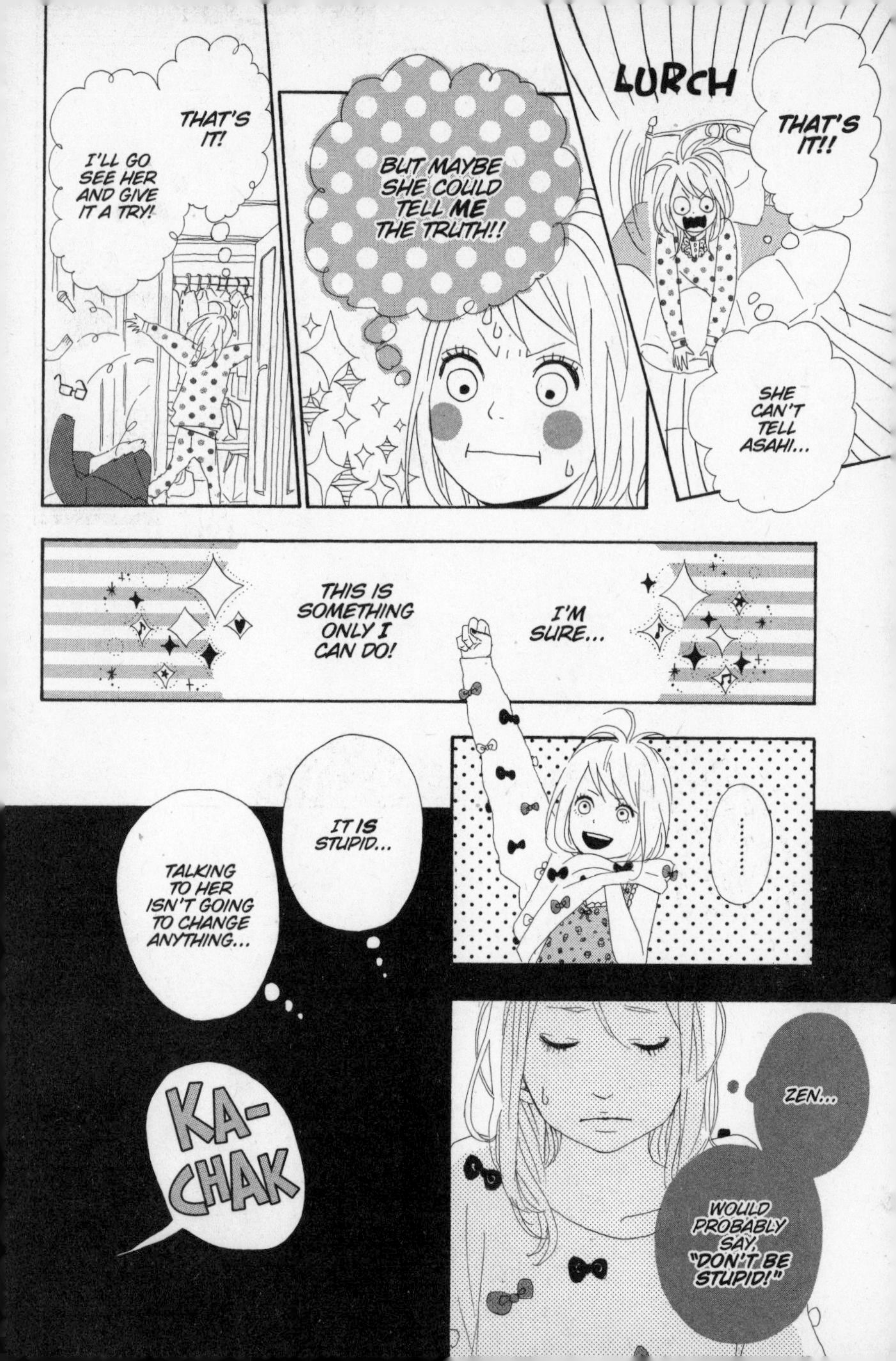
LURCH
THAT'S IT!!
SHE CAN'T TELL ASAHI...
BUT MAYBE SHE COULD TELL ME THE TRUTH!!
THAT'S IT!
I'LL GO SEE HER AND GIVE IT A TRY!
I'M SURE...
THIS IS SOMETHING ONLY I CAN DO!
......
ZEN...
WOULD PROBABLY SAY, "DON'T BE STUPID!"
IT IS STUPID...
TALKING TO HER ISN'T GOING TO CHANGE ANYTHING...
KA-CHAK

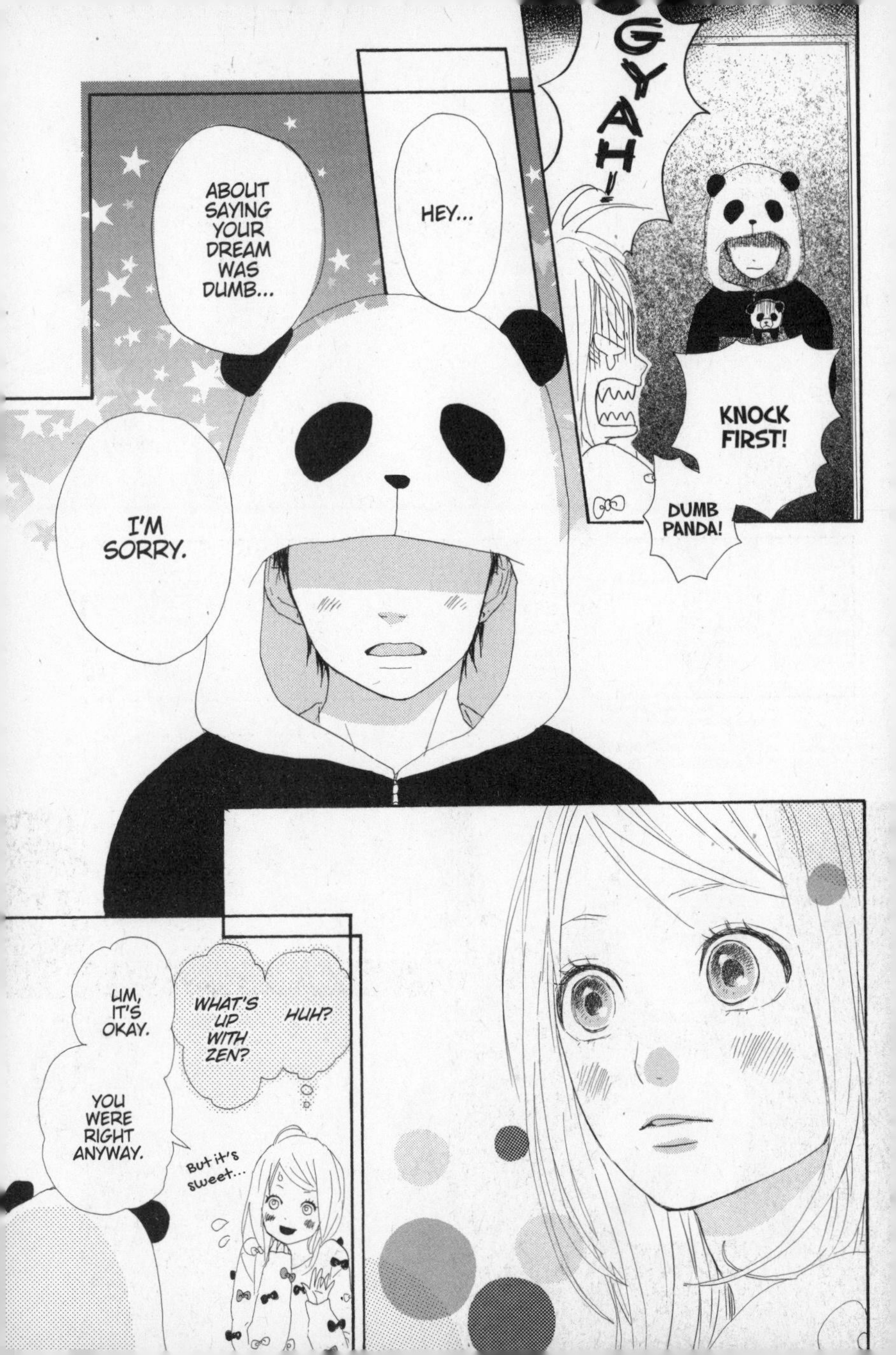
GYAH!!
KNOCK FIRST!
DUMB PANDA!
HEY...
ABOUT SAYING YOUR DREAM WAS DUMB...
I'M SORRY.
HUH?
WHAT'S UP WITH ZEN?
UM, IT'S OKAY.
YOU WERE RIGHT ANYWAY.
But it's sweet...

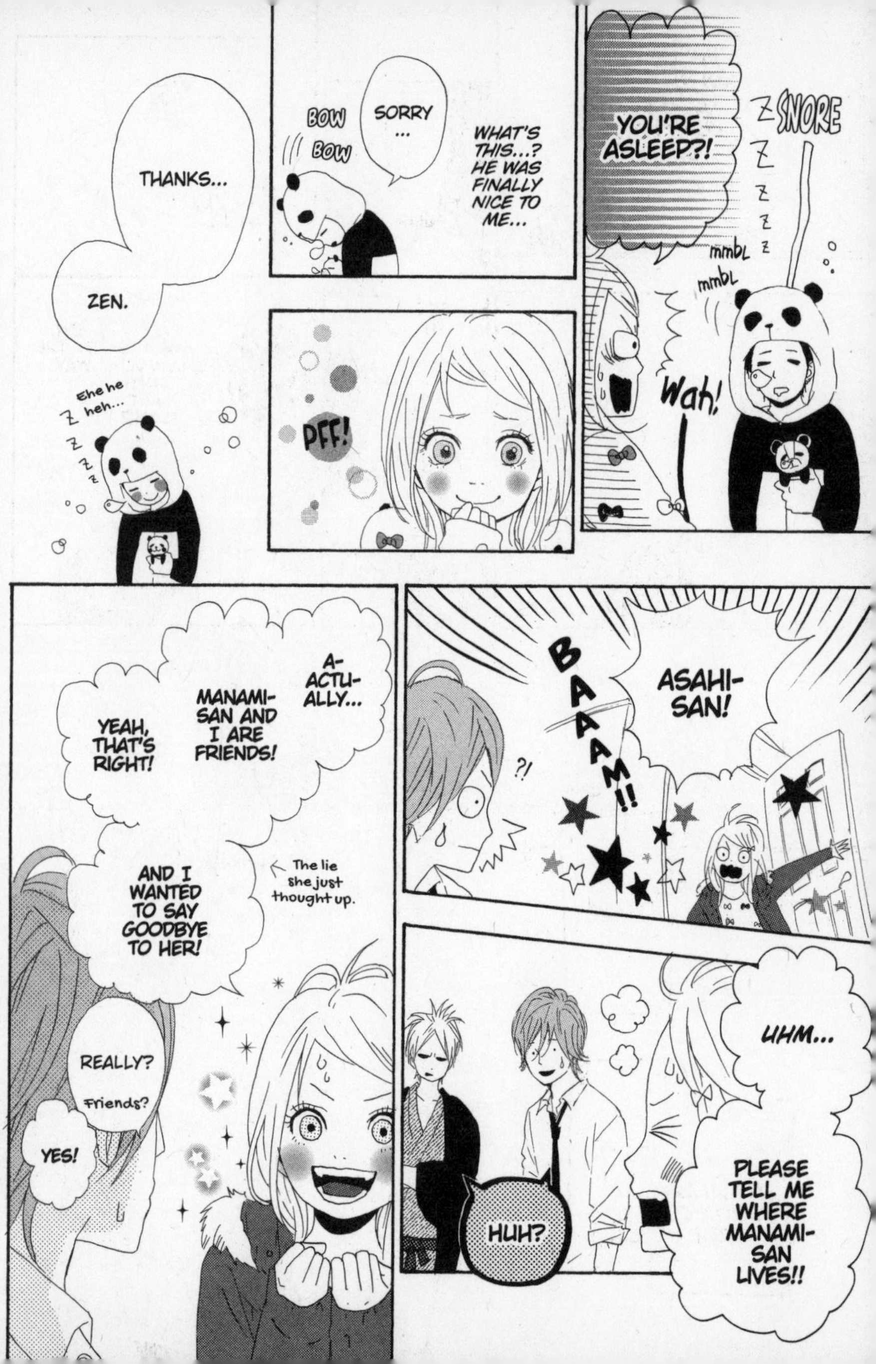
YOU'RE ASLEEP?!
SNORE
Z Z Z Z Z
mmbL
mmbL
Wah!
SORRY ...
BOW
BOW
WHAT'S THIS...? HE WAS FINALLY NICE TO ME...
PFF!
THANKS... ZEN.
Ehe he heh...
BAAAM!!
ASAHI-SAN!
?!
UHM...
PLEASE TELL ME WHERE MANAMI-SAN LIVES!!
HUH?
A-ACTUALLY...
MANAMI-SAN AND I ARE FRIENDS!
YEAH, THAT'S RIGHT!
AND I WANTED TO SAY GOODBYE TO HER!
The lie she just thought up.
REALLY?
Friends?
YES!

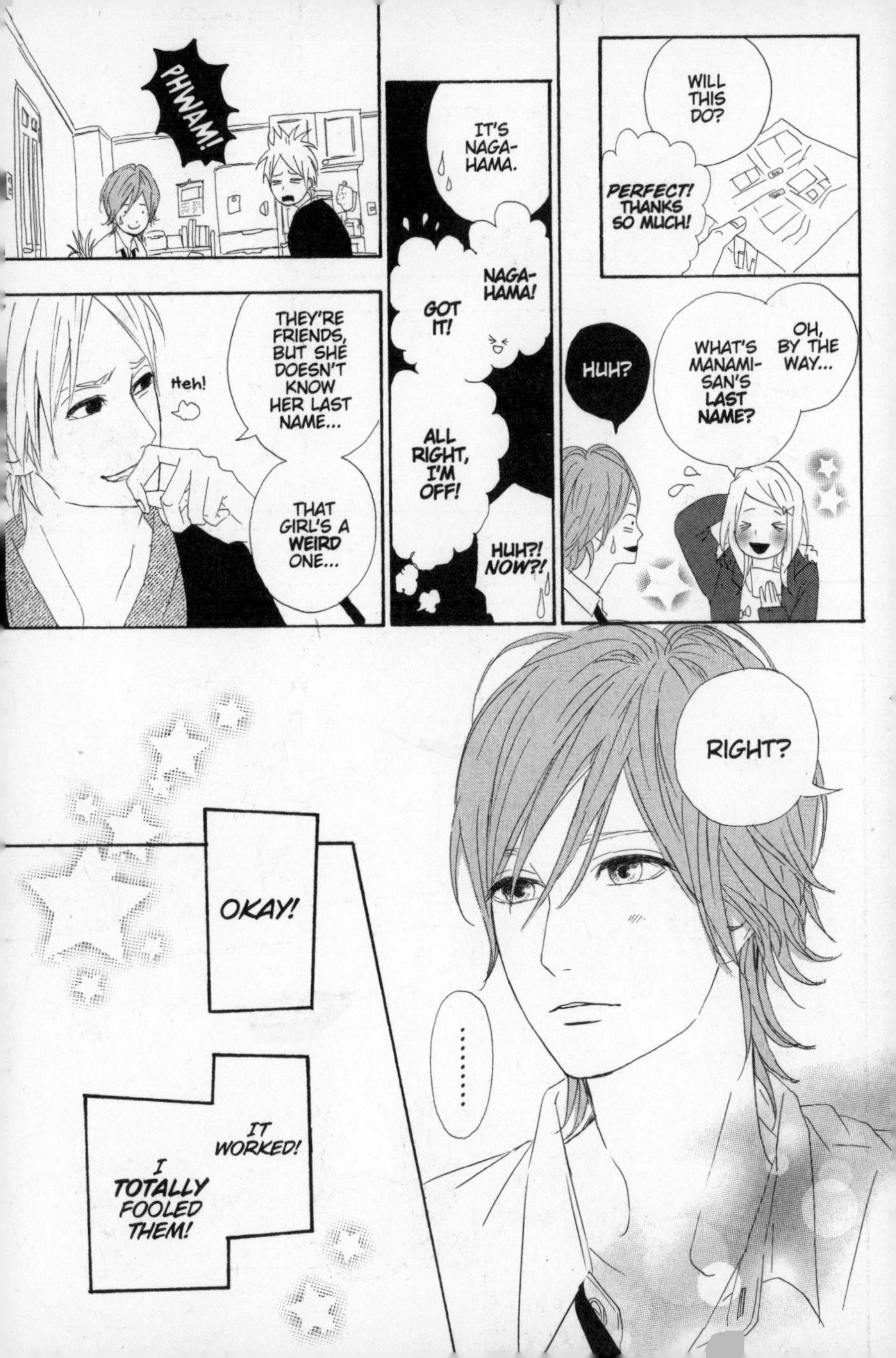
WILL THIS DO?
PERFECT! THANKS SO MUCH!
OH, BY THE WAY...
WHAT'S MANAMI-SAN'S LAST NAME?
HUH?
IT'S NAGA-HAMA.
NAGA-HAMA!
GOT IT!
ALL RIGHT, I'M OFF!
HUH?! NOW?!
PHWAM!
THEY'RE FRIENDS, BUT SHE DOESN'T KNOW HER LAST NAME...
Heh!
THAT GIRL'S A WEIRD ONE...
RIGHT?
......
OKAY!
IT WORKED!
I TOTALLY FOOLED THEM!

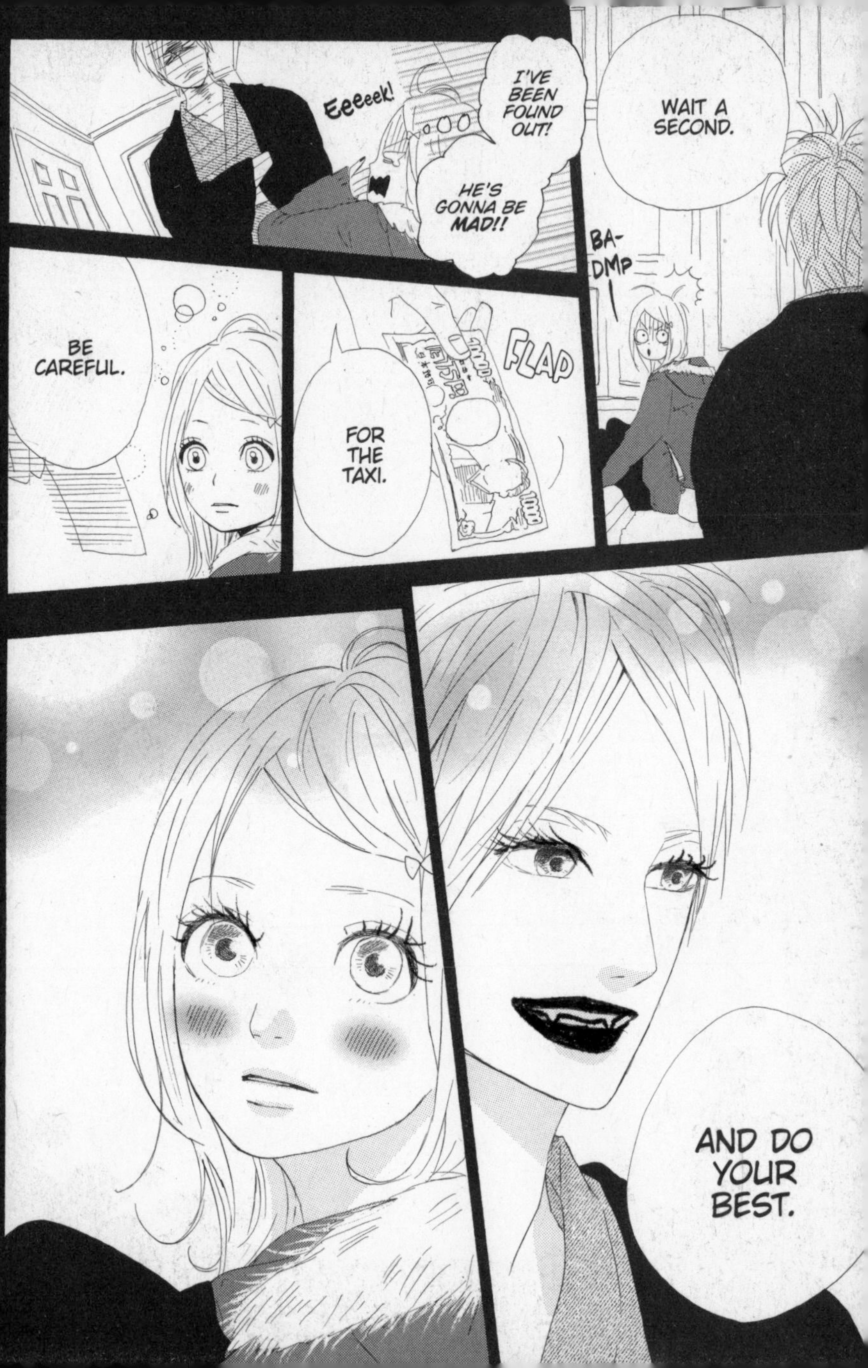
WAIT A SECOND.
BA-DMP
I'VE BEEN FOUND OUT!
Eeeeek!
HE'S GONNA BE MAD!!
FLAP
FOR THE TAXI.
BE CAREFUL.
AND DO YOUR BEST.

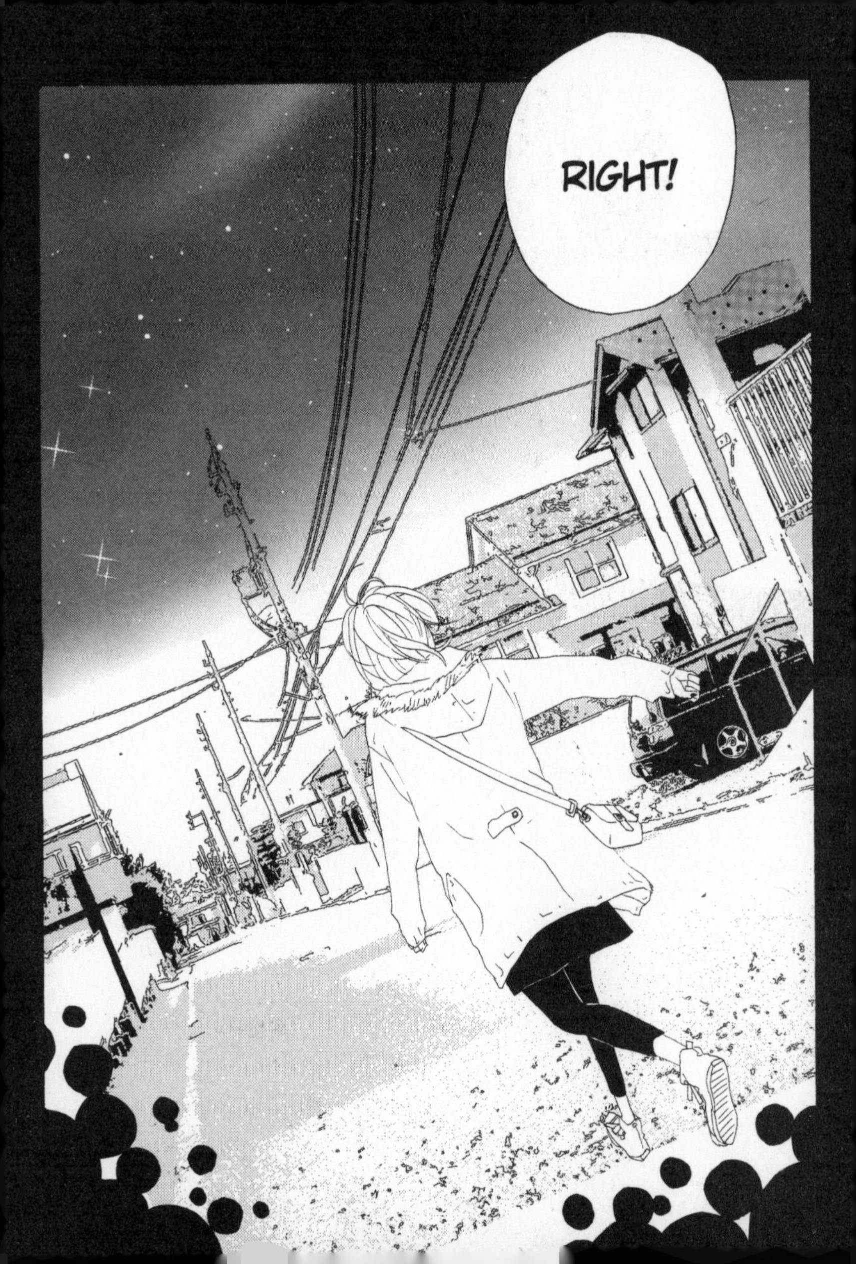
RIGHT!

Meaningless Doodle

Ah!

I should get a refill.

EXCUSE me, waiter!

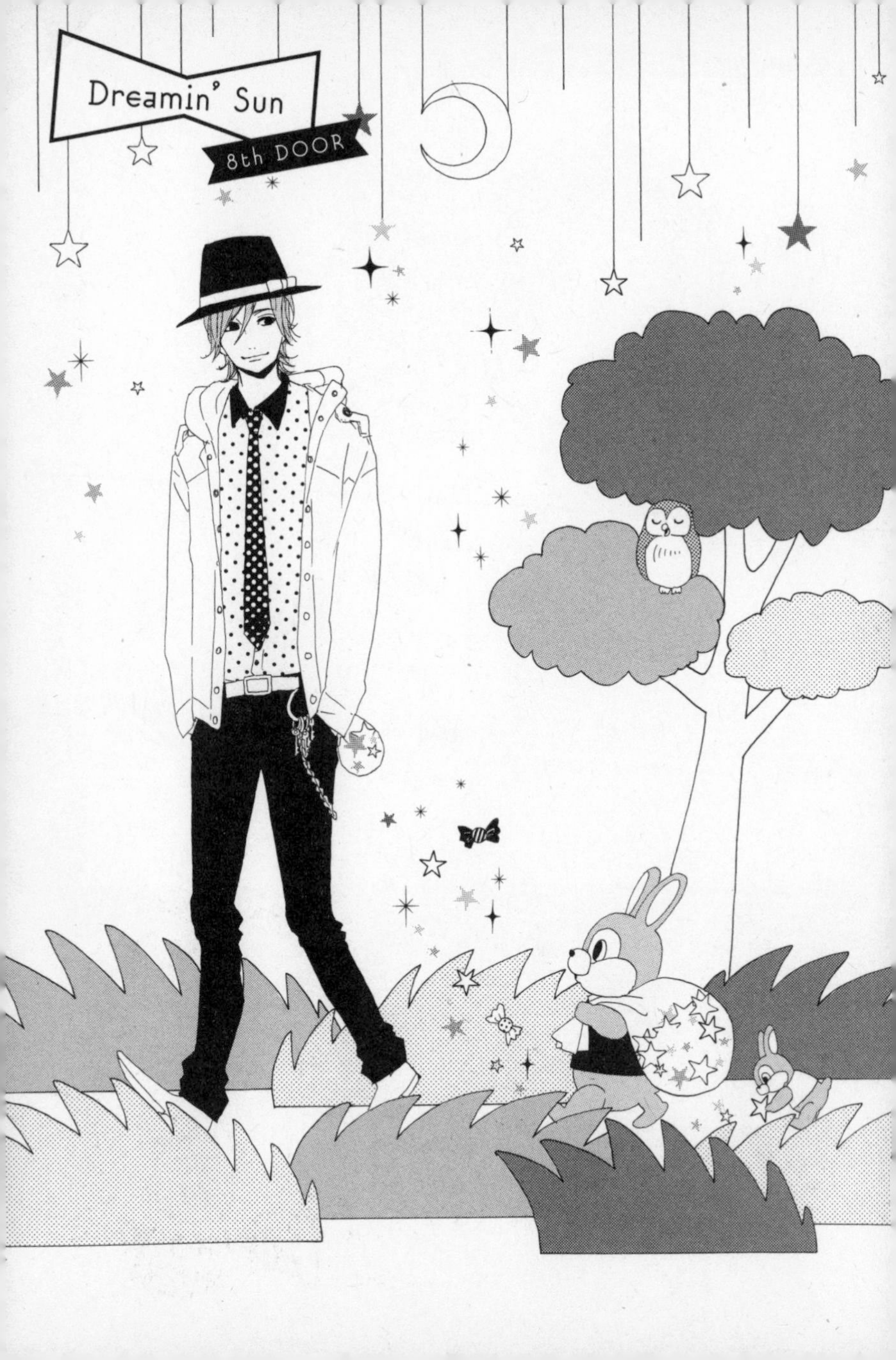
Dreamin' Sun
8th DOOR

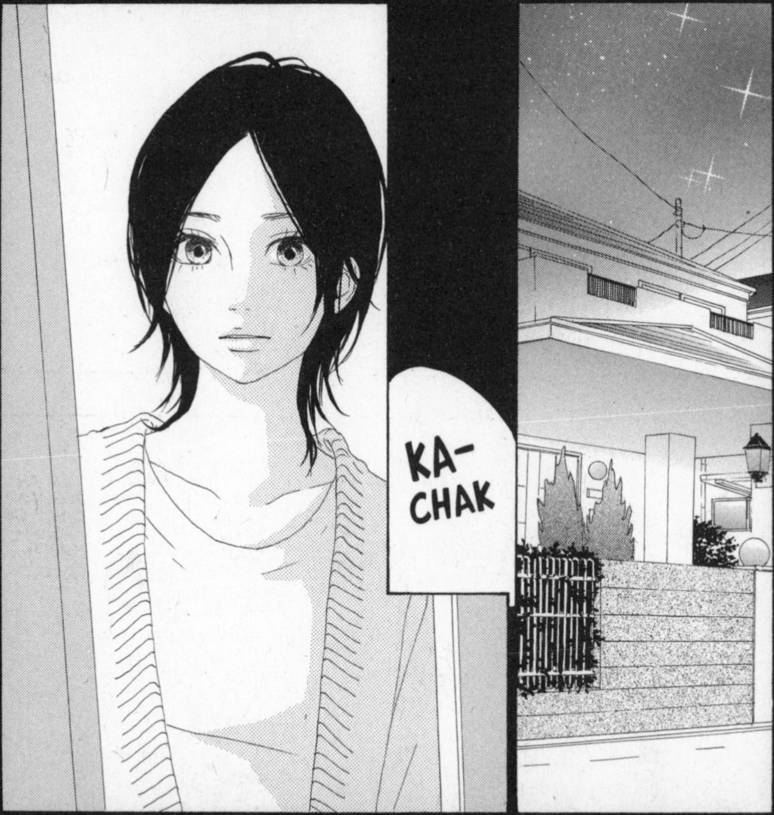
KA-
CHAK

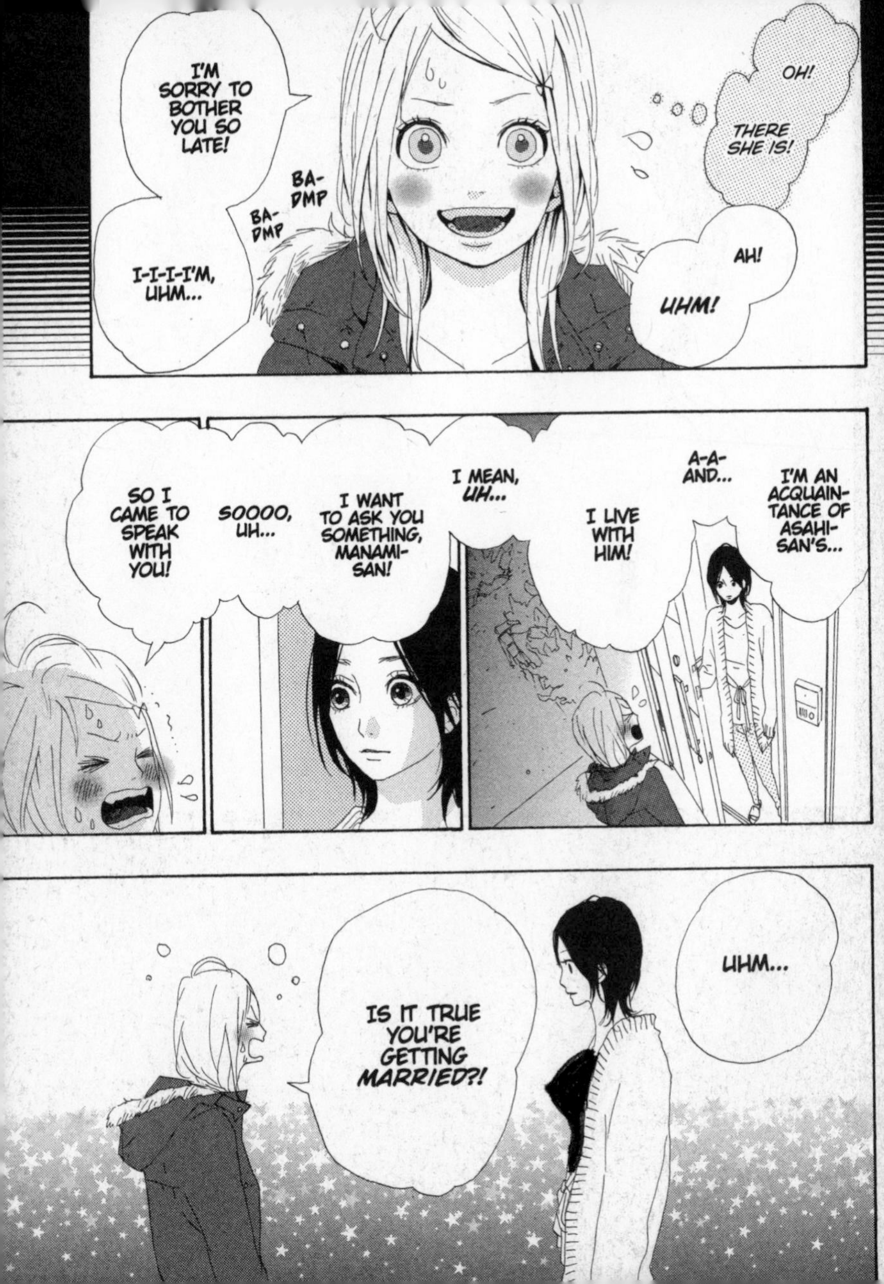
OH! THERE SHE IS!
AH! UHM!
I'M SORRY TO BOTHER YOU SO LATE!
BA-DMP
BA-DMP
I-I-I-I'M, UHM...
I'M AN ACQUAINTANCE OF ASAHI-SAN'S...
A-A-AND...
I LIVE WITH HIM!
I MEAN, UH...
I WANT TO ASK YOU SOMETHING, MANAMI-SAN!
SOOOO, UH...
SO I CAME TO SPEAK WITH YOU!
UHM...
IS IT TRUE YOU'RE GETTING MARRIED?!

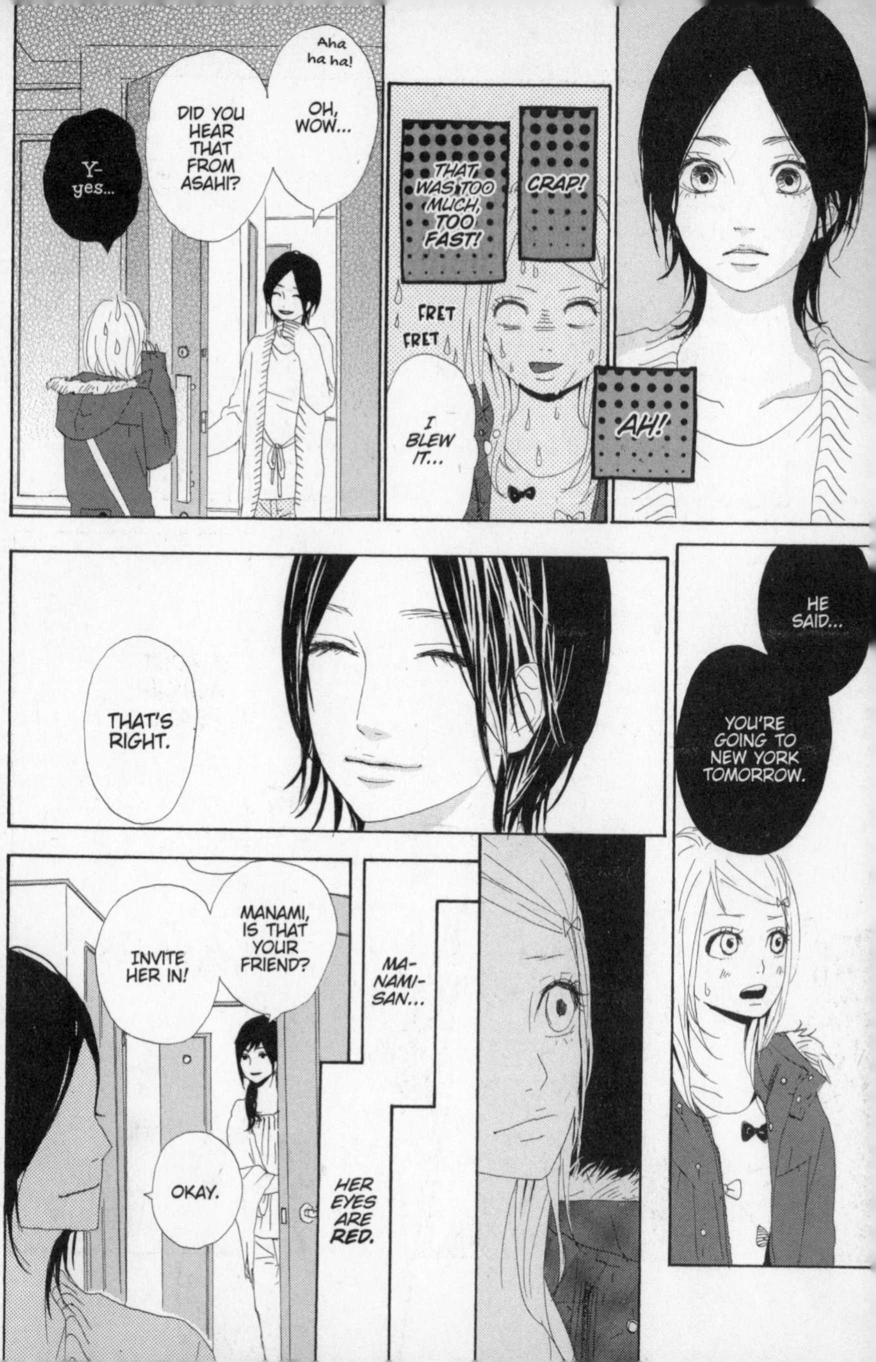
AH!
CRAP!
THAT WAS TOO MUCH, TOO FAST!
FRET FRET
I BLEW IT...
Aha ha ha!
OH, WOW...
DID YOU HEAR THAT FROM ASAHI?
Y- yes...
HE SAID...
YOU'RE GOING TO NEW YORK TOMORROW.
THAT'S RIGHT.
MA- NAMI- SAN...
HER EYES ARE RED.
MANAMI, IS THAT YOUR FRIEND?
INVITE HER IN!
OKAY.

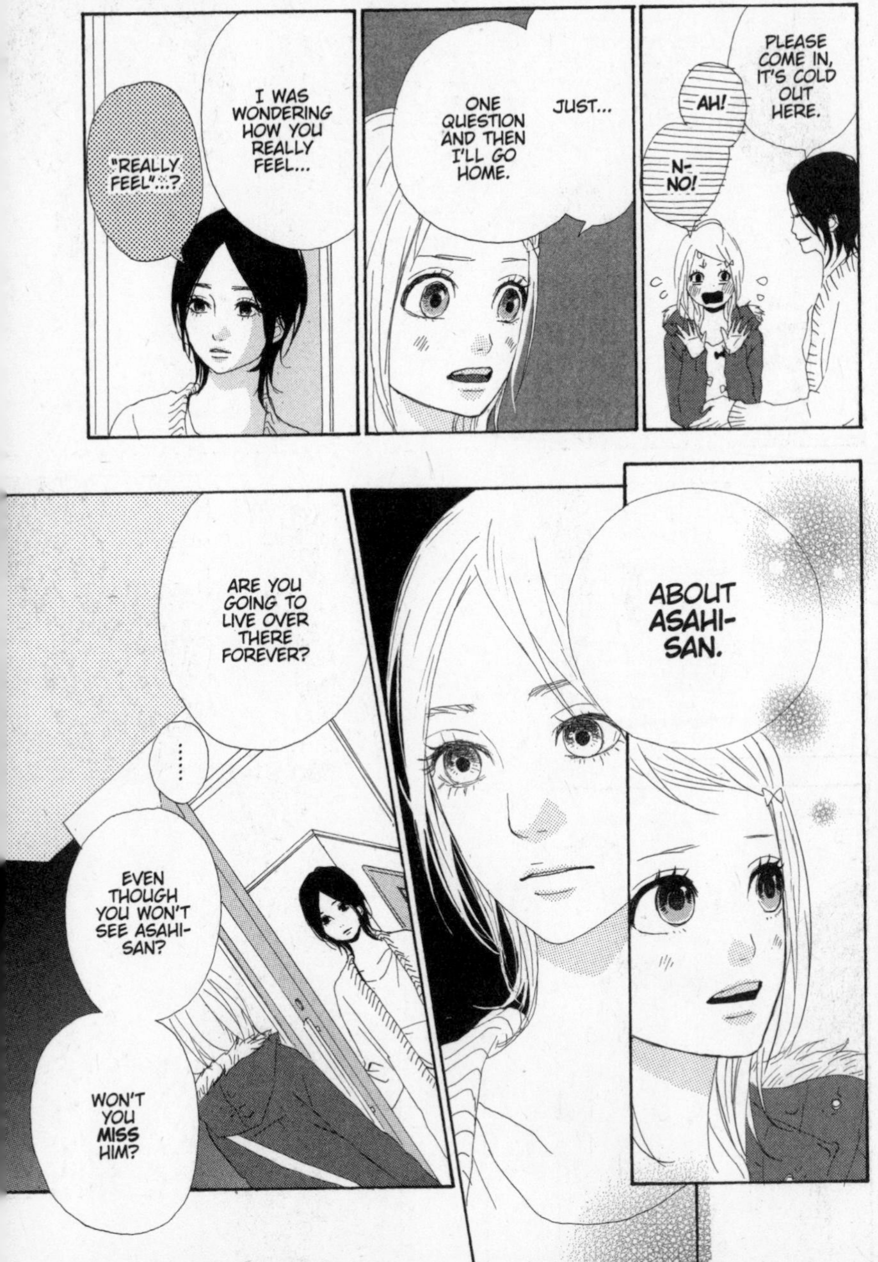
PLEASE COME IN, IT'S COLD OUT HERE.
AH!
N-NO!
JUST...
ONE QUESTION AND THEN I'LL GO HOME.
I WAS WONDERING HOW YOU REALLY FEEL...
"REALLY FEEL"...?
ABOUT ASAHI-SAN.
ARE YOU GOING TO LIVE OVER THERE FOREVER?
......
EVEN THOUGH YOU WON'T SEE ASAHI-SAN?
WON'T YOU MISS HIM?

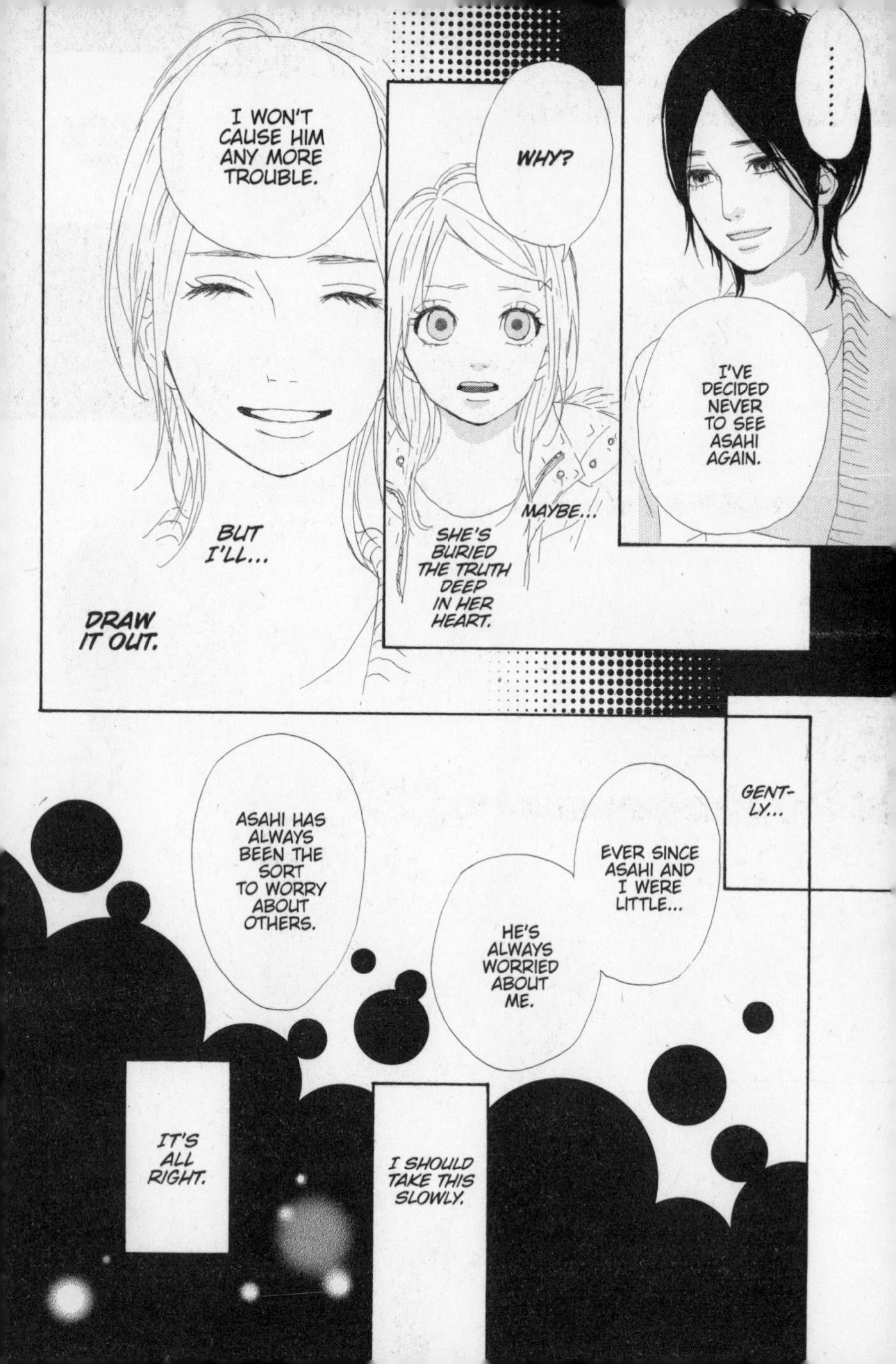
......
I'VE DECIDED NEVER TO SEE ASAHI AGAIN.
WHY?
MAYBE...
SHE'S BURIED THE TRUTH DEEP IN HER HEART.
I WON'T CAUSE HIM ANY MORE TROUBLE.
BUT I'LL...
DRAW IT OUT.
GENT-LY...
EVER SINCE ASAHI AND I WERE LITTLE...
HE'S ALWAYS WORRIED ABOUT ME.
ASAHI HAS ALWAYS BEEN THE SORT TO WORRY ABOUT OTHERS.
I SHOULD TAKE THIS SLOWLY.
IT'S ALL RIGHT.

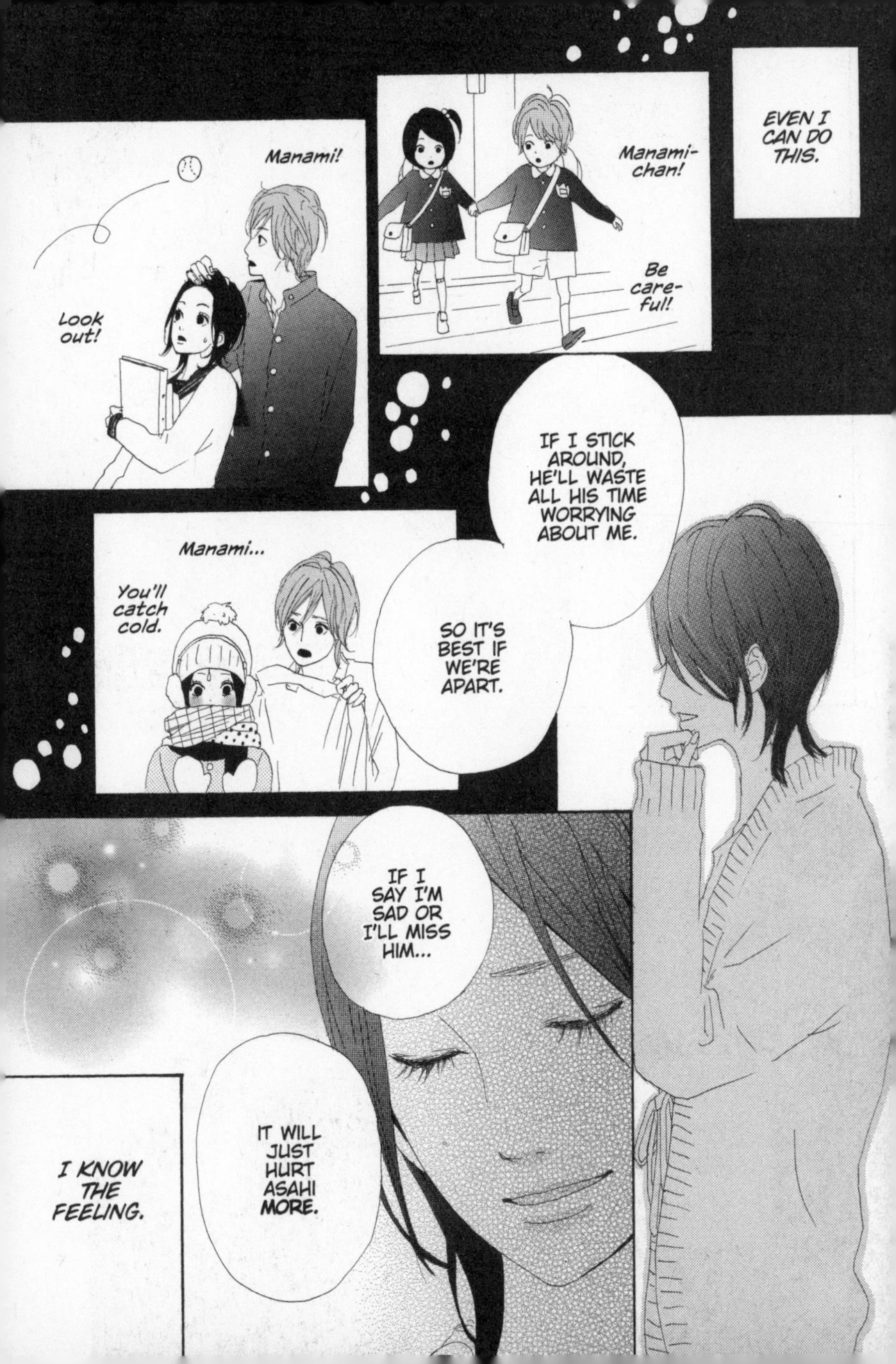
EVEN I CAN DO THIS.
Manami-chan!
Be careful!
Manami!
Look out!
Manami...
You'll catch cold.
IF I STICK AROUND, HE'LL WASTE ALL HIS TIME WORRYING ABOUT ME.
SO IT'S BEST IF WE'RE APART.
IF I SAY I'M SAD OR I'LL MISS HIM...
IT WILL JUST HURT ASAHI MORE.
I KNOW THE FEELING.

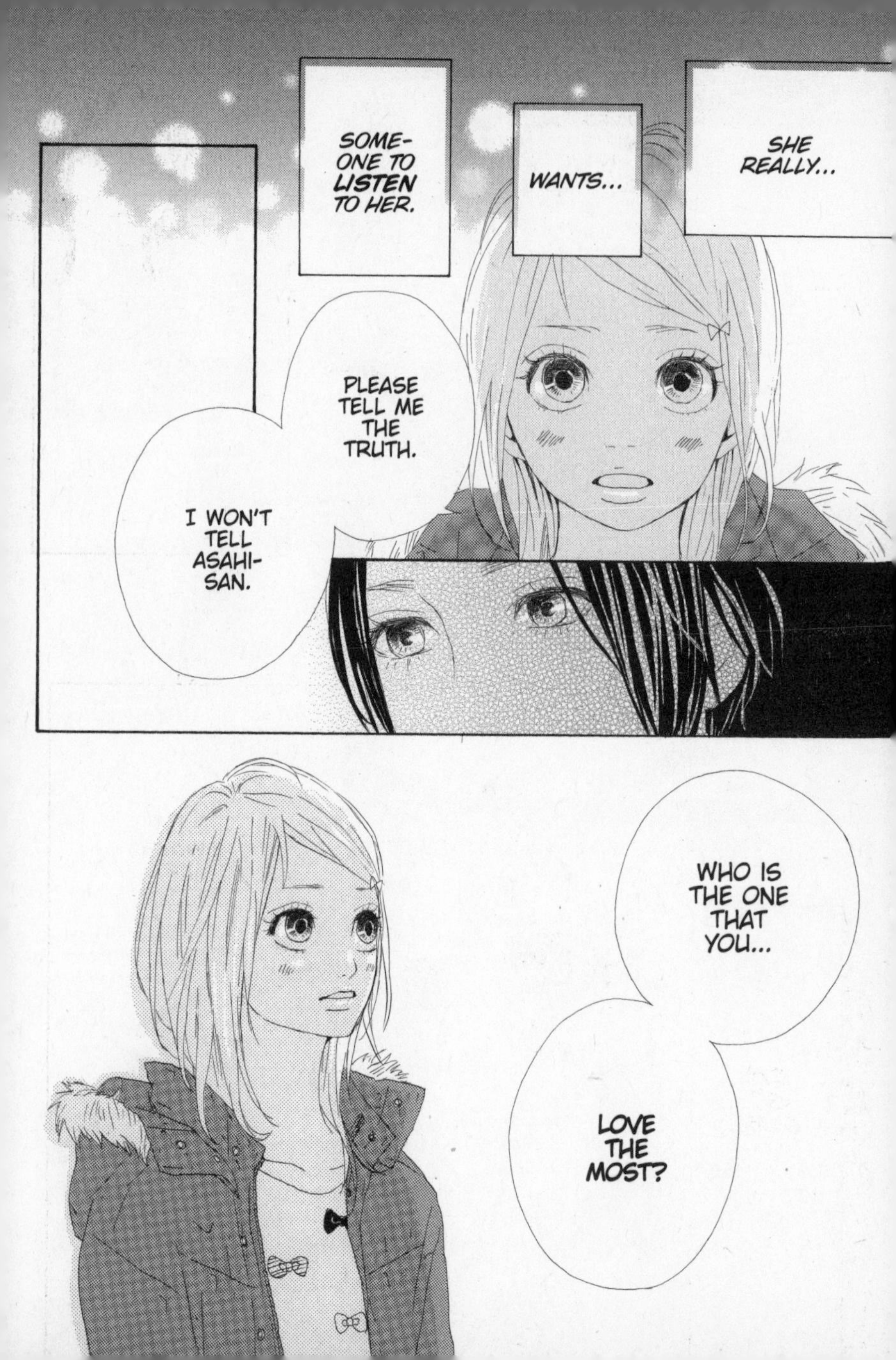
SHE REALLY...
WANTS...
SOME-ONE TO LISTEN TO HER.
PLEASE TELL ME THE TRUTH.
I WON'T TELL ASAHI-SAN.
WHO IS THE ONE THAT YOU...
LOVE THE MOST?

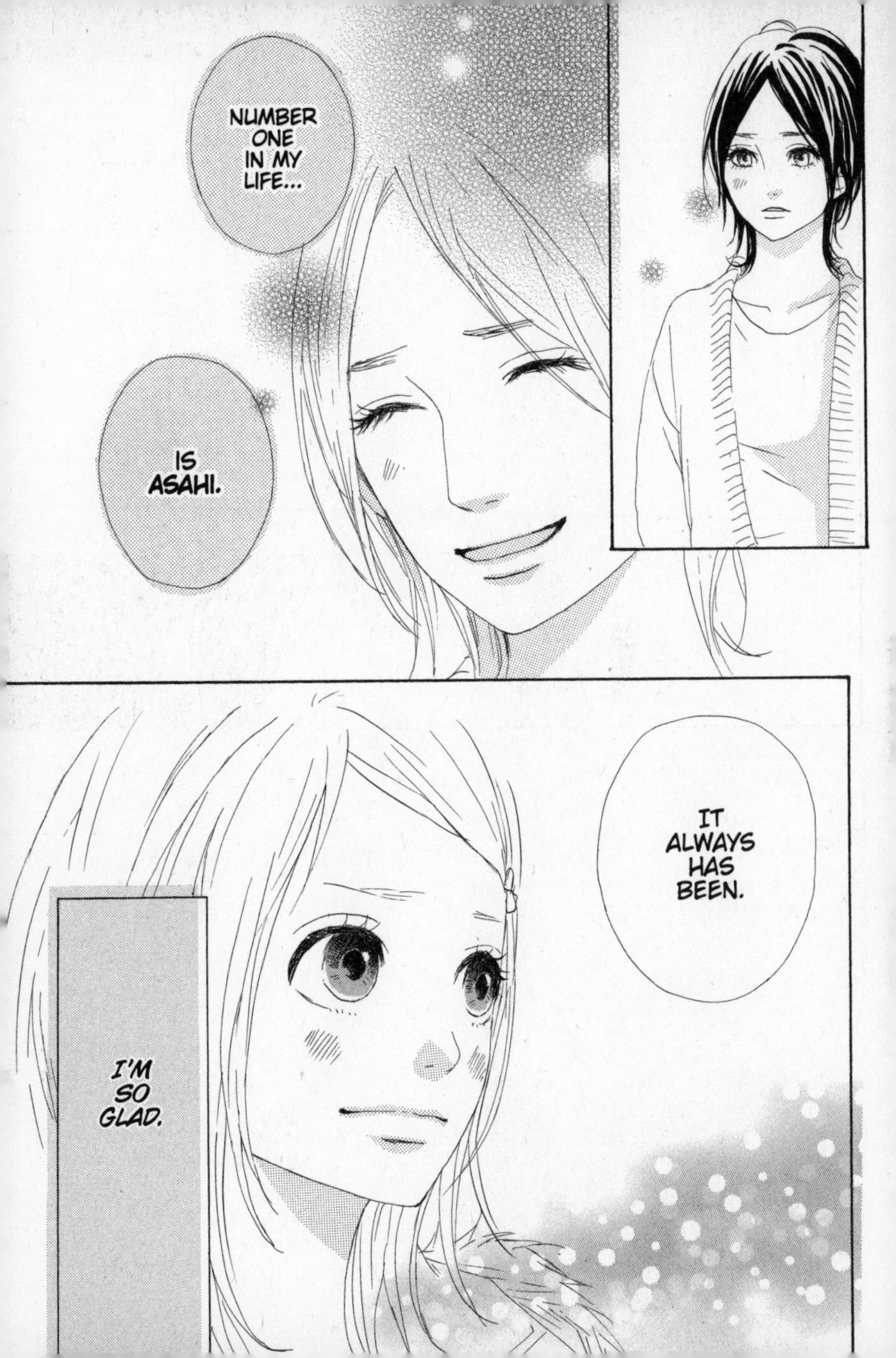
NUMBER ONE IN MY LIFE...
IS ASAHI.
IT ALWAYS HAS BEEN.
I'M SO GLAD.

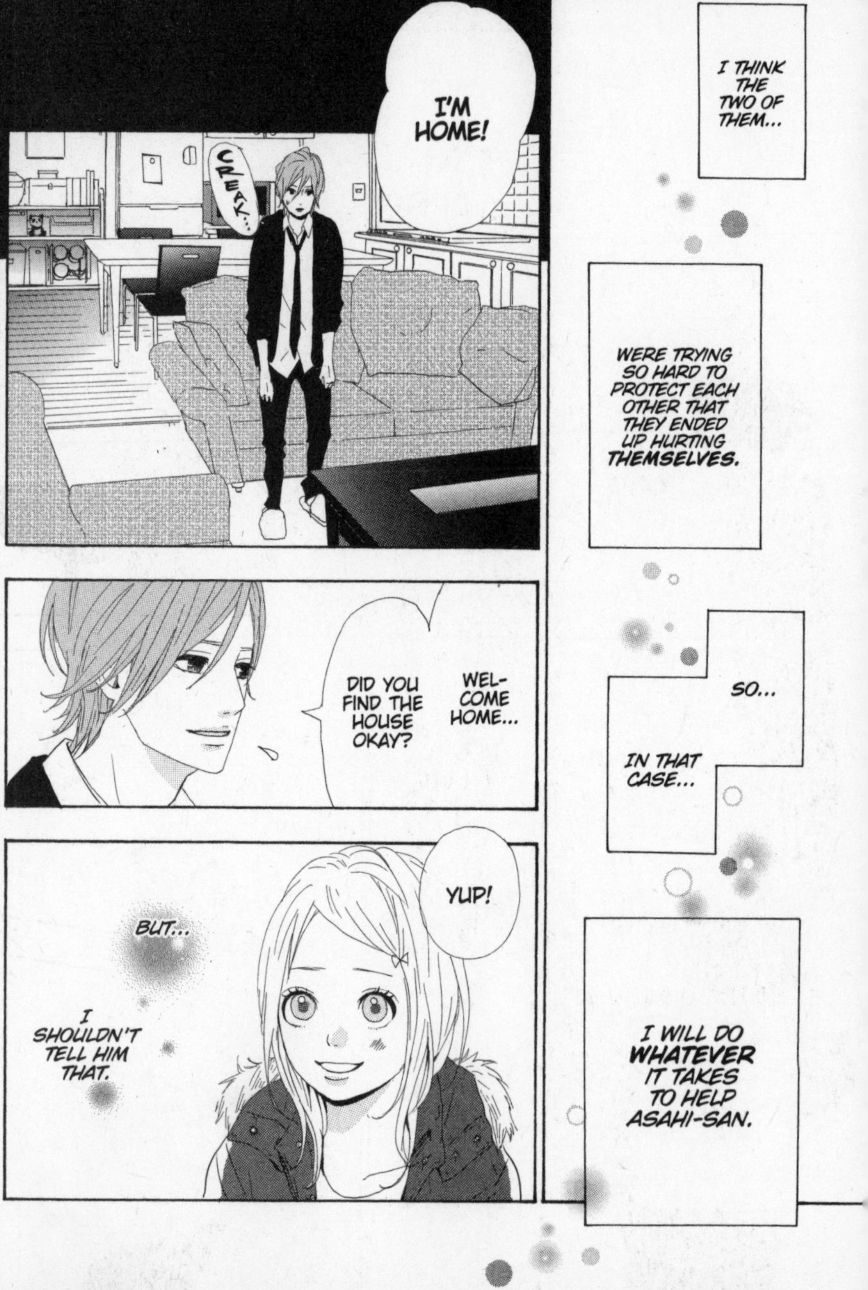

I THINK THE TWO OF THEM...
WERE TRYING SO HARD TO PROTECT EACH OTHER THAT THEY ENDED UP HURTING THEMSELVES.
SO...
IN THAT CASE...
I WILL DO WHATEVER IT TAKES TO HELP ASAHI-SAN.
I'M HOME!
CREAK...
WEL-COME HOME...
DID YOU FIND THE HOUSE OKAY?
YUP!
BUT...
I SHOULDN'T TELL HIM THAT.

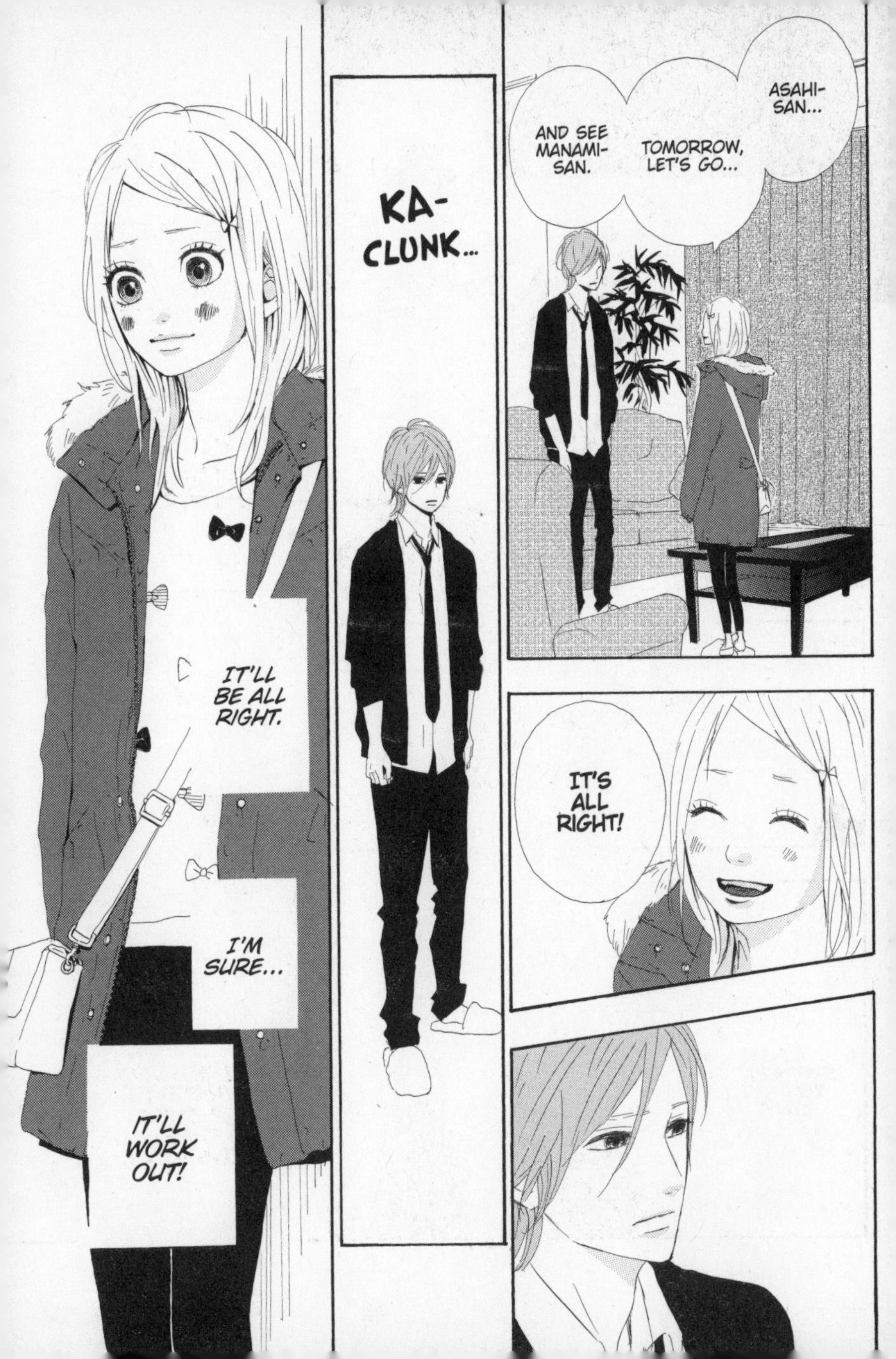
ASAHI-SAN...
TOMORROW, LET'S GO...
AND SEE MANAMI-SAN.
IT'S ALL RIGHT!
KA-CLUNK...
IT'LL BE ALL RIGHT.
I'M SURE...
IT'LL WORK OUT!

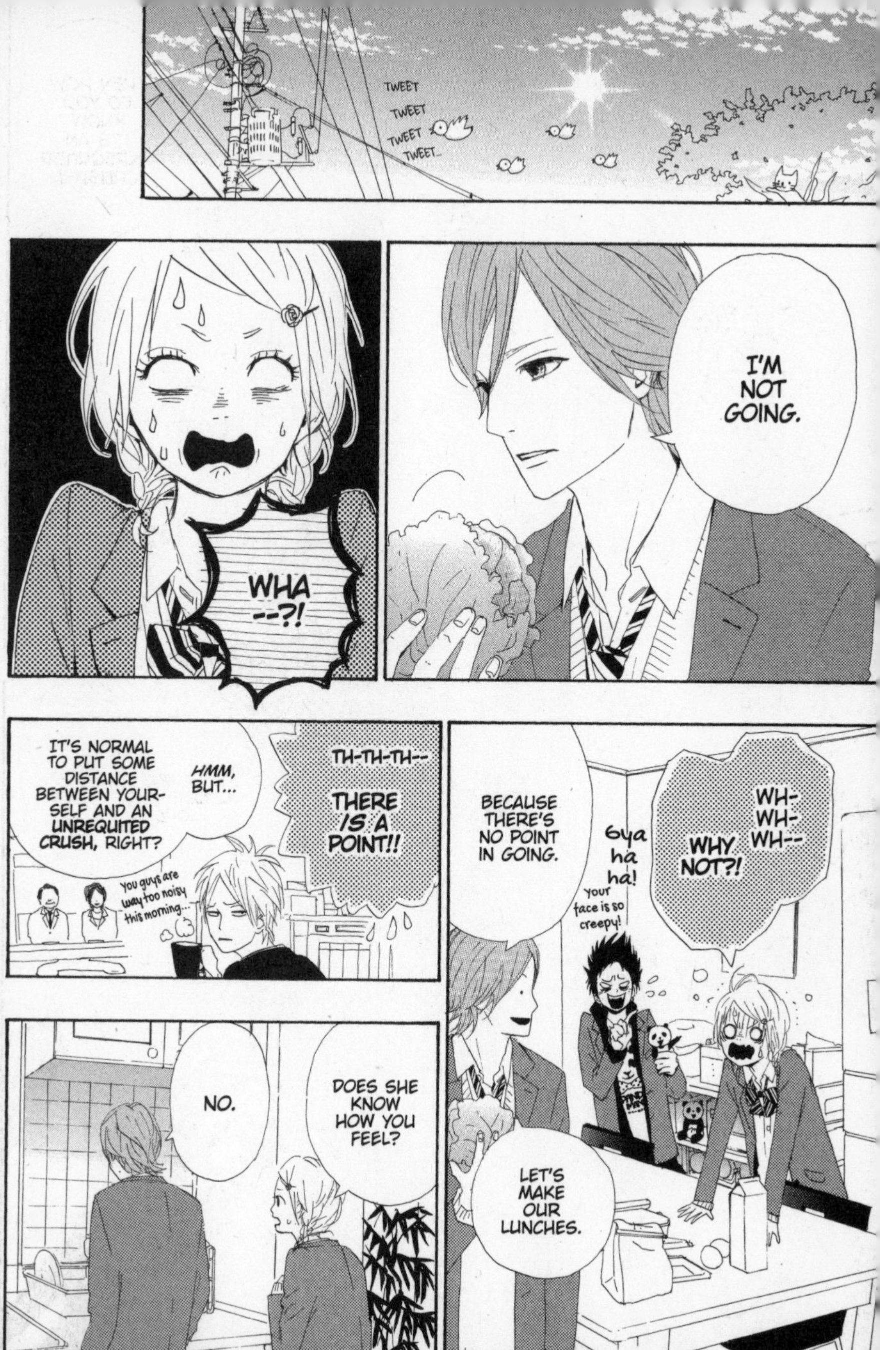
TWEET
TWEET
TWEET
TWEET...
I'M NOT GOING.
WHA--?!
BECAUSE THERE'S NO POINT IN GOING.
WH- WH- WH--
WHY NOT?!
Gya ha ha!
your face is so creepy!
LET'S MAKE OUR LUNCHES.
TH-TH-TH--
THERE IS A POINT!!
HMM, BUT...
IT'S NORMAL TO PUT SOME DISTANCE BETWEEN YOURSELF AND AN UNREQUITED CRUSH, RIGHT?
You guys are way too noisy this morning...
DOES SHE KNOW HOW YOU FEEL?
NO.

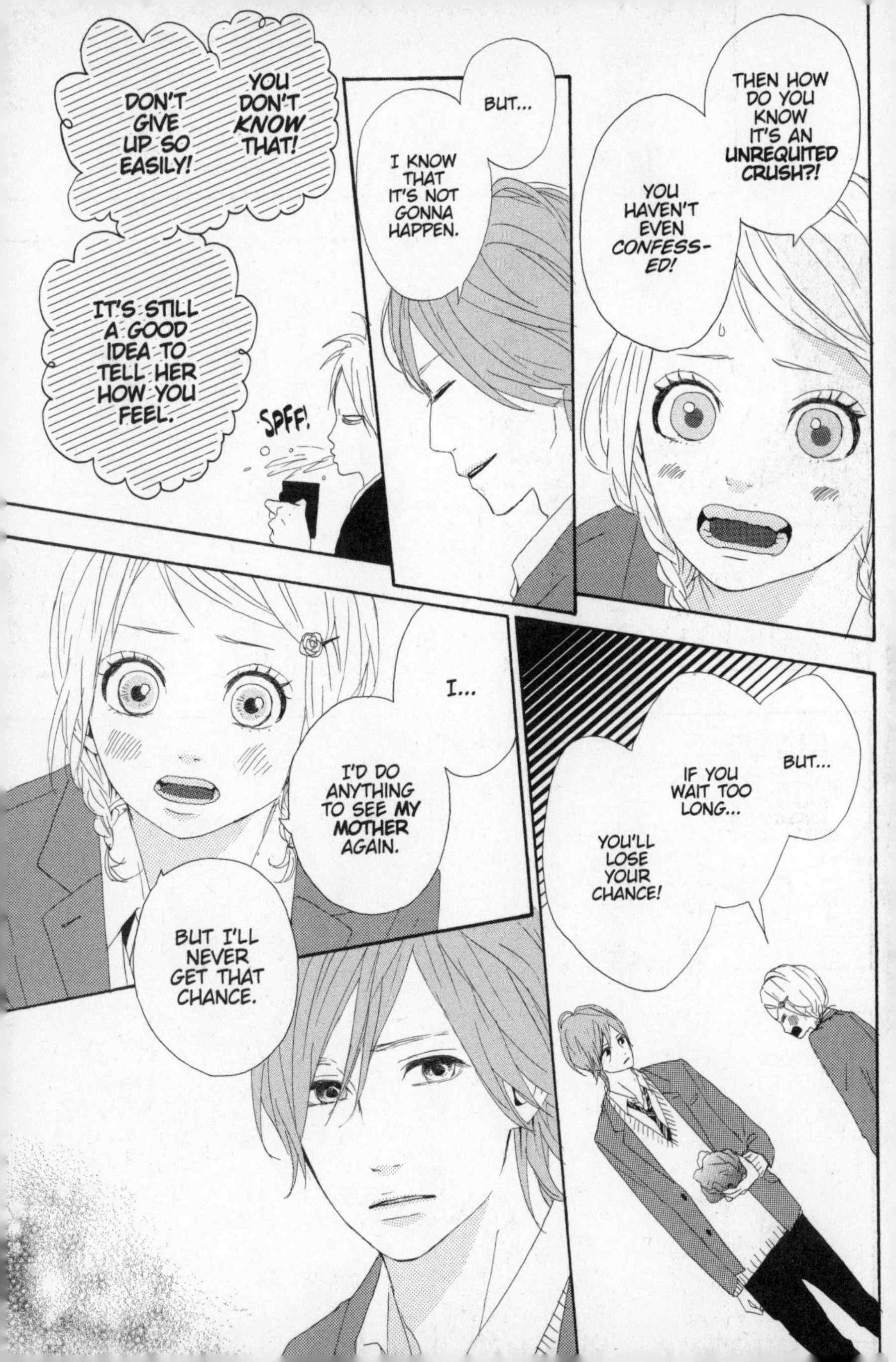
THEN HOW DO YOU KNOW IT'S AN UNREQUITED CRUSH?!
YOU HAVEN'T EVEN CONFESSED!
BUT...
I KNOW THAT IT'S NOT GONNA HAPPEN.
YOU DON'T KNOW THAT!
DON'T GIVE UP SO EASILY!
IT'S STILL A GOOD IDEA TO TELL HER HOW YOU FEEL.
SPFF!
BUT...
IF YOU WAIT TOO LONG...
YOU'LL LOSE YOUR CHANCE!
I...
I'D DO ANYTHING TO SEE MY MOTHER AGAIN.
BUT I'LL NEVER GET THAT CHANCE.

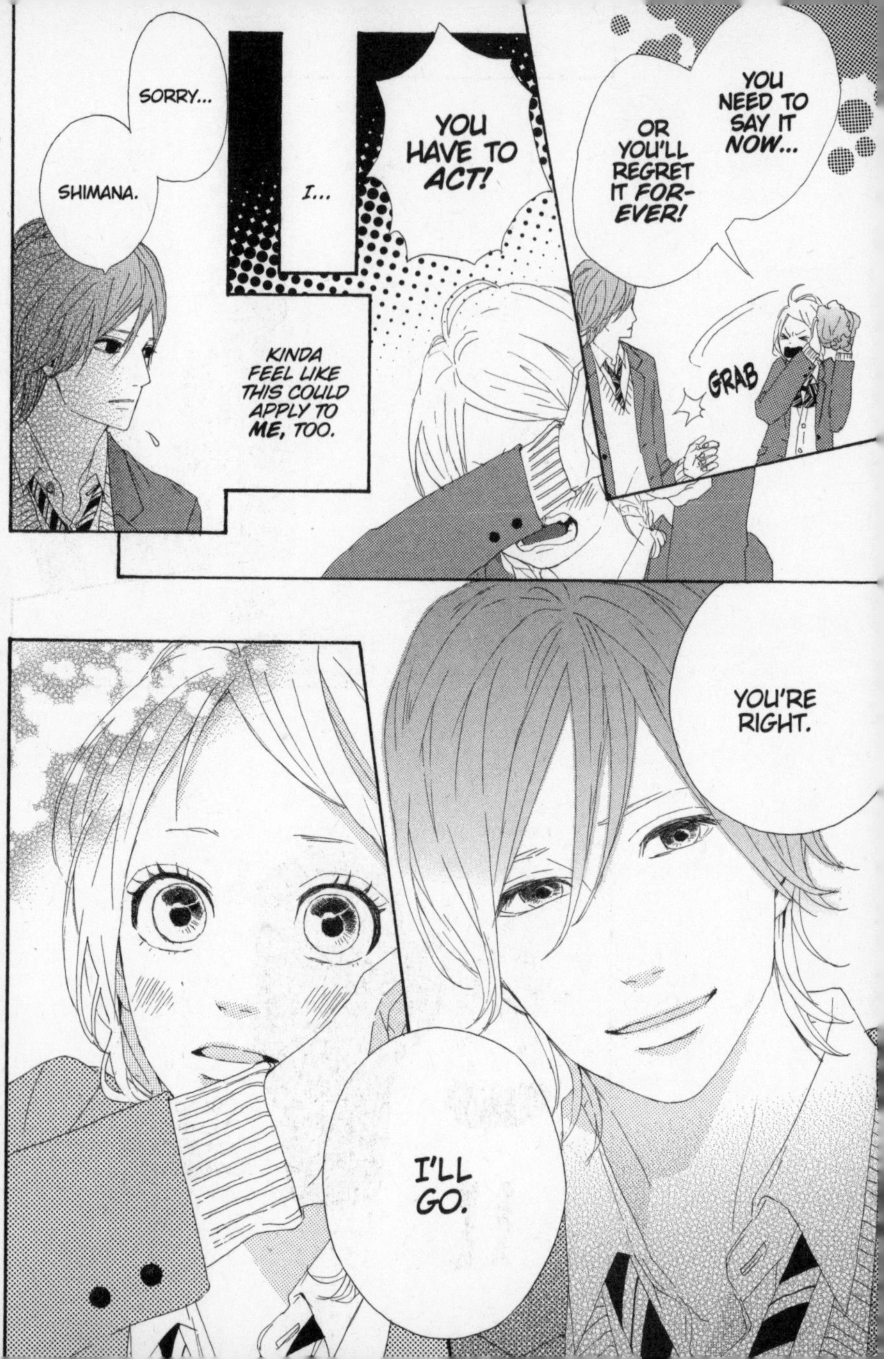
YOU NEED TO SAY IT NOW...
OR YOU'LL REGRET IT FOREVER!
GRAB
YOU HAVE TO ACT!
I...
KINDA FEEL LIKE THIS COULD APPLY TO ME, TOO.
SORRY...
SHIMANA.
YOU'RE RIGHT.
I'LL GO.

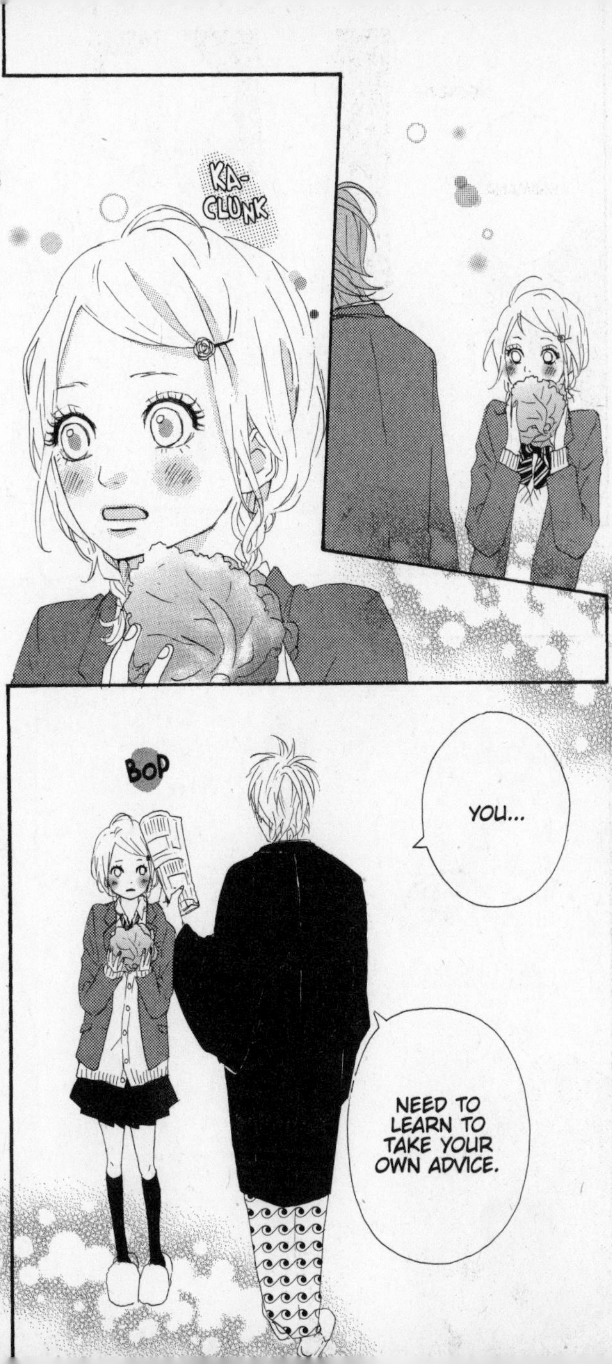
KA-CLUNK
BOP
YOU...
NEED TO LEARN TO TAKE YOUR OWN ADVICE.

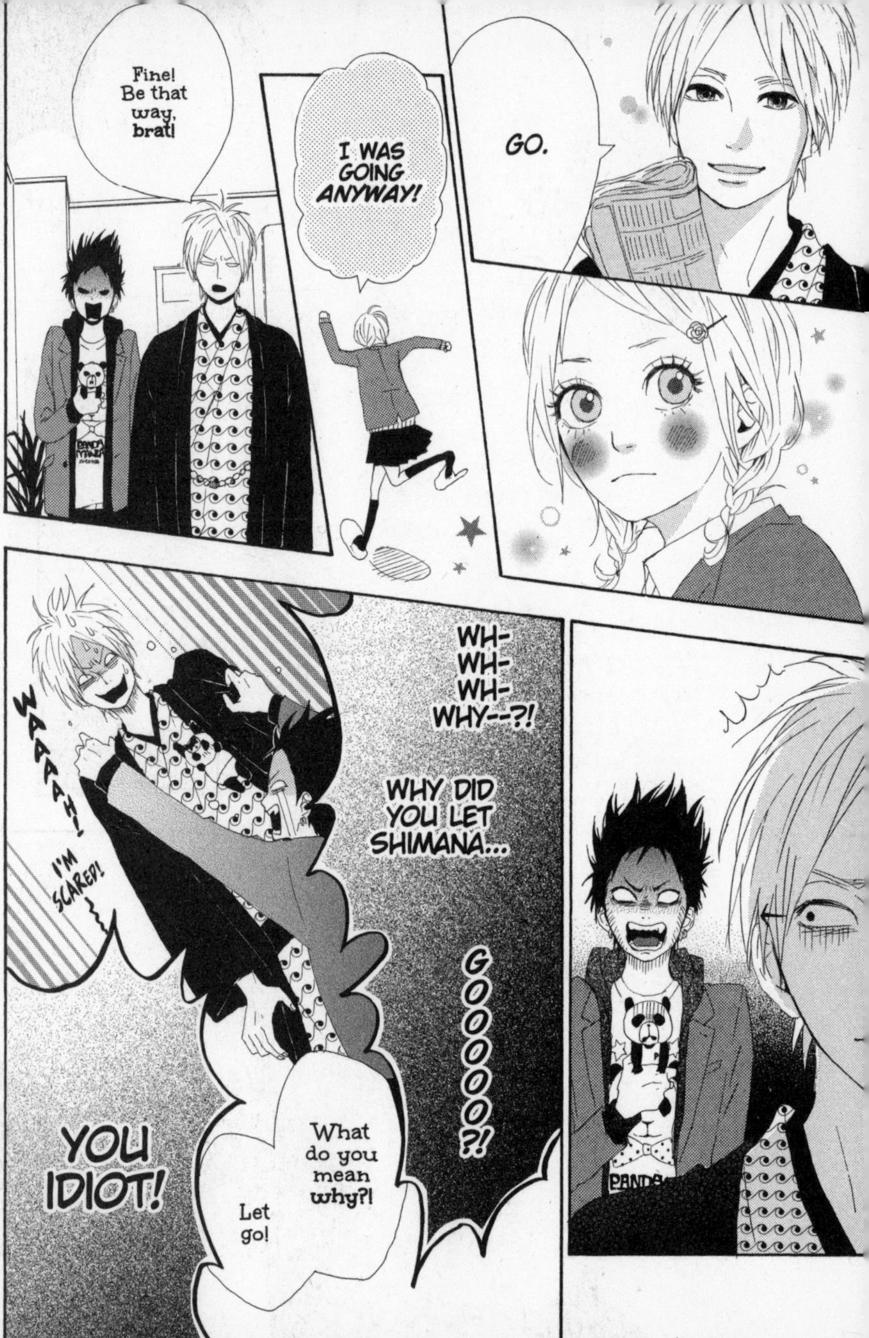
GO.
I WAS GOING ANYWAY!
Fine! Be that way, brat!
WH-WH-WH-WHY--?!
WHY DID YOU LET SHIMANA...
GOOOOOOO?!
WAAAAH!
I'M SCARED!
What do you mean why?!
Let go!
YOU IDIOT!

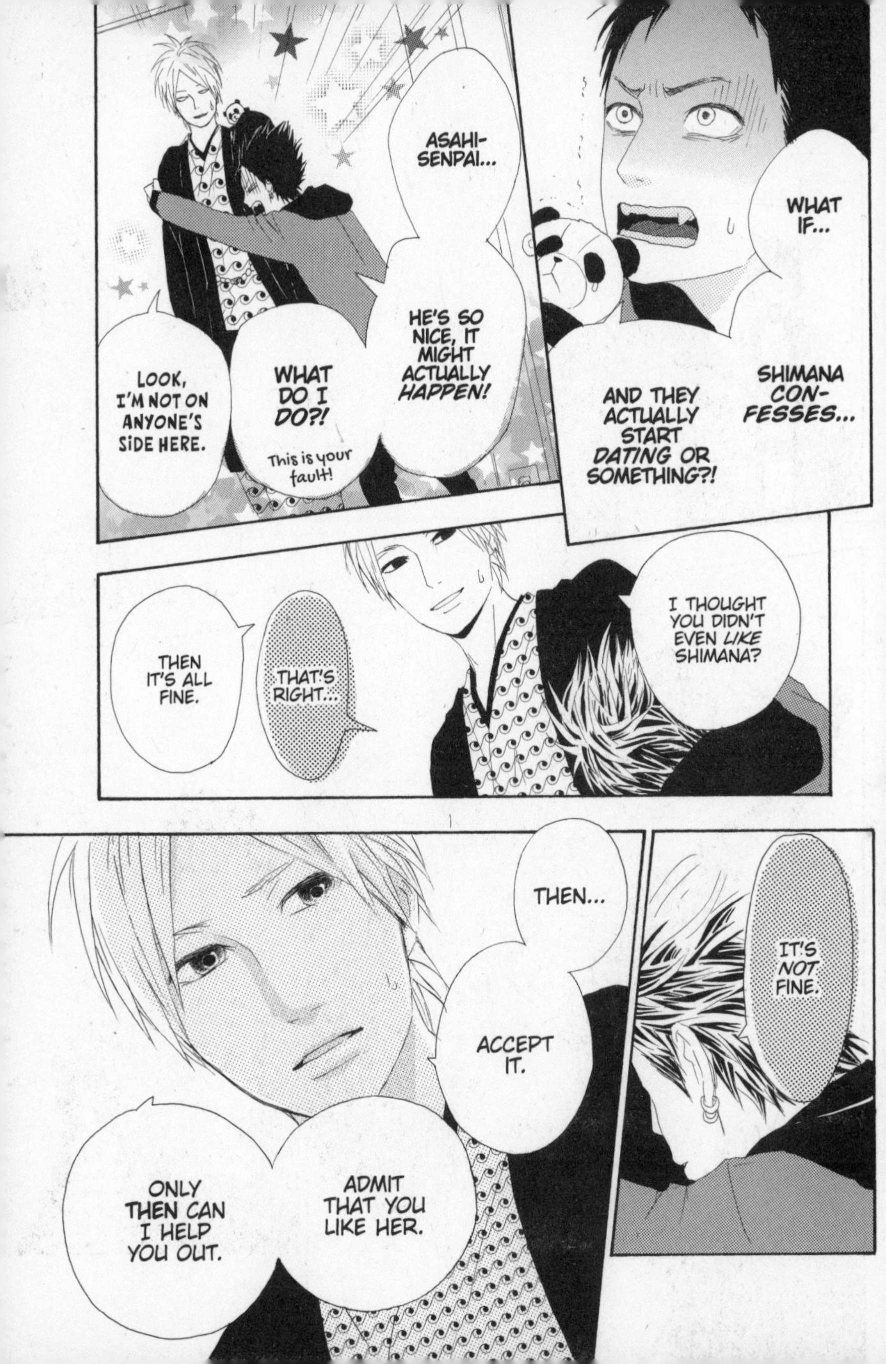
WHAT IF...
SHIMANA CON-FESSES...
AND THEY ACTUALLY START *DATING* OR SOMETHING?!
ASAHI-SENPAI...
HE'S SO NICE, IT MIGHT ACTUALLY *HAPPEN!*
WHAT DO I *DO?!*
This is your fault!
LOOK, I'M NOT ON ANYONE'S SIDE HERE.
I THOUGHT YOU DIDN'T EVEN *LIKE* SHIMANA?
THAT'S RIGHT...
THEN IT'S ALL FINE.
IT'S *NOT* FINE.
THEN...
ACCEPT IT.
ADMIT THAT YOU LIKE HER.
ONLY THEN CAN I HELP YOU OUT.

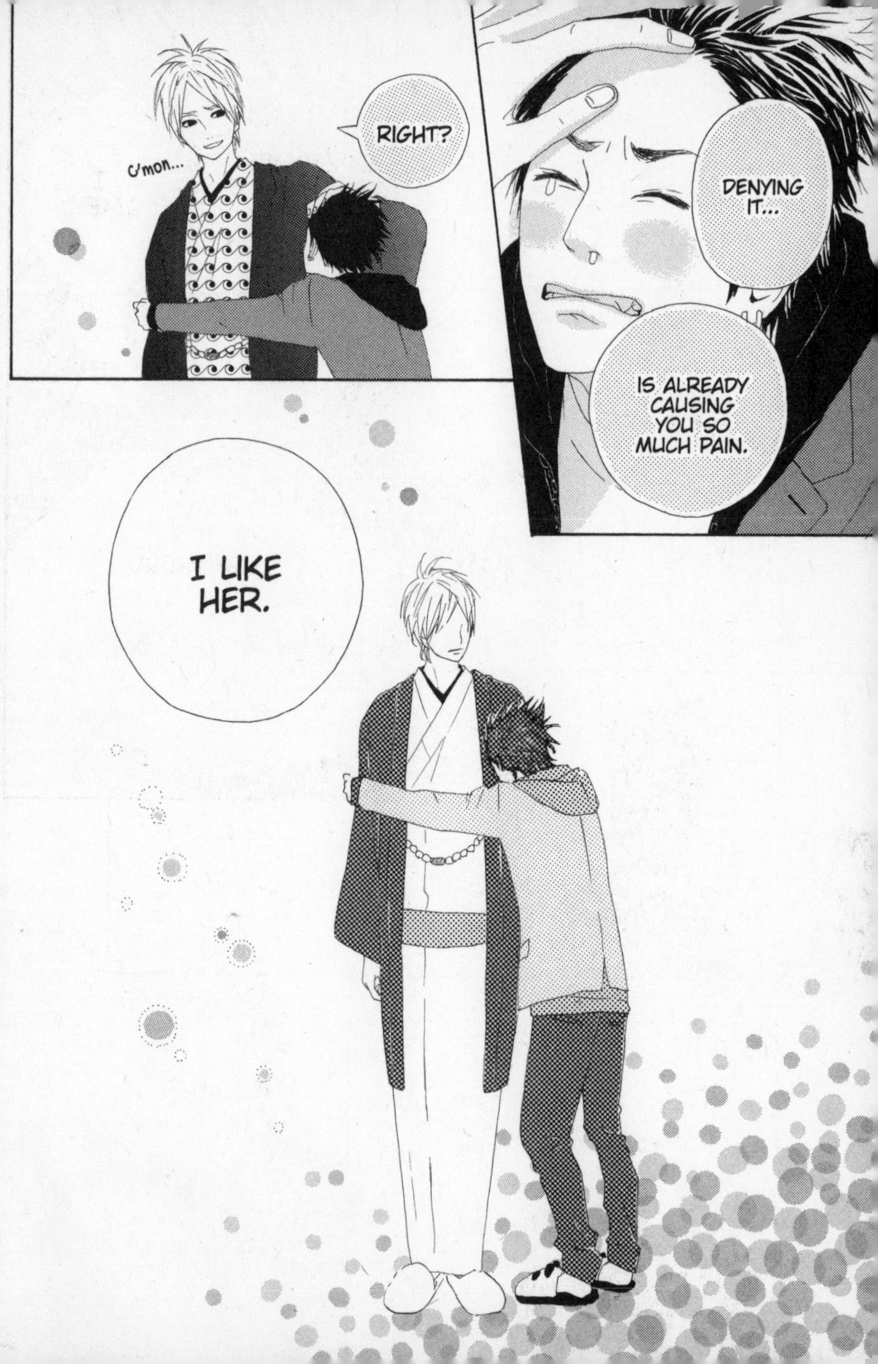
DENYING IT...
IS ALREADY CAUSING YOU SO MUCH PAIN.
RIGHT?
C'mon...
I LIKE HER.

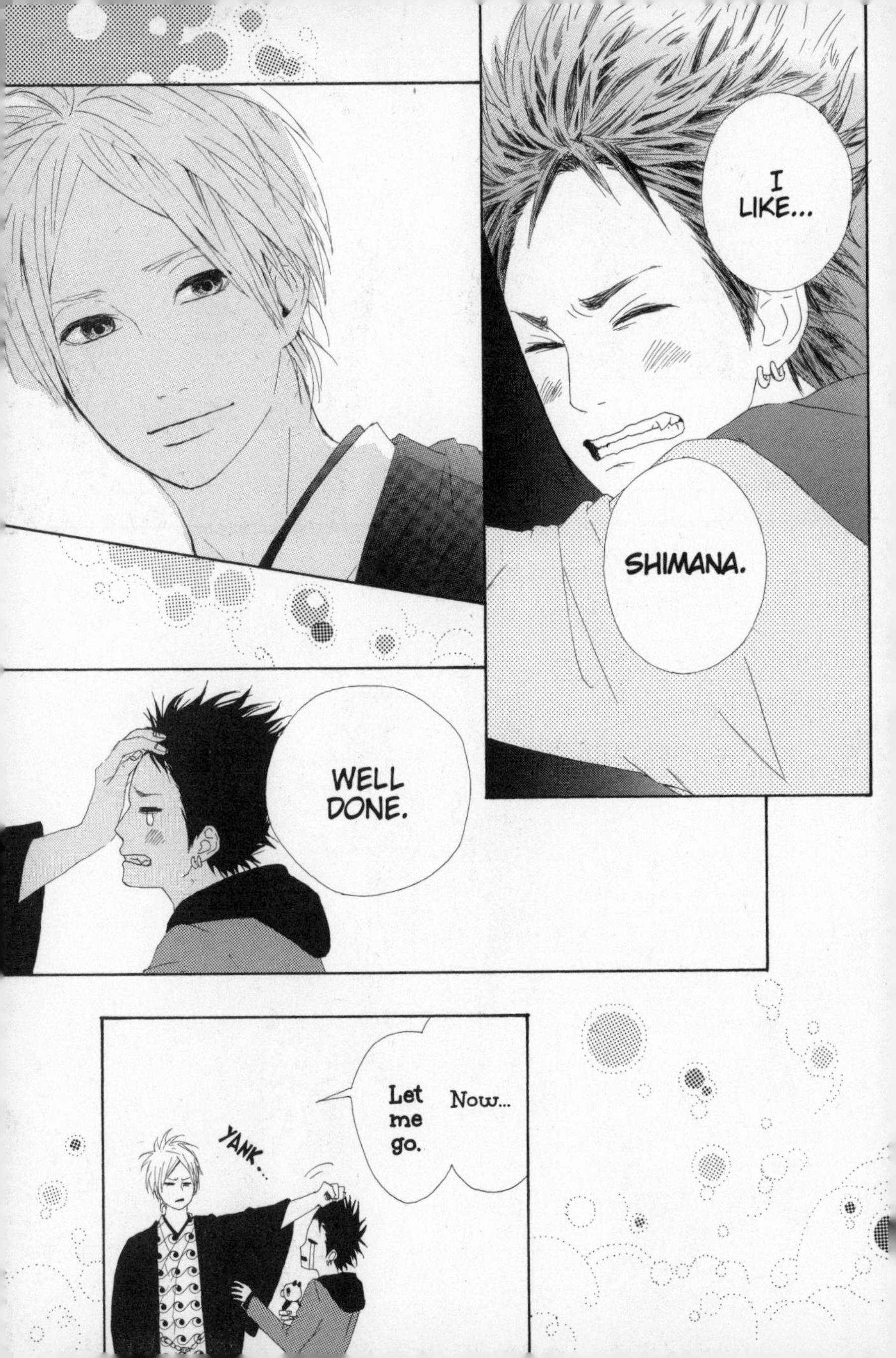
I LIKE...
SHIMANA.
WELL DONE.
Now...
Let me go.
YANK...

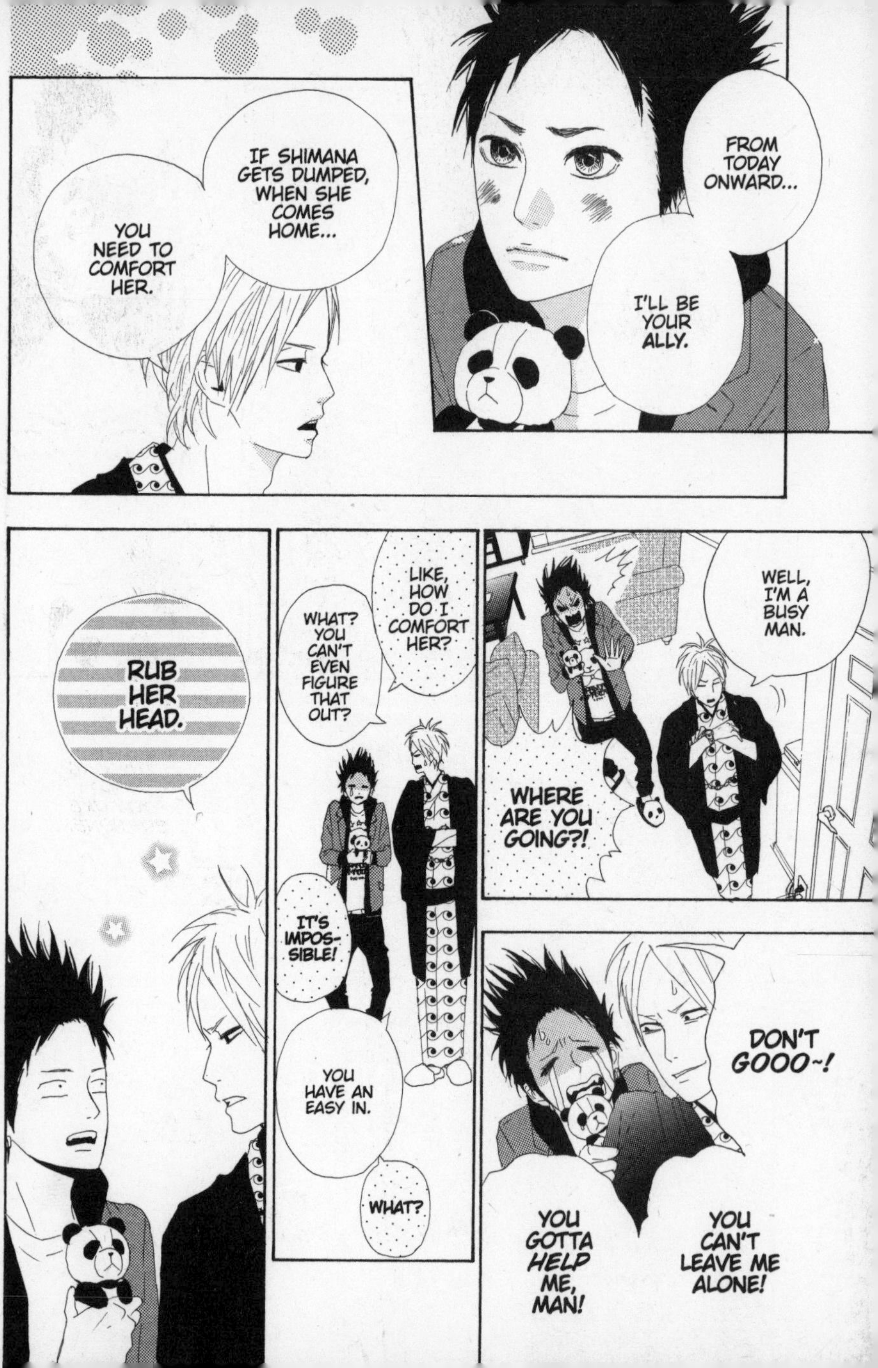
FROM TODAY ONWARD...
I'LL BE YOUR ALLY.
IF SHIMANA GETS DUMPED, WHEN SHE COMES HOME...
YOU NEED TO COMFORT HER.
WELL, I'M A BUSY MAN.
WHERE ARE YOU GOING?!
DON'T GOOO~!
YOU CAN'T LEAVE ME ALONE!
YOU GOTTA HELP ME, MAN!
LIKE, HOW DO I COMFORT HER?
WHAT? YOU CAN'T EVEN FIGURE THAT OUT?
IT'S IMPOSSIBLE!
YOU HAVE AN EASY IN.
WHAT?
RUB HER HEAD.

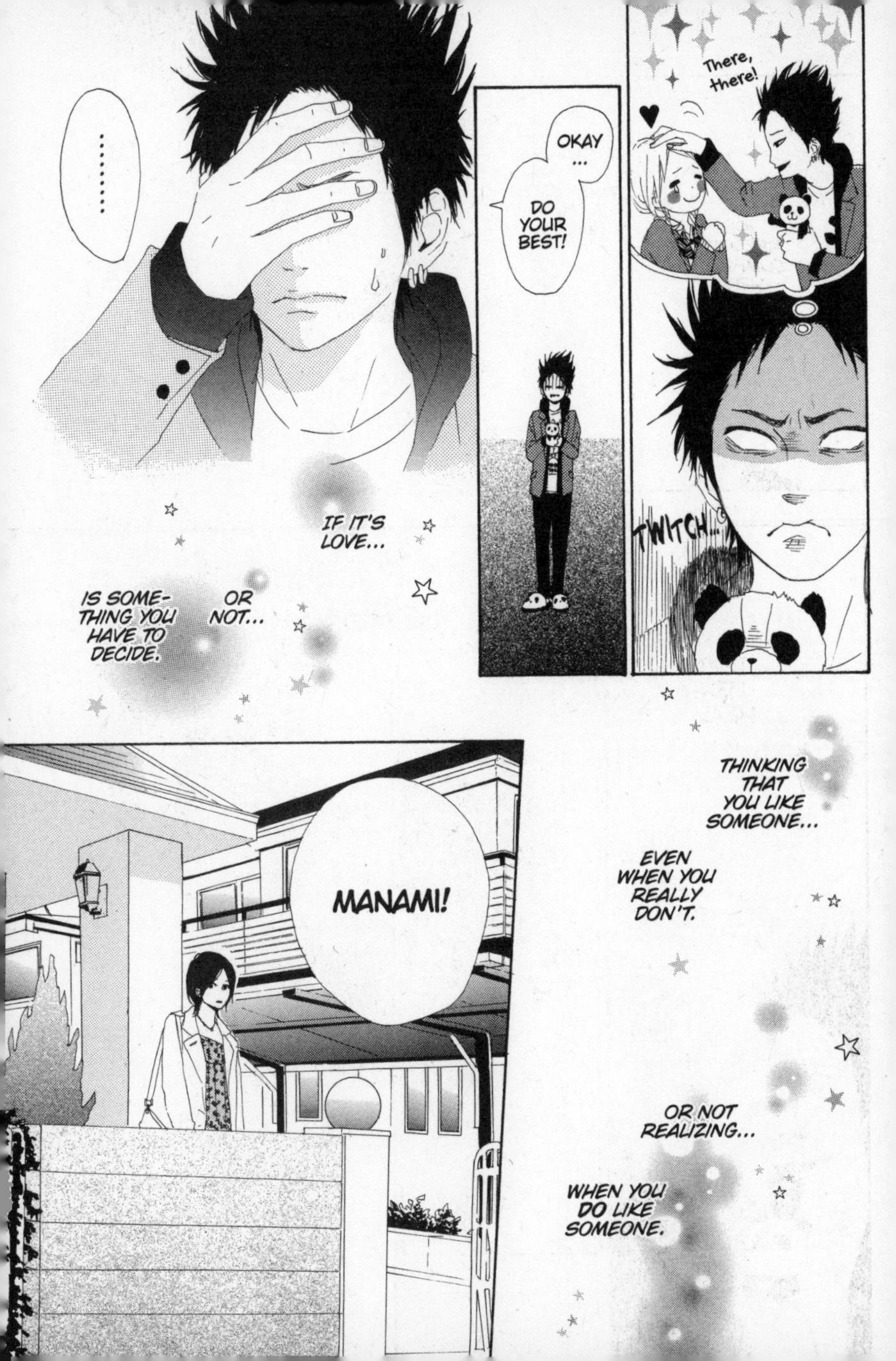

There, there!
TWITCH...
OKAY ... DO YOUR BEST!
......
IF IT'S LOVE...
OR NOT...
IS SOMETHING YOU HAVE TO DECIDE.
THINKING THAT YOU LIKE SOMEONE...
EVEN WHEN YOU REALLY DON'T.
OR NOT REALIZING...
WHEN YOU DO LIKE SOMEONE.
MANAMI!

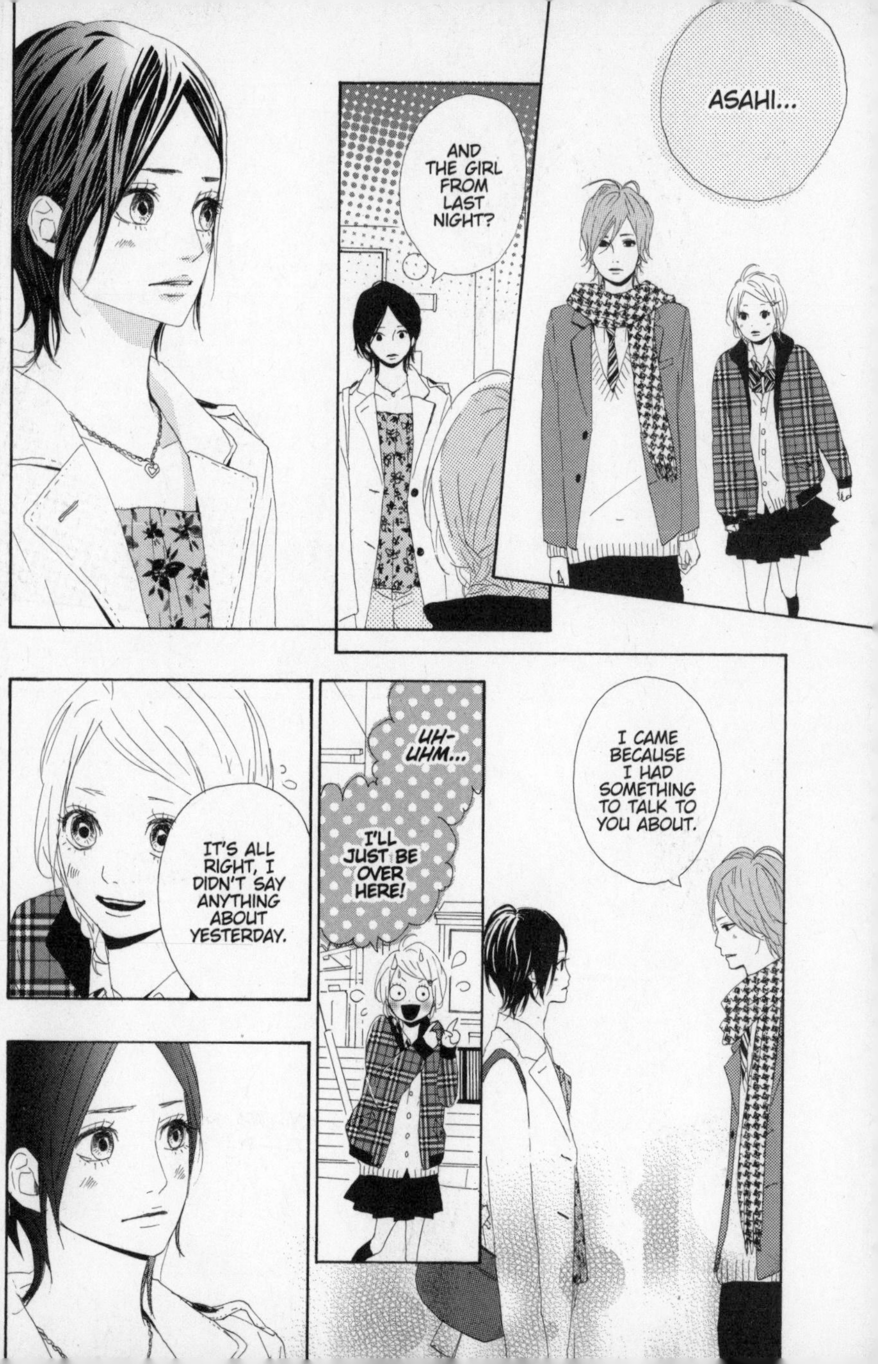
ASAHI...
AND THE GIRL FROM LAST NIGHT?
I CAME BECAUSE I HAD SOMETHING TO TALK TO YOU ABOUT.
UH-UHM...
I'LL JUST BE OVER HERE!
IT'S ALL RIGHT, I DIDN'T SAY ANYTHING ABOUT YESTERDAY.

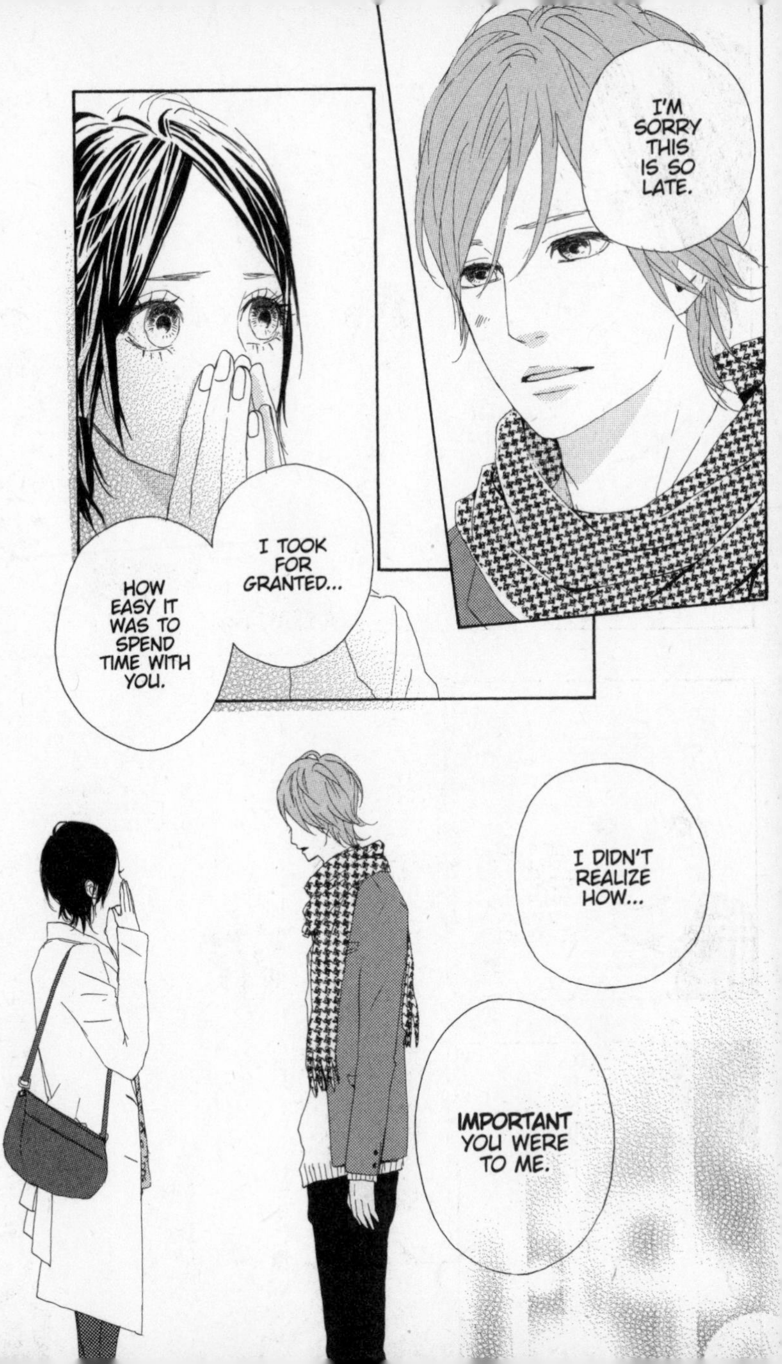
I'M SORRY THIS IS SO LATE.
I TOOK FOR GRANTED...
HOW EASY IT WAS TO SPEND TIME WITH YOU.
I DIDN'T REALIZE HOW...
IMPORTANT YOU WERE TO ME.

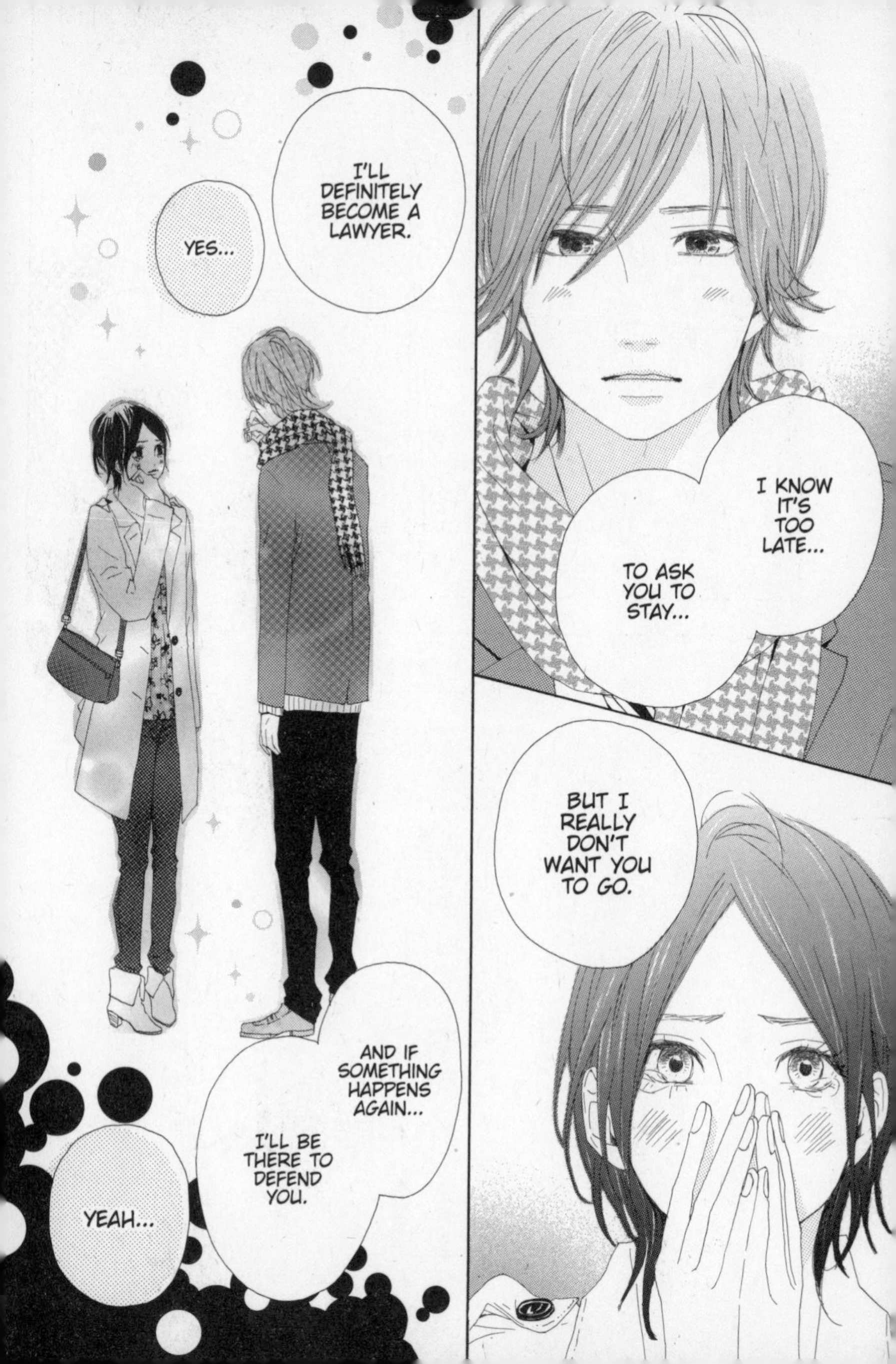
I KNOW IT'S TOO LATE...
TO ASK YOU TO STAY...
BUT I REALLY DON'T WANT YOU TO GO.
I'LL DEFINITELY BECOME A LAWYER.
YES...
AND IF SOMETHING HAPPENS AGAIN...
I'LL BE THERE TO DEFEND YOU.
YEAH...

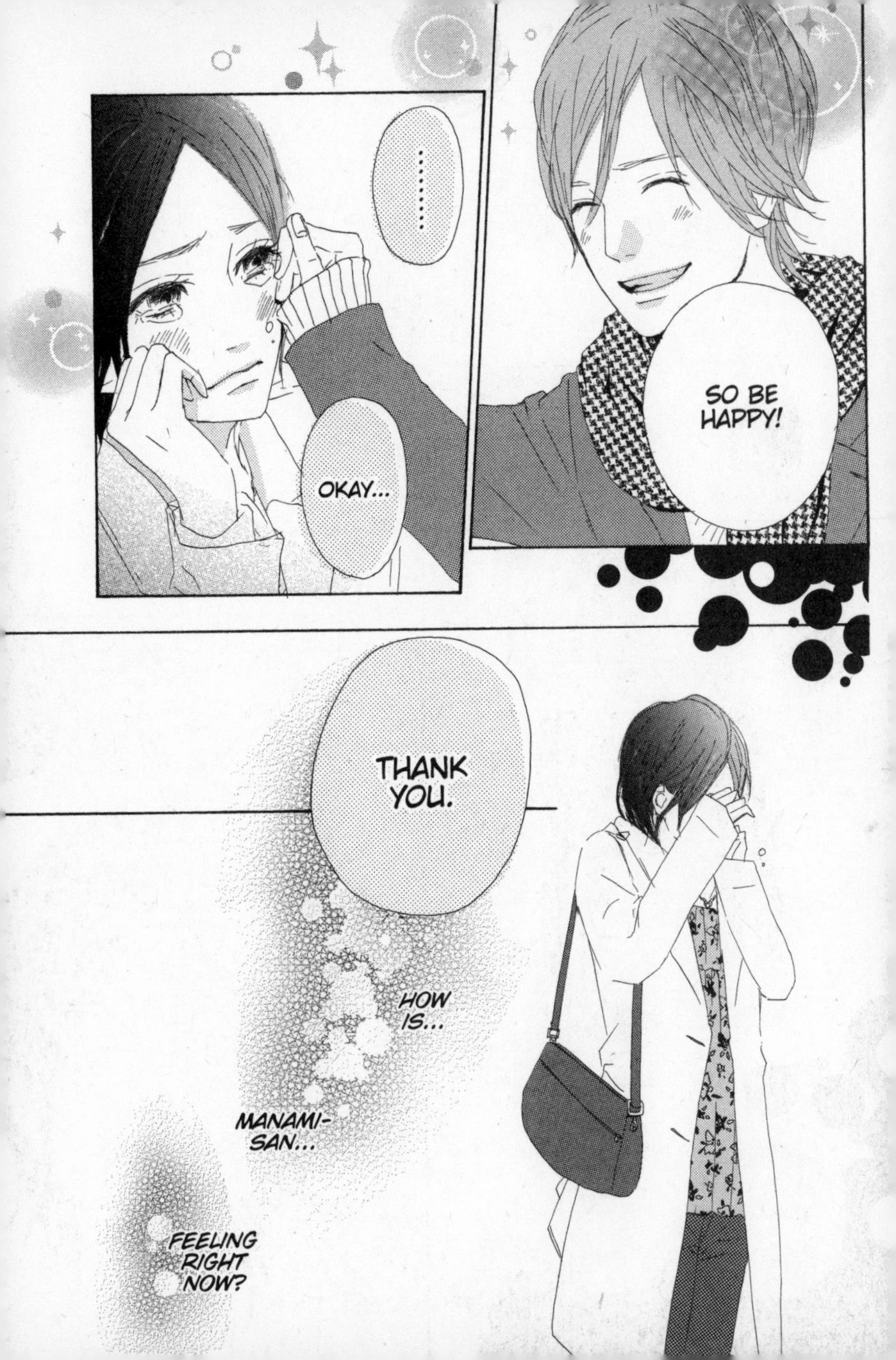
SO BE HAPPY!
......
OKAY...
THANK YOU.
HOW IS...
MANAMI-SAN...
FEELING RIGHT NOW?

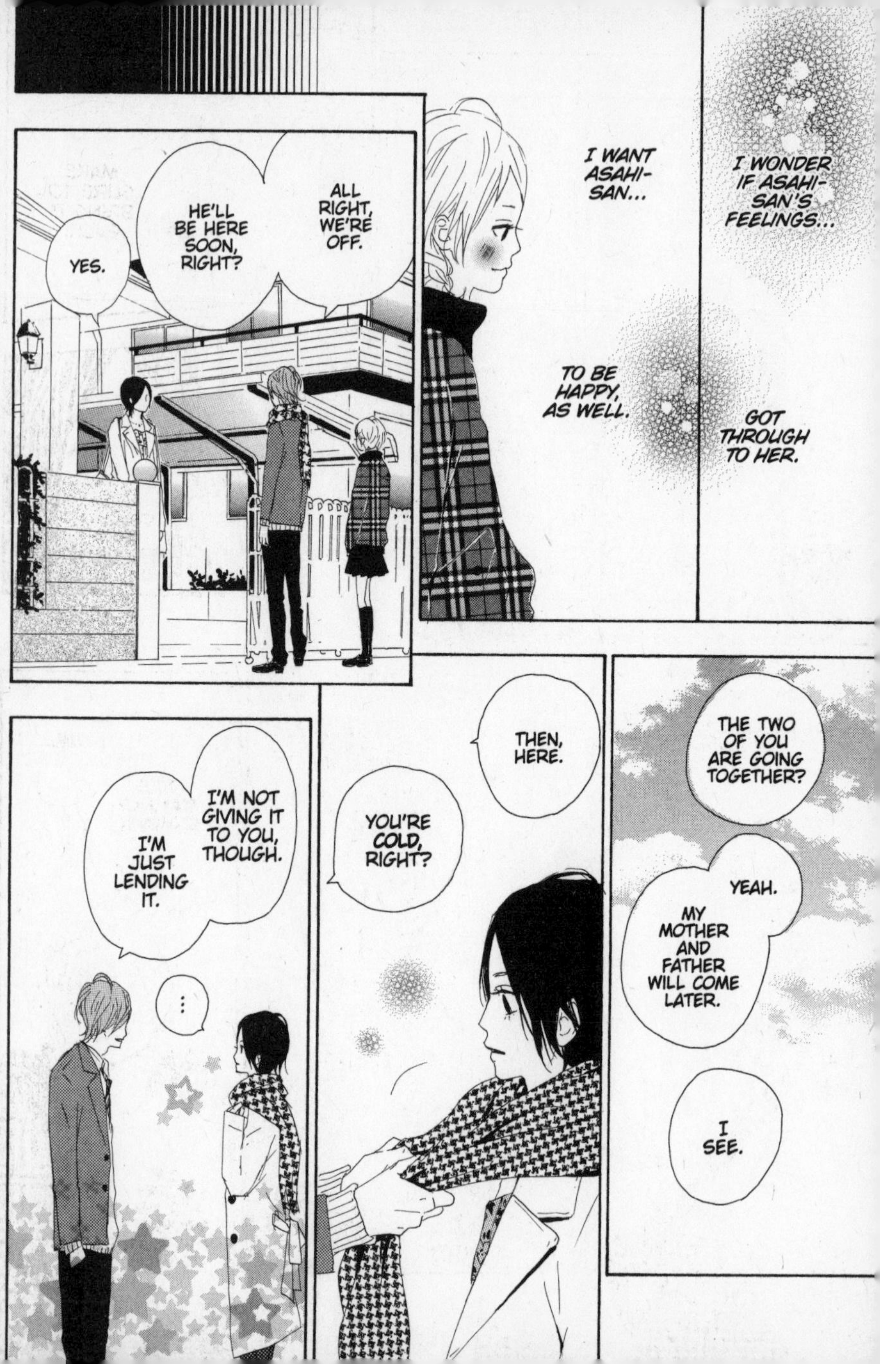
I WONDER IF ASAHI-SAN'S FEELINGS...
GOT THROUGH TO HER.
I WANT ASAHI-SAN...
TO BE HAPPY, AS WELL.
ALL RIGHT, WE'RE OFF.
HE'LL BE HERE SOON, RIGHT?
YES.
THE TWO OF YOU ARE GOING TOGETHER?
YEAH.
MY MOTHER AND FATHER WILL COME LATER.
I SEE.
THEN, HERE.
YOU'RE COLD, RIGHT?
I'M NOT GIVING IT TO YOU, THOUGH.
I'M JUST LENDING IT.
...

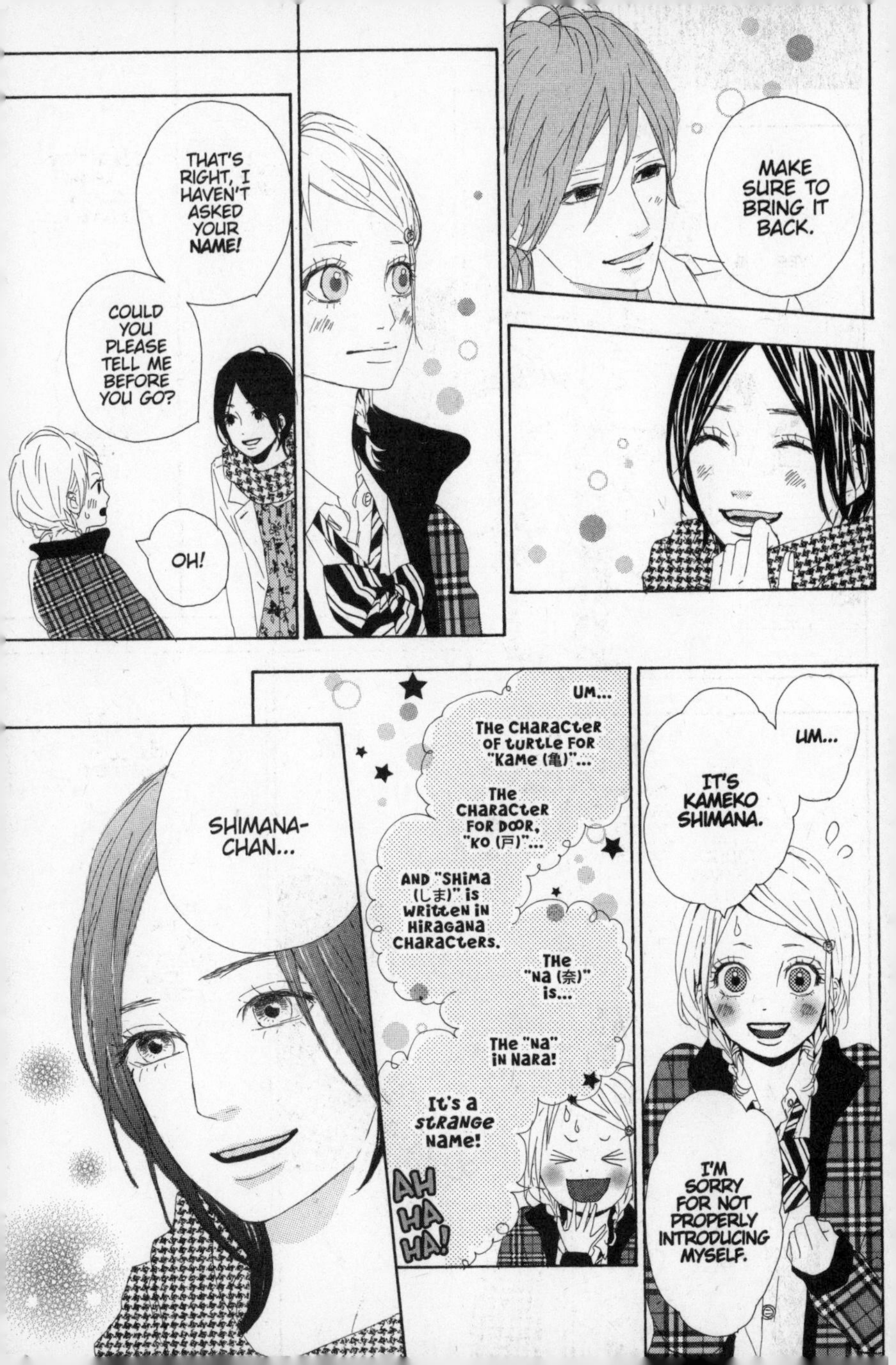
MAKE SURE TO BRING IT BACK.
THAT'S RIGHT, I HAVEN'T ASKED YOUR NAME!
COULD YOU PLEASE TELL ME BEFORE YOU GO?
OH!
UM...
IT'S KAMEKO SHIMANA.
I'M SORRY FOR NOT PROPERLY INTRODUCING MYSELF.
UM...
THE CHARACTER OF TURTLE FOR "KAME (亀)"...
THE CHARACTER FOR DOOR, "KO (戸)"...
AND "SHIMA (しま)" IS WRITTEN IN HIRAGANA CHARACTERS.
THE "NA (奈)" IS...
THE "NA" IN NARA!
IT'S A STRANGE NAME!
AH HA HA!
SHIMANA-CHAN...

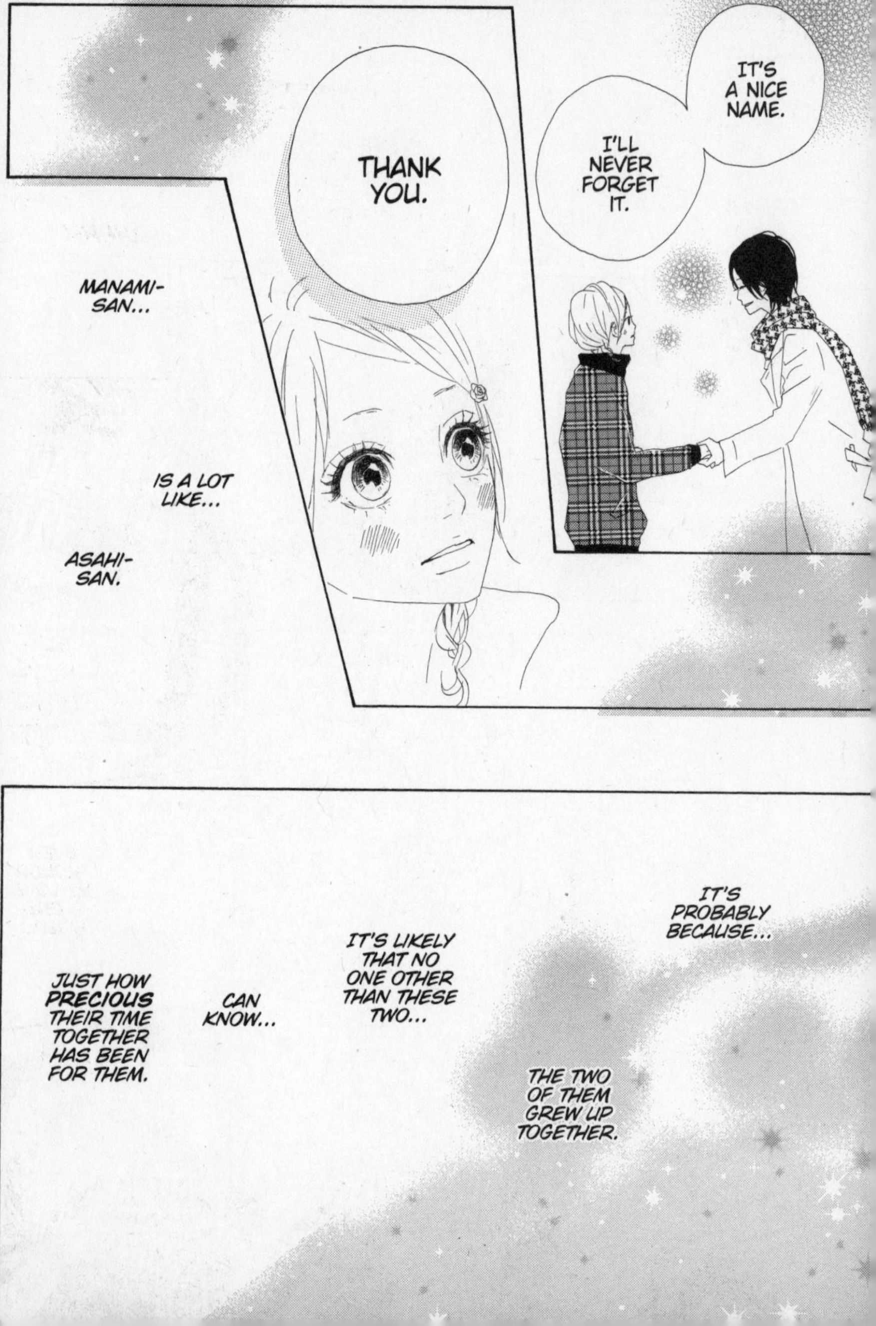
IT'S A NICE NAME.
I'LL NEVER FORGET IT.
THANK YOU.
MANAMI-SAN...
IS A LOT LIKE...
ASAHI-SAN.
IT'S PROBABLY BECAUSE...
THE TWO OF THEM GREW UP TOGETHER.
IT'S LIKELY THAT NO ONE OTHER THAN THESE TWO...
CAN KNOW...
JUST HOW PRECIOUS THEIR TIME TOGETHER HAS BEEN FOR THEM.

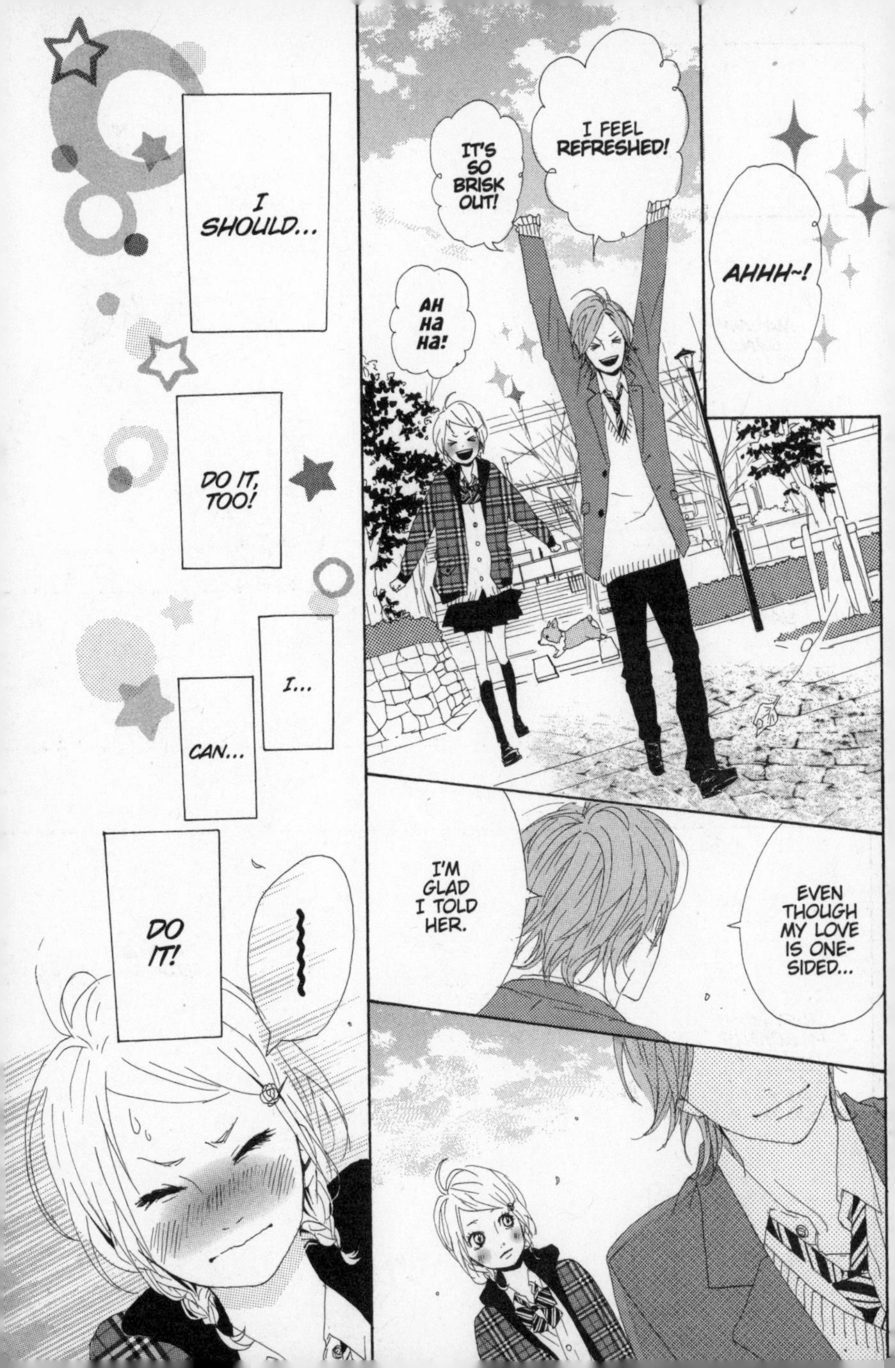
AHHH~!
I FEEL REFRESHED!
IT'S SO BRISK OUT!
AH HA HA!
EVEN THOUGH MY LOVE IS ONE-SIDED...
I'M GLAD I TOLD HER.
I SHOULD...
DO IT, TOO!
I...
CAN...
DO IT!

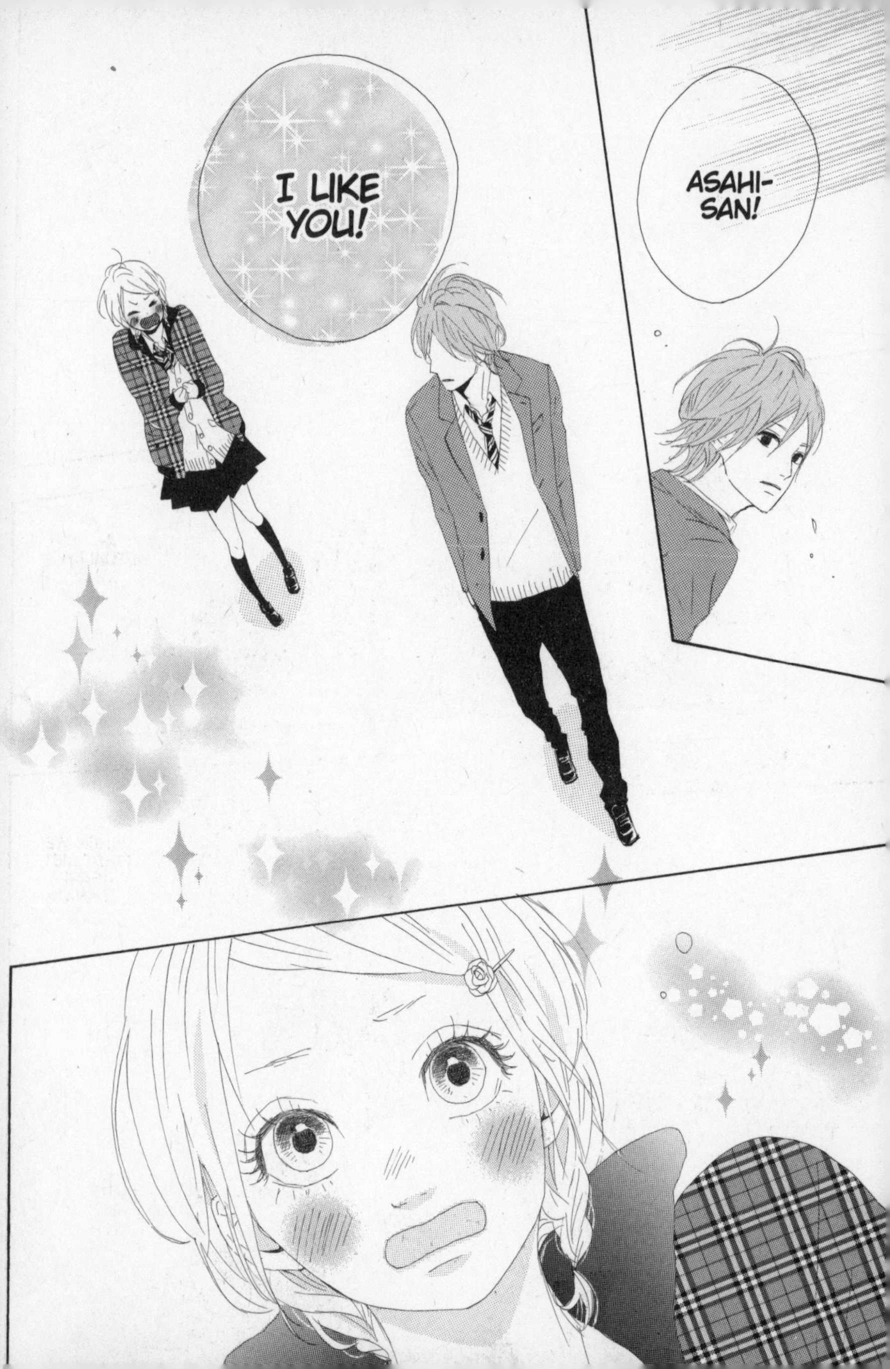
ASAHI-SAN!
I LIKE YOU!

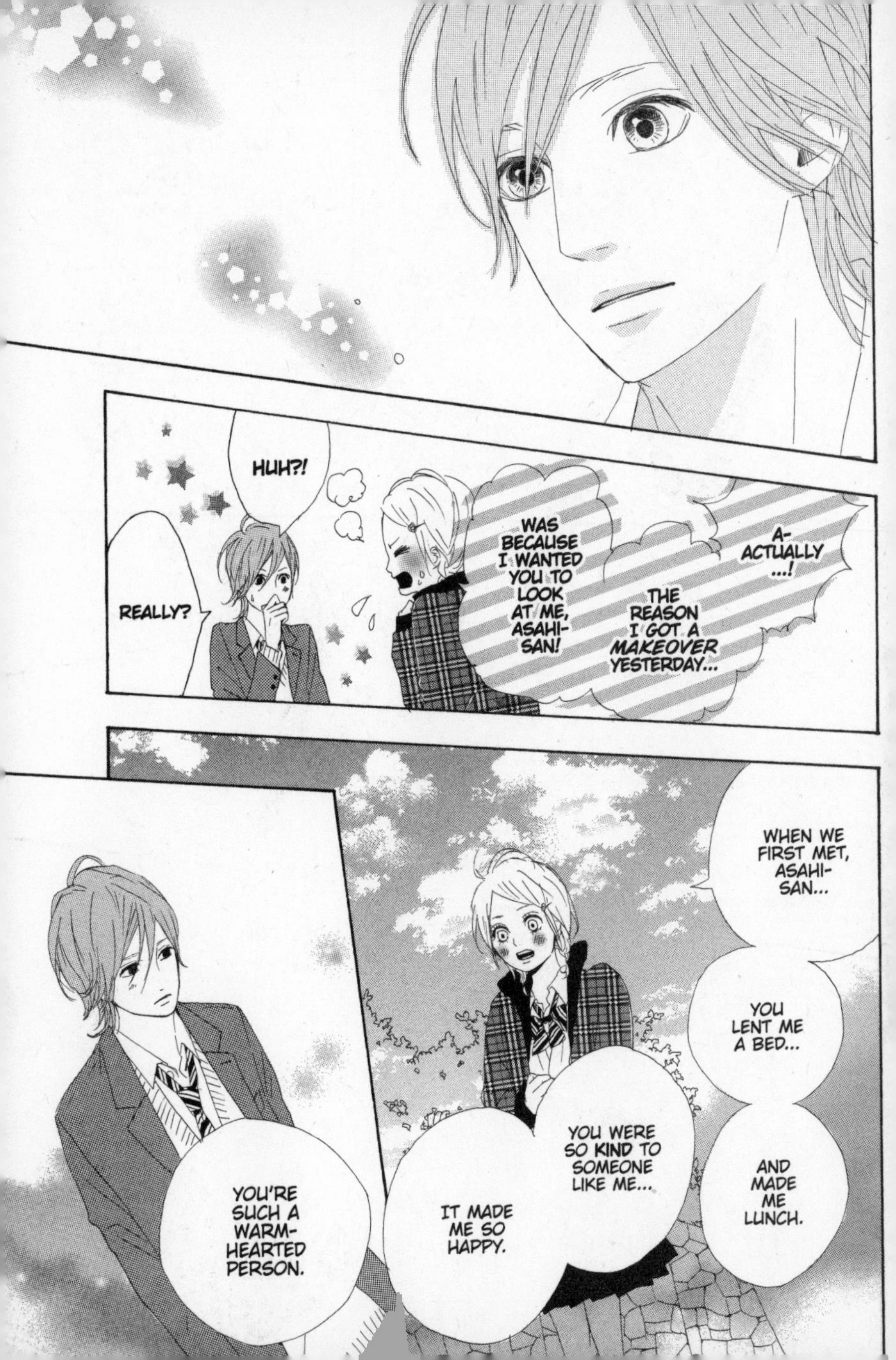
A-ACTUALLY...!
THE REASON I GOT A *MAKEOVER* YESTERDAY...
WAS BECAUSE I WANTED YOU TO LOOK AT ME, ASAHI-SAN!
HUH?!
REALLY?
WHEN WE FIRST MET, ASAHI-SAN...
YOU LENT ME A BED...
AND MADE ME LUNCH.
YOU WERE SO KIND TO SOMEONE LIKE ME...
IT MADE ME SO HAPPY.
YOU'RE SUCH A WARM-HEARTED PERSON.

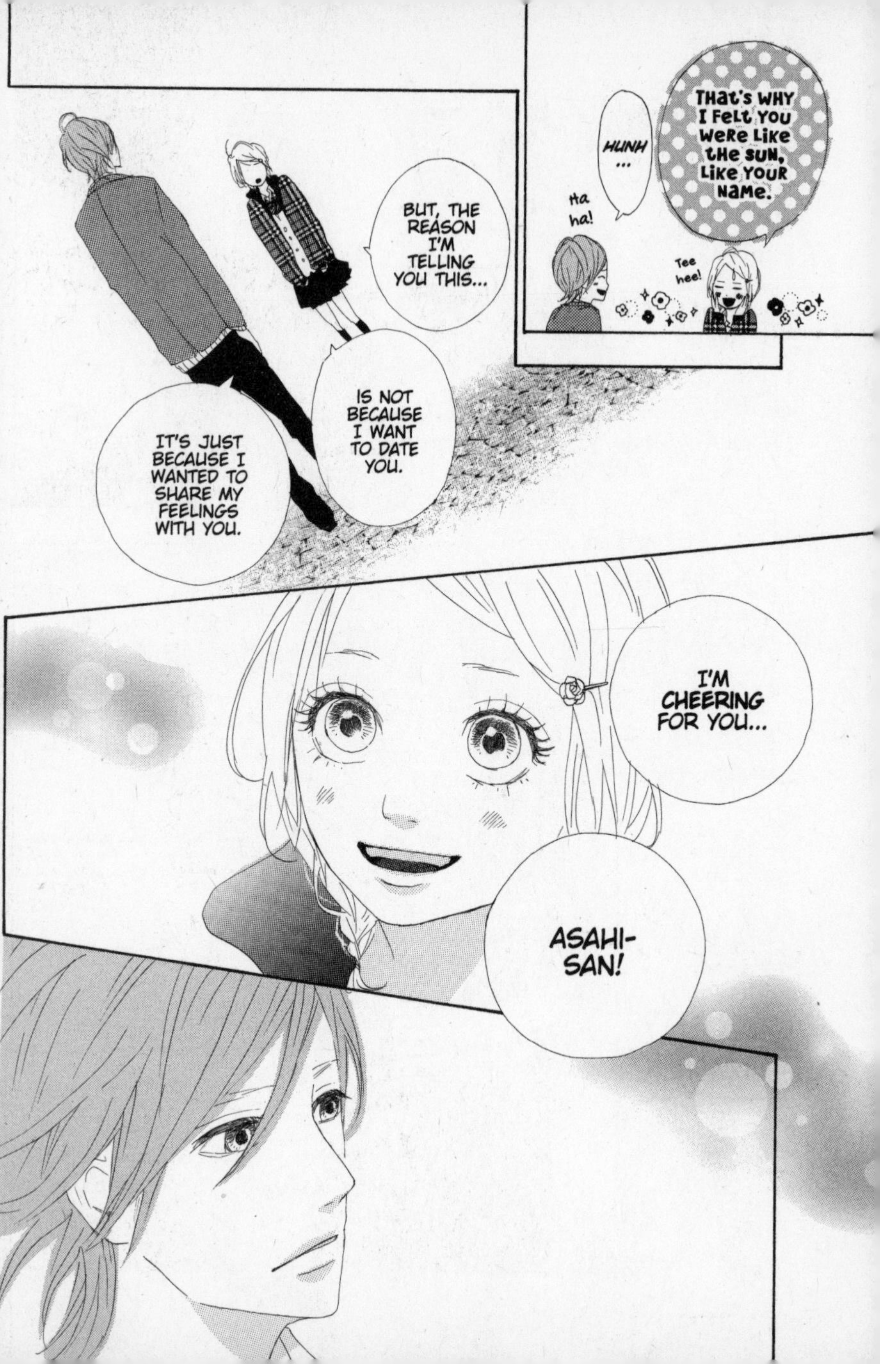
That's why I felt you were like the sun, like your name.
Hunh...
Ha ha!
Tee hee!
But, the reason I'm telling you this...
Is not because I want to date you.
It's just because I wanted to share my feelings with you.
I'm cheering for you...
Asahi-san!

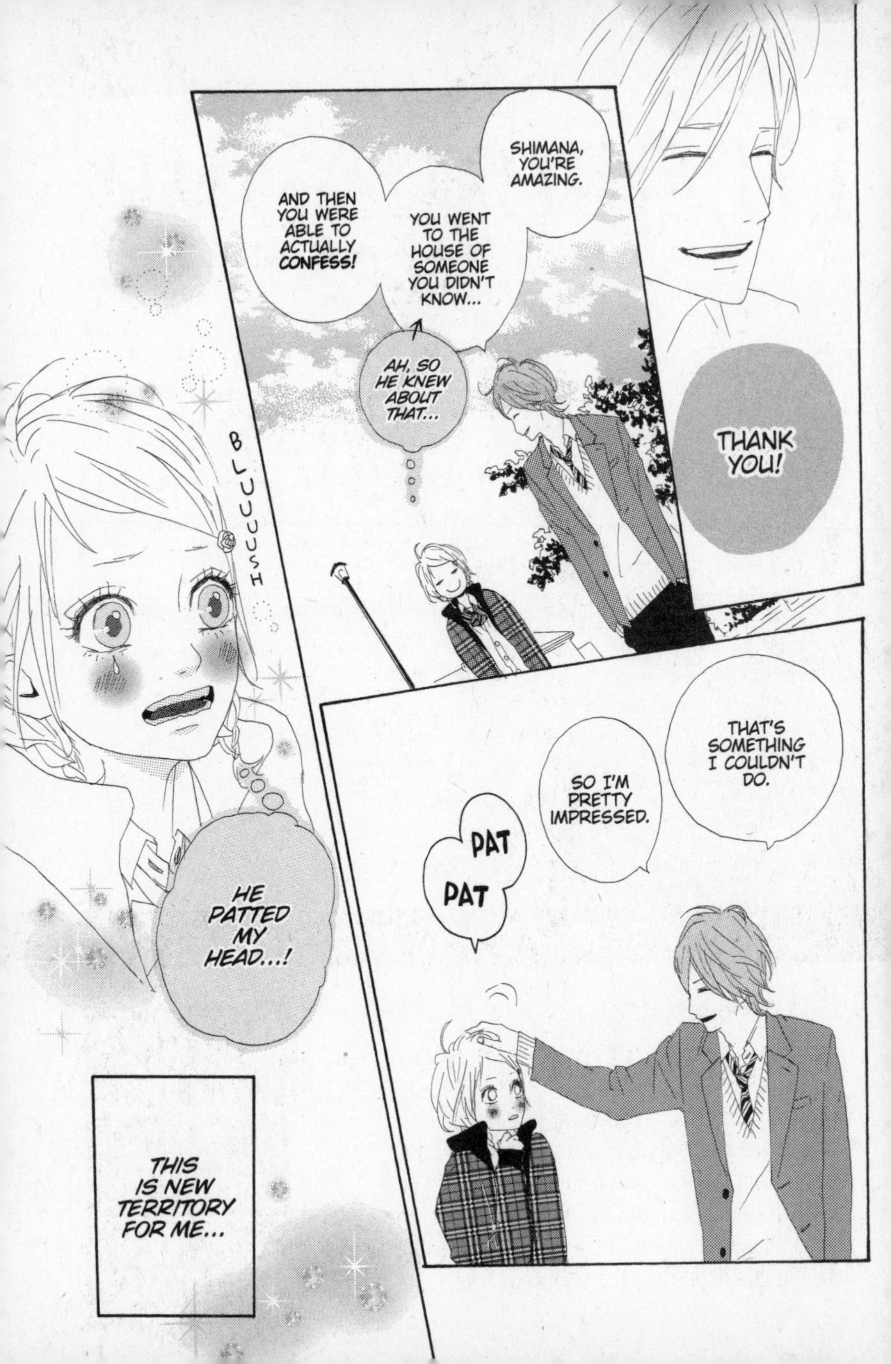
SHIMANA, YOU'RE AMAZING.
YOU WENT TO THE HOUSE OF SOMEONE YOU DIDN'T KNOW...
AND THEN YOU WERE ABLE TO ACTUALLY CONFESS!
AH, SO HE KNEW ABOUT THAT...
THANK YOU!
THAT'S SOMETHING I COULDN'T DO.
SO I'M PRETTY IMPRESSED.
PAT
PAT
BLUUUUSH
HE PATTED MY HEAD...!
THIS IS NEW TERRITORY FOR ME...

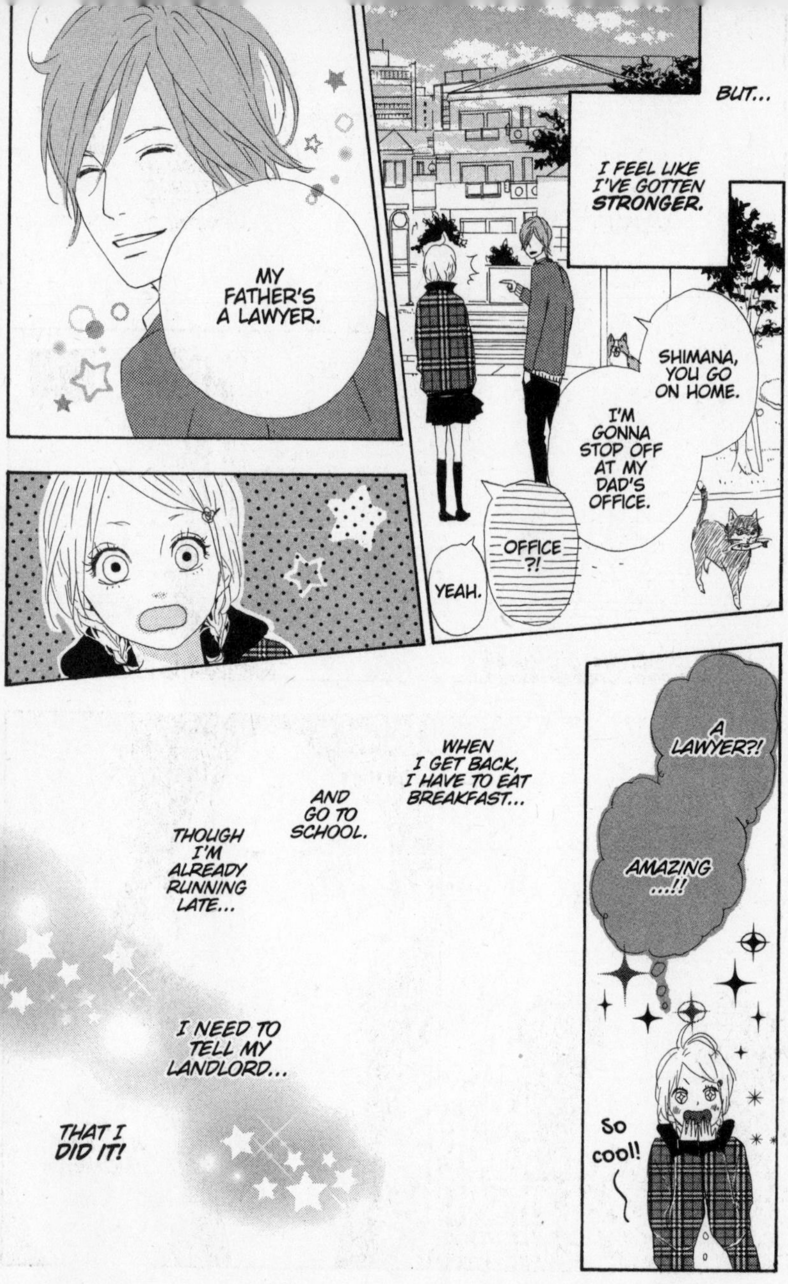
BUT...
I FEEL LIKE I'VE GOTTEN STRONGER.
SHIMANA, YOU GO ON HOME.
I'M GONNA STOP OFF AT MY DAD'S OFFICE.
OFFICE?!
YEAH.
MY FATHER'S A LAWYER.
A LAWYER?!
AMAZING ...!!
So cool!!
WHEN I GET BACK, I HAVE TO EAT BREAKFAST...
AND GO TO SCHOOL.
THOUGH I'M ALREADY RUNNING LATE...
I NEED TO TELL MY LANDLORD...
THAT I DID IT!

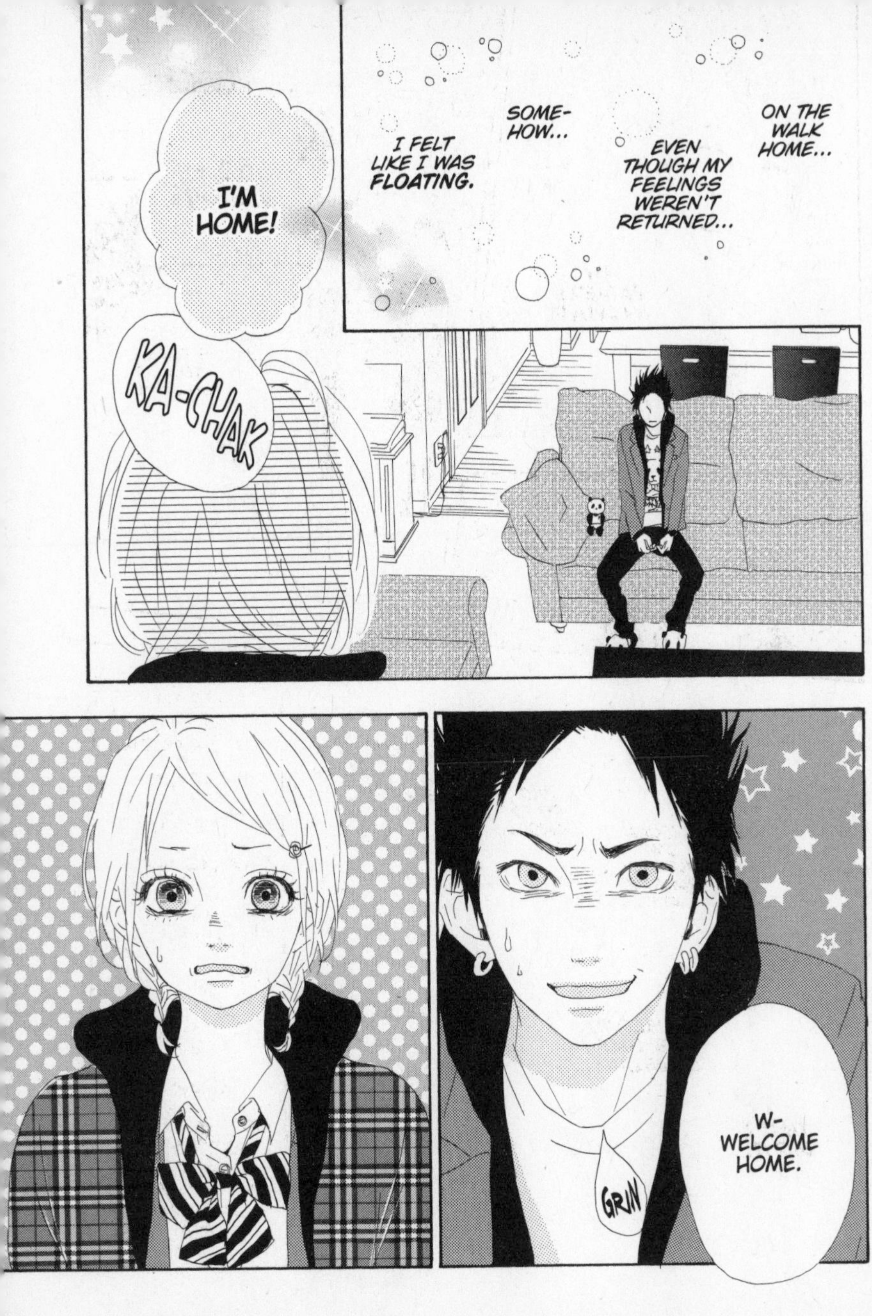
ON THE WALK HOME...
EVEN THOUGH MY FEELINGS WEREN'T RETURNED...
SOME-HOW...
I FELT LIKE I WAS FLOATING.
I'M HOME!
KA-CHAK
GRIN
W-WELCOME HOME.

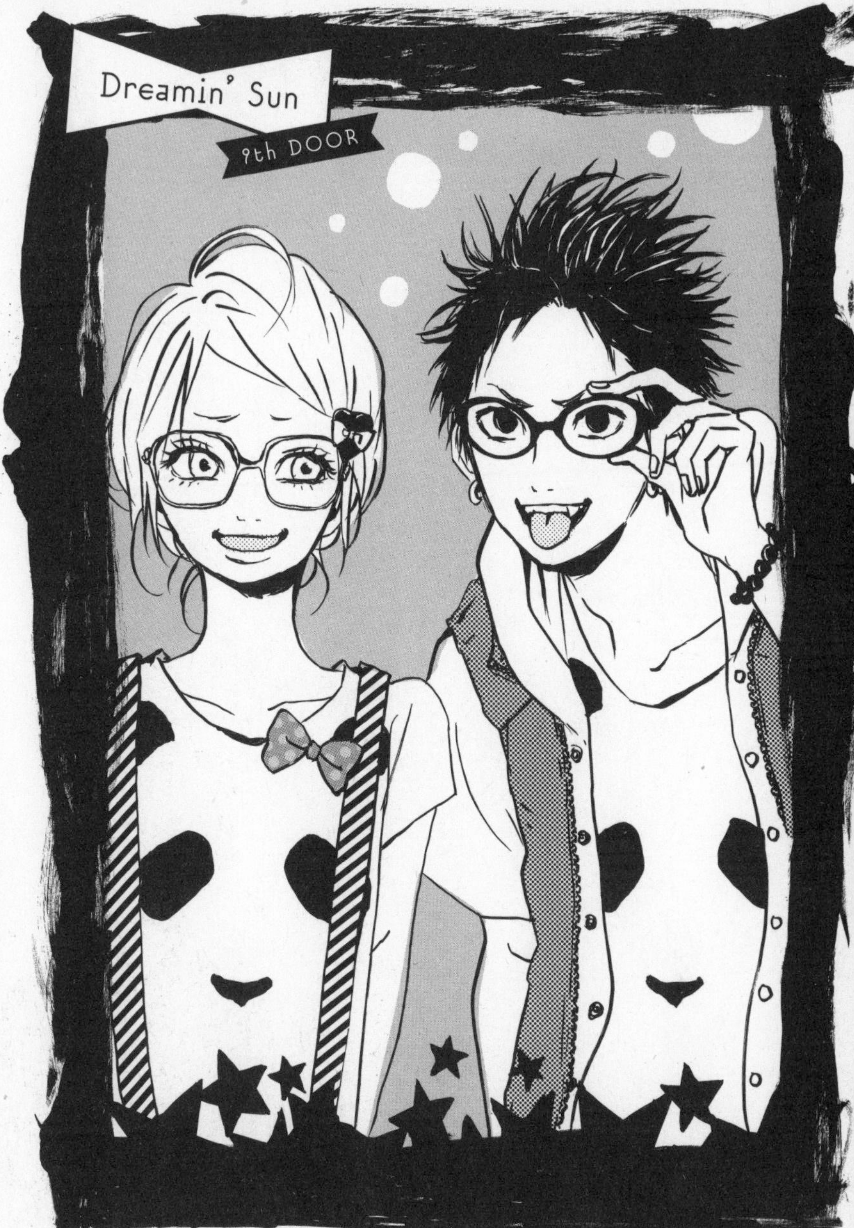
Dreamin' Sun
9th DOOR

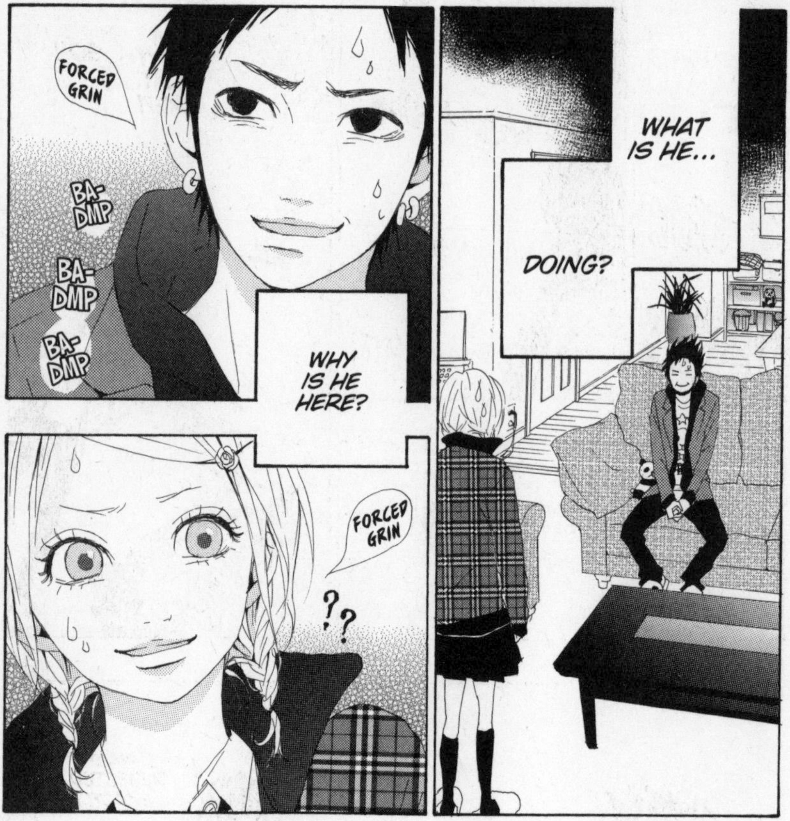
WHAT IS HE...
DOING?
FORCED GRIN
BA-DMP
BA-DMP
BA-DMP
WHY IS HE HERE?
FORCED GRIN
??

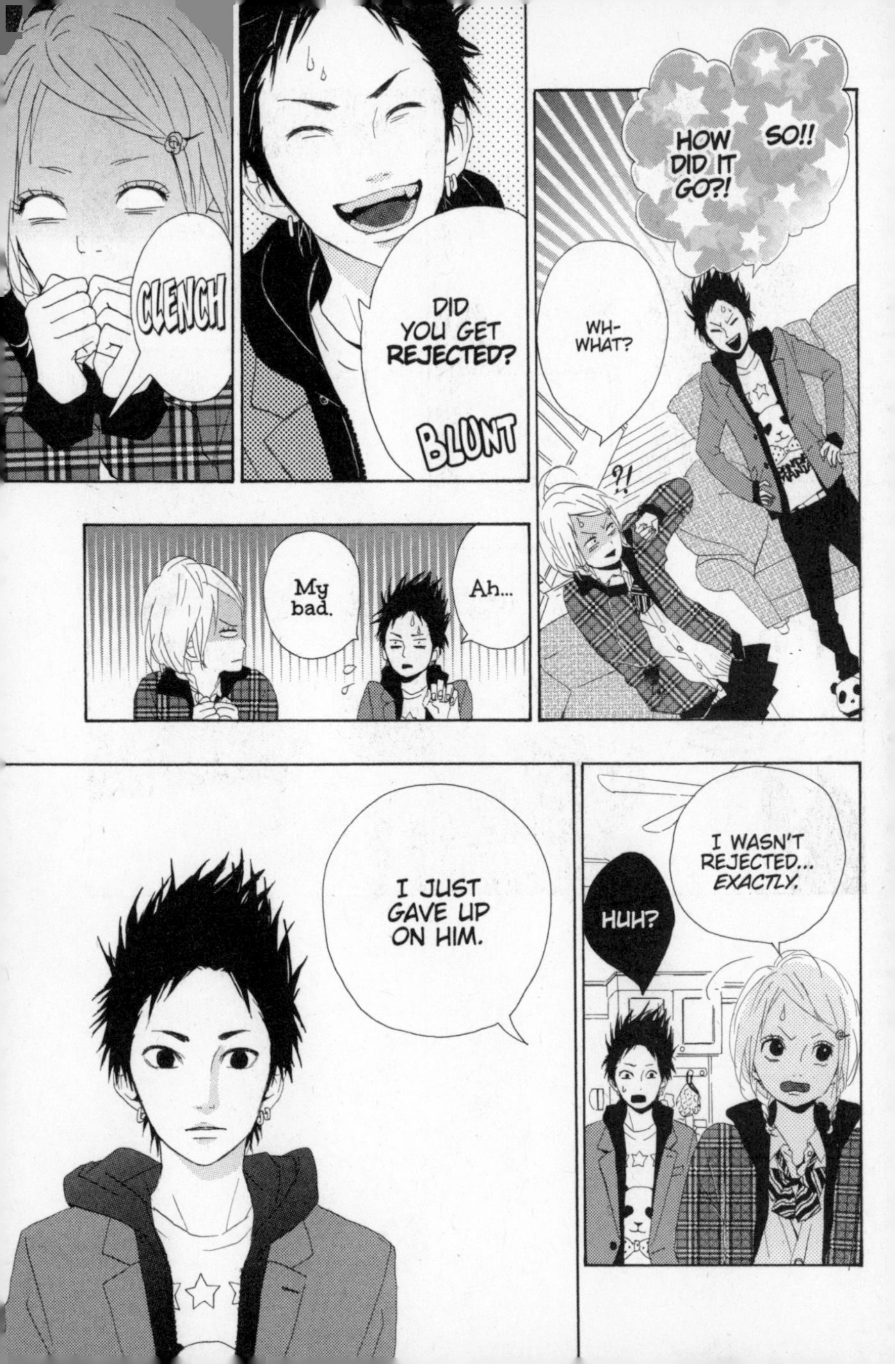
SO!!
HOW DID IT GO?!
WH- WHAT?
?!
DID YOU GET REJECTED?
BLUNT
CLENCH
Ah...
My bad.
I WASN'T REJECTED... *EXACTLY.*
HUH?
I JUST GAVE UP ON HIM.

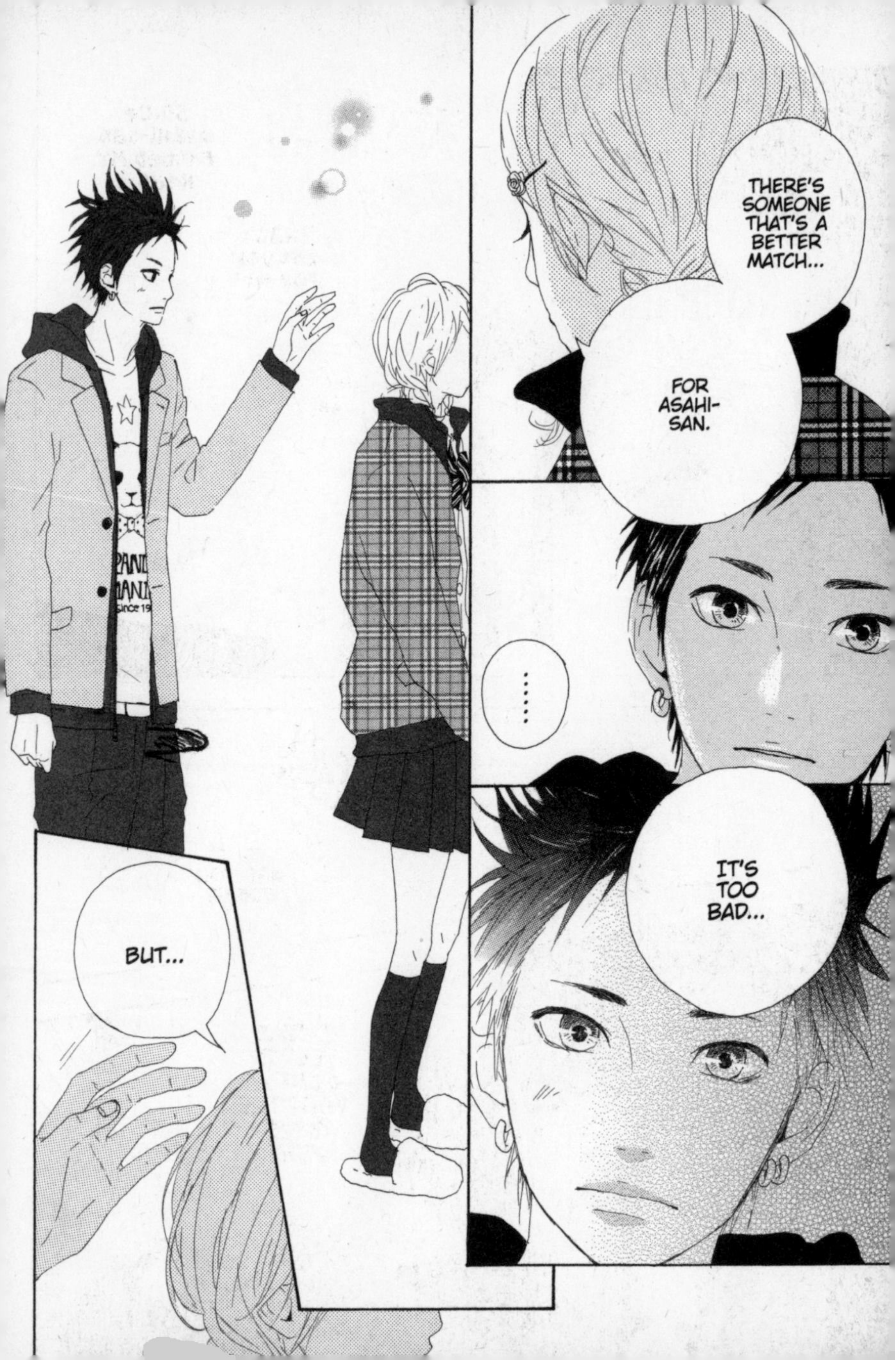
THERE'S SOMEONE THAT'S A BETTER MATCH...
FOR ASAHI-SAN.
......
IT'S TOO BAD...
BUT...

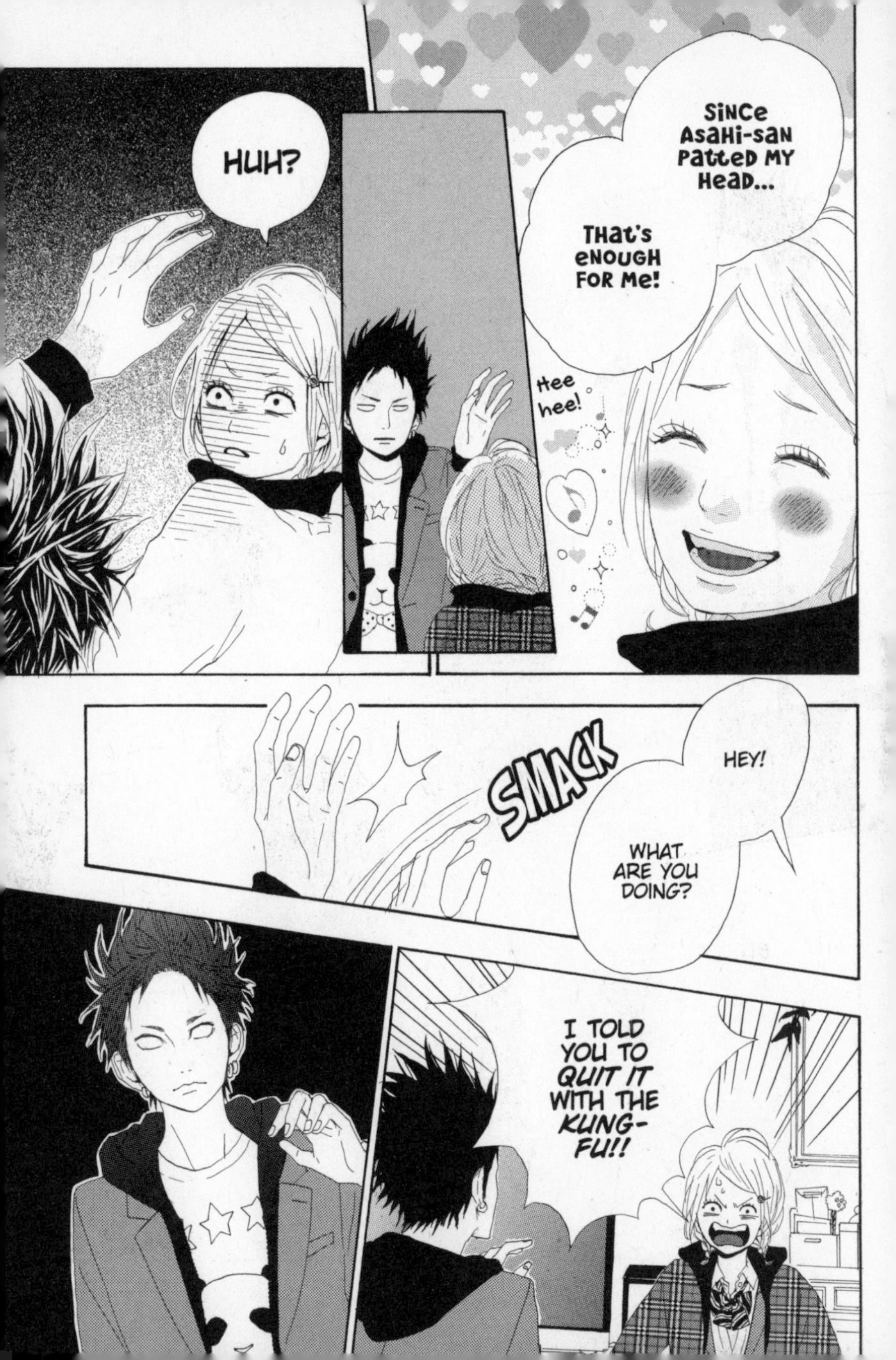
Since Asahi-san patted my head...
That's enough for me!
Hee hee!
HUH?
HEY! WHAT ARE YOU DOING?
SMACK
I TOLD YOU TO QUIT IT WITH THE KUNG-FU!!

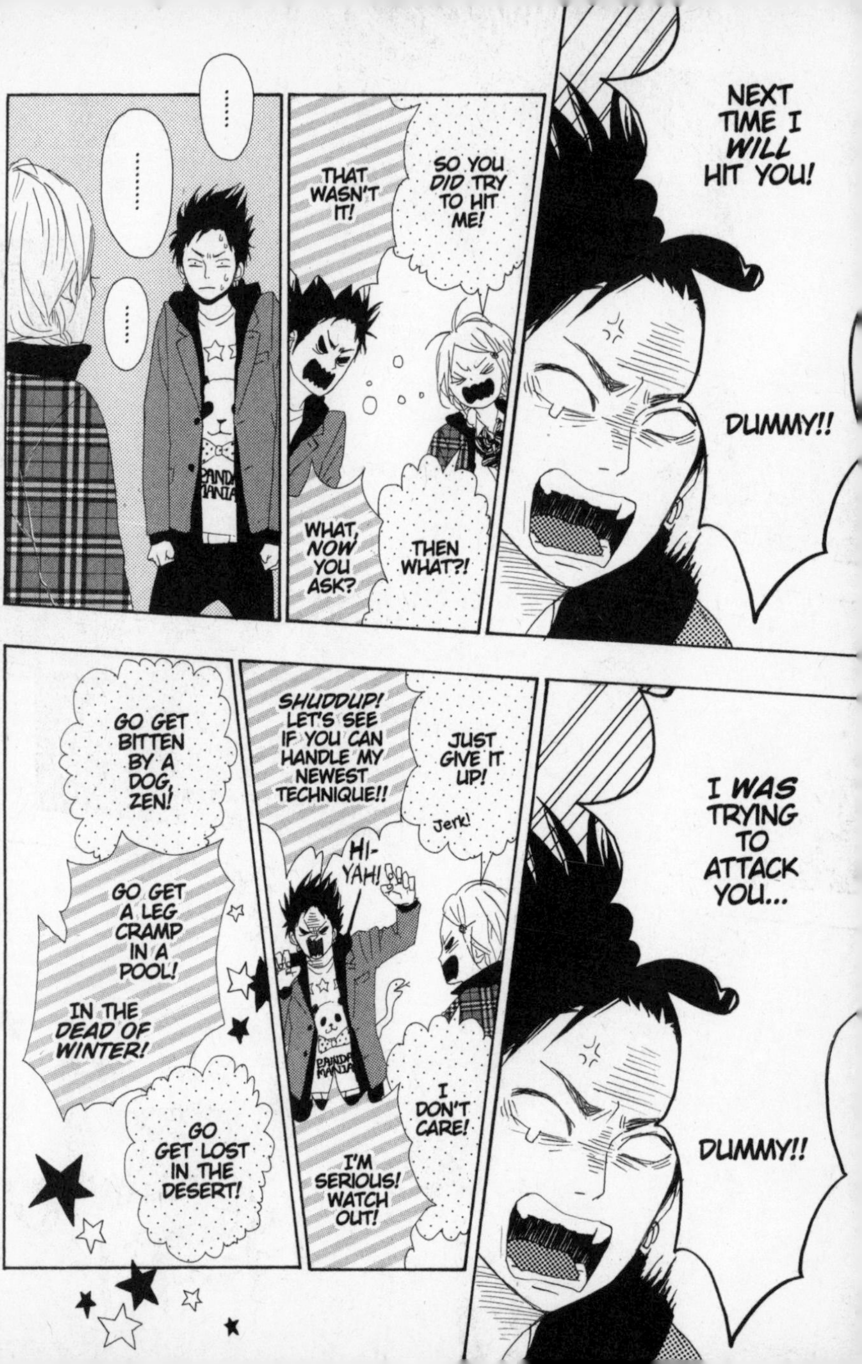
NEXT TIME I *WILL* HIT YOU!
DUMMY!!
SO YOU *DID* TRY TO HIT ME!
THAT WASN'T IT!
THEN WHAT?!
WHAT, *NOW* YOU ASK?
......
......
......
I *WAS* TRYING TO ATTACK YOU...
DUMMY!!
JUST GIVE IT UP!
SHUDDUP! LET'S SEE IF YOU CAN HANDLE MY NEWEST TECHNIQUE!!
Jerk!
HI-YAH!
I DON'T CARE!
I'M SERIOUS! WATCH OUT!
GO GET BITTEN BY A DOG, ZEN!
GO GET A LEG CRAMP IN A POOL!
IN THE *DEAD OF WINTER!*
GO GET LOST IN THE DESERT!

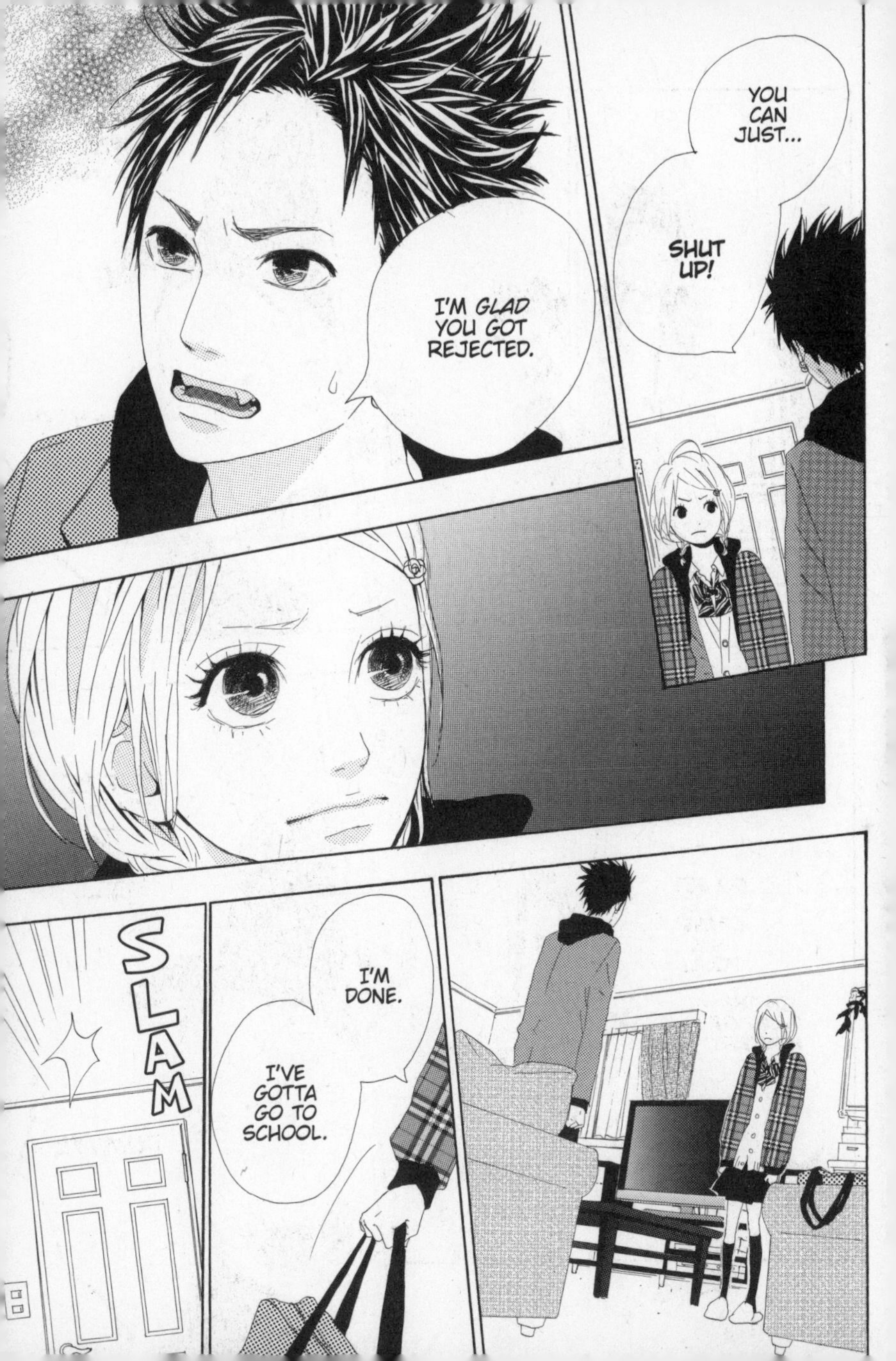
YOU CAN JUST...
SHUT UP!
I'M GLAD YOU GOT REJECTED.
I'M DONE.
I'VE GOTTA GO TO SCHOOL.
SLAM

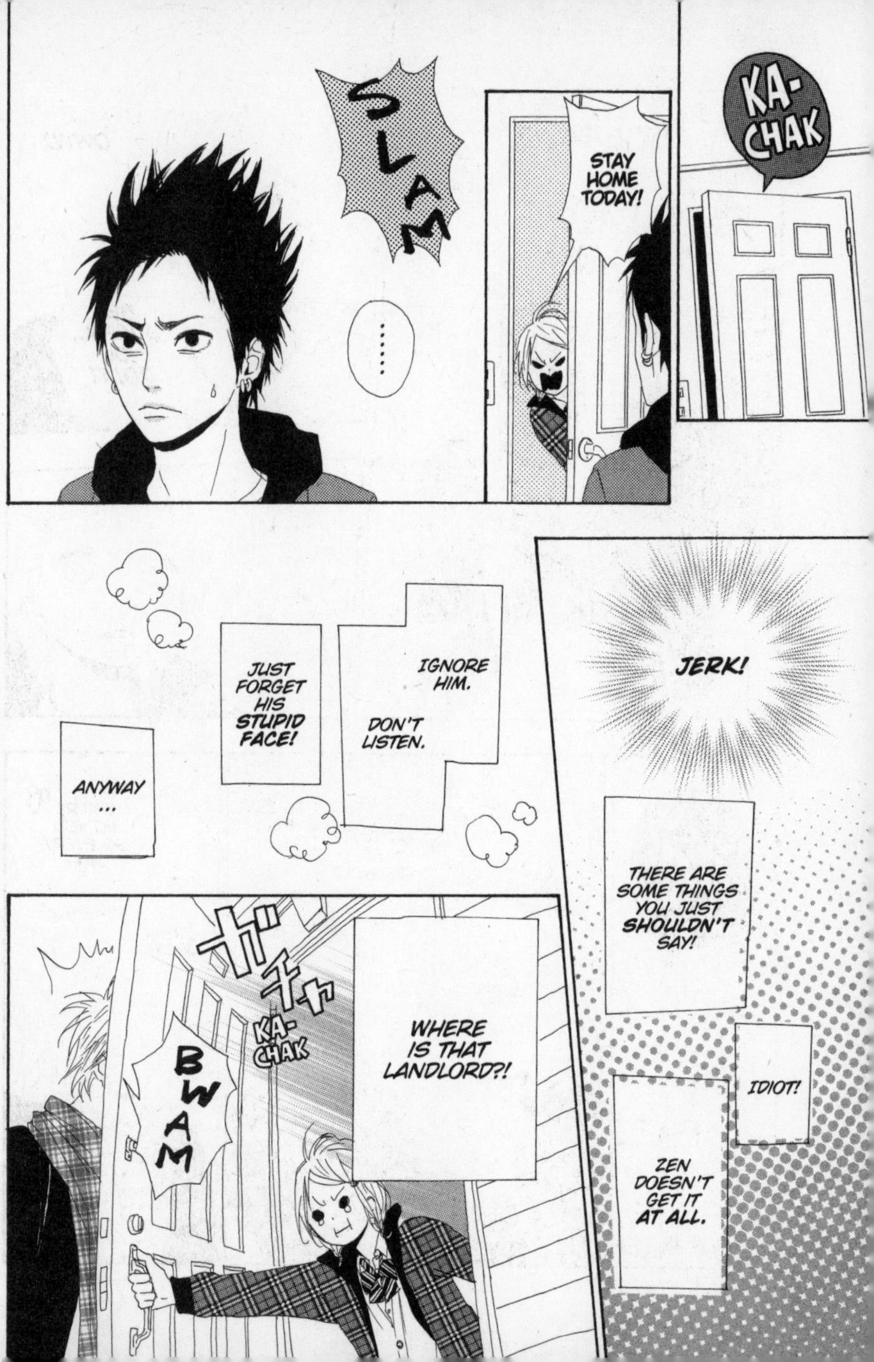
KA-CHAK
STAY HOME TODAY!
SLAM
......
JERK!
THERE ARE SOME THINGS YOU JUST SHOULDN'T SAY!
IDIOT!
ZEN DOESN'T GET IT AT ALL.
IGNORE HIM.
DON'T LISTEN.
JUST FORGET HIS STUPID FACE!
ANYWAY ...
ガチャ
KA-CHAK
BWAM
WHERE IS THAT LANDLORD?!

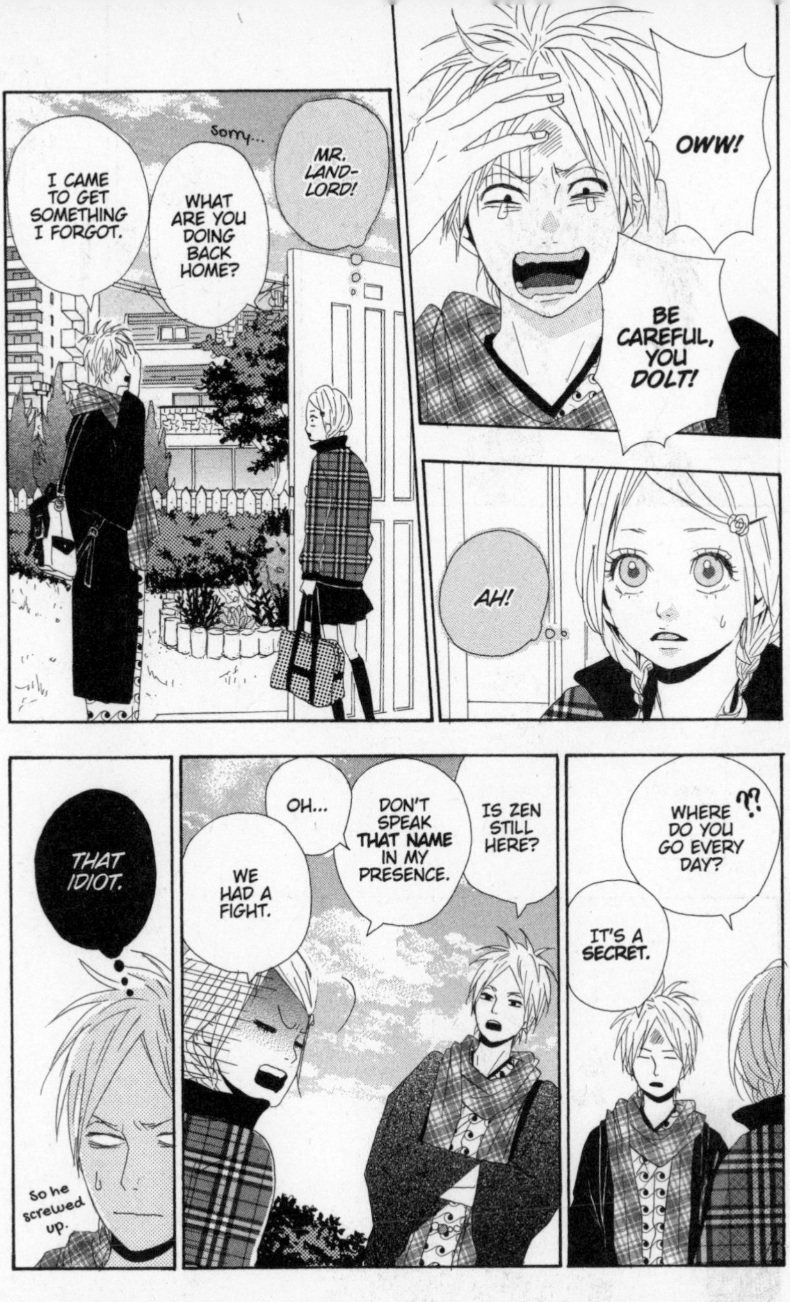
OWW!
BE CAREFUL, YOU DOLT!
AH!
MR. LAND-LORD!
WHAT ARE YOU DOING BACK HOME?
Sorry...
I CAME TO GET SOMETHING I FORGOT.
WHERE DO YOU GO EVERY DAY?
??
IT'S A SECRET.
IS ZEN STILL HERE?
DON'T SPEAK THAT NAME IN MY PRESENCE.
OH...
WE HAD A FIGHT.
THAT IDIOT.
So he screwed up.

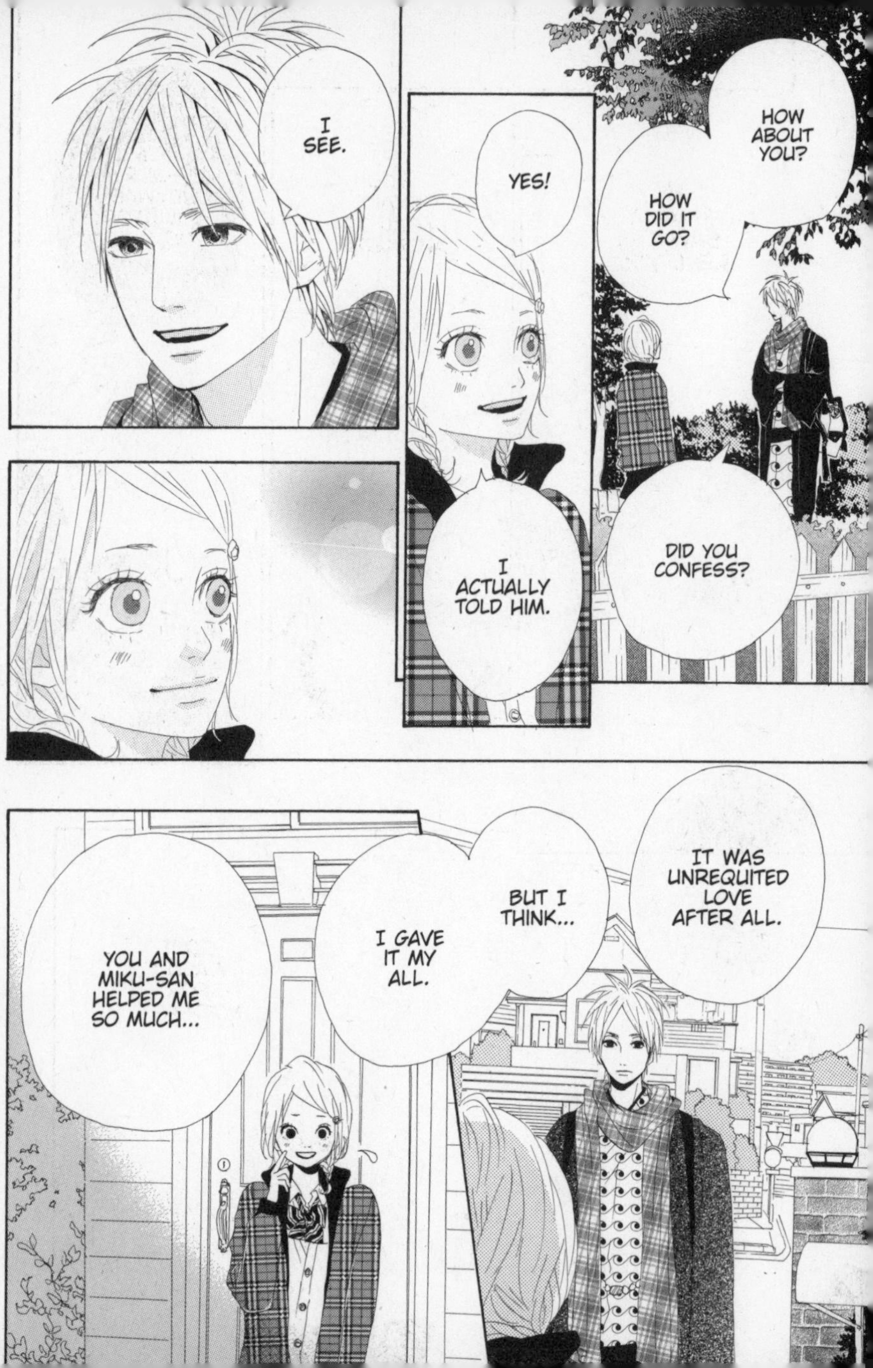
HOW ABOUT YOU?
HOW DID IT GO?
DID YOU CONFESS?
YES!
I ACTUALLY TOLD HIM.
I SEE.
IT WAS UNREQUITED LOVE AFTER ALL.
BUT I THINK...
I GAVE IT MY ALL.
YOU AND MIKU-SAN HELPED ME SO MUCH...

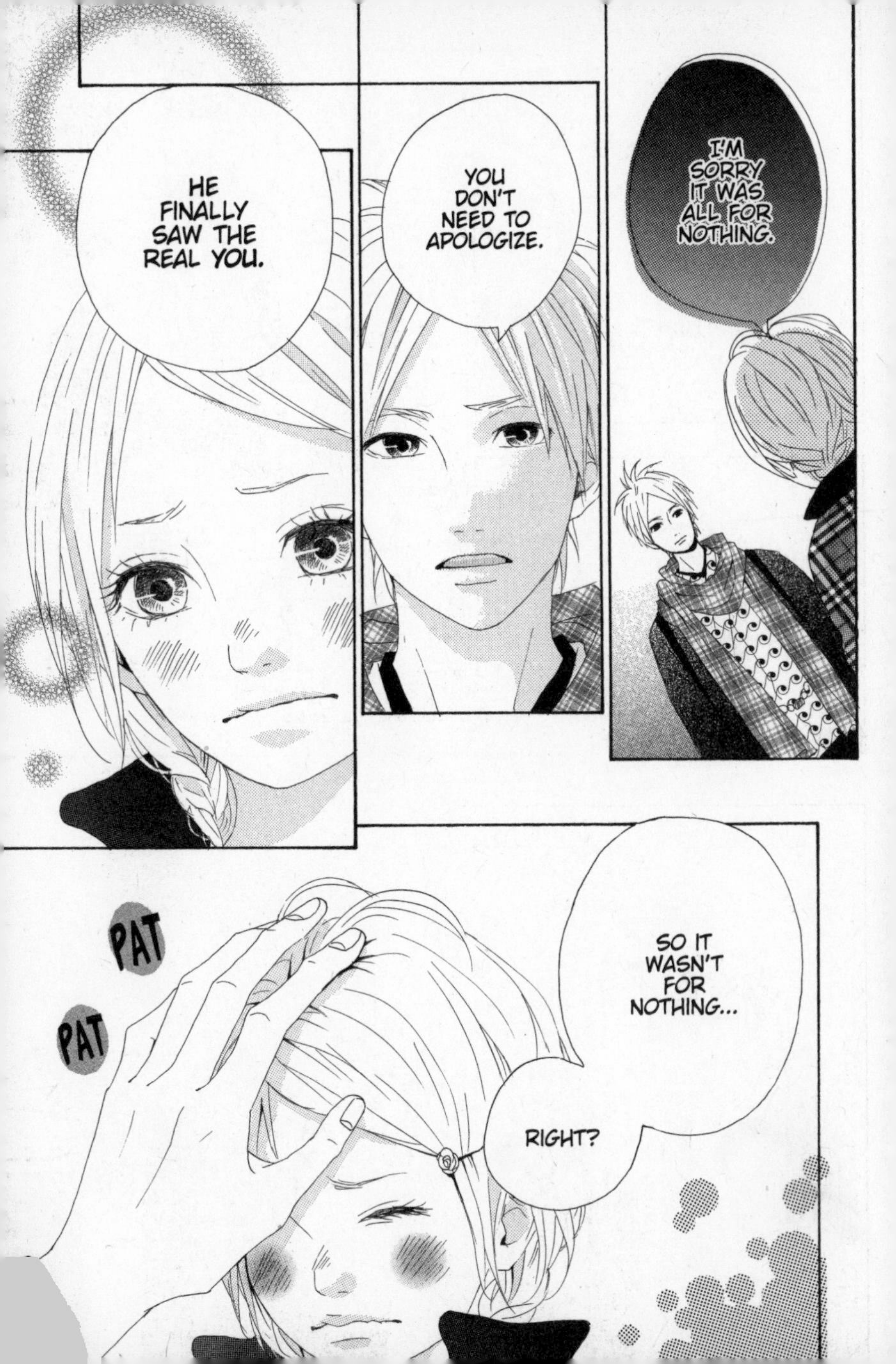
I'M SORRY IT WAS ALL FOR NOTHING.
YOU DON'T NEED TO APOLOGIZE.
HE FINALLY SAW THE REAL YOU.
SO IT WASN'T FOR NOTHING...
RIGHT?
PAT
PAT

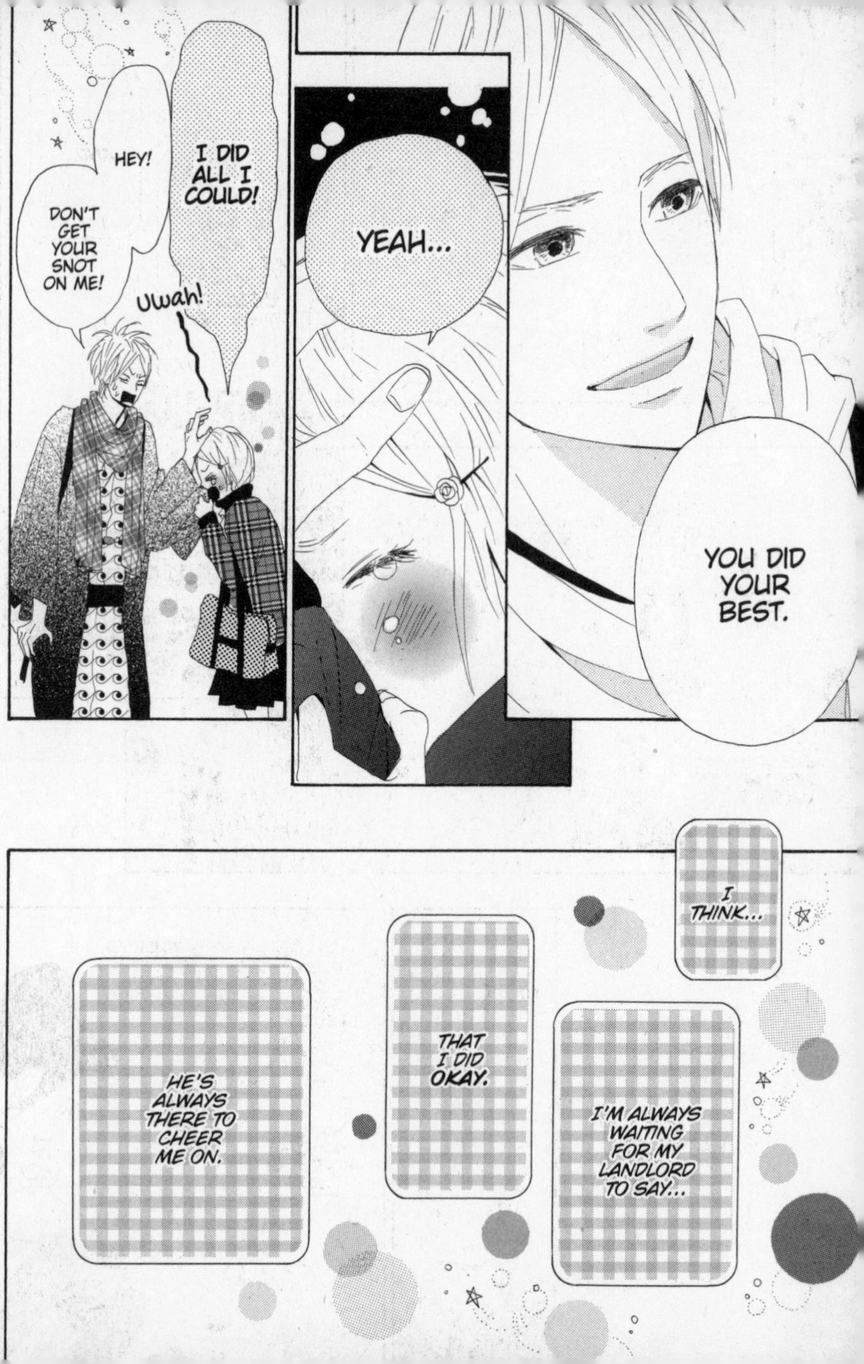
YOU DID YOUR BEST.
YEAH...
I DID ALL I COULD!
HEY!
DON'T GET YOUR SNOT ON ME!
Uwah!
I THINK...
I'M ALWAYS WAITING FOR MY LANDLORD TO SAY...
THAT I DID OKAY.
HE'S ALWAYS THERE TO CHEER ME ON.

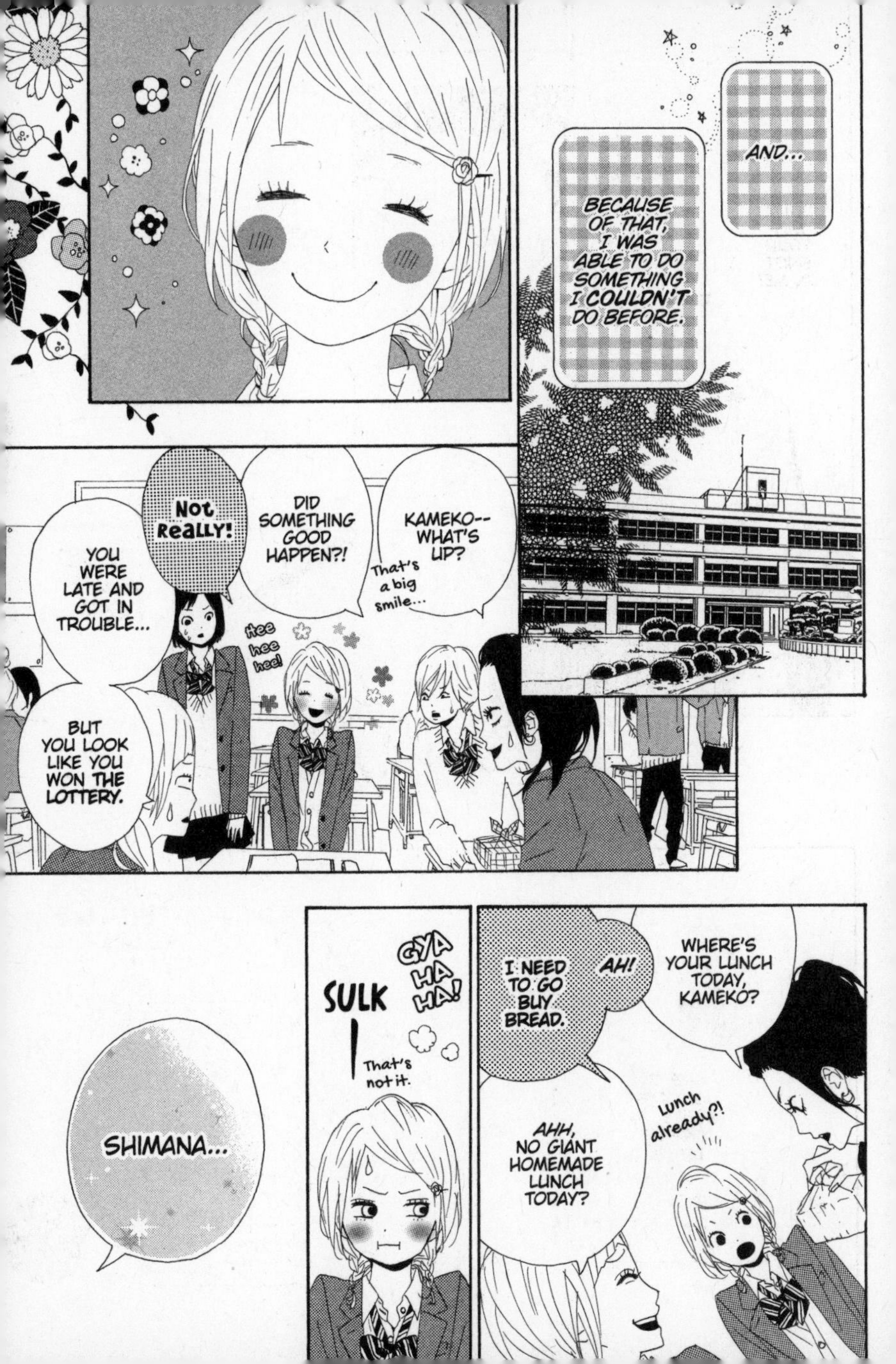
AND...
BECAUSE OF THAT, I WAS ABLE TO DO SOMETHING I COULDN'T DO BEFORE.
KAMEKO-- WHAT'S UP?
That's a big smile...
DID SOMETHING GOOD HAPPEN?!
Not Really!
Hee hee hee!
YOU WERE LATE AND GOT IN TROUBLE...
BUT YOU LOOK LIKE YOU WON THE LOTTERY.
WHERE'S YOUR LUNCH TODAY, KAMEKO?
AH!
I NEED TO GO BUY BREAD.
Lunch already?!
AHH, NO GIANT HOMEMADE LUNCH TODAY?
GYA HA HA!
SULK
That's not it.
SHIMANA...

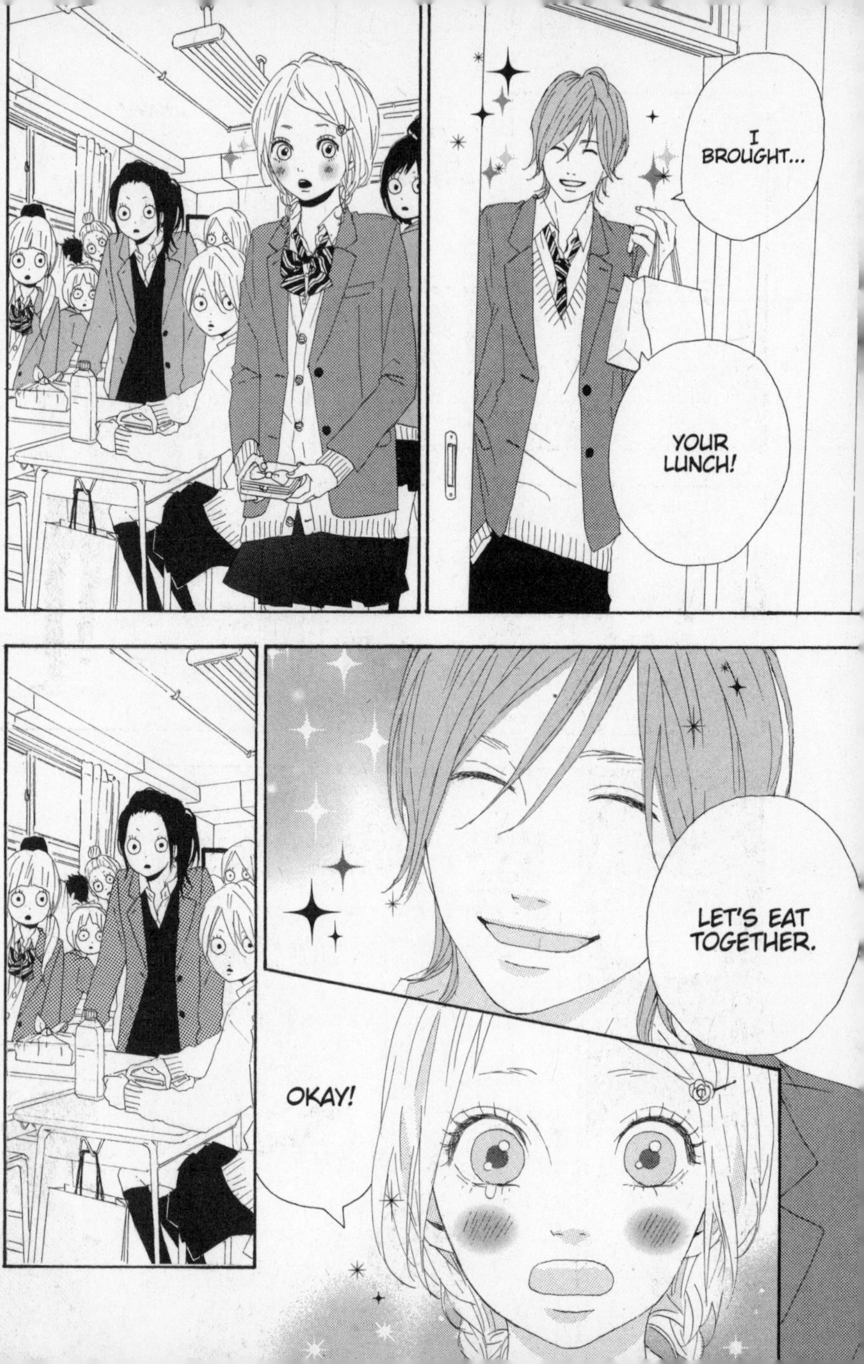
I BROUGHT...
YOUR LUNCH!
LET'S EAT TOGETHER.
OKAY!

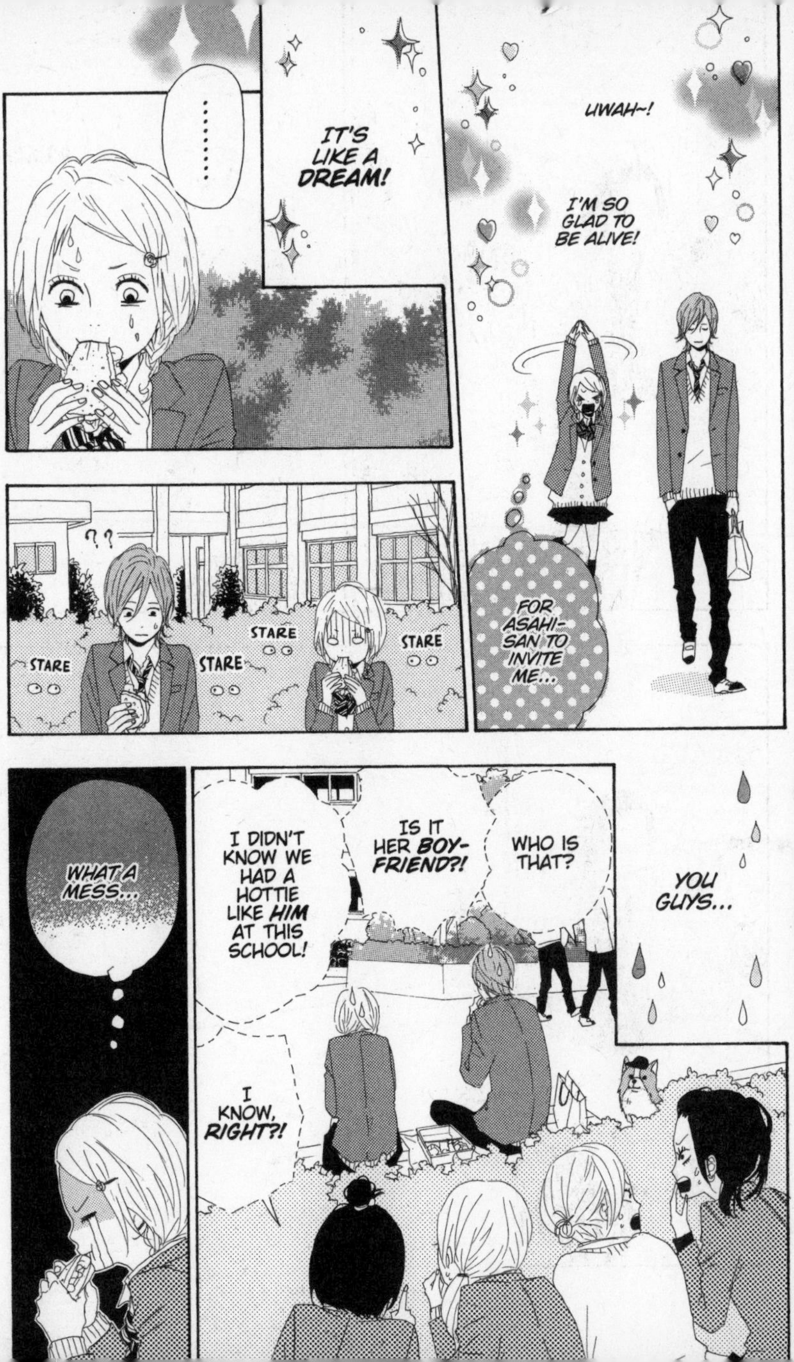
UWAH~!
I'M SO GLAD TO BE ALIVE!
FOR ASAHI-SAN TO INVITE ME...
IT'S LIKE A DREAM!
......
??
STARE
STARE
STARE
STARE
YOU GUYS...
WHO IS THAT?
IS IT HER BOY-FRIEND?!
I DIDN'T KNOW WE HAD A HOTTIE LIKE HIM AT THIS SCHOOL!
I KNOW, RIGHT?!
WHAT A MESS...

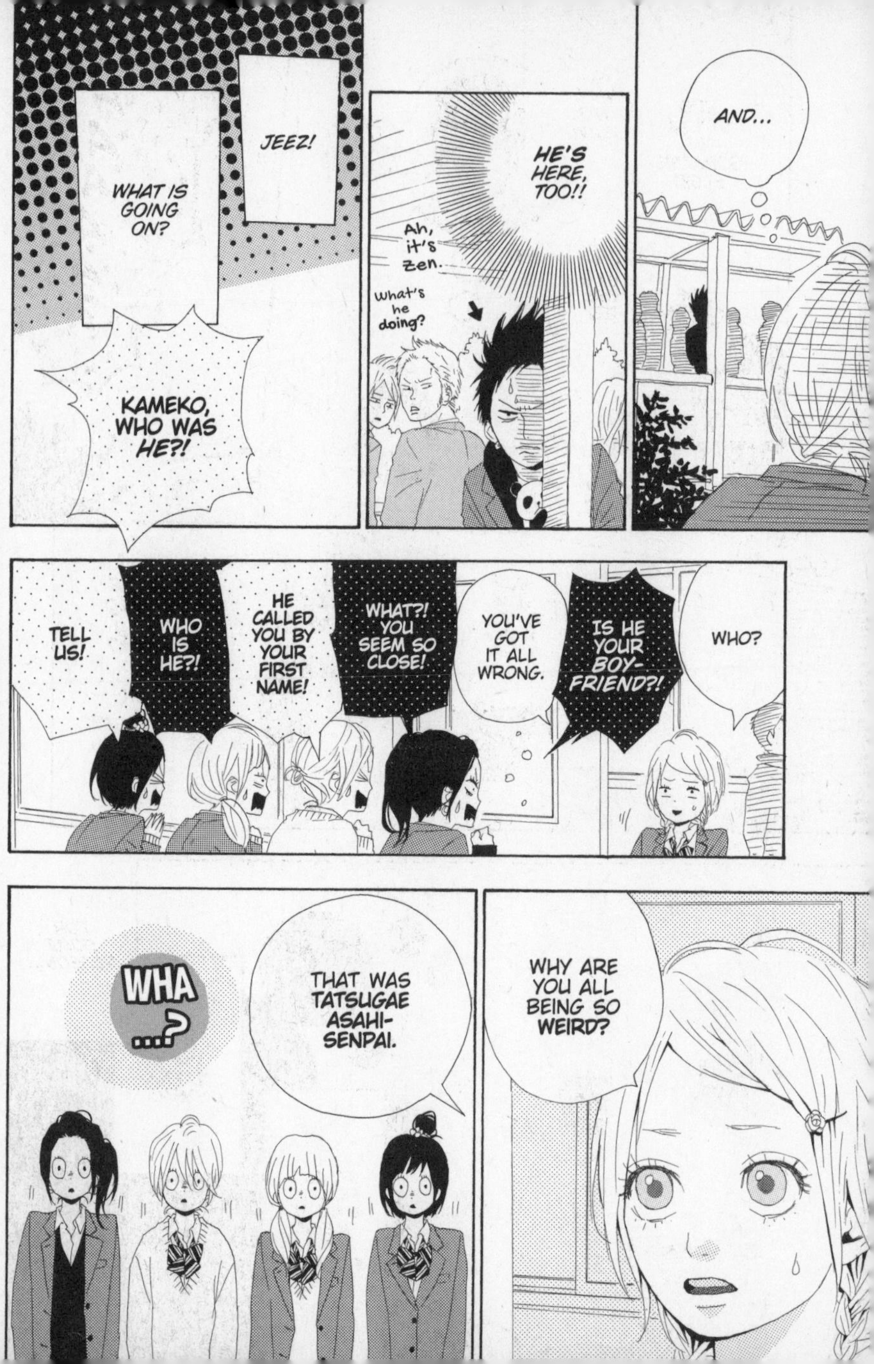
AND...
HE'S HERE, TOO!!
Ah, it's Zen.
What's he doing?
JEEZ!
WHAT IS GOING ON?
KAMEKO, WHO WAS HE?!
WHO?
IS HE YOUR BOY-FRIEND?!
YOU'VE GOT IT ALL WRONG.
WHAT?! YOU SEEM SO CLOSE!
HE CALLED YOU BY YOUR FIRST NAME!
WHO IS HE?!
TELL US!
WHY ARE YOU ALL BEING SO WEIRD?
THAT WAS TATSUGAE ASAHI-SENPAI.
WHA ...?

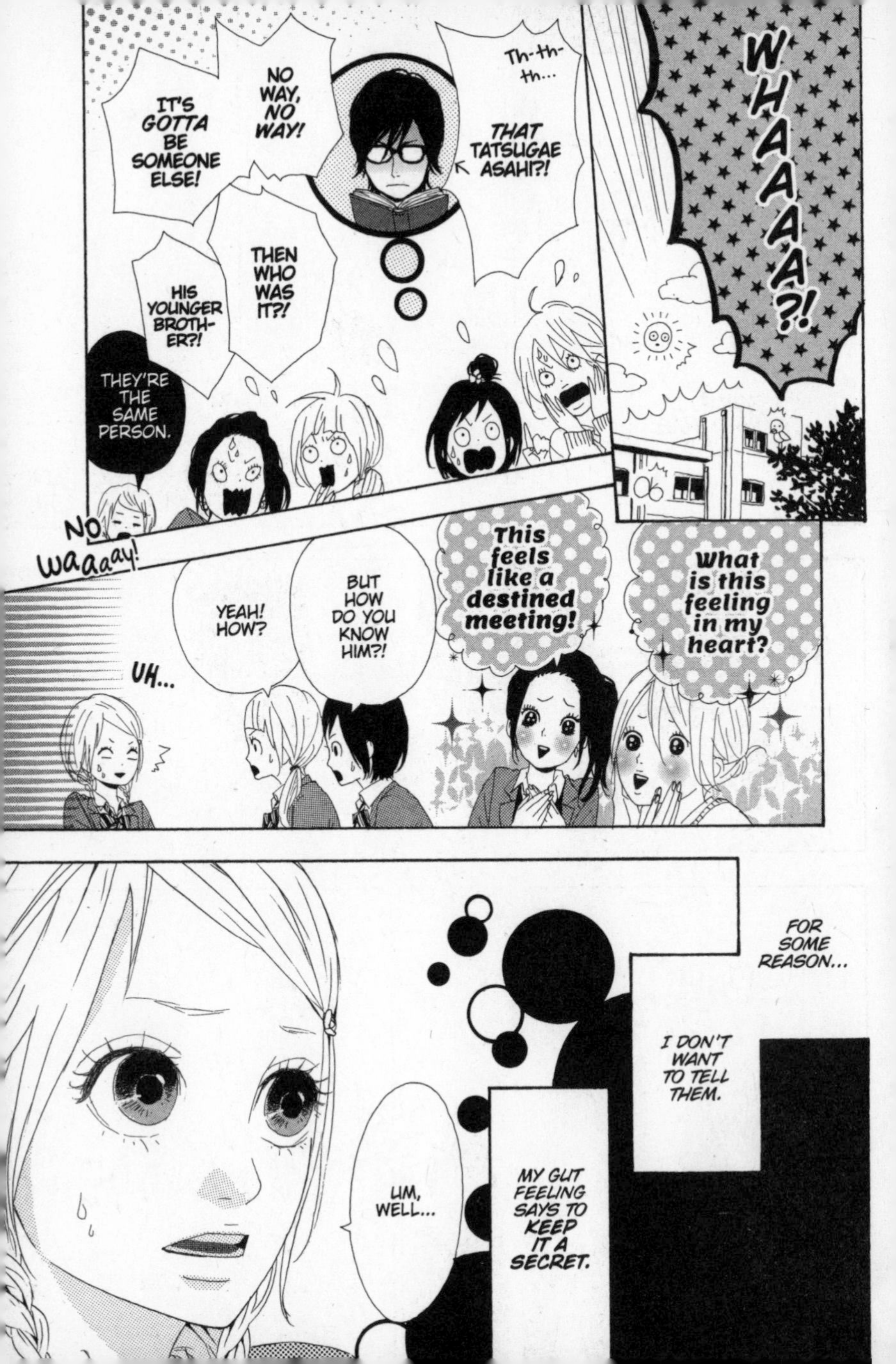
WHAAAAA?!
Th-th-th...
THAT TATSUGAE ASAHI?!
NO WAY, NO WAY!
IT'S GOTTA BE SOMEONE ELSE!
THEN WHO WAS IT?!
HIS YOUNGER BROTHER?!
THEY'RE THE SAME PERSON.
NO waaaay!
What is this feeling in my heart?
This feels like a destined meeting!
BUT HOW DO YOU KNOW HIM?!
YEAH! HOW?
UH...
FOR SOME REASON...
I DON'T WANT TO TELL THEM.
MY GUT FEELING SAYS TO KEEP IT A SECRET.
UM, WELL...

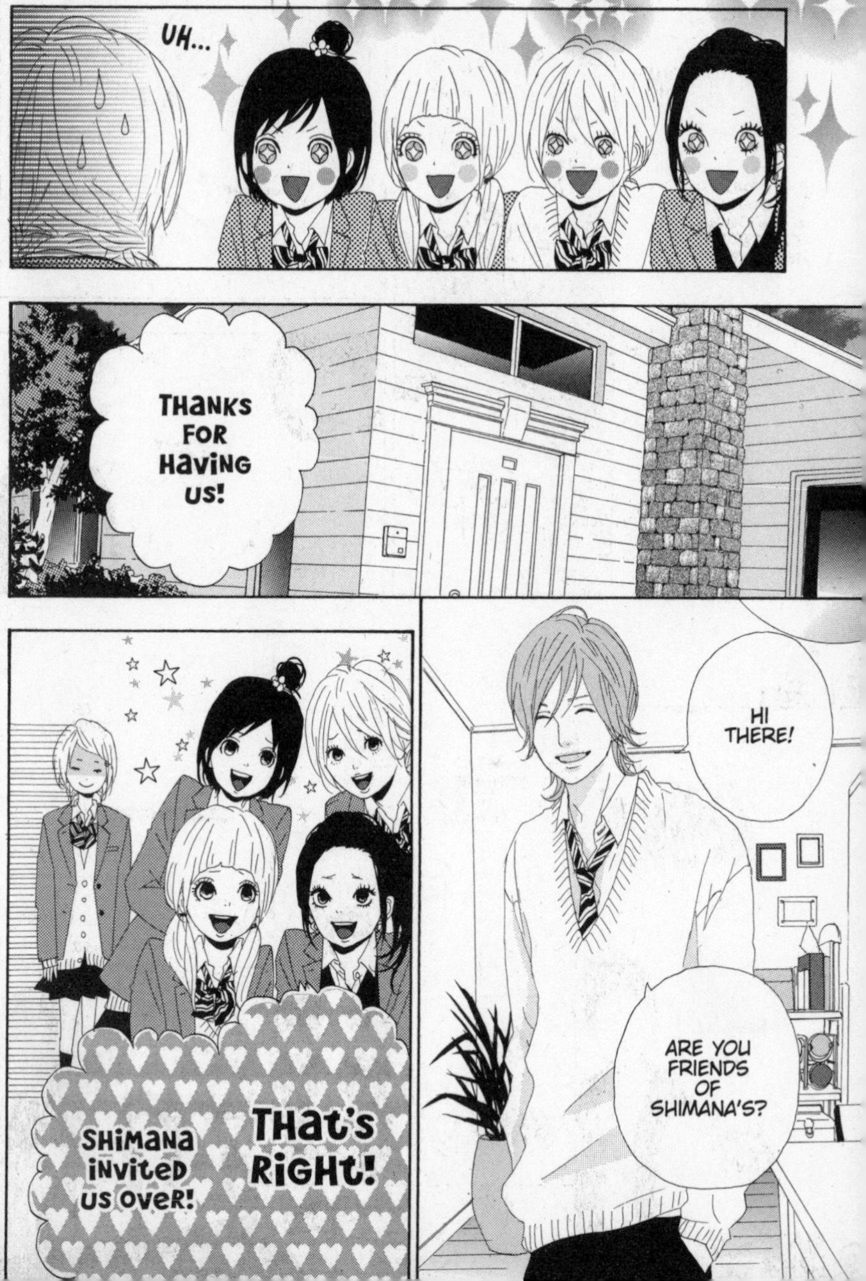
UH...
THANKS FOR HAVING US!
HI THERE!
ARE YOU FRIENDS OF SHIMANA'S?
THAT'S RIGHT!
SHIMANA INVITED US OVER!

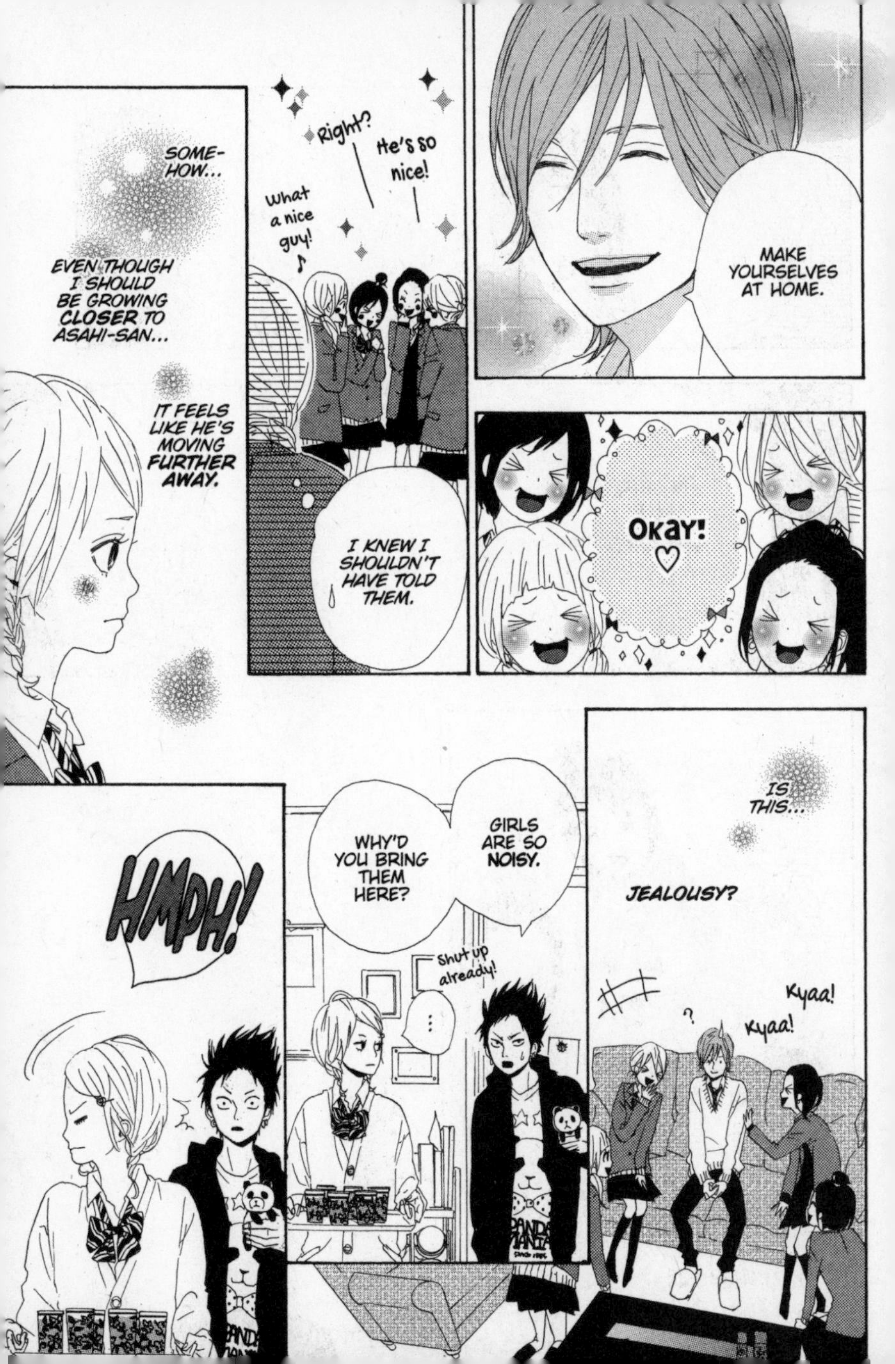
MAKE YOURSELVES AT HOME.
OKAY! ♡
He's so nice!
Right?
What a nice guy! ♪
I KNEW I SHOULDN'T HAVE TOLD THEM.
SOME-HOW...
EVEN THOUGH I SHOULD BE GROWING CLOSER TO ASAHI-SAN...
IT FEELS LIKE HE'S MOVING FURTHER AWAY.
IS THIS...
JEALOUSY?
Kyaa!
Kyaa!
?
GIRLS ARE SO NOISY.
WHY'D YOU BRING THEM HERE?
Shut up already!
...
HMPH!

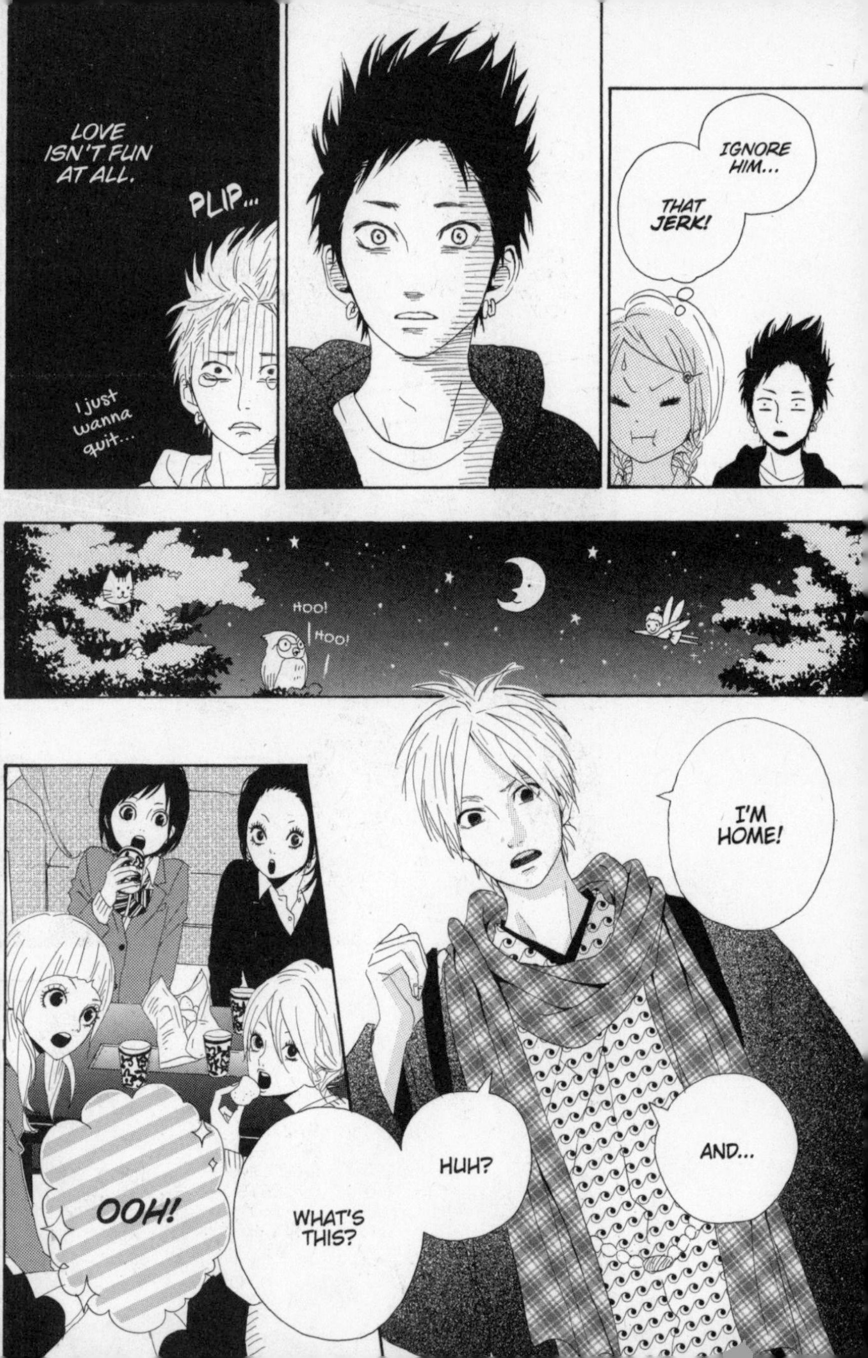
IGNORE HIM...
THAT JERK!
LOVE ISN'T FUN AT ALL.
PLIP...
I just wanna quit...
HOO!
HOO!
I'M HOME!
AND...
HUH?
WHAT'S THIS?
OOH!

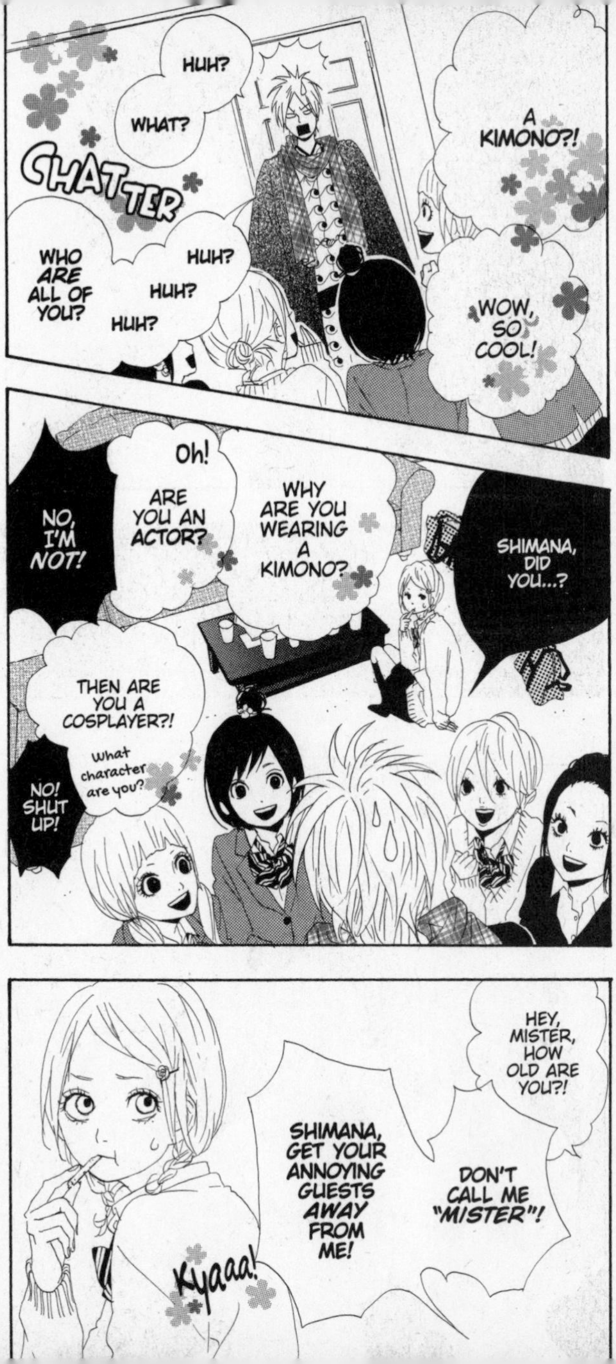
A KIMONO?!
WOW, SO COOL!
HUH?
WHAT?
CHATTER
HUH?
HUH?
HUH?
WHO ARE ALL OF YOU?
SHIMANA, DID YOU...?
WHY ARE YOU WEARING A KIMONO?
Oh! ARE YOU AN ACTOR?
NO, I'M NOT!
THEN ARE YOU A COSPLAYER?!
What character are you?
NO! SHUT UP!
HEY, MISTER, HOW OLD ARE YOU?!
DON'T CALL ME "MISTER"!
SHIMANA, GET YOUR ANNOYING GUESTS AWAY FROM ME!
Kyaaa!

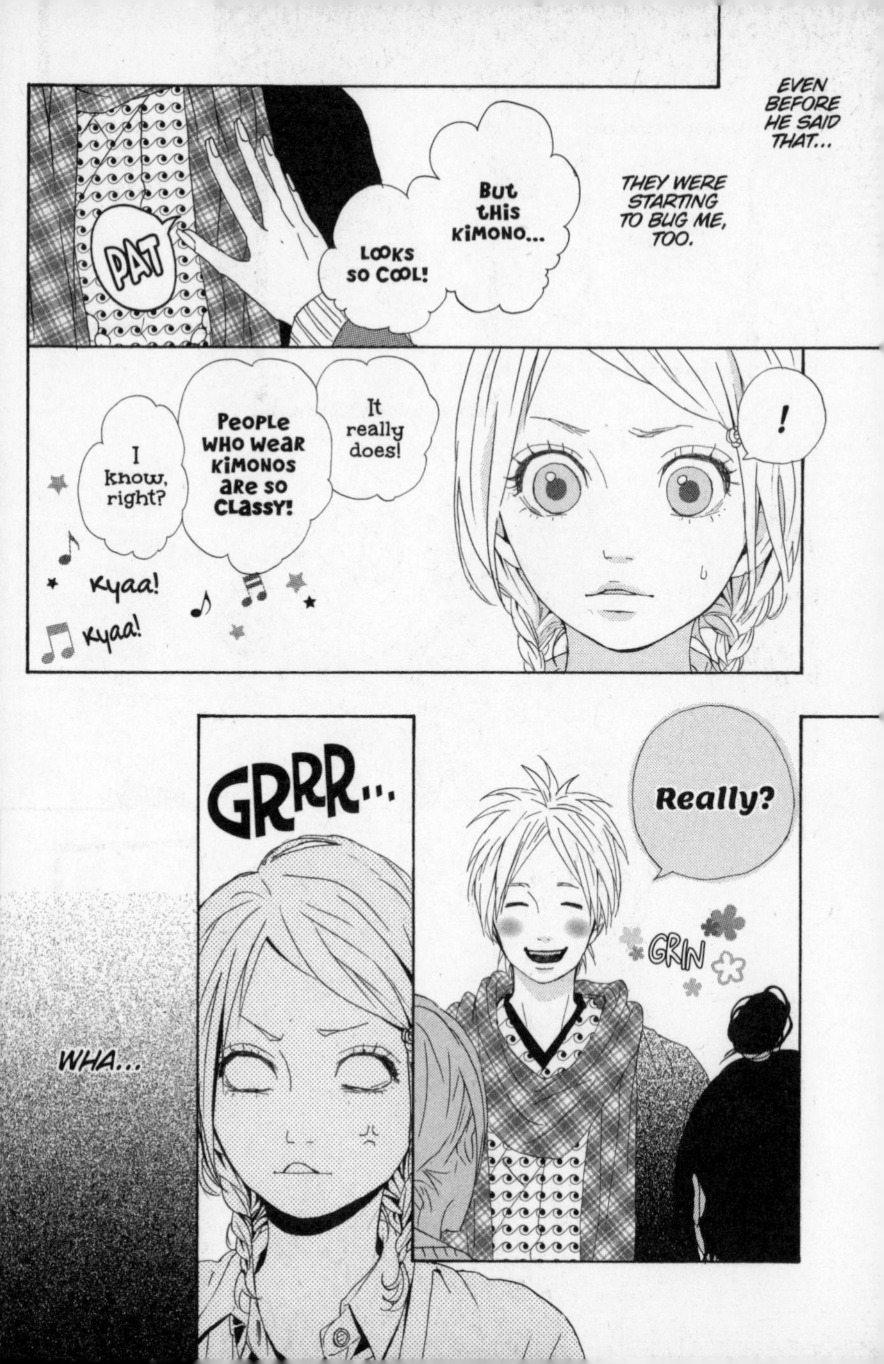
EVEN BEFORE HE SAID THAT...
THEY WERE STARTING TO BUG ME, TOO.
But this kimono...
Looks so cool!
PAT
!
It really does!
People who wear kimonos are so classy!
I know, right?
Kyaa!
Kyaa!
Really?
GRIN
GRRR...
WHA...

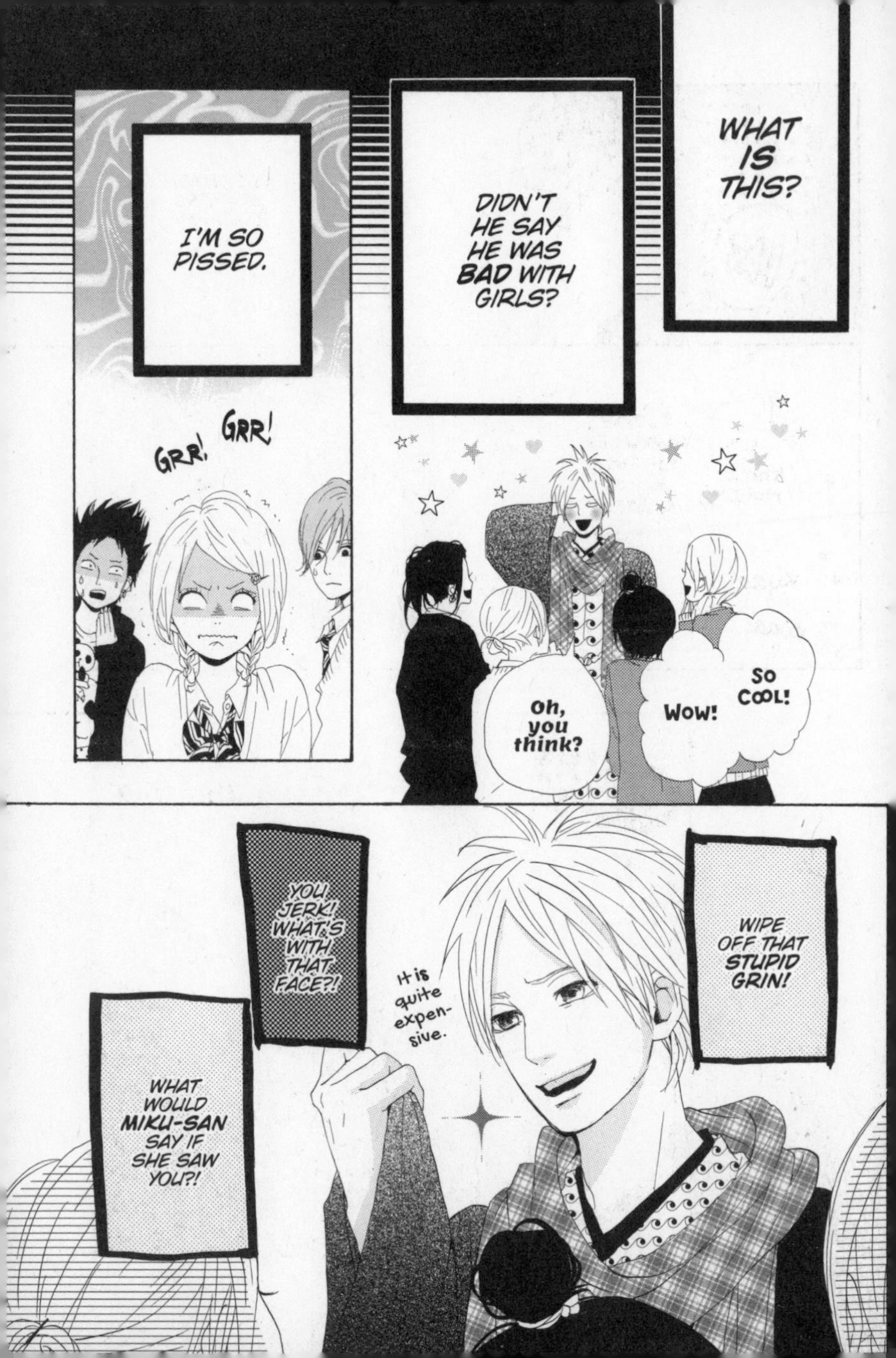
WHAT IS THIS?
DIDN'T HE SAY HE WAS BAD WITH GIRLS?
SO COOL!
WOW!
Oh, you think?
I'M SO PISSED.
GRR!
GRR!
WIPE OFF THAT STUPID GRIN!
It is quite expen-sive.
YOU JERK! WHAT'S WITH THAT FACE?!
WHAT WOULD MIKU-SAN SAY IF SHE SAW YOU?!

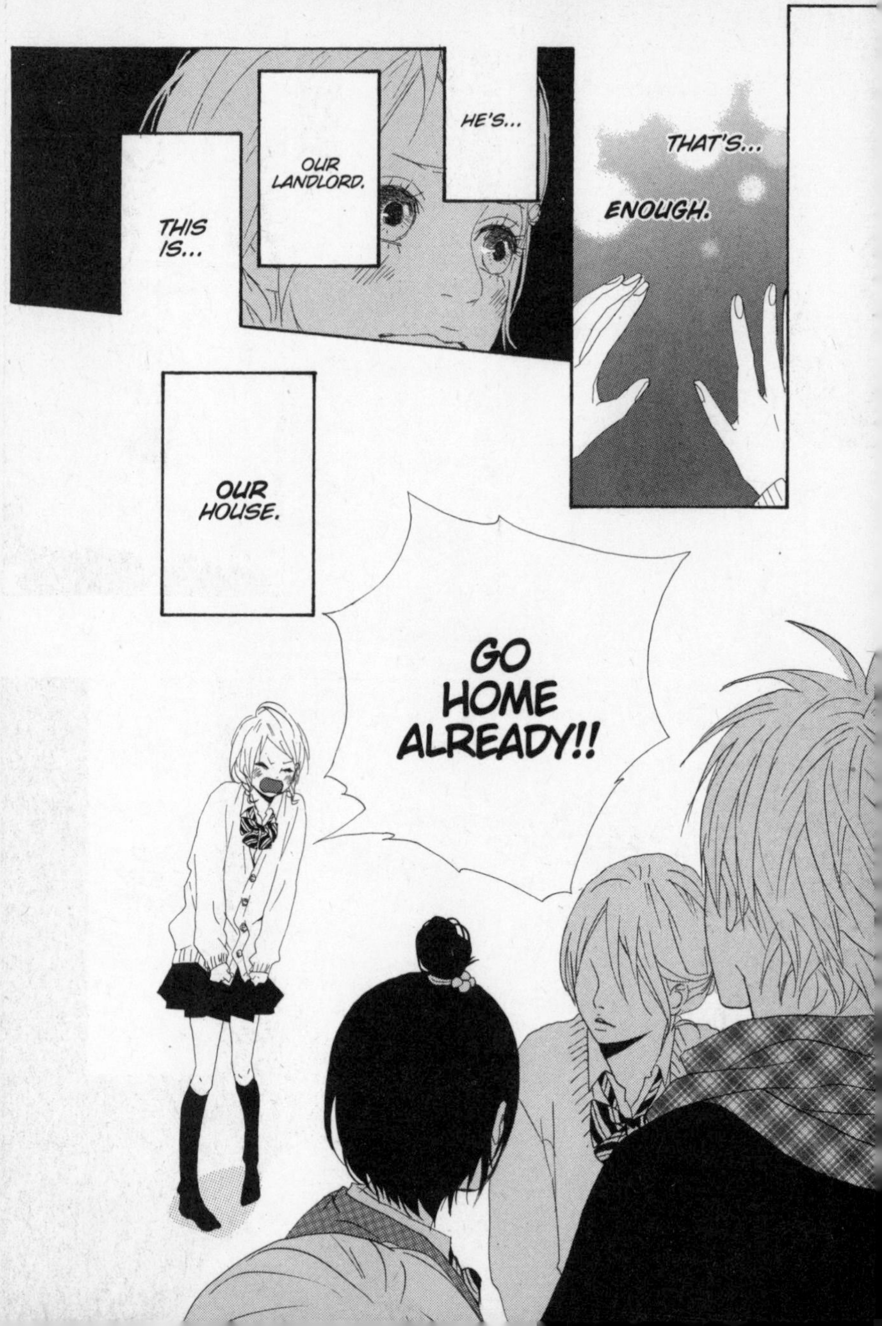
THAT'S...
ENOUGH.
HE'S...
OUR LANDLORD.
THIS IS...
OUR HOUSE.
GO HOME ALREADY!!

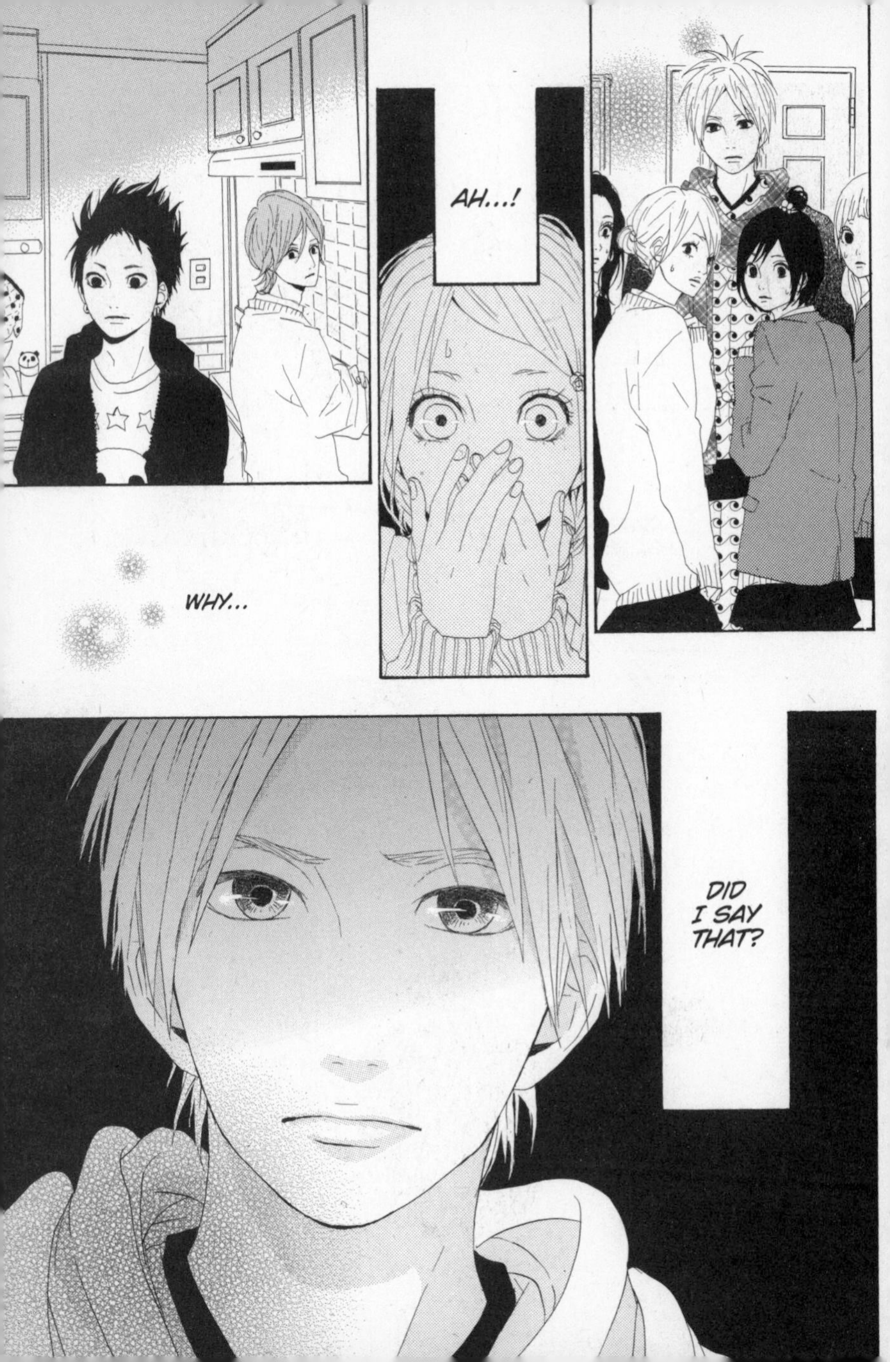
AH...!
WHY...
DID I SAY THAT?

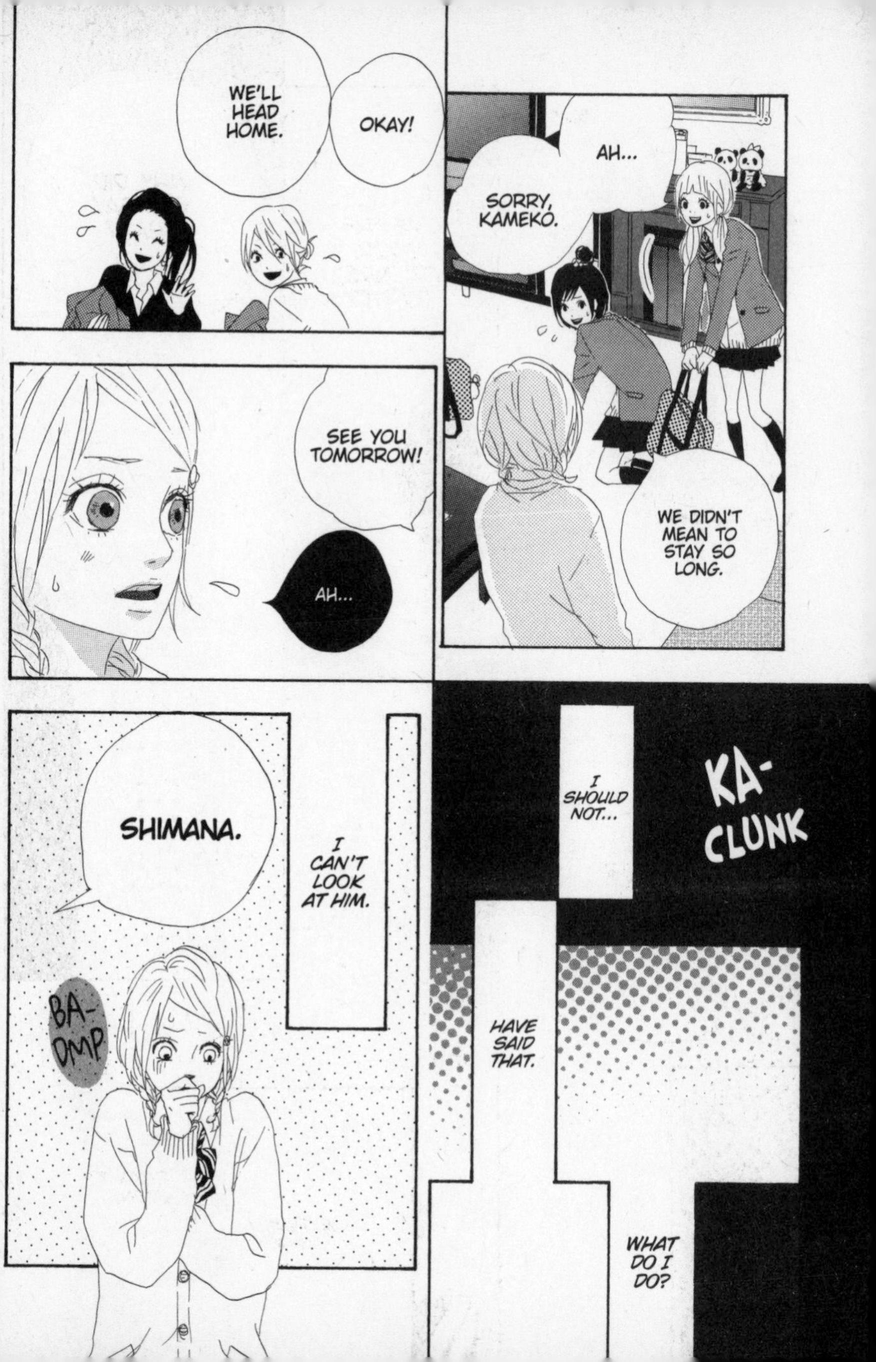
AH...
SORRY, KAMEKO.
WE DIDN'T MEAN TO STAY SO LONG.
WE'LL HEAD HOME.
OKAY!
SEE YOU TOMORROW!
AH...
KA-CLUNK
I SHOULD NOT...
HAVE SAID THAT.
WHAT DO I DO?
SHIMANA.
I CAN'T LOOK AT HIM.
BA-DMP

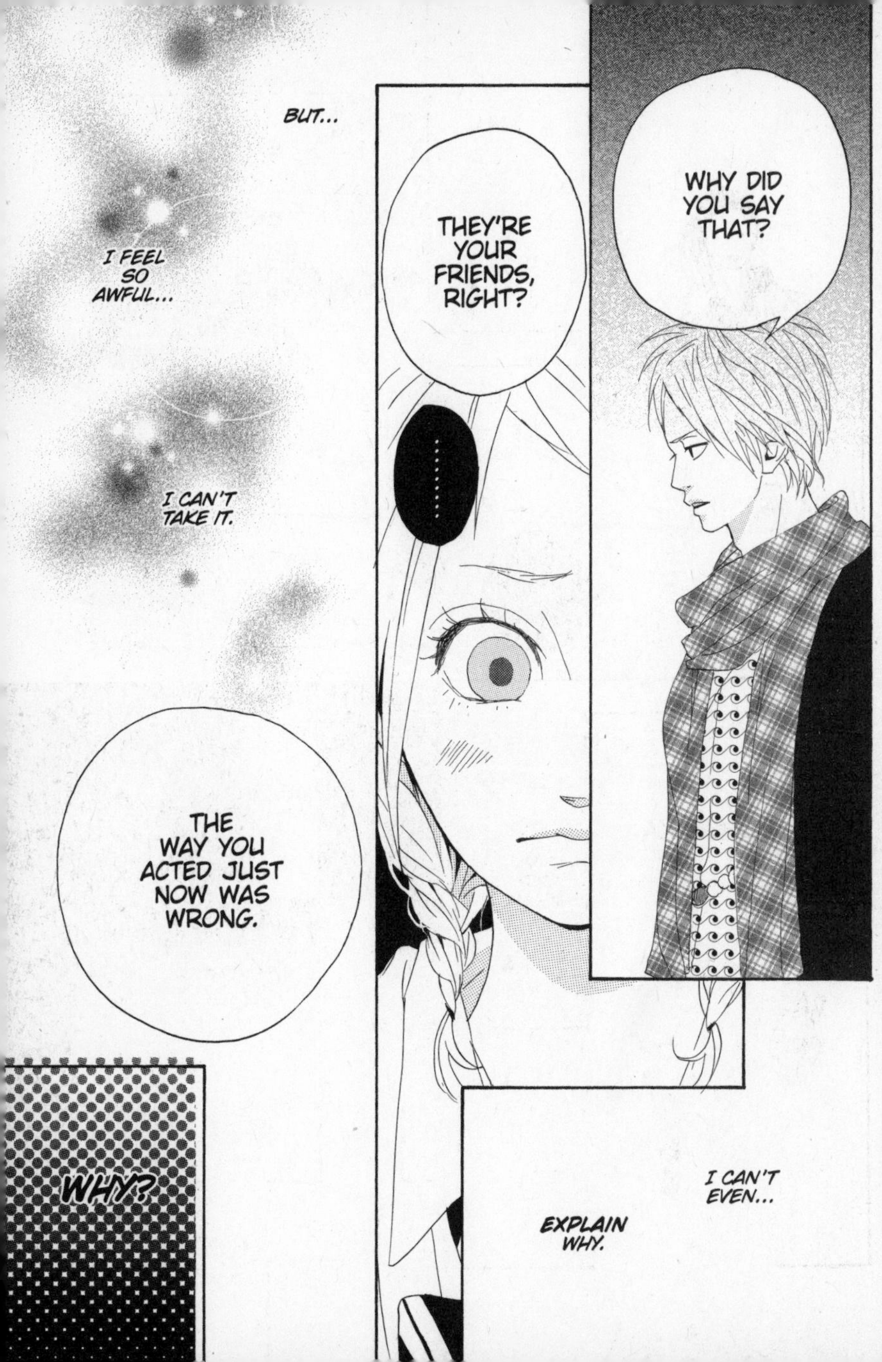
WHY DID YOU SAY THAT?
THEY'RE YOUR FRIENDS, RIGHT?
BUT...
I FEEL SO AWFUL...
I CAN'T TAKE IT.
THE WAY YOU ACTED JUST NOW WAS WRONG.
I CAN'T EVEN...
EXPLAIN WHY.
WHY?

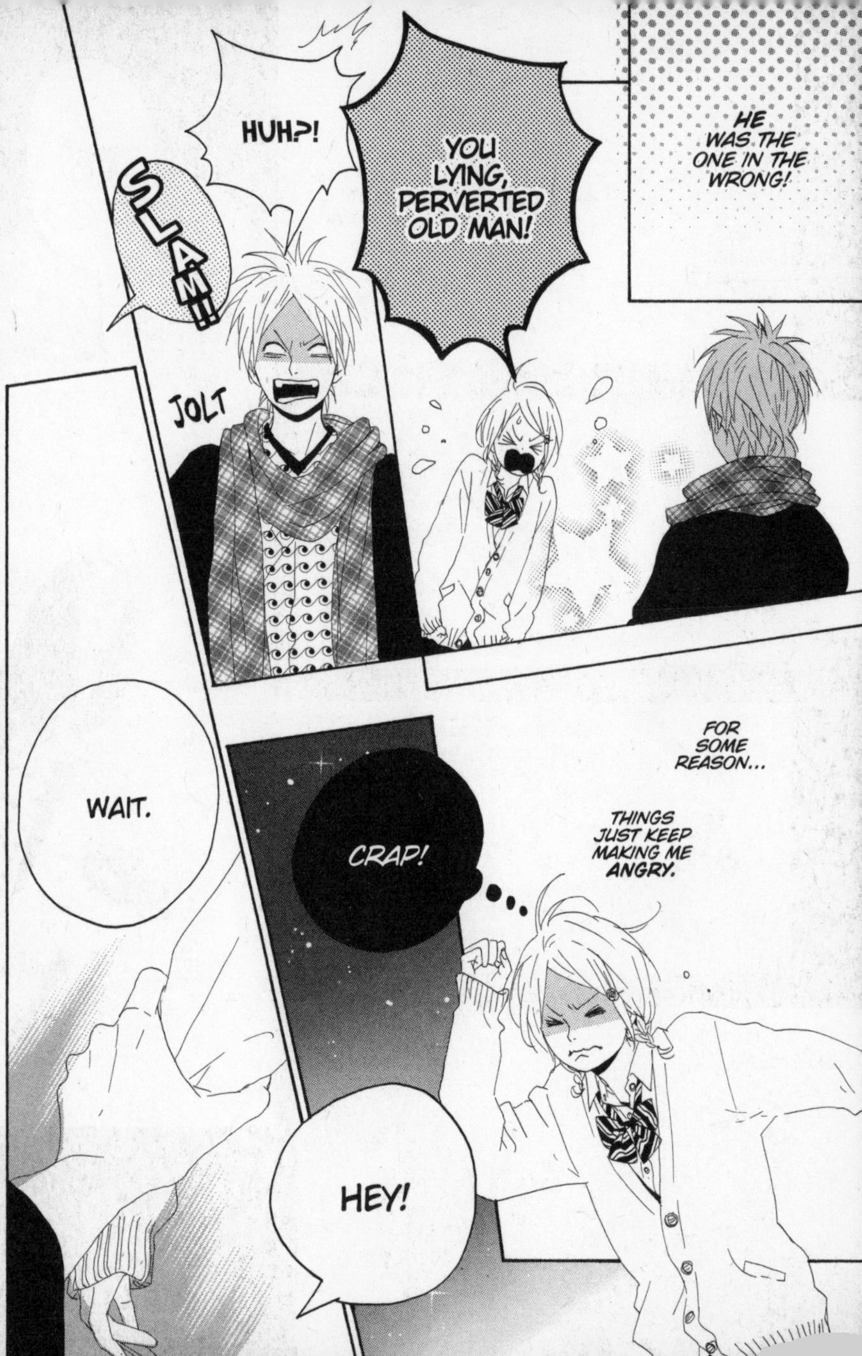
HE WAS THE ONE IN THE WRONG!
YOU LYING, PERVERTED OLD MAN!
HUH?!
SLAM!!
JOLT
FOR SOME REASON...
THINGS JUST KEEP MAKING ME ANGRY.
CRAP!
HEY!
WAIT.

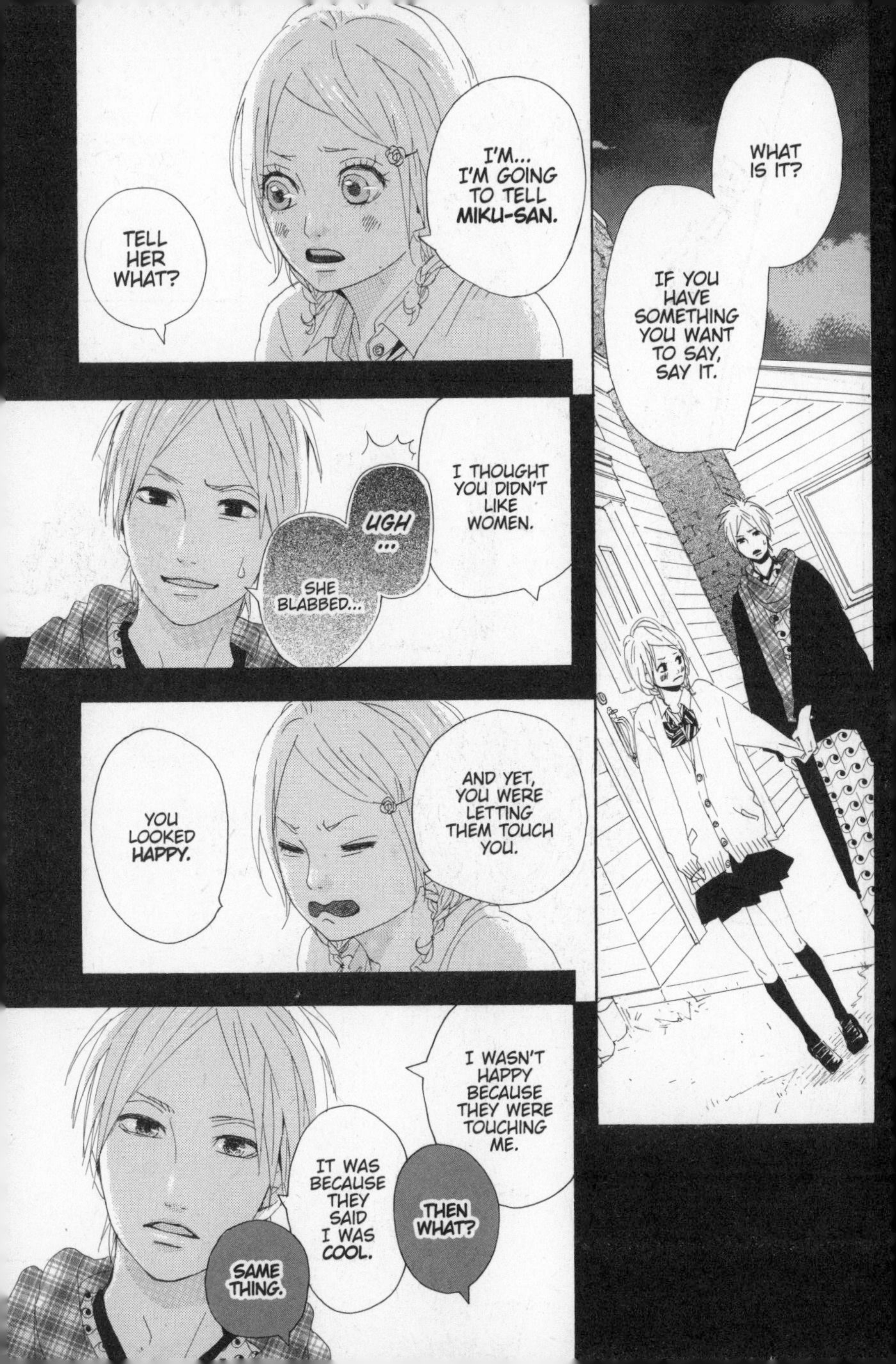
WHAT IS IT?
IF YOU HAVE SOMETHING YOU WANT TO SAY, SAY IT.
I'M... I'M GOING TO TELL MIKU-SAN.
TELL HER WHAT?
I THOUGHT YOU DIDN'T LIKE WOMEN.
UGH ...
SHE BLABBED...
AND YET, YOU WERE LETTING THEM TOUCH YOU.
YOU LOOKED HAPPY.
I WASN'T HAPPY BECAUSE THEY WERE TOUCHING ME.
THEN WHAT?
IT WAS BECAUSE THEY SAID I WAS COOL.
SAME THING.

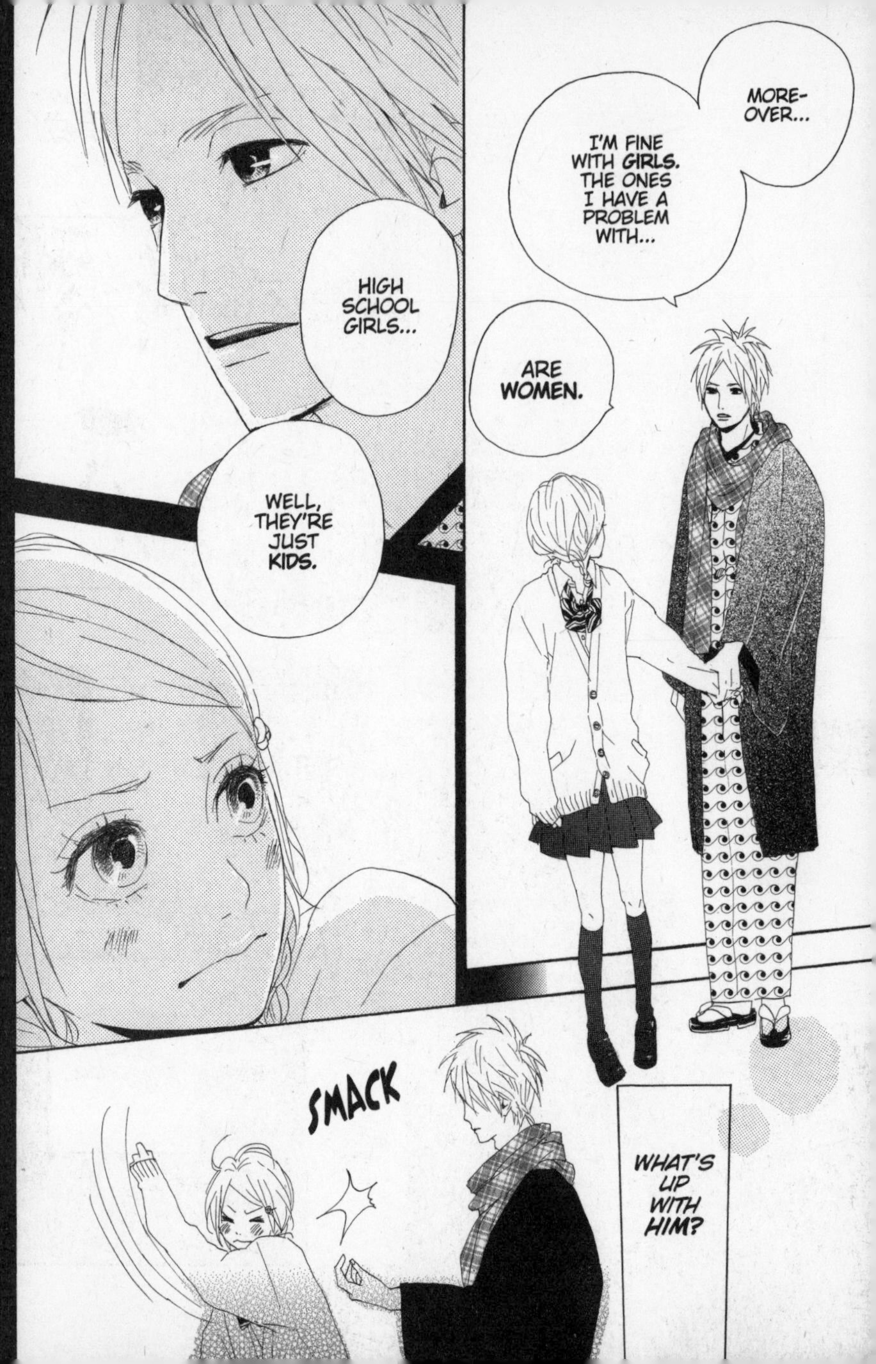
MORE-OVER...
I'M FINE WITH GIRLS. THE ONES I HAVE A PROBLEM WITH...
ARE WOMEN.
HIGH SCHOOL GIRLS...
WELL, THEY'RE JUST KIDS.
WHAT'S UP WITH HIM?
SMACK

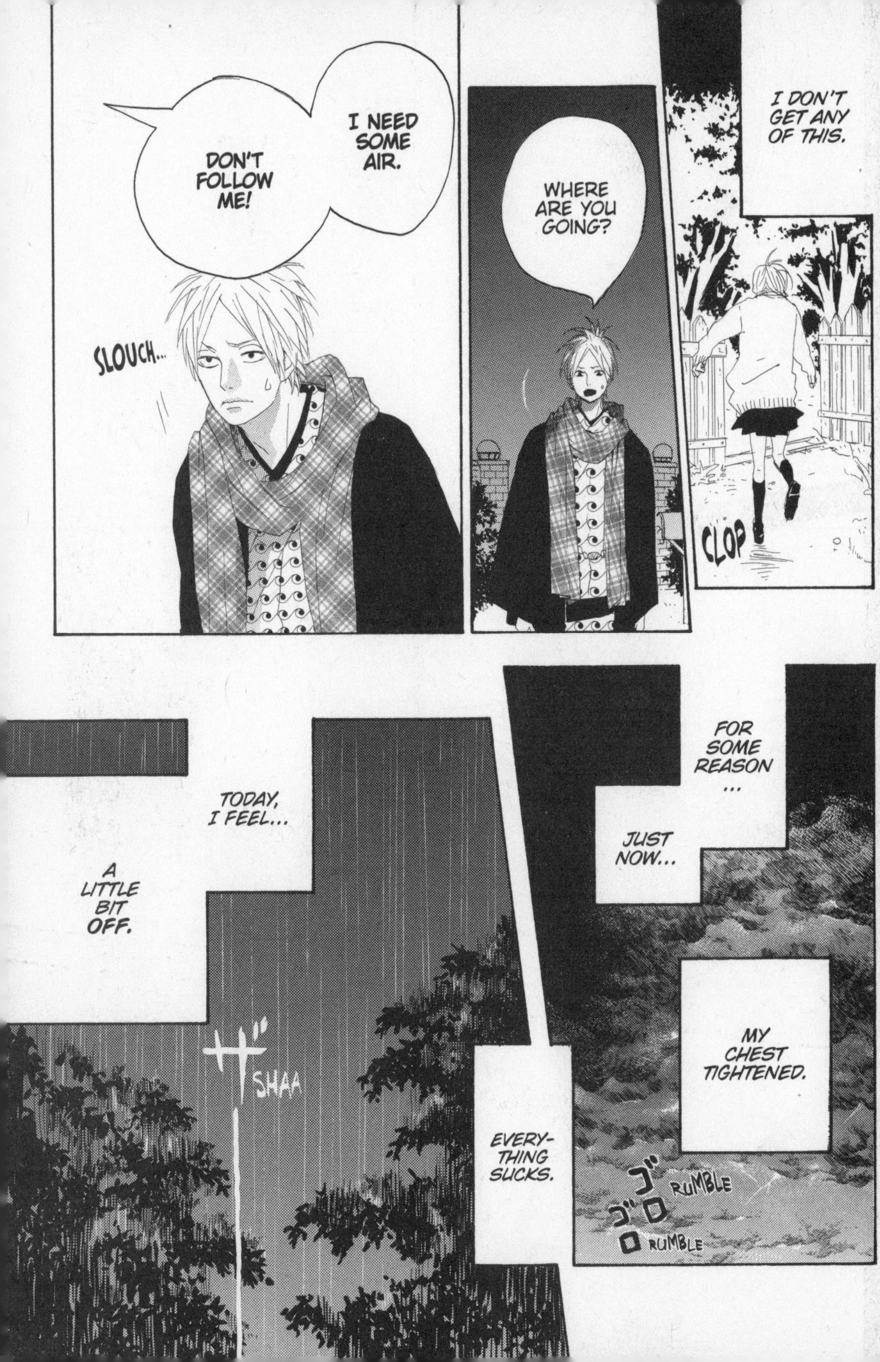
I DON'T GET ANY OF THIS.
CLOP
WHERE ARE YOU GOING?
I NEED SOME AIR.
DON'T FOLLOW ME!
SLOUCH...
FOR SOME REASON ...
JUST NOW...
MY CHEST TIGHTENED.
EVERY-THING SUCKS.
ゴロゴロ
RUMBLE
RUMBLE
TODAY, I FEEL...
A LITTLE BIT OFF.
ザ
SHAA

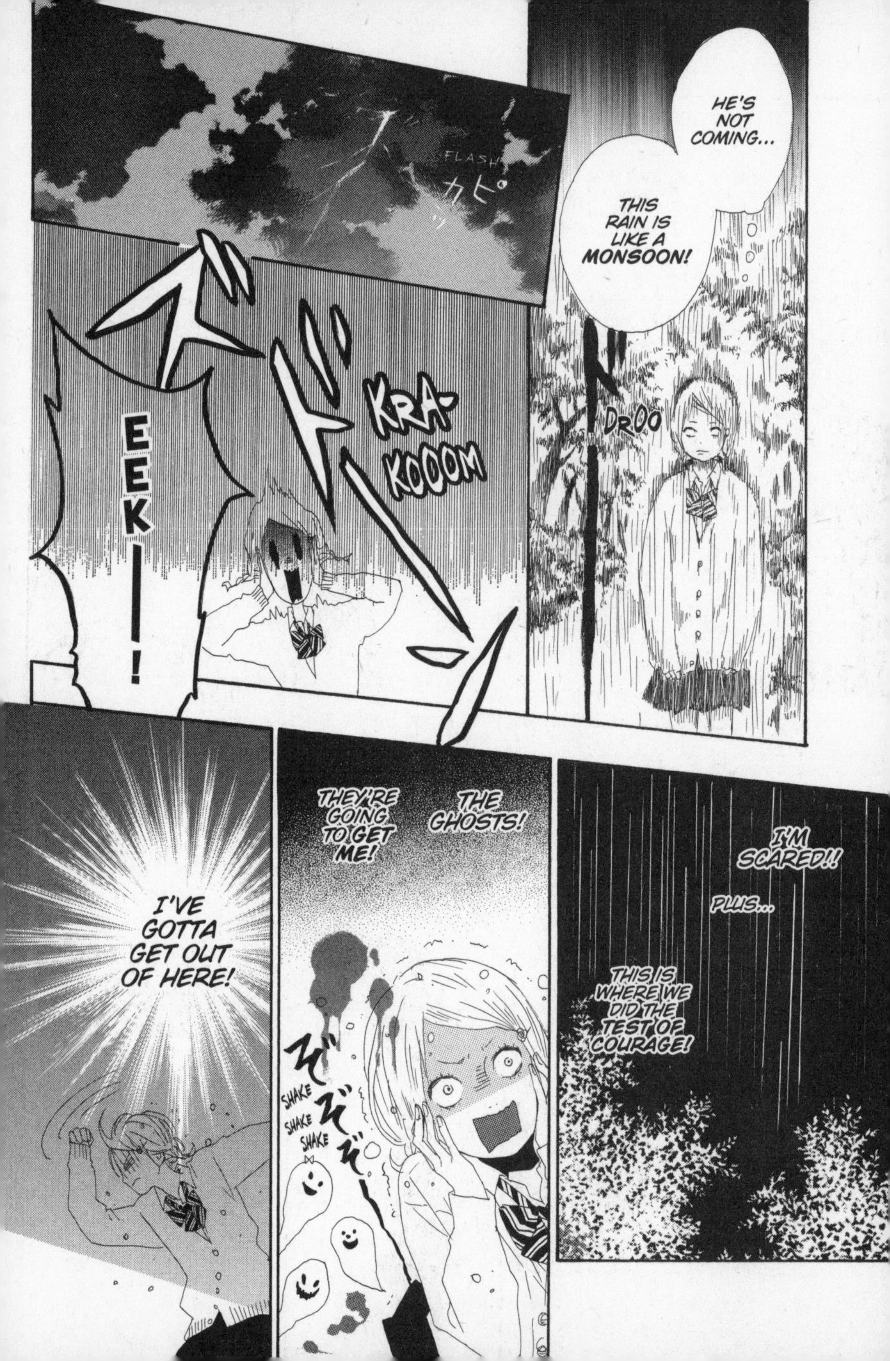
HE'S NOT COMING...
THIS RAIN IS LIKE A MONSOON!
DROO
FLASH
KRA-KOOOM
EEK!!
I'M SCARED!!
PLUS...
THIS IS WHERE WE DID THE TEST OF COURAGE!
THE GHOSTS!
THEY'RE GOING TO GET ME!
SHAKE SHAKE SHAKE
I'VE GOTTA GET OUT OF HERE!

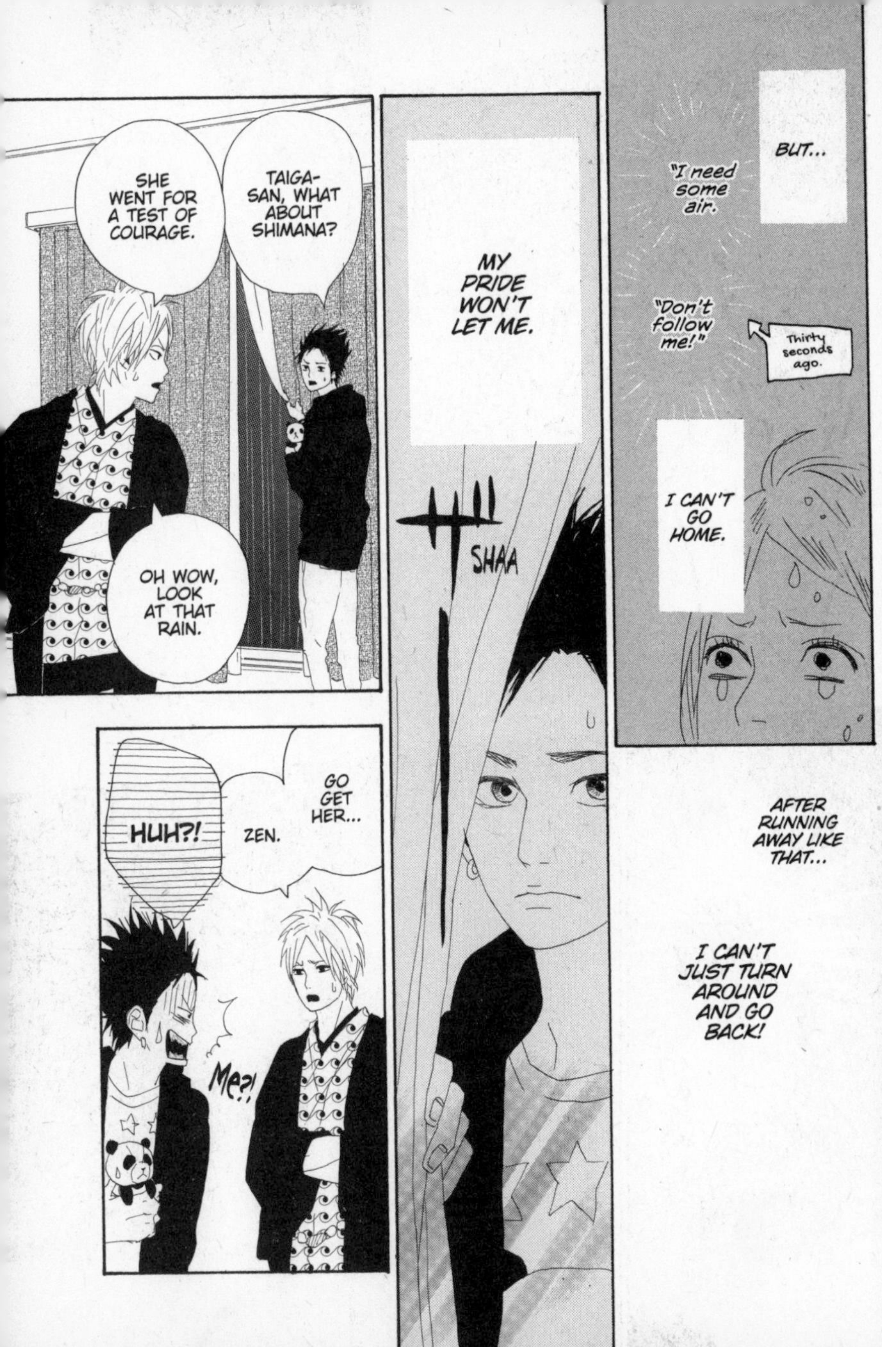
BUT...
"I need some air."
"Don't follow me!"
Thirty seconds ago.
I CAN'T GO HOME.
AFTER RUNNING AWAY LIKE THAT...
I CAN'T JUST TURN AROUND AND GO BACK!
MY PRIDE WON'T LET ME.
SHAA
TAIGA-SAN, WHAT ABOUT SHIMANA?
SHE WENT FOR A TEST OF COURAGE.
OH WOW, LOOK AT THAT RAIN.
GO GET HER... ZEN.
HUH?!
Me?!

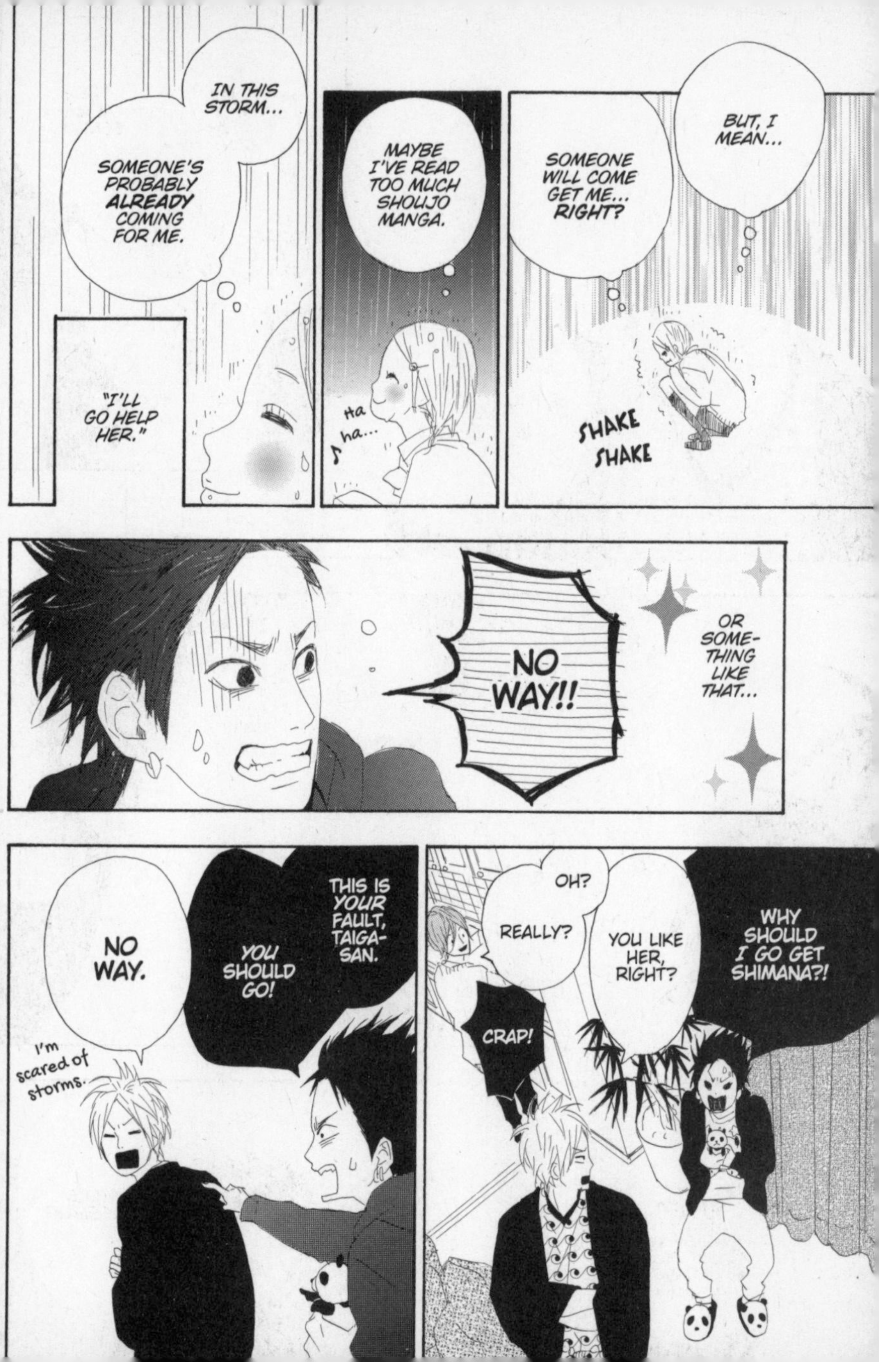
BUT, I MEAN...
SOMEONE WILL COME GET ME... RIGHT?
SHAKE SHAKE
MAYBE I'VE READ TOO MUCH SHOUJO MANGA.
Ha ha...
IN THIS STORM...
SOMEONE'S PROBABLY ALREADY COMING FOR ME.
"I'LL GO HELP HER."
OR SOMETHING LIKE THAT...
NO WAY!!
WHY SHOULD I GO GET SHIMANA?!
YOU LIKE HER, RIGHT?
OH?
REALLY?
CRAP!
THIS IS YOUR FAULT, TAIGA-SAN.
YOU SHOULD GO!
NO WAY.
I'm scared of storms.

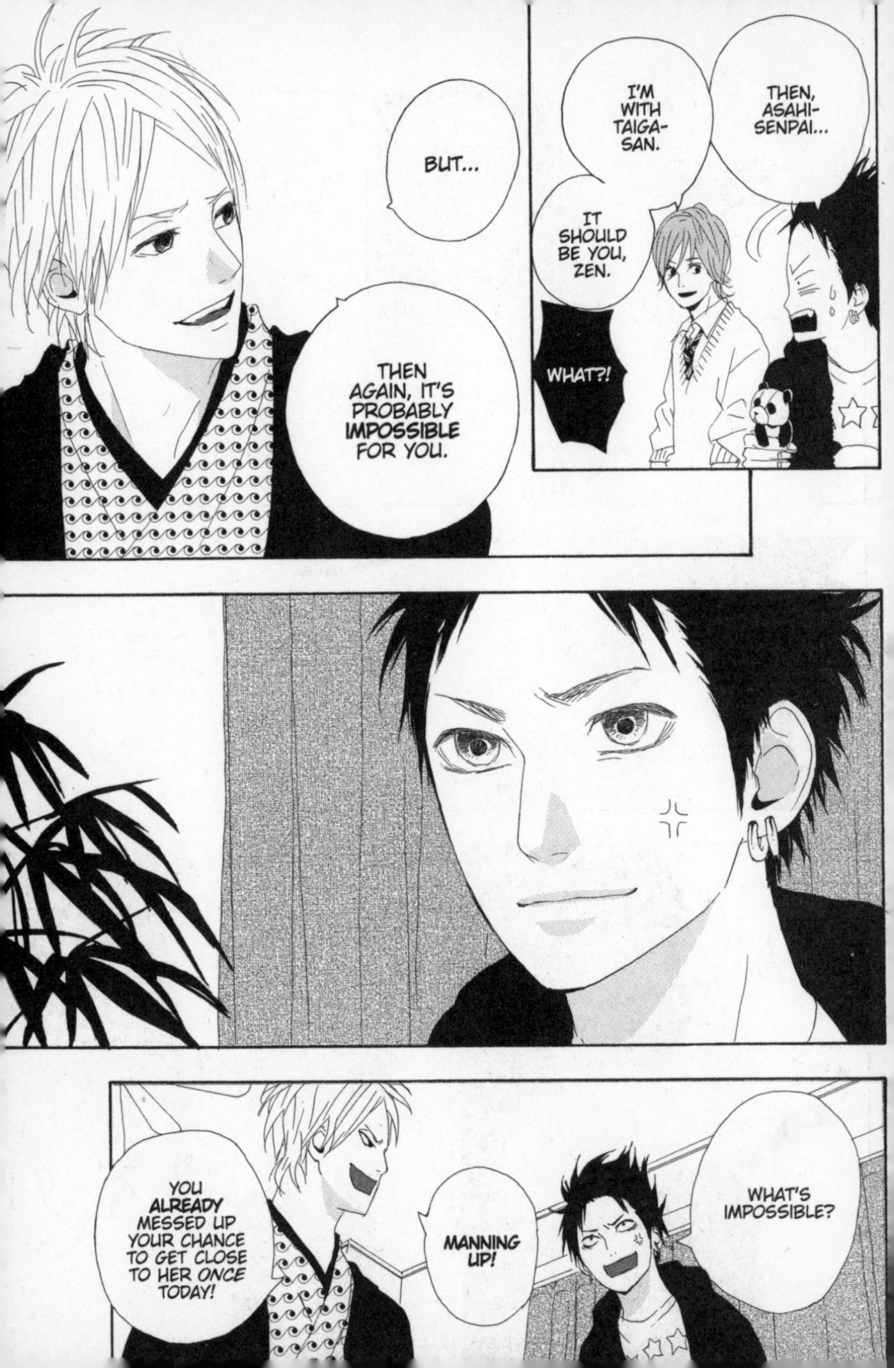
THEN, ASAHI-SENPAI...
I'M WITH TAIGA-SAN.
IT SHOULD BE YOU, ZEN.
WHAT?!
BUT...
THEN AGAIN, IT'S PROBABLY IMPOSSIBLE FOR YOU.
WHAT'S IMPOSSIBLE?
MANNING UP!
YOU ALREADY MESSED UP YOUR CHANCE TO GET CLOSE TO HER ONCE TODAY!

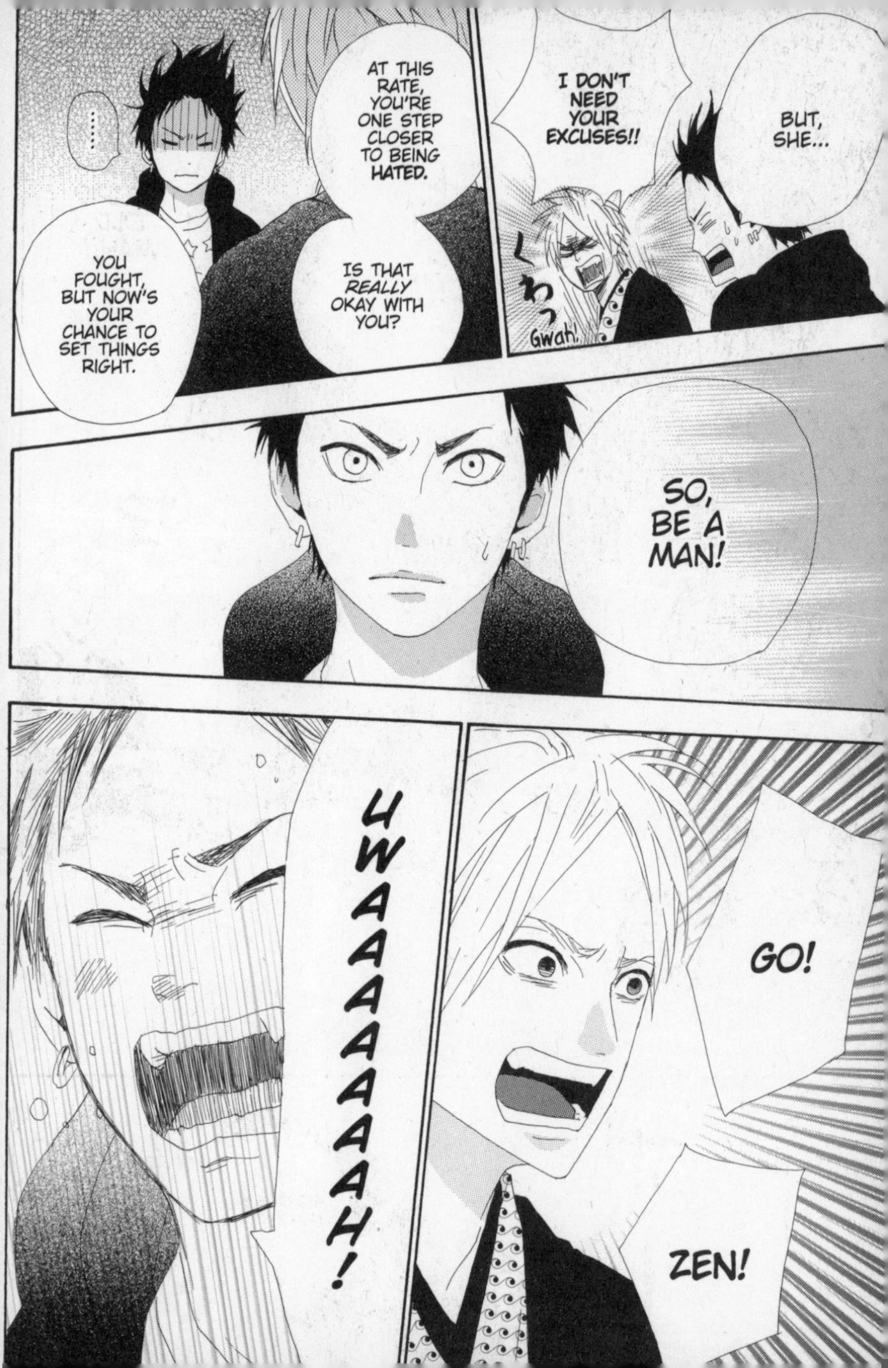
BUT, SHE...
I DON'T NEED YOUR EXCUSES!!
くわっ
Gwah!
AT THIS RATE, YOU'RE ONE STEP CLOSER TO BEING HATED.
......
IS THAT *REALLY* OKAY WITH YOU?
YOU FOUGHT, BUT NOW'S YOUR CHANCE TO SET THINGS RIGHT.
SO, BE A MAN!
GO!
ZEN!
UWAAAAAAAH!

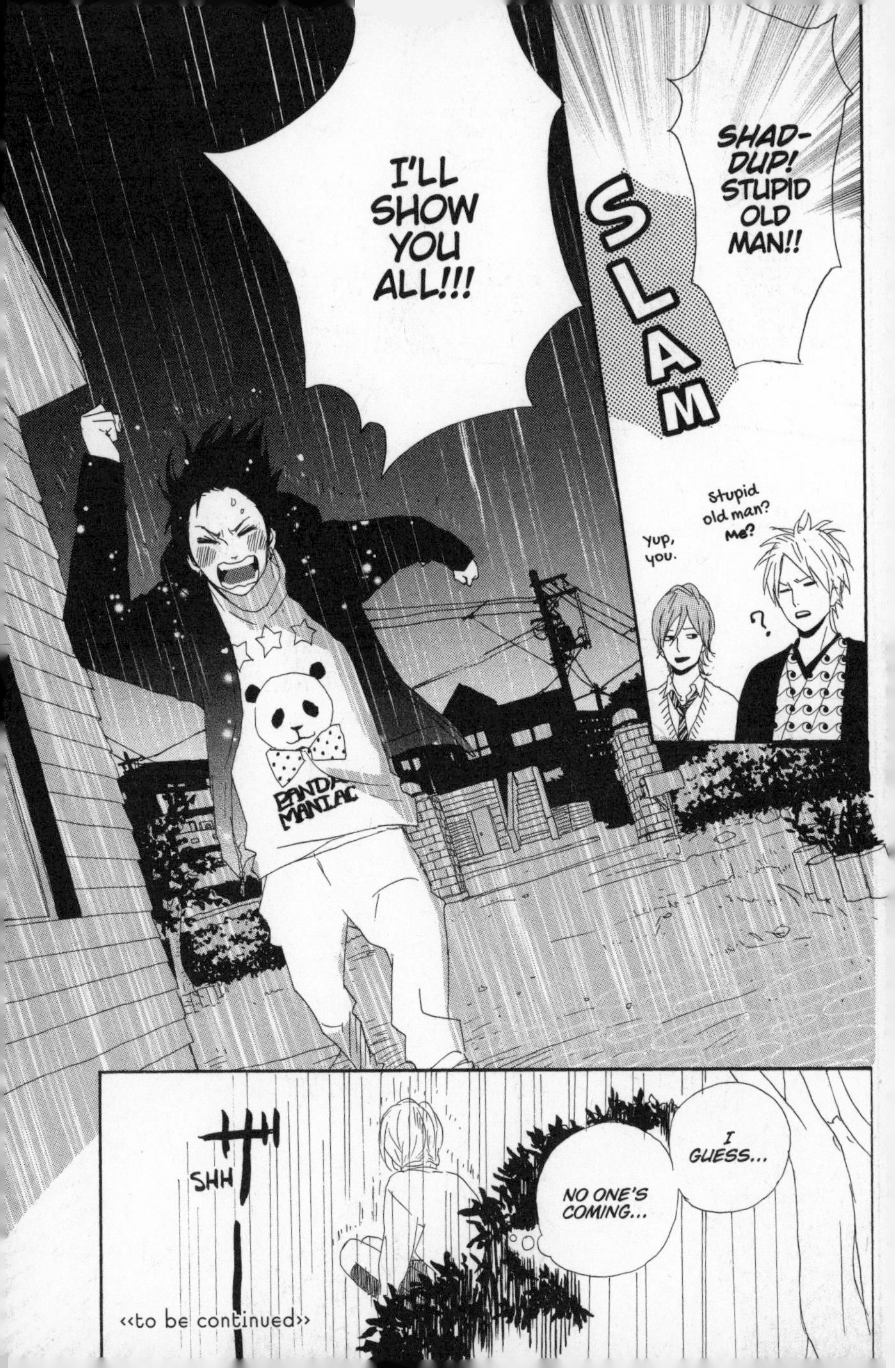
SHAD-DUP! STUPID OLD MAN!!
SLAM
Stupid old man? Me?
Yup, you.
I'LL SHOW YOU ALL!!!
PANDA MANIAC
I GUESS...
NO ONE'S COMING...
SHH
‹‹to be continued››

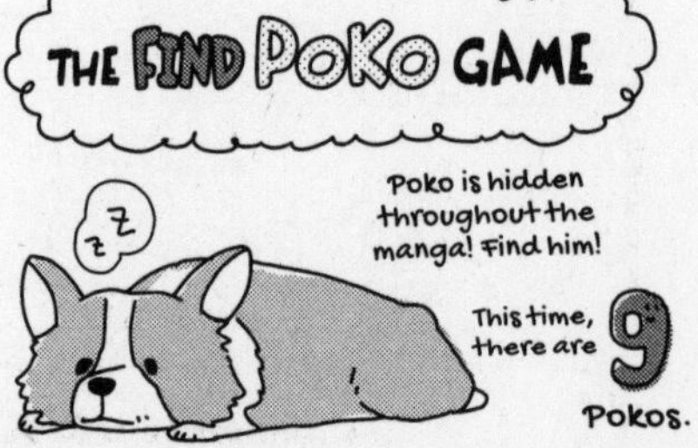
THE FIND POKO GAME
Poko is hidden throughout the manga! Find him!
This time, there are 9 Pokos.
z z
Corgi (♂)

BONUS MANGA

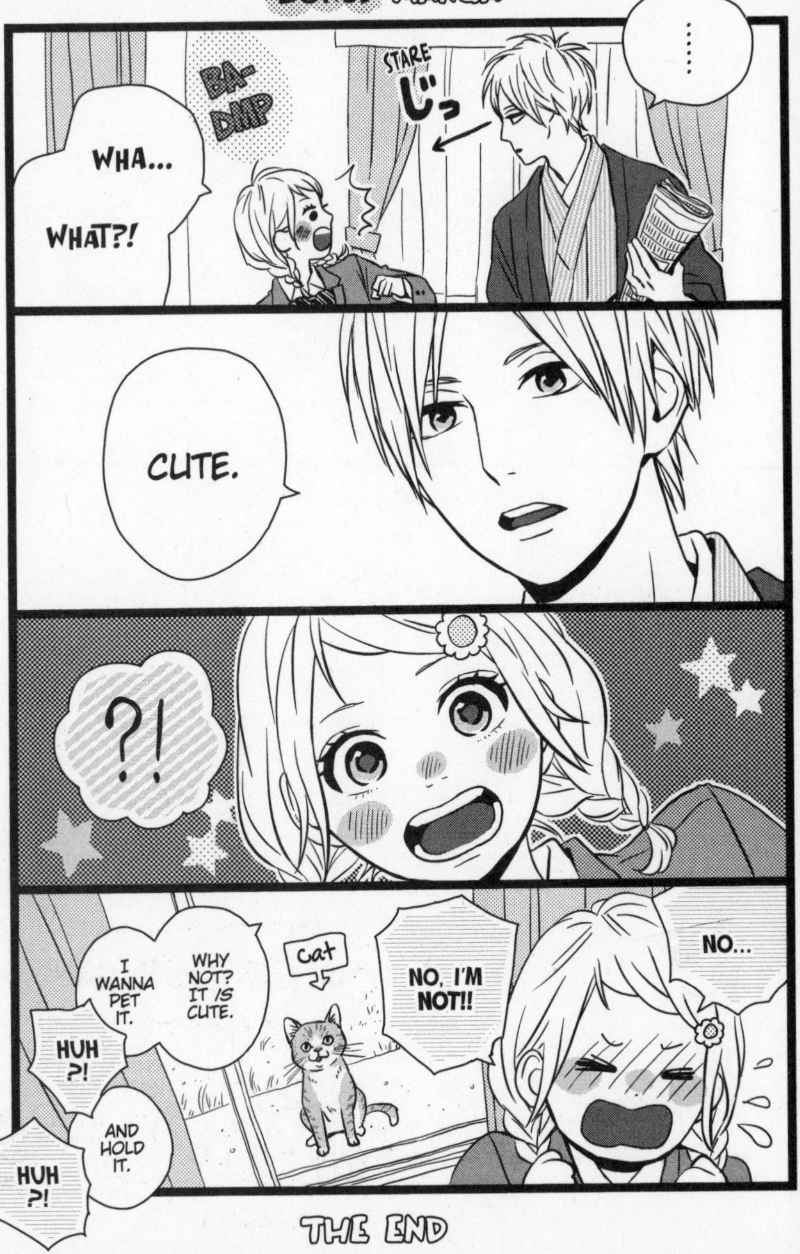
......
STARE
じっ
BA-DMP
WHA...
WHAT?!
CUTE.
?!
NO...
NO, I'M NOT!!
Cat
WHY NOT? IT IS CUTE.
HUH?!
I WANNA PET IT.
HUH?!
AND HOLD IT.

THE END

The New Release Version of the Hit Romantic Comedy!

With its redrawn artwork, it's even cuter than before!

★

"We're kind of like a family."

Shimana yelled at her school friends to leave her home after seeing her woman-hating landlord getting friendly with them. She runs off into the rainstorm, but Zen finds her and brings her back inside. When he comes down with a high fever the next day, Shimana feels responsible and offers to nurse him back to health. While caring for him, she learns a surprising secret...

Includes *Dreamin' Sun* chapters 10~14!

★

Ichigo Takano presents
Dreamin' Sun 3

Coming Soon!

Story & Art by *orange*'s Ichigo Takano!

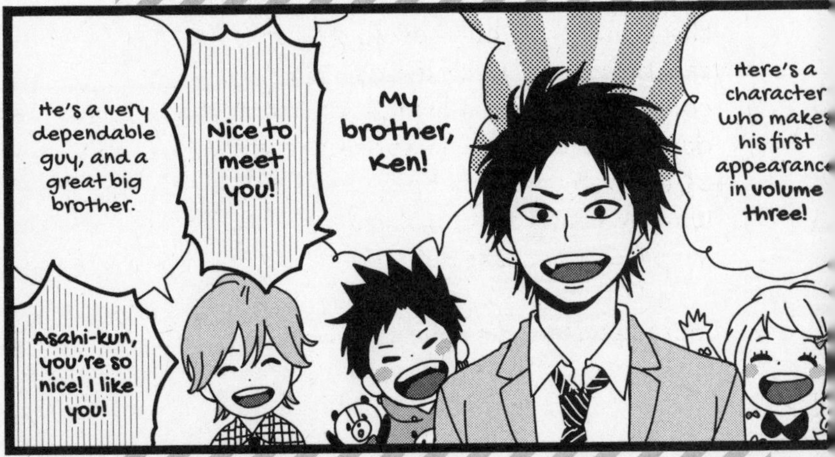
Here's a character who makes his first appearance in volume three!
My brother, Ken!
Nice to meet you!
He's a very dependable guy, and a great big brother.
Asahi-kun, you're so nice! I like you!

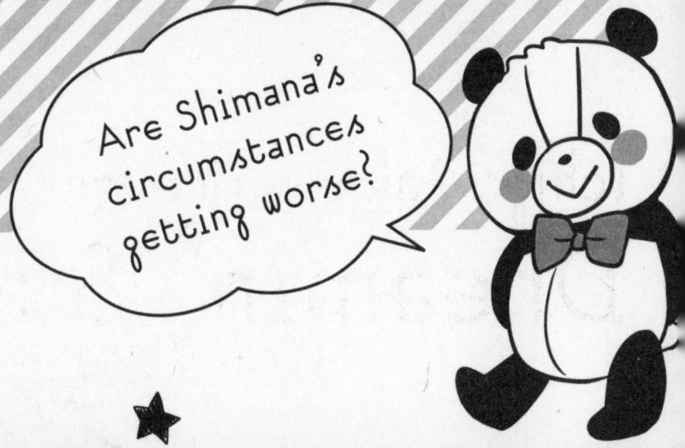
Are Shimana's circumstances getting worse?

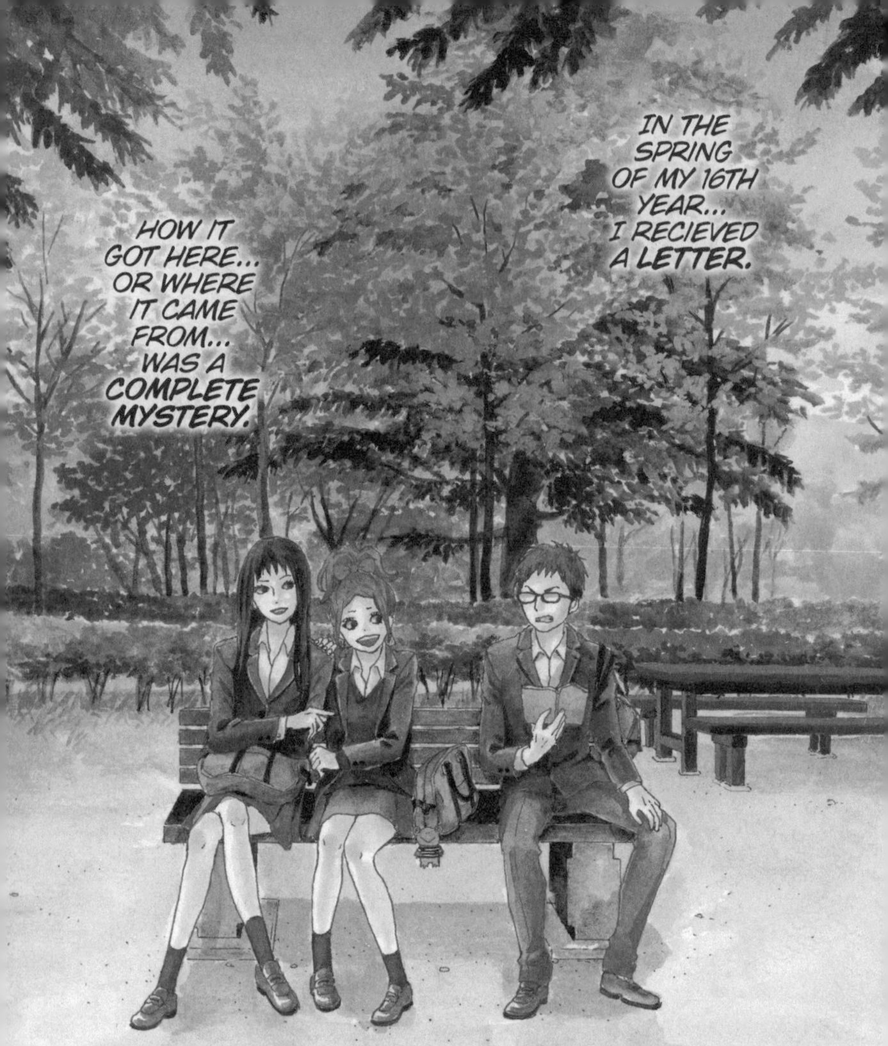
IN THE SPRING OF MY 16TH YEAR... I RECIEVED A LETTER.
HOW IT GOT HERE... OR WHERE IT CAME FROM... WAS A COMPLETE MYSTERY.

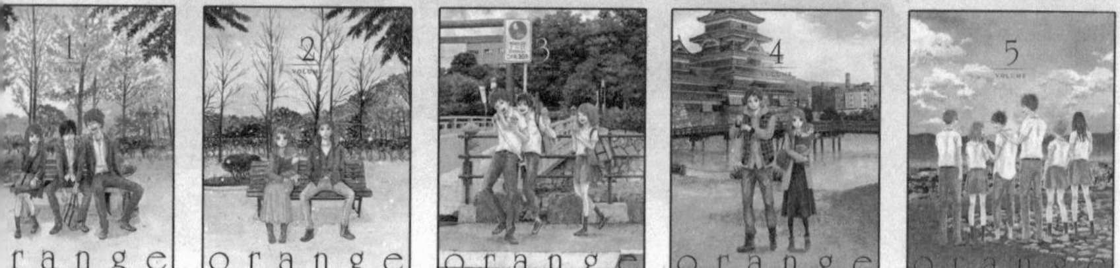
2
orange
ICHIGO TAKANO
3
orange
ICHIGO TAKANO
4
orange
5

The *New York Times'* manga bestseller—a story of love and friendship that trancends time and tragedy.

orange

story & art by ICHIGO TAKANO

The complete five-volume series is available now in omnibus print and digital editions from **Seven Seas Entertainment**

SEVEN SEAS ENTERTAINMENT PRESENTS

Dreamin' Sun

story and art by ICHIGO TAKANO VOLUME 2

TRANSLATION
Amber Tamosaitis

ADAPTATION
Shannon Fay

LETTERING AND RETOUCH
Lys Blakeslee

COVER DESIGN
Nicky Lim

PROOFREADER
Danielle King
Holly Kolodziejczak

ASSISTANT EDITOR
Jenn Grunigen

PRODUCTION ASSISTANT
CK Russell

PRODUCTION MANAGER
Lissa Pattillo

EDITOR-IN-CHIEF
Adam Arnold

PUBLISHER
Jason DeAngelis

First published in Japan in 2016 by Futabasha Publishers Ltd., Tokyo.
English version published by Seven Seas Entertainment, LLC.
under license from Futabasha Publishers Ltd.

ISBN: 978-1-626925-27-4

Printed in Canada

First Printing: July 2017

10 9 8 7 6 5 4 3 2 1

READING DIRECTIONS

This book reads from ***right to left***, Japanese style. If this is your first time reading manga, you start reading from the top right panel on each page and take it from there. If you get lost, just follow the numbered diagram here. It may seem backwards at first, but you'll get the hang of it! Have fun!!

1
2
3
4
5
6
7
8
9

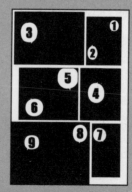